*Pension and Retirement Policies
in Colleges and Universities*

The Commission on College Retirement

Oscar M. Ruebhausen, General Editor

Pension and Retirement Policies in Colleges and Universities

An Analysis and Recommendations

 Jossey-Bass Publishers

San Francisco • Oxford • 1990

PENSION AND RETIREMENT POLICIES IN COLLEGES AND UNIVERSITIES
An Analysis and Recommendations
by The Commission on College Retirement

Copyright © 1990 by: Jossey-Bass Inc., Publishers
350 Sansome Street
San Francisco, California 94104
&
Jossey-Bass Limited
Headington Hill Hall
Oxford OX3 0BW

Library of Congress Cataloging-in-Publication Data

Commission on College Retirement.
      Pension and retirement policies in colleges and universities : an
analysis and recommendations / the Commission on College Retirement;
Oscar M. Ruebhausen, general editor. — 1st ed.
      p.   cm. — (The Jossey-Bass higher education series)
      ISBN 1-55542-224-1 (alk. paper)
      1. College teachers — Pensions — United States.   2. Universities and
colleges — Employees — Pensions — United States.   I. Ruebhausen, Oscar M.
II. Title.   III. Series.
LB2334.C8275   1990
331.25'2913781'20973 — dc20   90-4342
                                                                    CIP

Manufactured in the United States of America

The paper in this book meets the guidelines for
permanence and durability of the Committee on
Production Guidelines for Book Longevity of
the Council on Library Resources.

JACKET DESIGN BY WILLI BAUM

FIRST EDITION

Code 9054

The Jossey-Bass Higher Education Series

Contents

Preface   xix

Acknowledgments   xxv

Commission Members   xxvii

The Authors   xxix

**Part One: Transferability of Funds Invested
   with TIAA-CREF: The Legal Issues   1**

1.1   Policy Statement of the Commission   7

1.2   Transferability of Funds from TIAA and CREF   14
      Spencer L. Kimball

      1.2.1 Introduction   14

      1.2.2 The Contracts   16

            1.2.2.1 Description of the Funds   16

                    1.2.2.1.1 CREF   18

                    1.2.2.1.2 TIAA   19

1.2.2.2 Relevant Terms of the TIAA and
CREF Contracts   23

1.2.2.2.1 TIAA   23

1.2.2.2.2 CREF   24

1.2.2.3 Conceptualization of the Relationships   25

1.2.2.3.1 CREF   27

1.2.2.3.2 TIAA   30

1.2.2.3.3 ERISA Preemption of
New York Trust Law   32

1.2.3 Transferability of Funds   34

1.2.3.1 The Handling of New Money   35

1.2.3.2 Practical Problems with Old
Money   36

1.2.3.2.1 CREF   36

1.2.3.2.2 The Fairness Problem   39

1.2.3.2.3 TIAA   40

1.2.3.3 Legal Problems, Including In-
surance Law Problems   45

1.2.3.3.1 CREF   45

1.2.3.3.2 TIAA   45

1.2.4 Conclusions   49

1.3 Applicability of New York Law to
Transferability of Funds from TIAA and
CREF: Opinion of Elias Clark   53

1.3.1 Elements of Trust Present in TIAA-
CREF's Holding of Funds   54

1.3.2 Section 513(a) of the Not-for-Profit Cor-
       poration Law Is Not Applicable   60

1.3.3 Applicability of EPTL Section 7-1.9   61

1.4   Transfers of TIAA and CREF Annuity Con-
      tract Interests: Opinion of Dewey, Ballantine,
      Bushby, Palmer and Wood   64

       1.4.1 The Retirement Annuity Contracts Do
              Not Create or Constitute a Trust Entity   65

       1.4.2 TIAA-CREF's Retirement Annuity Con-
              tracts Are Subject to the Provisions of
              New York Insurance Law   69

       1.4.3 Section 7-1.9 of the New York Estates,
              Powers and Trusts Law Has No Ap-
              plication to TIAA-CREF's Retirement
              Annuity Contracts   71

       1.4.4 Errors, Omissions, and Other Aberra-
              tions of the Clark Opinion   75

              1.4.4.1 Errors Regarding Contract
                       Terms   75

              1.4.4.2 Confusion of Fiduciary Obliga-
                       tions and "Elements of Trust"
                       with Creation of Express Trusts   77

              1.4.4.3 Improper Reliance on *Community
                       Services, Incorporated* v. *United States*   78

              1.4.4.4 Failure to Consider Controlling
                       Statutes and Numerous Judicial
                       Authorities   79

              1.4.4.5 Failure to Identify What Property
                       or Amounts Would Be Subject to
                       the Proposed Requirement for
                       Premature Transfers, or to
                       Discuss the Enormous Problems
                       Relating Thereto   80

1.4.4.6 Confusion of a Statutory Grant
of Authority to Delegate Responsibility with an Assumed Requirement So to Delegate   83

1.4.4.7 Omission of Any Consideration
of ERISA Problems   84

Appendix   89

1.5 Additional Opinion   90
     Elias Clark

1.5.1 Assumptions in the Dewey Opinion That
Are Either Erroneous or Inconsistent
with Positions Taken by TIAA-CREF in
the Past   91

1.5.1.1 The Commission's Recommenda-
tion Concerned the Investment of
Contributions Prior to the
Teacher's Retirement, Not to the
Pay Out of an Annuity Purchased
Upon Retirement   92

1.5.1.2 TIAA-CREF Operates During
the Accumulation Phase in the
Manner of a Trust; Previous
Recognition of the Trust Analogy
by TIAA-CREF   93

1.5.2 Reaffirmation of the Argument That
CREF Operates in the Manner of a
Trust and That New York EPTL Section
7-1.9 Is Available to Obtain a Transfer
of Funds   96

1.5.3 Transferability of Funds Is Not Barred
by the Preemption Provisions of ERISA   98

Epilogue   105

**Part Two: Retirement Ages for
College and University Personnel   107**

2.1   Policy Statement on Retirement Ages for Col-
      lege and University Personnel   110

      2.1.1 Chronological Age as a Criterion for
             Faculty   112

      2.1.2 The Tenure System   113

2.2   Age as a Criterion for the Retirement of
      Tenured Faculty   115
      Oscar M. Ruebhausen

      2.2.1 The Retirement Arrangement   117

      2.2.2 The Fairness of Age as a Criterion   120

      2.2.3 Is There Another Criterion Better Than
             Age?   123

      2.2.4 Who Should Determine the Criterion to
             Use?   127

      2.2.5 Should Government Intervene in This
             Determination?   129

      2.2.6 Is the Use of Age as a Criterion Barred
             by Federal Law?   133

      2.2.7 Is the Use of Age as a Criterion Barred
             by State Law?   135

      2.2.8 Conclusion   137

2.3   Laws Governing Involuntary Retirement of
      Tenured College and University Faculty by
      Reason of Age,   141
      Joan Ehrenworth Erdman

      2.3.1 Federal Age Discrimination Law   142

2.3.2 State Age Discrimination Laws   146

2.3.2.1 State Laws Requiring Retirement
of Faculty at Colleges and
Universities   149

2.3.2.2 State-by-State Analysis   149

Epilogue   165

**Part Three: A Pension Program for
College and University Personnel**   **167**

3.1   Current Retirement Plans for College and
University Employees   172

3.1.1 Retirement Income Goals   172

3.1.1.1 Establishing the Initial Benefit   173

3.1.1.1.1 Social Security   175

3.1.1.1.2 Employer Pension
Plans   175

3.1.1.2 Maintaining the Value of Benefits
After Retirement   177

3.1.2 Retirement Plans in Higher Education 180

3.1.2.1 Social Security   180

3.1.2.2 Pension Benefits at Private Institutions   181

3.1.2.2.1 Coverage   181

3.1.2.2.2 Contributions   183

3.1.2.2.3 Assessment of TIAA-
CREF Plans   185

3.1.2.2.4 Summary of Defined
Contribution Plans   189

3.1.2.3 Pension Benefits at Public
        Institutions   190

        3.1.2.3.1 Coverage and Benefits
                  Under Public Defined
                  Plans   190

        3.1.2.3.2 Assessment of Public
                  Defined Benefit Plans   191

        3.1.2.3.3 Summary of Public
                  Defined Benefit Plans   193

3.1.2.4 TIAA-CREF for Employees at
        Public Institutions   200

3.1.3 Conclusion   200

3.2 The Recommendations   203

**Part Four: A Plan to Create Comprehensive
Group Long-Term-Care Insurance
for College and University Personnel   213**

4.1 Findings of the Commission   217

4.2 Goals of a College and University Sponsored
     Long-Term Care Insurance Plan   221

4.3 The Proposed Plan   224

     4.3.1 The Plan in Brief   225

           4.3.1.1 Full Plan   225

           4.3.1.2 Basic Plan   226

     4.3.2 Program Administration   227

     4.3.3 Employer Participation   229

     4.3.4 Employee Participation   230

4.3.5   Spouse Coverage   231

4.3.6   Premiums   231

4.3.7   Portability   234

4.3.8   Criteria for Benefit Eligibility   236

4.3.9   Benefits   239

4.3.10 System Management   241

4.3.11 Reimbursement of Providers   244

4.3.12 Financing   246

4.3.13 Adjustment for Inflation   246

4.3.14 Adjustment for Unexpected
        Developments   247

4.3.15 Preliminary Cost Estimates   249

4.3.16 Transition Issues   252

4.3.17 Employer-Sponsored Plans   252

4.3.18 Other Considerations   253

Epilogue   255

Appendix   257

Part Five: Financial Planning   263

5.1 Implementing Financial Planning, Information,
     and Administrative Services   265

Epilogue   271

**Part Six: Encouraging
Continued Activity After Retirement   273**

6.1 Working Paper on Continued Activity   275

Contents

Postscript   281

Notes   285

Case Index   339

Subject Index   343

Preface

Changes in American society have affected the ways in which college faculty and staff think about retirement and about what constitutes desirable retirement planning. Principal among these changes are the erosion of the concept of involuntary retirement, a period of inflation, an uncertain economy, the increasing longevity of both men and women, changes in social security, the increasing percentages of both older people and older retirees in the population, the introduction of new financial vehicles for retirement savings and payouts, changes in the tax laws, and increasing individual, institutional, and governmental restlessness over the control and management of pension assets.

The Commission on College Retirement was formed in 1984 in response to these changes. The commission was asked to review the role and functioning of college and university retirement programs and make recommendations for improvements in such programs for the future. Although the commission received financial support from four major foundations (the Carnegie Corporation of New York, the Ford Foundation, the William and Flora Hewlett Foundation, and the Andrew W. Mellon Foundation), it was created as an independent entity. The opinions and conclusions in the commission's reports, accordingly, are solely those of the commission itself.

The charge to the commission was broad. The focus of the charge was explicitly on the retirement needs and aspira-

tions of academic institutions and on personnel in the context
of their educational responsibilities. Consistent with the thrust
of that charge, the commission resisted suggestions that it focus
primarily on Teachers Insurance and Annuity Association
(TIAA) and its affiliate, the College Retirement Equities Fund
(CREF), or, specifically, on TIAA-CREF's past performance.*
Instead, the commission concentrated its examination on retirement policies and programs that would be sound for higher
education in the decades ahead. However, the commission had
to pay close attention to the extent to which its recommended
policies and programs were consistent with existing TIAA-CREF
operating practices.

　　In most instances, those operating practices and the available services of TIAA-CREF were consistent with the commission's recommendations. In a few important instances, however — most notably with respect to the transferability of funds
to third parties either during the accumulation period for investment or later for annuitization — TIAA-CREF's operating
practices conflicted with the commission's recommendations.
When such conflicts occurred, the commission discussed them
with TIAA-CREF management and reflected them in its reports.

　　This volume brings together the separate reports issued
by the commission. Each of the reports speaks as of the date
of its original issue. Included also are other materials considered
by the commission and relevant to its conclusions.

　　In its first report, "Retirement Ages for College and
University Personnel," (Part Two of this volume), issued in
January 1986, the commission addressed the issues of retirement age policy in light of federal and state laws, the tenure
system, and the provision of sound and sensible retirement programs for college and university personnel. One of its purposes
was to point a path toward relief of the potential tension between

---

*Almost all college and university faculty in private institutions are covered by
pension plans carried out by TIAA-CREF. In addition, there are state pension
plans for public institutions. In the great majority of the states, faculty members
who work for public institutions have the option of joining TIAA-CREF. Thus,
although the college and university system in this country is extraordinarily diver-
sified, the system can be seen as bound together through one predominant pension provider.

the tenure system and the age discrimination laws, without weakening either. The issues involved have not yet been settled, but academic institutions and government authorities are intensively reviewing them.

The commission's second report was entitled "Transferability of Funds Being Accumulated by TIAA-CREF for the Benefit of College and University Personnel," published in May 1986. The report recommended that as a matter of sound pension policy, funds be transferable from TIAA and CREF to approved third-party investment managers and to approved third-party providers of annuities. The report also described a newly identified legal right to compel such transferability if it is requested both by an individual participant using TIAA and CREF services and by the participant's relevant employing institution.

The policy of transferability recommended by the commission and the legal right to compel transferability, which the commission introduced, sparked a wide examination of the newly identified legal right and the TIAA-CREF investment management policies. The management of TIAA and CREF opposed the commission's recommendation urging transferability of the funds held by TIAA-CREF during their accumulation phase. Within weeks of publication of the commission's report, TIAA-CREF publicly released a legal opinion it had obtained from a New York law firm. That opinion expressed sweeping disagreement with and condemnation of the legal right to compel transferability as identified by the commission and as supported by the commission's consultant, Professor Elias Clark of the Yale Law School.

The commission responded in May 1987 by reissuing its policy statement on transferability of funds and by supplementing it with a fresh analysis of the legal issues involved. Spencer L. Kimball, a member of the commission and professor of law at the University of Chicago Law School, wrote the analysis. Included also with the reissue of the commission's policy statement were the opinion of TIAA-CREF's New York law firm and a response to it from Professor Clark (see Part One of this volume).

TIAA-CREF came under new leadership in 1987. In a

reversal of its earlier position, TIAA-CREF announced, in April 1988, the adoption of a policy that carried out the commission's recommendation and policy statement with respect to the transferability of funds.

The commission's third report, also issued in May 1986, was entitled "A Pension Program for College and University Personnel" (Part Three of this volume). That report points out the advantages and disadvantages of the two different pension approaches currently in use — one a defined contribution plan, the other a defined benefit plan — and makes recommendations for the improvement of both. Central to the report is the distinction it makes between a core pension plan, with required annuitization to provide lifetime income, and supplementary plans with greater flexibility in investment and payout options. The objective of the recommendations is to enable individuals to have and achieve a target retirement benefit to maintain their preretirement standard of living.

A discussion paper of July 1986, on "Implementing Financial Planning, Information, and Administrative Services" (Part Five of this volume), constituted the commission's fourth report. It was intended to show the way in which academic institutions and their faculty and staff could be helped to resolve increasingly complex pension-related issues. The commission's recommendation that pension accumulations be transferred among approved investment managers during the accumulation phase, and its proposal for an individualized target benefit approach for retirement planning, added to this complexity. The need of institutions and participants to have clear, unbiased, individualized financial information available to them has become ever more pressing.

This need for improved information and benefit forecasting services was an early concern of the commission, which conducted a financial planning pilot study on twenty-one college and university campuses. Participants in that study found that broader financial planning information improved their knowledge of retirement planning needs. The commission concluded that retirement planning can be improved if conducted in the context of general financial planning and integrated with the pension programs of college and university campuses. Left for further study and discussion by the academic community was the question of how best to implement this conclusion. The commission proposed the creation of a permanent, independent organization to assist in implementation.

The commission's fifth report was also issued as a discussion draft in July 1986. It was entitled "A Plan to Create Comprehensive Group Long-Term Care Insurance for College and University Personnel" (Part Four of this volume) and was the first of its kind to outline the framework of such an insurance plan. Early in its deliberations, the commission became concerned with the perhaps 15 percent of college and university retirees who face heavy financial burdens as a result of expenses associated with long-term care services. The commission concluded that it would not be wise for individual faculty and staff members to try to save adequate funds to meet these potentially catastrophic expenses. Instead, the commission has proposed that protection against long-term care expenses be provided through group, employment-based insurance.

The commission recognized that before a plan, such as the one it outlined, could be put into effect, further careful consideration by and among the colleges and universities was essential. After such discussion, it was the commission's hope that an improved version of its plan would be developed and initially put into effect, at least on a pilot basis, by a small group of academic institutions. To continue this work, the commission looked to Harvard University and to the Commission on Long-Term Care, which Harvard established with the financial support of the Carnegie Corporation.

The five reports of the commission, which are republished in this volume and which speak only as of the dates of their issue, are accompanied by introductory material, epilogues, and a postscript. These supplementary essays are designed to put the reports into fuller context and to add the perspective provided by events that immediately followed.

Although these supplementary essays are believed to reflect the perceptions of the commission — and in some instances actually draw on language prepared by members of the commission — they are the responsibility of the editor.

Although conditions in the future are inherently uncertain,

the commission — informed by the past, by its collective experience, and by its work together and with its staff — has endeavored to put before the academic community, and before those concerned with its continued effectiveness, certain recommendations concerning retirement programs that it believes to be significant. It is the commission's hope that its recommendations will help academic institutions and their personnel meet their retirement needs and fulfill their aspirations.

New York, N. Y.   Oscar M. Ruebhausen, General Editor
April 1990

Acknowledgments

This volume would not have been possible without the initiative and financial support of four major foundations: Carnegie Corporation of New York, the Ford Foundation, the William and Flora Hewlett Foundation, and the Andrew W. Mellon Foundation. Their foresight and concern led to the formation of the Commission on College Retirement in 1984. These four foundations maintained liaison with the commission through David Z. Robinson, then executive vice president of Carnegie Corporation. The word *liaison* does not, however, adequately reflect the unflagging attention and support he provided. He was a valued participant in the work of the commission, rigorous in his analysis and wise in his commentary. The commission (and especially I, as its chair) are grateful.

The commission's staff was effectively recruited and led by Thomas C. Woodruff, executive director. I extend a warm thank you to him and to Marion Basta, Joan Erdmann, Barbara Fehrenbach, Antonio Poglianich, Zenali Tirado, Pamela Ward, and Julie Winskie. Together they gathered and organized material for the commission's study and evaluation, retained and guided the work of consultants, and ably served the commission in its deliberations and reports.

A list of the people who contributed materially to the development of the commission's conclusions and recommendations would be a long one. I must expressly acknowledge, however, the Health Policy Center at Brandeis University for the extensive contribution it made to the development of the commission's plan for creating comprehensive, group, long-term health care insurance for college and university personnel. Jay Greenberg, Stanley Wallack, Christine Bishop, Sarita Karon, Marc Cohen, and their colleagues at the Health Policy Center merit the special thanks of the commission for their intensive and creative work.

And I owe a special tribute to the individual members of the commission. It is not simply that they were rewarding to work with: knowledgeable, talented, committed, creative, and generous of spirit. Each gave unstintingly to the common endeavor. They actively participated in the drafting and redrafting of the commission's recommendations and reports. The quality of their individual contributions is perhaps epitomized by the scholarly and definitive essay by Spencer Kimball, included in this volume, on "Transferability of Funds from TIAA and CREF." No chair could be more appreciative than I am for the opportunity to participate with each of the members of the commission in responding to our charge.

Finally, I wish to thank Rachel Anderson, Gale Erlandson, and Laura Baxter of Jossey-Bass for their efforts in ensuring the smooth production of this volume and to Jeannine Marschner for her most essential editorial assistance.

OMR

Commission Members

Oscar M. Ruebhausen, Chair
Counsel, Debevoise & Plimpton

Robert M. Ball
Former U.S. Commissioner of Social Security

Boris I. Bittker
Professor of Law, Emeritus, Yale Law School

Colin G. Campbell
President, Wesleyan University

Lisle C. Carter, Jr.
Attorney, Verner, Liipfert, Bernhard and McPherson, Chartered

William T. Golden
Corporate Director and Trustee

Mary W. Gray
Professor of Mathematics, American University

Spencer L. Kimball
Professor, University of Chicago Law School

Note: Titles indicated are those in effect at the time each member joined the commission. John H. Biggs, President and Chief Executive Officer, Centerre Trust Company, and Andrew F. Brimmer, President, Brimmer and Company, Inc., both resigned as members of the commission in August 1986.

Alicia H. Munnell
Senior Vice President and Director of Research,
Federal Reserve Bank of Boston

Thomas O'Brien
Financial Vice President, Harvard University

Matilda White Riley
Associate Director, National Institute on Aging

Alfredo de los Santos, Jr.
Vice Chancellor for Educational Development,
Maricopa County Community Colleges

Harold T. Shapiro
President, University of Michigan

John B. Shoven
Vice Chairman, Department of Economics, Stanford University

Laurence A. Tisch
Chief Executive Officer, Loews Corporation

The Authors

Elias Clark is Lafayette S. Foster Professor of Law at Yale University. He received his B.A. degree (1943) in history, his LL.B. degree (1947) and his M.A. degree (1957) in law from Yale University.

Joan Ehrenworth Erdman practices law in Richmond, Virginia. She received her B.S. degree (1974) in business administration from Boston University and her J.D. degree (1977) from the University of Virginia.

Spencer L. Kimball is Seymour Logan Professor of Law, Emeritus, University of Chicago, practicing law as of counsel to the Washington, D.C., law firm of Spiegel & McDiarmid. He received his B.S. degree (1940) in mathematics from the University of Arizona, his B.C.L. degree (1949) from Oxford University, and his S.J.D. degree (1958) from the University of Wisconsin.

Oscar M. Ruebhausen is retired presiding partner of the New York City law firm of Debevoise & Plimpton. He received his A.B. degree (1934) from Dartmouth College and his L.L.B. degree (1937) from Yale University.

*Pension and Retirement Policies
in Colleges and Universities*

Part One

Transferability of Funds Invested with TIAA-CREF: The Legal Issues

The issue of transferability of funds from TIAA and CREF, while not a new one, was of growing concern when the Commission on College Retirement issued its report in May 1986. That report had an immediate impact in part because of its policy recommendations but even more so because it identified a new legal remedy whereby both TIAA and CREF might be compelled to permit transferability of funds invested with them when participating academic institutions and their employees join in seeking a transfer.

The setting for the policy issues surrounding transferability of funds and the legal remedy the commission introduced are described in the preface to the commission's May 1987 reissue of its policy statement. The following are relevant excerpts.

Billions of dollars are currently being set aside by colleges and universities to provide lifetime retirement income for faculty and other personnel. Substantial additional sums are also contributed regularly by these employees themselves to add to the funds being held, invested and accumulated for their individual benefit.

The funds being accumulated and managed for the college world are huge in absolute terms. They are equally huge in their significance to the individuals for whose benefit the funds are being accumulated and invested. By the time of retirement the sums so accumulated for the benefit of individual faculty members typically represent the major asset saved from a lifetime

1

of work. For many, it is their only significant surviving asset, apart from equity in a home.

It is not surprising, accordingly, that the investment management of the funds being accumulated to provide lifetime retirement income for college faculty is a matter of acute concern to those who are the beneficial owners of the funds involved.

The predominant organization in managing accumulating funds in furtherance of college and university pension plans is TIAA-CREF. TIAA-CREF, although one organization, is in fact two not-for-profit companies with a single management, but separate boards of trustees. One company, Teachers Insurance and Annuity Association (TIAA) was created in 1918 by the Carnegie Foundation for the Advancement of Teaching to serve the college world; the other, College Retirement Equities Fund (CREF), its affiliate, was formed by TIAA in 1952. Seven individuals, acting as trustees for the college world, control both TIAA and CREF. These seven individuals are referred to by TIAA-CREF as its "top board."

Together, TIAA and CREF today manage more than 50 billion dollars of funds for the college world. The great bulk of these funds is being invested and accumulated during the working lives of their owners. This period, prior to retirement and prior to applying the funds to the purchase of one of several types of annuities designed to provide lifetime retirement income, is known as the accumulation phase.

The accumulation phase for each participant normally lasts for decades; and normally ends with death or retirement. If death occurs first, the funds accumulated are available to be paid out to survivors. Upon retirement, however, at least 90 percent of the accumulated funds must be applied to the purchase of an annuity.

The college world, accordingly, is significantly dependent on TIAA-CREF investment management for the lifetime retirement income of its employees. TIAA-CREF is not only the sole manager of the sums placed with it, but it manages them on average for decades. The size of the funds being managed by TIAA-CREF, the duration of that investment management, and the importance of those funds to the academic retirees for whom the funds are being managed have naturally attracted critical attention.

That attention has been sharpened by what is perceived as the rigidity of TIAA-CREF's investment management policies. Under TIAA-CREF policy, once funds have been placed with it for management, those funds are, with minor exceptions, permanently locked under TIAA-CREF management. Further, the beneficiaries of the funds locked into TIAA-CREF management have only two investment choices: one is CREF which is largely an indexed equity fund, and the other is TIAA, essentially a relatively illiquid fixed income fund. More than this, although transfers of accumulating funds from CREF to TIAA are permitted by TIAA-CREF policy during the accumulation phase, the reverse is not true. Thus funds once transferred to TIAA's fixed income management are essentially locked permanently into that investment mode. Lastly, for funds managed by TIAA-CREF the only annuity options available to the beneficiaries are those offered by TIAA-CREF.

Thus, once funds have been placed with TIAA-CREF, they are subjected, in effect, to a multiple lockup, regardless of performance. With this policy of lockup, TIAA-CREF has assured itself of, in effect, a permanent monopoly in the management of funds once they are placed in its care.

These TIAA-CREF investment limitations have been a source of genuine concern — particularly in recent years when a wide variety of investment vehicles has been made available by other investment managers. By contrast, TIAA-CREF has resisted change: it has not contracted with other investment managers to provide a wider range of investment choice for the TIAA-CREF beneficiaries; it has not provided such a range of investment choice under its own management; and it has refused to permit fund transfers to other investment managers (who will maintain the commitment to ultimate annuitization of the accumulating funds). Frustration, accordingly, has added to the existing concerns of the TIAA-CREF beneficiaries.

The Commission on College Retirement, in a policy statement issued in May 1986, recommended that under certain conditions, the funds held by CREF and TIAA as fiduciaries during the accumulation phase should be transferable, in whole or in part, not only between TIAA and CREF, but to third party investment managers to be held in trust to secure for the beneficial owners a lifetime retirement income from an annuity issued either by TIAA or CREF or by a third party.

The policy of transferability recommended by the commission would meet the concern about the limited investment choice now available from TIAA-CREF during the accumulation phase. It would also change the perceived inequity of both the multiple lockup and the TIAA-CREF maintenance of its monopoly.

The recommended policy, if adopted, would also tend to relieve the present frustration in academia with what is perceived as TIAA-CREF's lack of responsiveness — a frustration that is encouraging institutions of higher education to place *future* contributions of retirement funds for their faculties with investment managers other than TIAA-CREF. Further, the present frustration, if not relieved, is almost certain at some point to force academic institutions to seek legal relief from TIAA-CREF's present multiple lockup of the funds previously so contributed.

The commission, in formulating its recommendations, was aware that TIAA-CREF has consistently rejected the recommended change in policy. The commission hoped that TIAA-CREF would reconsider, even though the commission was not encouraged by the then management of TIAA-CREF to believe that TIAA-CREF would favor a more flexible policy. The commission, accordingly, in its policy statement believed it important to identify a legal remedy which would enable colleges and universities, and their faculties, as a last resort, to compel investment policy changes desired by them for the presently "locked up" funds.

The legal rationale identified by the commission has stimulated considerable interest. Obviously, the policy issue of investment flexibility is not an issue that requires a legal remedy in order to be put into effect. It could be directly implemented by TIAA-CREF's "top board," those seven individuals who are in control of, and who are accountable for, TIAA-CREF's discharge of its responsibilities to the college world. The commission recommended this latter course in its May 1986 policy statement when it urged that

> the seven individual trustees who control both TIAA and CREF proceed affirmatively with TIAA and CREF to provide for the transferability of the funds now being accumulated for the benefit of college and university personnel. It is neither sound nor sensible for those who are acting as trustees for the college world to wait for such transferability to be ordered by the courts after litigation.

Although litigation is clearly an alternative, it is not the most desirable means of devising workable policies that meet institutional and individual retirement objectives. It would be unfortunate if the difficult task of policy-making for the transferability of accumulating retirement funds were left to the expensive, time consuming and adventitious intervention of the courts. Nevertheless, the legal issue of whether a remedy exists to compel desirable policy changes cannot be ignored.

The legal issues raised by the commission's policy statement were new. They are important. They had not previously been publicly analyzed or discussed. In the year since the commission's policy statement was prepared, however, legal commentary has appeared directed not only to the existence of a legal remedy but to analysis of the legal relationship, during the accumulation phase, of TIAA-CREF with the individuals and institutions that look to TIAA-CREF for investment management. These legal materials are of interest to all academic institutions utilizing the service of TIAA-CREF and to all faculty members, and others, who are the beneficiaries of those services in furtherance of the pension plans adopted by their institutions. . . .

The legal issues precipitated by the commission's policy statement deal with remedies. Remedies are secondary, however, to the basic policy recommendation for greater flexibility in the investment management of the billions of dollars being accumulated and invested by TIAA-CREF for the college world.

A policy of greater flexibility as recommended by the commission stands on its own feet. It is a policy which could be rewarding for institutions of higher education and for their retirees. A policy of greater flexibility will also enhance the ability of TIAA-CREF better to fulfill its responsibilities as trustees for the college world.

There is no doubt that there will be practical problems in putting a policy of investment flexibility into effect. What is most needed, however, is the will on the part of TIAA-CREF to do so.

The commission's policy statement follows, along with the legal materials that accompanied its reissue in May 1987.

1.1

Policy Statement of the Commission

Teachers Insurance and Annuity Association (TIAA) and College Retirement Equities Fund (CREF) are, and for decades have been, the dominant vehicles for the execution and administration of the defined contribution pension plans adopted by institutions of higher education.

The primary purpose of these pension plans, and of TIAA-CREF, is to provide lifetime income for retired personnel. (See TIAA-CREF Ad Hoc Committee Report on Goals and Objectives (1984), p. 15, hereinafter referred to as the Ad Hoc Committee Report.) To achieve this goal annuity contracts are entered into, generally at the time of retirement. Although the provisions of the annuity contracts vary — for example with respect to the coverage of spouses and the payout arrangements — when they are finally entered into they govern the payouts to retirees.

Prior to the annuity phase, however, there is an accumulation phase in which the potential retiree builds up funds in an investment account for use in the ultimate purchase of an annuity. During the accumulation phase, funds are set aside by colleges and universities, as well as by their personnel, to establish accounts for the benefit of those personnel when they retire. These funds are remitted to TIAA and CREF to be held and to be invested, during the accumulation phase, for the benefit of specifically identified personnel. Those personnel remain the beneficial owners of the funds held and invested on their behalf.

7

For purposes of this accumulation phase, each college or university could have accumulated the funds itself and acted as a trustee for the benefit of its own personnel. Alternatively, each college could have set the funds aside in a separate trust, with a third party as trustee for the beneficial owners, to hold, invest and ultimately to apply the accumulated funds to the purchase of the desired individual annuities. It is readily understandable why colleges did not follow either of these courses. Entrusting an accumulation of funds and the trustee's functions to a single, non-profit organization, TIAA-CREF, was and remains a more efficient and attractive alternative than either of the other two courses of action.

Under the TIAA-CREF system, all of the pension contributions can be pooled, held, invested and accumulated, and the detailed accounting records for each beneficiary maintained, under the management of a single fiduciary pending the purchase of an annuity upon the retirement of the individual beneficial owners.

Both CREF and TIAA keep a separate record of, but do not physically segregate, the pension funds contributed by or for the benefit of an individual. The funds are held and invested by CREF or TIAA for the ultimate benefit, and at the risk, of the individual who is their beneficial owner. Net earnings on the funds are credited to the account maintained for each beneficial owner. Any investment loss or appreciation is separately charged or credited to each individual beneficial owner's account.[1]

This accumulation phase — during which funds are held, invested and accumulated by CREF or TIAA for the risk and account of the beneficial owner — lasts until the accumulated funds are to be paid out either as a death benefit or used to purchase an annuity.

Thus, under the present system TIAA and CREF have two distinct and separate responsibilities: the *first* is to hold and manage the pension contributions being set aside and entrusted to them for the ultimate purchase of an annuity (or payment of a death benefit in the event of death before retirement); the *second* is to provide a lifetime income to the retiree under one or more forms of an annuity contract purchased by the retiree with the accumulated contributions.

Lifetime retirement income for college and university personnel is one of the fundamental fiduciary obligations of both CREF and TIAA under the college and university pension plans that they implement. Both CREF and TIAA have been sensitive to this obligation.[2] TIAA and CREF have repeatedly made clear their conviction that it would be a breach of "fiduciary responsibilities"[3] either to permit lump-sum cashouts [except as a death benefit] of the accumulated contributions or to permit loans of these accumulations to their beneficial owners. This sense of fiduciary obligation to the college world in adhering to the purpose of applying accumulated funds to the provision of lifetime retirement income is soundly based. It is fully supported by the commission.

The question remains, however, whether these accumulating funds, when once remitted to TIAA-CREF, must continue to be managed only by TIAA-CREF during the entire accumulation phase before annuitization.

The commission *recommends that the funds held by CREF and TIAA as fiduciaries during the accumulation phase should be transferable, in whole or in part, not only between TIAA and CREF, but to third party investment managers to be held in trust to secure for the beneficial owners a lifetime retirement income from an annuity issued either by TIAA or CREF or by a third party.*

The commission, as a matter of sound policy for institutions of higher education and for their personnel, believes that four conditions should be placed on the transfer of funds during the accumulation phase. The *first* is that such a transfer of funds be approved either specifically or generally by the relevant college or university as an option exercisable with respect to funds contributed for the benefit of their employees and exercisable by those who are the beneficial owners of such funds; the *second* is that the new investment manager, functioning as a fiduciary, and any new provider of annuities be similarly so approved and so opted for; the *third* is that any new investment manager be subject to the same commitment to annuitization as TIAA and CREF now are for core pension funds; and the *fourth* condition is that any such transfer not adversely affect the funds credited to the accounts of those beneficial owners who are not making such a transfer.[4]

The transferability which the commission recommends is more than a sound policy alternative for TIAA and CREF to adopt. The commission is persuaded that such transferability may be required as a matter of law,[5] if it is appropriately requested by a college or university and by a beneficial owner under that institution's pension plan.

The legal basis for the commission's conclusion is outlined in the opinion of its consultant, Professor Elias Clark of the Yale Law School. Professor Clark's opinion is attached as Appendix A to this report.

The commission finds the legal basis for permitting transferability to other trustees during the accumulation phase a compelling one. The policy considerations are equally so. Thus:

1. Reason and equity combine in support of the proposition that beneficial owners of accumulating funds, who bear the investment risk during the accumulation phase, should have some say as to who is to manage those funds while they are accumulating.
2. Prudence also suggests that the entire pension accumulation of college and university personnel should not be required to be concentrated with a single investment manager, no matter how astute or qualified, if the beneficial owners desire diversification.
3. The diversity of the college and university population, and the diversity of individual needs during a normal career and life course, call for greater flexibility in investment objectives than that now afforded by TIAA (a somewhat illiquid bond and mortgage fund) or CREF (an equity fund largely indexed to the Standard & Poor's 500).
4. Choice, at the end of the accumulation phase, of the terms and conditions under which life income is to be paid to retirees and their spouses, and the amounts of such payments, beyond the choices then currently offered by TIAA and CREF annuities, should, through competition, bring additional material benefits.

5. Transferability of the accumulating pension funds would bring benefits to TIAA and CREF as well as to the college world. The dominant position now occupied by TIAA-CREF in managing defined contribution pension funds gives it many of the attributes of a monopoly. The transferability that the commission recommends would bring both productive tension to TIAA-CREF's management of the accumulating pension funds and a new, pragmatic form of accountability. These, in turn, should lift the level of TIAA-CREF performance and encourage both TIAA and CREF to add to the range and usefulness of their services to the college world.

6. Recognition by TIAA and CREF of a right to transferability should substantially reduce some of the current disaffection of the beneficial owners and their institutions with the present TIAA-CREF "lockup" of their pension funds.

Both TIAA and CREF have thus far rejected transfers of accumulated funds ("roll-overs") to others than themselves even if, apparently, the transferred funds are to be held in trust for the purpose of providing the desired lifetime retirement income.

Once funds are, at the designation of the beneficial owner, transferred to TIAA, for example, those funds under present TIAA policy are "locked up."[6] They cannot even be transferred thereafter back to CREF. They can, however, be cashed out for a death benefit or, on retirement, used to purchase a TIAA annuity.

CREF is only slightly less rigid. CREF funds are transferable to TIAA but, as of now, nowhere else, although plans have been announced for funds to which transfers might be made from CREF.

The boards of trustees of TIAA-CREF and their ad hoc committee[7] have also rejected the conclusions which the commission has reached. Neither TIAA, nor CREF, nor the ad hoc committee, however, appear to have considered the legal analysis which the commission finds to be persuasive.

The bulk of the ad hoc committee discussion concerns the problems of the illiquidity of the funds held by TIAA, and of the differences between market and book value of the TIAA securities, apparently compelled by insurance law. The commission agrees with the TIAA-CREF ad hoc committee that this is a significant problem. At certain times accordingly, the commission's fourth condition for transferability (that remaining participants should not be hurt by the transfer) might not be met.

Moreover, the ad hoc committee in rejecting transferability of the funds held by CREF, did so in the analytical context of dealing, *at the same time* and as if there were no differences, not only with *both* TIAA and CREF, but also *both* with lump-sum cashouts and with transfers to another trustee. This blurs the analysis. It remains unclear, for example, whether the ad hoc committee report would use the same reasoning and reach the same conclusion, if it examined separately the option to transfer CREF funds to a new trustee to be accumulated and held for ultimate annuitization.[8]

Thus, if the ad hoc committee's report had dealt separately with CREF on this issue of transferability of funds, it might well have shared our conclusions:

1. that there are no legal barriers to the transferability of the beneficial owner's funds under the conditions we propose.
2. that sound policy recommends such transferability, and
3. that prevailing trust law supports such transferability.

The commission's conclusion with respect to the transferability of TIAA's accumulation of funds held for the beneficial owners is the same as it is for the CREF funds. However, the problems of disintermediation and of insurance law must be dealt with. There are a number of possible solutions. Thus, TIAA could allow transfer only during periods of time when the allowable charges for transfer would mean that current TIAA holders would not be harmed (for example, since in New York a 7 percent charge can be made, one insurance company allows transfers at the lesser of book or market whenever the market value is above 93 percent of book value). Or, transfers could be limited in ways that would make them in fact "de minimis" in character, while accepting the overarching principle of transferability. Or, investment practices could be adjusted to reduce the impact of disintermediation without materially or adversely affecting yields.

The commission also recognizes that permitting transferability of funds during the accumulation phase, and at annuitization, will increase the pressures on, and the decisional burdens of, the colleges and universities. They will be called upon to decide when, to what extent, under what conditions, and for what purposes transferability will be requested or approved by them. While recognizing this increased burden of responsibility, the commission is satisfied that colleges and universities can devise effective procedures to respond successfully without jeopardizing the fundamentals of the pension system now in place.

In consideration of all of the foregoing, it is the further recommendation of the commission that the seven individual trustees who control both TIAA and CREF proceed affirmatively with TIAA and CREF to provide for the transferability of the funds now being accumulated for the benefit of college and university personnel. It is neither sound nor sensible for those who are acting as trustees for the college world to wait for such transferability to be ordered by the courts after litigation.

The commission believes that TIAA-CREF, consistent with its history as trustee for the college and university world, will move constructively and promptly to establish a fair and equitable mechanism of transfer that will meet the needs of educational institutions and their employees, and fulfill the fiduciary responsibility that TIAA undertook when it was established almost seventy years ago.

1.2

Transferability of Funds from TIAA and CREF

Spencer L. Kimball

1.2.1 Introduction

In 1905, the Carnegie Foundation for the Advancement of Teaching was established with a $15 million endowment for the purpose of giving free pensions to college teachers. Such provision for all retired educators being beyond Carnegie's financial capacity, "Teachers Insurance and Annuity Association (TIAA) was founded by the Carnegie Foundation for the Advancement of Teaching in 1918 and was operated as a part of the Foundation until 1936."[1] TIAA is structured as an insurance company under the insurance laws of New York to provide retirement annuities on a self-supporting and financially sound basis for teachers in institutions of higher education.

In part to respond to the ravages of inflation on annuities based on portfolios consisting mainly of debt instruments, and in part to permit greater diversification of investment, the New York legislature, by a 1952 special act, created College Retirement Equities Fund (CREF) as a companion organization to

Note: I wish to express appreciation to Boris Bittker, Walter Blum, Elias Clark, Francis Gunning, David Robinson, Oscar Ruebhausen, and Thomas Woodruff for many helpful comments on earlier drafts. I especially appreciate the challenges to positions in the earlier drafts that led me to reconsider some of them. None of the above is responsible for any errors or mistaken judgments in the final product. In some instances I have exercised a willful author's prerogative of refusing to be persuaded of error, however egregious readers may consider such error to be.

TIAA, and thus provided "the first unit-valued variable annuity with the objective of providing an equity-based investment component for college pension plans."[2]

Together, TIAA and CREF now operate one of the largest nongovernmental pension programs in the world. TIAA alone is, whether measured by assets or by premium income, among the largest life insurers in the United States and even in the world.[3] Though technically a life insurer, TIAA's size results from its annuity business; its life insurance business is limited.

TIAA and CREF are legally separate but closely linked. Common trustees hold all the (nondividend-paying) stock of TIAA and, as the sole members of CREF, control that fund as well. The active managements overlap; they operate essentially as a single organization.

TIAA and CREF receive contributions during the working lives of the individual participants — contributions paid mainly by the educational institutions that employ them. Sometimes individual participants also contribute; the arrangements for contributions vary from one institution to another in amount and degree of participation. Even for those plans in which an individual participant decides little about the arrangement except what proportion of the contributions should be in TIAA and what proportion in CREF, the contributions are always identified as attributable in specific amounts to individual participants. The latter become owners of the contributions made in their behalf, subject to certain restrictions discussed below.[4] At retirement, the accumulated amounts are annuitized and provide lifetime income to the individual participants.

This paper will examine the accumulation phases of TIAA and CREF and will discuss the extent to which the funds accumulated are and should be irretrievably locked up in TIAA and CREF. Conversely, we will examine the extent to which individual participants may now make, or should be permitted to make, transfers of parts or all of the accumulations to other managers pending annuitization and to use other vehicles for annuitization. And we will explore whether the consent or cooperation of TIAA-CREF and of the institutions that contribute to the individuals' accumulations is necessary or should be necessary for such transfers. Further, because a fairness issue has been raised regarding transfers from CREF to managers other than TIAA, while transfers from TIAA are not allowed, I shall give attention to the question of whether there should be parallel treatment of participants in TIAA and CREF.

I have been a member of the Commission on College Retirement since it was formed in April 1984 as an independent entity to study and to make recommendations for improving the functioning of college retirement programs. The commission had no preconceived positions; we reached our conclusions after extensive discussion and after receiving help from appropriate experts. Because of the dominance of TIAA-CREF in the academic retirement field, that institution received special attention during the commission's deliberations.

I agree with the relevant policy recommendations of the commission, though in minor respects I would have stated them differently.[5] I seek here mainly to explore the practical and legal obstacles to implementation of the policy recommendation that transferability during the accumulation phase should be facilitated from both TIAA and CREF to other reliable and effective managers of funds, to the extent consistent with the commission's position, also strongly held by TIAA-CREF and by most educational institutions, that the funds should only be available (though not necessarily to the last dollar) to assure a lifetime income by annuitization at the time of retirement.[6] TIAA-CREF management has emphasized the supposed obstacles to transferability and has energetically argued that they cannot be overcome; to initial appearances, outside legal advisers of that management seem to support the management position.[7]

The initial part of this inquiry will describe the actual arrangements made by TIAA-CREF with participating institutions and, through them, with individual participants.

1.2.2 The Contracts

1.2.2.1 Description of the Funds

For each participant in TIAA and CREF, there is an accumulation phase and a payout phase. The phases can be sharply separated, both factually and conceptually, by the act of annuitization. At annuitization, the aggregate amount of the accumulated funds determines the amount of the annuity, and payment begins. Generally this occurs at the time of retirement, though there need not be exact correspondence of annuitization and retirement. In some circumstances there may be partial annuitization, marking the separation of the phases only for those funds annuitized. When annuitization occurs, whether total or partial, it is irrevocable.

The transition from accumulation to payout provides a sharply defined point at which the relationships between the parties change. CREF recognizes the clear distinction by converting accumulation units into annuity units at that point. For analytical purposes, a simple matrix consists of four distinct segments of the TIAA-CREF program (see Figure 1.1).

Figure 1.1. Phases of the TIAA-CREF Funds.

	TIAA	CREF
Accumulation phase		
Payout phase		

In this paper, I am not interested in the payout phases of TIAA and CREF; from the point of retirement on, it clearly seems most appropriate to consider the relationship to be one based on an individual retirement annuity, a form of insurance contract. That aspect of mortality risk that is insured by annuities — the risk of living too long — becomes important at the moment when the money flow changes direction from in to the insurer to out to the annuitant. Prior to that point, the relevant mortality risk is only of premature death, which would be covered (if at all) by life insurance contracts. The aspect of mortality risk relevant to annuities having come into existence and having been assumed by TIAA or CREF upon retirement, insurance law should now govern. Even if there were possibilities under insurance law of providing for transfer or cashout after the annuity begins, the commission would not suggest that either transfers or cashouts in any amount should be allowed after annuitization.

In the accumulation phases, however, it is not clear without closer scrutiny that it is most appropriate, for either TIAA or CREF, to describe the relationship as one based on a retirement annuity contract; it is particularly doubtful for CREF. Though TIAA and CREF are closely linked, they present distinct problems and should be separately considered.

For both TIAA and CREF, there is an "understanding" that at retirement the accumulated funds will be annuitized.[8] In CREF's case, the accumulations may be transferred in whole or in part to TIAA for conversion to an annuity based on a portfolio made up mainly of bonds and mortgages; what is not transferred will be converted into a variable annuity within CREF, based on equities. In neither case is there an option to transfer funds to some other institution for annuitization. For both TIAA and CREF, accumulated funds may be paid out in a lump sum (or in alternative ways) if there is death before retirement. And for both TIAA and CREF, there is an option to withdraw up to 10 percent of the accumulation in cash at retirement — the so-called Retirement Transition Benefit (RTB).[9] The understanding about annuitization is contained in the written instruments governing the arrangement; the limited cashout is a "benefit" not provided in the contracts but allowed by TIAA-CREF on the mistaken notion that it is de minimis.[10] Annuitization is imposed involuntarily on individual participants by the agreement between the institutional contributors and TIAA-CREF. There are no cash surrender values, rollovers, transfers, or loan values.[11]

Deposits by the contributors, whether institutions or individual participants, are credited to individual accounts and create explicit interests of each individual participant in the TIAA or the CREF portfolio, however those interests may be conceptualized. It is reasonable to assume that the contributing institutions desire that the agreed annuitization take place, but the institutions have no further property interest in funds once they are paid over to TIAA-CREF.[12]

1.2.2.1.1 CREF. TIAA was created as an insurance company when inflation was not perceived as a serious problem and no way to deal with it had been devised. There had been a long period of comparative stability in the value of the dollar, and expectations for the future did not contemplate troublesome inflation. TIAA annuities were based upon a portfolio consisting, in the main, of long-term bonds and mortgages. They were similar to fixed-dollar annuities, though participation in excess investment earnings caused them to increase over time rather than remain fixed in amount.

CREF was created in part to provide the annuitant with a hedge against inflation when inflation had become a pervasive fact of life — in part to provide for more diversification and in part to offer a chance at a better return (though with a higher risk). Its holdings have been primarily in equities. The CREF annuity is a variable annuity measured in annuity (or payout) units, the dollar value of which changes in relation to the market value of the investment portfolio. In the accumulation phase, CREF operates no differently than would a mutual fund that primarily holds equities, except for the so-called spendthrift provision (or understanding) about annuitization upon retirement, the limitation on the right to transfer (to TIAA only), and no right to withdraw more than the *de minimis* 10 percent RTB.

During accumulation, the individual participant's interest in CREF is measured in accumulation units; the number of accumulation units acquired through a contribution is essentially the dollar amount of the contribution divided by the dollar value of each accumulation unit at the time of contribution. The dollar value of each accumulation unit is the market value of the total CREF portfolio attributable to the accumulation phase divided by the number of accumulation units then existing. At any moment, it is possible to calculate the value of the interests of any individual participant by multiplying the number of accumulation units held by the current value of each unit. Each figure can be precisely calculated. Speaking colloquially, one can say exactly how much one's "ownership" interest in the CREF portfolio is worth, to a fraction of a penny.

1.2.2.1.2 TIAA. The TIAA accumulation phase is in some respects like a program of regular savings in a hypothetical mutual savings bank that permanently guarantees interest at 3 percent, builds a contingent reserve to back that guarantee by making charges against the participants' accounts, and also provides full participation in excess earnings. The differences are the spendthrift provision of the TIAA contract that requires annuitization (with correlative provisions limiting withdrawal from TIAA) and the method of valuing the assets and the payouts provided for.

Certain guarantees exist in the TIAA accumulation phase. Insurance law requires that investment returns be guaranteed to be at least 3 percent (formerly 2.5 percent) on the amounts contributed, plus any additional amounts credited to the individual's account;[13] excess earnings are credited to the individual accounts. The amounts contributed plus excess earnings so credited, all with investment returns at 3 percent, are guaranteed as a death benefit if death occurs prior to retirement.[14] The guarantee applies no matter what the market value of the individual's account may be. At retirement, there is also the cashout privilege previously mentioned (the RTB) for 10 percent of the account as thus valued, whatever its market value. (CREF has no similar investment guarantees; the individual participant earns whatever the portfolio earns, gets a death benefit equal to his share of the portfolio, measured in accumulation units translatable into dollars, and gets a 10 percent RTB valued at market.) The TIAA guarantees represent transfers from the individual to TIAA as en entity of *investment* risk, not of *mortality* risk.[15]

TIAA points to Section 38 of the Retirement Annuity Contract as a transfer of mortality risk. That section provides a rate schedule for the computation of benefits (changeable from time to time on three months' notice, as to future accumulations only). The general description in the contract says that "Each premium paid to TIAA for your annuity buys a definite amount of lifetime income for you."

In a formal sense, the contention is plausible. If the participant's life continues to the time of annuitization, TIAA has promised to pay certain sums periodically thereafter until death, irrespective of the length of the annuitant's life. That appears to be a transfer of mortality risk. Yet it must be asked what risk there is that the participant will live too long. The answer is, in the context of a retirement benefit program, none, until he or she first lives to the time of annuitization. Until that date, the participant's risk is of premature death. Even at retirement, the risk of living too long is small initially, becoming greater as time passes. Annuities convert accumulated savings into periodic payments to the annuitant, on average paying back the premiums paid in plus investment earnings. The paybacks seldom exceed that amount by large proportions, as they sometimes do in life insurance. In any event, in the context of a retirement benefit program the mortality risk relevant to annuities comes into existence and is transferred only when the annuities are calculated and payments start.

Section 38 specifies an interest rate and a mortality table to be used in computing the annuity on annuitization. This aspect of Section 38, while indeed a guarantee, is not in itself a transfer of the individual's mortality risk but, instead, of the risk that the mortality experience of the TIAA population will change. It is much more like investment risk than it is like mortality risk, and some of what is said below about investment risk is applicable to it. The same is true of all deferred annuity contracts, of course; TIAA-CREF is not peculiar in this respect. Nor do I suggest that such a guarantee has no value, though it is not clear in advance whether the value, as to a particular cohort of participants, is positive or negative. That depends on what happens over time to the mortality experience of the TIAA population. The guarantee is funded by transfers between generations, not by any TIAA funds, for TIAA has no funds of its own to use for that purpose.

Mortality risk is transferred to TIAA (and to CREF) only when the accumulations are used to fund a retirement annuity. That division is sharp; only at that point does TIAA (or CREF) assume the risk of too-long life.

The significance of the limited transfer of investment risk is repeatedly overestimated; in relation to the amounts at stake, the guarantees are minimal. The recent history of the economy is such that a guarantee of 3 percent in nominal and not real terms, is inconsequential; with TIAA's careful investment program, the probabilities of failure to earn that rate for the forseeable future are small. Although inflation has been much reduced, there is little likelihood that it has been, or in the near future will be, reduced to zero or that there will be deflation. The risk transferred in the other guarantees (except that in Section 38) is identical; it is investment risk. The risk transferred by Section 38 is similarly inconsequential.

Second, and more important, even the unlikely failure to achieve the 3 percent rate of earnings does not mean that TIAA as an entity would somehow absorb the losses and protect the participants. Except for the nominal amount of capital ($1 million) supplied by Carnegie Corporation, TIAA has no funds of its own to make up any deficiency in earnings.[16] Such a deficiency would result first in the drawdown of contingency reserves, which are built up by deductions from the contributions of individual participants and their employers rather than by capital invested by shareholders.[17] After exhaustion of those reserves, insolvency would result in the casting of the losses rateably onto the individual participants — except to the extent that other life insurers, whether voluntarily or through guaranty funds, "bailed out" the insolvent TIAA. The transfer of investment risk to TIAA is purely formal; the true investment risk remains on the individual participants (with the qualification that some backup may be provided by the life insurance industry).[18]

Many life insurance companies issue contracts similar to the TIAA contract, but usually without the spendthrift rule precluding cashout above 10 percent and without the TIAA practice prohibiting transfer to anyone else. Formerly, the annuity considerations of such companies, like the premiums of traditional life insurance contracts, were fixed in amount rather than based on a percentage of salary as are the TIAA contributions. But it is now common for life insurers to issue contracts for retirement annuities with flexible periodic contributions or "premiums."[19]

The investment portfolios of CREF and TIAA differ substantially, so that one fund is suitable for variable annuities based on equities, the other for annuities based on a portfolio made up primarily of debt instruments. The latter annuities have a guaranteed base payment that has increased as a result of excess earnings.[20] In addition, a few other differences exist between the accumulation phases of TIAA and CREF. Under present TIAA practice, the market values of the individual participants' interests cannot be ascertained with the precision possible for CREF, but that does not matter because it is never necessary to ascertain market value for TIAA. No commitments of TIAA, either during accumulation or during payout, depend for their amounts on market value; commitments are measured and paid in terms of book value, ascertained under the conventional accounting methods of insurance regulation. The most important such convention is that long-term bonds are not valued at market but on an amortization basis.[21]

The amortization method makes sense for assets funding long-term obligations that are guaranteed as to minimum amount (supplemented by excess earnings) when the assets sufficiently, though not necessarily closely, match the obligations. In a period of unusually high interest rates, market valuation would make such an insurer appear insolvent, even if it could still comfortably perform its obligations over both the short and the long terms. An insurer that can meet all its obligations as they become due is sound. Thus, though TIAA's portfolio is estimated to have been worth on the market, in January 1982, only 63 percent of book value, it was presumably as sound both then and now, when the portfolio is said by common report to have a market value well in excess of 100 percent of book;[22] it will be able to meet all its obligations as they mature despite market fluctuations. At least, TIAA manages to earn consistently high ratings from Best's Reports, the bible of the insurance industry. Further, to one familiar with the insurance accounting or valuation conventions, TIAA will also appear to be sound so long as there is sufficient matching of assets and obligations.

1.2.2.2 Relevant Terms of the TIAA and CREF Contracts

1.2.2.2.1 TIAA. The relevant provisions of the contracts and practices of TIAA-CREF are simplest with TIAA. Contributions once made to TIAA are locked in until paid out as

annuities, with minor exceptions upon death before retirement or upon termination of employment while the accumulated funds are still truly *de minimis* (under the Employee Retirement Income Security Act [ERISA] of 1974, the present value of accumulations must be under $3,500).[23] Two other exceptions are considerably more important. One permits withdrawal at the time of retirement of up to 10 percent of the funds accumulated under the basic contract, at book value. This withdrawal (the RTB) cannot properly be called *de minimis,* and it should not have been created. The other exception is an unlimited right of withdrawal of those funds accumulated under the voluntary supplemental retirement annuities (SRAs). This policy presents no problems for CREF but can create serious inequities in TIAA inasmuch as withdrawals are at book value rather than market value. A front end load for SRA contributions is intended to take care of administrative costs as well as the possible inequities in such withdrawals, but it cannot effectively do so.

TIAA has no provision for loans or cash values, though both are available in some conventional annuities issued by other insurers, and even in some flexible payment annuities.[24] At the time of retirement, the participant has a variety of choices among possible annuity options. But, with the exceptions noted above, there must be annuitization, and it must be in TIAA.

1.2.2.2.2 CREF. The CREF terms and practices are slightly more liberal. In addition to the options mentioned for TIAA (and annuitization in CREF in a variable annuity with options parallel to those available in TIAA), it is permissible to transfer out all or any part of the CREF accumulations at market value, though only to TIAA. (The reverse transfer is not permitted; once the transferred funds are in TIAA, they are locked in as tightly as if they originally had been placed there.) The transfer from CREF may be made at the end of any month by a letter postmarked on or before the last day of the month. The letter may even be posted after the markets are closed so that the transferor knows exactly how the markets stand at that point and therefore knows, within a narrow range, how the transfer will fare. While the exact value of a CREF accumulation unit cannot easily be known for some days, a telephone call to an 800 number on the last day of the month — the only day on which transfers are currently permitted — will give the value at the end of the previous month and the estimated difference, in percentage terms, from that value as of the close of the previous business day. This is not difficult for CREF to do because about 80 percent of the CREF portfolio is passively managed and reasonably closely tracks important market indices, especially the S&P 500.

1.2.2.3 Conceptualization of the Relationships

In communications to the commission, TIAA-CREF has assumed, without examination, that both CREF and TIAA contracts are individual retirement annuities (a form of insurance contract), even during the accumulation phase.[25] But in other contexts, where other stakes are involved, TIAA-CREF has described the relationship differently; in dealing with Congress on pending tax legislation, it has sought the advantage of being taxed no more than a pension trust, which would be zero, and has repeatedly said it is governed by charitable trust law.[26]

Outside counsel for management, the Dewey, Ballantine firm of New York (hereafter, Dewey), has also taken the position that the TIAA and CREF relationships with participants are based on individual retirement annuities and, indeed, has assumed that without discussion. The lengthy opinion letter supplied by Dewey assumes from start to finish that there is "a retirement annuity contract," not bothering to ask whether that is an apt description.[27] In considering that unasked question, one must distinguish sharply between TIAA and CREF, which Dewey does only in passing, and between the accumulation and payout phases, which Dewey glosses over — apparently without seeing that there may be a crucial difference.[28] Not perceiving the differences in the four cell matrix, Dewey assumes that the same analysis is appropriate for all cells in the matrix and that a retirement annuity contract exists in all four settings. In that way, Dewey has continuously begged the basic questions — what is the proper (or best) conceptualization of each of the four phases and whether the same conceptualization is best for all purposes and must be used for all purposes. This weakness appears throughout the opinion. [29]

It is most helpful and realistic to think of the CREF and TIAA accumulation phases as sui generis. Indeed, TIAA-CREF took essentially that position in its dealings with the Congress on the tax question described above. The question then is reduced to how the accumulation phases should be conceptualized for particular purposes. It is clear that they can easily be conceived in terms other than those of an insurance contract. Professor Elias Clark of the Yale Law School has argued, quite plausibly, that the relationship of TIAA-CREF with the participants is a trust relationship and that pursuant to trust law, the grantor can change the trustee with the consent of all beneficiaries. [30] While that contention is not totally free from difficulty, at least with respect to TIAA, it deserves far more respectful treatment and penetrating analysis than the condescending dismissal (albeit in forty pages) it gets in the singularly unpersuasive Dewey opinion letter. The trust analysis of Professor Clark seems especially compelling for the accumulation phase of CREF; it would be supererogatory to repeat it here. [31]

In analyzing the nature of the relationships in question, it is crucial to keep in mind that TIAA-CREF is no more than a useful vehicle created to serve the higher education community, not an entity entitled to pursue its own interests. Whatever conceptualization is given, the relationship must subordinate TIAA-CREF to the interests and control of the parties who do have legitimate interests.

TIAA-CREF itself generally stands on the high moral ground — that it is the vehicle through which higher educational institutions and their employees achieve their desires for a satisfactory program of lifetime retirement income. TIAA-CREF is not and does not claim to be a profit-seeking entrepreneur that has a right to preserve for itself the benefits of bargains it has made. It is no more than a servant, a vehicle, for a community whose interests it exists to advance. This general (and proper) position is betrayed by the view expressed, apparently seriously, in the Dewey opinion letter, that the nontransferability and control of accumulated funds somehow becomes a substantive right of TIAA-CREF, of which it cannot be deprived without its consent.[32] It is hard to see how TIAA-CREF can have any rights that are inconsistent with the desires of participants, save for the sole purpose of protecting threatened interests of other participants.

Dewey does respond to some of Clark's points quite specifically. It argues that if the accumulation phase of either TIAA or CREF is a trust, it must be regarded as a single trust and that all beneficiaries must consent to any change in the trustee by the creator of the trust, under the New York Estates, Powers, and Trusts Law (hereafter, EPTL) Section 7-1.9(a).[33] The statute does require unanimous consent by all beneficiaries before the grantor may change the trustee or the trust terms. But the argument that TIAA or CREF is a single trust, with the trust res being the total portfolio (in which case it would clearly be impossible to get unanimous consent of all participants), is based by Dewey on the obvious inability to identify a separate trust res for each participant by tracing individual monthly contributions into identifiable assets.[34] Apparently, Dewey would have us believe that a trust res may never consist of a defined proportion of a portfolio. Yet, if the trust analysis is valid at all, the express contemplation by all contracting parties that assets and investments will be commingled would surely make the accumulation fund phases into common trust funds, even without the benefit of applicable statutes.[35]

1.2.2.3.1 CREF. Pursuant to CREF's established method of operation, a contribution purchases a determinable number of accumulation units in CREF. An individual's interest in CREF's portfolio can be precisely determined at any given moment as so many accumulation units (or shares) worth so much each; both numbers are susceptible to precise determination. That whole amount is payable without deductions to beneficiaries of participants on death or (subject to certain restrictions) may be paid in installments or annuitized — not as life insurance (no life contingencies are involved) but as an accumulated ownership interest in CREF's portfolio. The amount payable is not based on a promise but is a proportionate share of the CREF portfolio. By TIAA-CREF's own rules, it is transferable to TIAA, in part or in whole, at the end of any month and at the sole election of the participant, subject only to conformity to minor conditions on the method of requesting transfer. On retirement, 10 percent of the value of the interest can be taken by the participant in cash; the remainder must be annuitized. For any of these purposes, the value of the interest can be fixed with more certainty than that of any trust res consisting of a separate parcel of real property, which can unquestionably be a trust res.[36] Nor is the identity of this res any less certain.

The statute creating CREF provided that "The corporation (CREF) . . . shall have power (a) to acquire property . . . either absolutely *or in trust . . . without any obligation to segregate contributions, or the investment thereof,* of participating institutions or their teachers and other employees or both" (emphasis added).[37] While admittedly this does not establish that CREF is acting as a trustee of the contributed funds during the accumulation phase, or that there are a multitude of trusts, it surely does confirm the notion that CREF can be a trustee of funds, even though it has not segregated the assets for each individual trust.[38]

Professor Clark suggests[39] that CREF is a Type B corporation under the New York Not-for-Profit Corporation Law,[40] basing his suggestion on a filing to that effect by CREF under Section 113 of the law. If CREF is a Type B corporation, it becomes necessary to explain why Section 513(a) of that law, declaring that a Type B corporation is not to "be deemed a trustee of an express trust of such assets," is not applicable. The most cursory glance at the list of Type B purposes makes it clear why corporations of Type B should not be trustees but beneficial owners, even when there are restrictions on the uses to which they may put the property.

Without further analysis, Dewey eagerly seized upon the Clark suggestion, which is favorable to the other-than-tax-purposes position of TIAA-CREF, that CREF is not a trust. It is not obvious, however, that CREF is in fact a Type B corporation. Type C seems a more appropriate characterization, for CREF is a corporation organized for a lawful business purpose to achieve a lawful public or quasi-public objective. Section 201(c) of the law makes a corporation Type C if any of its purposes is within the Type C definition. Whether it is still possible to challenge the self-classification of CREF made long ago, even if the challenge is on behalf of participants for whose benefit CREF holds funds, is a question apparently never raised before. If the classification was erroneous when made, it is hard to see why a court should permit CREF to rely on its own error to avoid responding to the wishes of the individual and institutional participants whose servant CREF claims to be.[41]

If CREF is Type C, Section 513(a) does not apply, making Professor Clark's explanation unnecessary. Even if the characterization of CREF as a Type B corporation were correct, Professor Clark's interpretation of Section 513(a) is reasonable.[42] It is essentially reducible to the same argument as mine.

During the accumulation phase — until retirement — CREF exhibits none of the characteristics of insurance. Until retirement, nothing looks like an annuity. Neither investment risk nor mortality risk is transferred to CREF, the manager. As a result, the full market value of the participant's share of the CREF portfolio, without any deductions, remains available for such purposes as the arrangement contemplates or, indeed, for any other legitimate purposes. The relationship of the participant to CREF is different from that to a group of mutual funds only in the limitation of transfers to a single transferee and the spendthrift provision that requires annuitization of (all but 10 percent of) the funds accumulated. It is remarkably similar to a common trust fund, with CREF being the trustee. Both the possibility of a trust relationship and the commingling of the funds seem to be contemplated by the organic statute and by the contracts (which would be the trust instruments). The individual participant in CREF shares in the total portfolio rather than being merely a promisee of specific promises.

The primary argument to support the notion that the accumulation phase in CREF is an insurance contract is that the provisions respecting it are united in a single document with those respecting the payout phase, which is called an individual variable retirement annuity. Educational institutions that have made parallel arrangements for regulated investment companies to be managers during accumulation have often required, and are free to require, annuitization on retirement by purchase of an annuity from qualified institutions. Sometimes the annuitization has even been limited to TIAA and CREF themselves. In only unimportant formal ways is that different from the arrangement with CREF. It is elementary that a single document may combine various arrangements and define different relationships of parties for different circumstances or different time periods, such as a trust initially and a contract later.

A purely formal test based on the unity of the transaction document is a flimsy basis for calling the CREF accumulation phase insurance. As between the competing trust and insurance analogies, the similarities and differences weigh heavily on the side of the trust. Assuming an annuity agreement without careful analysis is an analytical error pervading the Dewey opinion. The trust analysis, for the reasons forcefully advanced by Professor Clark, makes better sense for the CREF accumulation phase, even as currently structured.

The important point with respect to CREF is that an analogy that competes powerfully with the annuity model is available. Legal decision makers such as courts, applying precedents to a new situation, must deal frequently with competing analogies — often because the subject phenomenon has enough similarity to each analogy and few enough differences that each would probably govern were it not for the other. There is no irresistible compulsion to choose one rather than another of the alternatives. Choice may be based on either the comparative degrees of similarity or (more likely in contemporary decision making) on the policy considerations involved.[43] The primary policy consideration here is the desirability of giving maximum control over accumulations for retirement to the contributors and to the beneficiaries affected by the decision — with TIAA-CREF regarded as a servant of the higher educational community and not as an entrepreneur with independent rights of its own.

1.2.2.3.2 TIAA. As with CREF, it matters not at all that a single document provides for both the accumulation and payout phases of TIAA. But because the mechanics of TIAA's operation, especially the valuation of assets, resemble those of insurance, and because they conform to usual insurance regulatory patterns, TIAA provides what in form is more like an insurance contract than does CREF. In substance and purpose, on the other hand, the TIAA accumulation phase is more like the CREF accumulation phase and a trust than it is like an insurance contract. It is only in a few areas of the modern law that form is elevated over substance; there is no reason to think this is such an area. As explained above, the reality is that no significant investment risk is transferred; that transfer is show, not substance. And while there is some pretense of transfer of mortality risk, there is in reality no such transfer in the accumulation phase. Until annuitization, the TIAA relationship looks only the slightest bit more like insurance than does the CREF relationship.

Both the CREF and the TIAA accumulation phases are sui generis; without distortion, they can be conceptualized either as contracts or as trusts. Characterizing them is an undertaking in which policy considerations, not form, should be decisive. The trust concept subordinates TIAA-CREF to the parties with the real interests; the insurance contract concept does not. There is another way to conceptualize them — a way apparently chosen by TIAA-CREF management and a way that shows the flexibility management really considers possible. That way is to speak of insurance contract when transferability is in issue and to emphasize subjection to charitable trust law when taxation is the question.[44]

It makes sense to follow TIAA-CREF's lead in approach, though not necessarily in result. There is no good reason to require that the accumulation phase of either TIAA or CREF be considered an annuity for all purposes or a trust for all purposes. Nothing is more familiar in law than a change in characterization as the purpose of the inquiry changes. Because it has been and still is contemplated that the accumulation phases of both TIAA and CREF will normally lead to an annuity, it is entirely appropriate for the Internal Revenue Service (IRS) to consider the accumulation phases of both to be annuities within the meaning of Section 403(b) of the Internal Revenue Code, as the service has done. Section 403(b) excludes the contributions of the employer from the employee's gross income "if an annuity contract is purchased." It does not matter that in another forum, for such unrelated purposes as protecting the employee's interests, an accumulation should be subjected to trust law or other body of law, so long as the goals of the tax law are not thereby subverted. They would not be in this case. The technical and sometimes artificial rules of the federal tax law create the problem that leads TIAA-CREF to fear the word *trust* in this context, though TIAA-CREF itself was using the word before anyone else did, and (perhaps surprisingly) was doing so in a tax context.

TIAA-CREF officials suggest that the consequence of having the accumulation phases of TIAA and CREF declared trusts to make transferability possible might "destroy this retirement system and . . . expose employees in higher education to huge tax liabilities." This would be the result, they say, because TIAA and CREF "could not meet the requirements of a regulated investment company" for purposes of Section 403(b)(7) of the Internal Revenue Code nor those of a qualified pension trust under Section 401(a). The tax exemption enjoyed under the TIAA-CREF system is based instead on their both providing annuity contracts under Section 403(b)(1).[45] Yet, because the IRS already has declared both to be annuities for tax purposes, TIAA-CREF's agreement to joint requests from institutions and individual participants for such transfers as Section 1035 of the Internal Revenue Code permits (and which are not unfair to other participants) would probably eliminate any prospect of the conceptual nature of the arrangement being questioned further for tax purposes. Nor should it be. Further, classification as an insurance company has its own perils, as TIAA-CREF has also discovered, leading to its heavy dependence on alleged subjection to New York charitable trust law.

1.2.2.3.3 ERISA Preemption of New York Trust Law.
Dewey has not shot its entire quiver of arrows with the foregoing arguments. Taking special aim at Professor Clark's reliance on New York trust law embodied in the EPTL (a focus responsive to the question the commission put to him), Dewey argues

that reliance on New York law is misplaced because the TIAA-CREF program is an employee benefit plan within the meaning of the Employee Retirement Income Security Act (hereafter, ERISA), and therefore that there is federal preemption of the New York trust law under Section 514 of that act.[46]

The preemption provision of ERISA does have an unusually broad sweep.[47] A New York court dealt with the problem at length in *Sasso* v. *Vachris;* the issue was whether Section 630 of the New York Business Corporation Law applied to an employee benefits trust fund.[48] The court analyzed the U.S. Supreme Court opinions and concluded that the New York statute would be preempted "notwithstanding the fact that it does not conflict with the general objectives of ERISA." Perhaps the same court would hold that EPTL Section 7-1.9 is preempted by ERISA. On the other hand, a federal district judge said in *Provience* v. *Valley Clerks Trust Fund* that "It now seems settled that where the state law has only an indirect effect on the plan *and* where it is one of general application which pertains to an area of important state concern, the court should find there has been no preemption" (emphasis in original).[49]

The conditions of *Provience* seem to be met in the TIAA-CREF case. The contrasting views of these two decisions on preemption (with the federal court taking the no-preemption position) creates uncertainty whether EPTL Section 7-1.9(a) would be preempted if the question were tested in an authoritative tribunal.

Assume, however, that ERISA Section 514 does supersede EPTL Section 7-1.9(a) and that a problem arises before a federal court to which, before ERISA, EPTL Section 7-1.9(a) would have applied. Does ERISA, because of its sweeping preemption provision, lessen the protection afforded to the participants in employee benefit plans? Or would the federal court ask whether EPTL Section 7-1.9 was only declaratory of a long-standing equitable principle? Professor Clark persuasively argues that it was declaratory.[50] If that is so, would the court then apply that long-standing principle to protect the participant rather than interpret ERISA to lessen the participant's protection inconsistently with ERISA's protective purposes?

Examination of ERISA reveals no provision plausibly intended to take the place of provisions like EPTL Section 7-1.9(a). If there is no substitute protective device in ERISA, what is the federal law? Fortunately, we do not need to speculate.

In *Hollenbeck* v. *Falstaff Brewing Corp.*,[51] the court had to deal with a so-called bad-boy provision that would have forfeited plaintiff's benefits. Missouri law prior to ERISA would have given the plaintiff a remedy. The court held the Missouri remedy was preempted by ERISA, but that "preemption does not eradicate a fraud or theft victim's remedies; rather, it only directs the victim to federal law for the source of his remedies."[52] Those remedies are to be found in "ERISA, and its supporting federal common law."[53] Another bad-boy case, *Montgomery* v. *Lowe*, first held there was preemption[54] and then that the preemption provision "means that Federal courts must develop substantive law for interpreting private retirement plans. . . . The Court need not abandon principles of common law which yield results consistent with ERISA's goals."[55]

1.2.3 Transferability of Funds

If the accumulation phases of TIAA and CREF are held to be trusts, the grantor and the beneficiary may change the trustee and the terms of the trust, subject to any restrictions necessary to protect the interests of other participants in the program. But if either is characterized as insurance, some technical problems of insurance law must be faced. Before addressing these technical issues, it will be useful to evaluate the practical problems, if any, that would be met in making transfers from TIAA and CREF.

The commission's examination of transferability was not the first time the question had been raised. In a year-long study during 1984, the TIAA-CREF Ad Hoc Committee on Goals and Objectives "studied in detail the possibility of fundamentally changing TIAA-CREF individual annuity contract provisions *retroactively* to enable funds to be cashed out or rolled over to the plan of another carrier. The proposition was rejected" (emphasis in original). The Committee found "such a change to be inconsistent with fundamental considerations of policy-holder equity and fairness, in potential violation of existing laws, a violation of contractual obligations, a threat to the financial integrity of TIAA, and a hindrance to the investment performance of TIAA."[56]

I ask here whether the Committee's finding may not have been greatly overstated.

1.2.3.1 The Handling of New Money

Any real difficulties center on the transfer of old money, meaning money already invested. There are fewer problems, and perhaps no serious ones, with the transfer of investment income from old investments. There is only one problem in placing new contributions initially with custodians other than TIAA and CREF — the possible increase in cost for the administration of the employing institutions' payroll or benefits offices. But experience has shown that except for some start-up cost, that increase does not amount to much. In this way, a large degree of flexibility could be attained. (The commission suggested that TIAA-CREF might help keep costs down by serving as a clearing house and administrative agent for money contributed for retirement plans, most but not all of which would go to TIAA-CREF itself. The suggestion was rejected.)

Any desired degree of flexibility for the investment of new money could be attained within the TIAA-CREF structure as well, if TIAA-CREF cooperated. The tentatively suggested money market and market-to-market bond funds within the CREF umbrella[57] would provide all the technical machinery for accumulation necessary to overcome all practical obstacles to transfer in the future — if only TIAA-CREF would redesign the contract (or change its practices) to authorize and facilitate transfer rather than attempt to prevent or hinder it. To achieve what I suggest for CREF, it would be necessary to make only one addition to the suggestion already made tentatively by the TIAA-CREF ad hoc committee, and that is to broaden the permissible transferees beyond TIAA and other CREF funds. No practical problems exist.

It is fairly asked, however, why it is necessary or even desirable to seek to induce TIAA-CREF to change its pattern of operation to permit free transfer. Is the simpler (and therefore better) solution to make various groups of mutual funds available as custodians for the accumulation phase, with annuitization by various appropriate vehicles upon retirement (TIAA-CREF as now constituted being among those vehicles but not the only ones)? Then the reluctance of TIAA-CREF to make changes would constitute no barrier to achieving what educational institutions want with respect to new money. Only the management of TIAA-CREF would lose by having a small part of its traditional clientele go elsewhere for the accumulation phase and perhaps also for the payout phase.

This course of action might sacrifice the additional return on investment thought to be the result of the current TIAA model's locking in of funds, for reasons discussed later. Whether that price is too high to pay for greater flexibility is best left to individual participants to decide. In support of paying that price for at least part of the accumulations is the importance of diversification — not only among types of investments but also among investment managers — in addition to the desirability of not being permanently locked into dependence on one manager, however good that manager may be at the time of investment. One does not have to be critical of current TIAA-CREF management to believe that it is unwise for a single institution to have a virtual monopoly of the retirement funds of the world of higher education, as TIAA-CREF has had in the past, or to believe it unwise for participants to be unable to escape to other systems. That quasi monopoly is now breaking down. Encouraging serious competition in this important market is a good thing. Further, the present TIAA model, with locked-in assets, would still be an option available for individual participants who wanted the added return enough to accept being locked in.[58]

1.2.3.2 Practical Problems with Old Money

1.2.3.2.1 CREF. Transfer of funds from CREF to TIAA or to any other fund manager presents no serious practical problems during the accumulation phase other than those artificially created by TIAA-CREF. Dewey claimed to see "enormous problems" in transferring sums from CREF.[59] The problems are imaginary; to insist that they exist is either disingenuous or evidence of misunderstanding. Calculation of the individual participant's share is practicable, down to a fraction of a penny. Mutual funds do it on a daily basis; CREF does it monthly, with some delay after the end of the month — a delay of almost two weeks (for informational purposes at least) in my personal experience of phoning the available 800 number to get the information. Perhaps better data processing induced by serious competition for the privilege of managing these funds would eventually motivate CREF to provide precise values routinely on a daily basis. Indeed, TIAA-CREF's own present plans contemplate daily valuation, at least for some of the new funds.[60]

Except for the limitation to a single transferee, the limitation to end of month transfers, and the failure to provide for telephonic transfers, none of which should be mechanically difficult to change, no criticism of TIAA-CREF has suggested any transfer of funds from CREF that CREF does not already make. It is true that CREF makes transfers only to TIAA, but TIAA is a separate corporation, and there are no legal or conceptual differences between (1) transfers from CREF to TIAA and (2) transfers from CREF to another fund from which annuitization is required. The enormous difficulties Dewey sees do not exist.

Fear that massive and disruptive demand for transfers from CREF will force such rapid liquidation of the portfolio as to force down its value seems unjustified. CREF expects to survive comfortably such transfers to TIAA and transfers among the various new CREF funds. Looking at the nature of the program and its participant population realistically, it is clear that trading in portfolios will be very limited. Most participants, present or forseeable, will be uninterested in the financial markets and content to leave their retirement investments alone for long periods. Those few with greater interest in shifting from one investment manager to another or from one form of investment to another will make varying judgments about when to do it.

After payout begins, no further transfers are possible, and none should be possible, either in or out. The normal inflow of funds to CREF from contributions and from dividends is immense and predictable for a considerable period into the future. A few transitional restrictions for the period immediately after the liberalization of transfer rules might be considered but will probably be unnecessary. Reasonable rules about permissible transfer times should suffice to prevent any troublesome demand for transfers. Should such transfers threaten to be substantial enough to create difficulty, such restrictions as tax laws permit on the amounts transferred on any single occasion and imposition of some delay on transfers (not unprecedented in the financial world) would keep the problem within bounds;[61] the possibility of imposing such restrictions could be reserved in the contracts. It is worth observing that a multitude of funds, including all those other than TIAA-CREF that universities use, seem to flourish without restrictions on transfers out.

One argument against transfer from CREF that Dewey suggests but does not discuss is the possibility of "adverse selection" prior to the annuity starting date.[62] It is not clear why that should be so any more in a transfer to an outside fund than it is in withdrawing money from a group of mutual funds or in transferring funds from CREF to TIAA. If annuitization were optional, there might be some adverse selection because of individuals' differing perceptions of their mortality risks, but there is none, or it is insignificant, if the option is only choosing of the investment vehicle.[63]

Perhaps the real fear is that the movement out of CREF of a large percentage of its participants might impose excessive administrative and transaction costs on those who remain. While this is not properly called adverse selection, the concern is, to a limited extent, superficially plausible. But it assumes what is surely unrealistic — a great rush to divest interests in CREF, requiring precipitous liquidation of the portfolio. If there were really sound grounds for such concern, the fair way to dispose of them would be to ensure that such costs be borne by those who cause them by departing.

1.2.3.2.2 The Fairness Problem. Let us then assume that transfer of old money from CREF is free from serious practical difficulty but that there are important practical difficulties in transferring old money out of TIAA. The ad hoc TIAA-CREF committee speaks of "unfairness" that would result from permitting transfers from CREF to managers outside the TIAA-CREF system when comparable transfers from TIAA are not permitted. The same document concedes that no inequity among CREF participants results from transfer from CREF to TIAA, because the CREF interests are valued at market, and there is thus no "asset/liability differential."[64] But wherever the money goes, there is no such differential. The interests transferred from CREF are exactly what the participant is entitled to; where they go should be of no concern to others.

Yet the notion of unfairness should not be dismissed so cavalierly. Unsystematic inquiry among TIAA-CREF participants about this possibility (reported to me but not made by me) led to expressions of indignation at the injustice of permitting CREF participants to escape while locking TIAA participants in. The stated ground was that participants might have made different allocations initially if they had forseen the possibility of such a change in the rules. Any sense of injustice by numbers of intelligent people should lead to concern. Yet the meaning and reality of the concern can and should be questioned. In this case, the indignation may reflect no more than a sense of injustice at being locked in to TIAA at all, without regard to what happens to participants in CREF. Because the initial allocations cannot be corrected at this date, that ground for indignation taken alone is not rational. Actual fairness may depend on whether transfer out of TIAA is merely inconvenient or difficult or whether it is impossible for technical reasons that cannot be overcome.

I believe that the expressions of concern are unjustified. If some are given a privilege that increases their welfare without harming those to whom it cannot be given for reasons that cannot be overcome, it is hard to discern any sound ground for complaint. While the funds to make the transfers do come from separate common pools, they represent individual interests. Each separate individual's interest is enhanced so far as possible. The aggregate welfare of the relevant community is increased, no individual's welfare is diminished, and no individual is denied a possible benefit. That consummation is a worthy goal, not to be regarded as somehow unjust in some abstract sense. If the disfavored class can also be given the privilege, so much the better; then its denial would be clear injustice, of course. In the end, the question reduces simply to whether TIAA funds are inextricably locked in. If so, there is no unfairness in giving relief to CREF participants alone.

To state it concretely in relation to this case, the only precondition that must be satisfied before allowing CREF transfers while denying TIAA transfers (if obstacles to the latter cannot be overcome) is that those who transfer out of CREF pay the full administrative and transaction costs of the transfers so that those who remain behind in CREF will suffer no harm. No TIAA participant will be disadvantaged by the CREF transfers. With all respect, I can see no inequity in transfer from CREF to another manager even if it is impossible to allow transfers from TIAA; the notion is, in my view, misconceived.

1.2.3.2.3 TIAA. Transfer from TIAA to CREF or to any other manager during the accumulation phase presents greater practical difficulties, mainly because of TIAA's use of the insurance method of asset valuation.

The market value of a bond fluctuates with changes in interest rates; the longer the duration of the bond, the greater the fluctuation. At its nadir, the TIAA portfolio had a market value of about 63 percent of its book value under the insurance valuation (amortization) method. Because all obligations of TIAA are cast in terms of accumulated contributions plus earnings allocated to them, market value is not even relevant for determining TIAA's obligations. But if transfer out of TIAA were permitted without revaluing the portfolio for the purpose, the individual participant who transferred out of TIAA at the bottom of the bond market would have received about 150 percent of the market value of the transferred interest. Rollover of the funds to another manager would thus have enabled the participant to increase his TIAA retirement accumulations by 50 percent. Then the financially sophisticated members of TIAA's academic community would be in a position to profit greatly, as arbitrageurs, at the expense of those who remained in TIAA.[65] If, in the extreme case, all members of the TIAA community simultaneously sought to transfer their accumulations out, there would be a 30 percent shortfall, even assuming perfect liquidity in the portfolio. And the portfolio is relatively illiquid. (The opportunity of gaining by such arbitrage can now occur with RTBs, SRAs, and death benefits, casting serious doubts on the fairness of those aspects of the present TIAA operation.)

Dewey correctly recognizes that ascertaining the amount to be transferred from TIAA, if that were permitted, might present special, though hardly "enormous," problems. Dewey misconceives the nature of the problems.[66] The actual calculations would be relatively simple. There is one exception of some importance. Evaluation of TIAA's real estate investments, whether in the actual ownership of real estate, in equity participation in connection with debt instruments, in the convertibility of debt to real estate equity, or in any other form, is admittedly difficult. Valuation of direct placement bonds, for which there is no market with quoted prices, would present problems too. But valuation to a reasonable approximation is sufficient for purposes of transferability and is now achieved for other purposes. A fair allowance for error charged to those who transfer is a proper price for the right to make the transfer. All that needs to be said here is that the valuation should be conservative enough for the risk of error to be borne by those who transfer out. Those who create the problems should bear the cost.

If transfer out of TIAA on a sound and fair basis is desired, there will have to be either (1) a revaluation of the portfolio at market, (2) a restriction of transfer to certain windows of opportunity when the market value of the portfolio is close to the book value, or (3) some structuring of the transfer (such as irrevocable spreading of the transfer over an extended period) to minimize the effect of calculated arbitrage. Legal difficulties may intrude, arising out of insurance law or from the restrictions of tax law. In addition, unless annuitization continues to be required and unless the requirement can be enforced effectively, tax traps too might face the unwary or unadvised individual participant who finds a way to cash out completely.

Frequent revaluation of the portfolio might be costly; occasional revaluation would not be a serious problem. In fact, the TIAA portfolio is now valued at market annually for internal purposes.[67] Limiting transfers to the time when that valuation is performed anyway would greatly limit the cost.

Ascertaining the market value of the individual participant's accumulation would not be conceptually difficult. One can start with the individual participants' accumulations for each vintage.[68] Then the aggregate book value of the portfolio attributed to each of the several vintages can be ascertained as the sum of the individual participants' accumulations for each vintage. Next, each vintage, both for the individual and for the aggregate accumulations, should be adjusted to market value, the primary determinant being the interest rate attributed to that vintage—perhaps not in its rounded-off form but in its more precise form. The individual's different vintage accumulations reduced to market value should then be summed to find the market value of the individual participant's total accumulations.

The above process assumes there is a single portfolio, with no separation by vintage. If separation by vintage has resulted in partial portfolios, identifiable even notionally, the process would be even simpler and more accurate. The partial portfolios could be valued directly at market instead of making adjustments on the basis of the interest allocations, which are at best rough, rounded approximations. The calculations should be at least as accurate as present vintage allocations, which are accurate enough to satisfy all reasonable needs, or at least so TIAA assumes by using them. An allowance for error, to the extent necessary, should be charged against those who depart, together with full administrative and (if any) transaction costs; each individual would presumably weigh those costs against the advantages of departing.

Ascertaining the market value of an individual's interest with acceptable precision is surely not beyond the capacities of the TIAA technical staff.

If the process roughly sketched above would not be possible at all or not possible at a reasonable cost or with acceptable precision, TIAA, having unique access to the information, ought to explain why. It somehow has managed to calculate individual accumulations by vintages and to attribute to the accumulations different interest rates based on those vintages. The calculations asked for here are similar. A simple assertion that they present serious difficulties should be received with skepticism. If the contention is instead that, though possible and legal, it would cost more than it would be worth, disclosure of the data and calculations that lead to that conclusion would enable others independently to weigh the cost against the value of freedom to transfer. If cost is initially excessive, it can be kept to a tolerable level by limiting the occasions on which transfers out of TIAA are permitted, such as those occasions when the dual valuation of the portfolio already exists; then valuation cost should be very small.

The guarantees in the TIAA contract of a 3 percent return on investment and of payout (whether the permissible 10 percent cashout at retirement, payment on death, or the gradual payout after annuitization) at book rather than at market value do not constitute an argument against transfer out. Once there is transfer out, the other claims no longer exist at any value; the transfer out overrides them all.

The effect of transferability on investment policy of TIAA-CREF has been presented as a serious practical problem. There is now minimal need for liquidity in the TIAA portfolio. The inflow of funds is huge and predictable, and there is unusual stability in the portfolio. In some small measure, the minimal need for liquidity and the resulting stability is a consequence of restricting transfers. Because of the unusual stability, TIAA investments vary, in extent though not in nature, from those made by other issuers of annuities based largely on debt. TIAA is said to be able to invest a larger share of its assets in direct placement loans and to arrange loans involving equity participation or convertibility of debt to equity more easily than can insurers that need greater liquidity.[69] This is said to produce a meaningfully higher return on invested assets. TIAA argues that relatively free transfer of accumulated funds out of TIAA would create enough additional risk of forced liquidation of assets at a sacrifice that these desirable investments would have to be curtailed somewhat, to the loss of participants. Because of the long time horizon for evaluating an annuity program, that higher return may produce annuity payments enough larger to make a real difference.

The argument, while plausible and perhaps having some validity, seems considerably overstated. As with CREF, the normal inflow of funds into TIAA from interest, maturing debt, and especially from contributions, is immense. Indeed, it is relatively greater than with CREF because long-term debt does mature and is paid off, whereas equities must be sold to realize their value.

That the change in rules would require a significant change in investment pattern is speculative. Even the possibility of a small reduction in return on the portfolio because of prudential restrictions on investments that have a uniquely high yield is a price to be weighed against participant freedom to transfer. But I would be greatly surprised if the reduction in return amounted to much. Because, however, the facts needed to form a judgment are peculiarly within the knowledge of TIAA and because the requisite technical expertise is also available there, TIAA ought to provide a careful estimate, accompanied by the relevant data, to support its position.

The TIAA case for the status quo now relies too much on unsupported assertions. In conversations, a difference of 0.1 percent per year in return on the portfolio has been suggested. If that can be supported, it is not trivial, but perhaps one may be indulged some skepticism about that number in the absence of proof. Even if accurate, it is modest compared with the differences in return among various possible investment managers, some of which have done much better than TIAA and some of which have done much worse. Whatever the measure of the reduction in return, it is a reduction that many would accept in return for the freedom to escape an operation in which, for good reason or for bad, they might not now have, or might in future lose, confidence. There have been times in the recent past when confidence in TIAA-CREF was at a low ebb.

As a counterweight to TIAA-CREF concern about constraints on investment policy or excessively rapid liquidation of the portfolio, there is also the possibility of a reverse flow of funds. If participants elect for the accumulation phase to transfer funds out of TIAA-CREF to accounts of regulated investment companies, or if they initially elect to use other accumulation vehicles as many have now begun to do, they will have need of an annuitization vehicle upon retirement; some educational institutions that permit alternative accumulation vehicles even require annuitization in TIAA-CREF. Recognizing the likely increase of accumulations in non-TIAA-CREF accounts, the TIAA-CREF ad hoc committee properly recommends facilitating transfer to TIAA-CREF for annuitization.[70] The inflow of funds for annuitization should partly balance out the outflow from transfer of old money to other managers for the accumulation phase. Further, giving more flexibility would be quite likely to increase voluntary contributions, one of the objects of the retirement programs.

1.2.3.3 Legal Problems, Including Insurance Law Problems

1.2.3.3.1 CREF. Only one legal obstacle can possibly exist to transfer of old money out of CREF to fund managers other than TIAA. That obstacle is the original contract manifesting the arrangement between TIAA-CREF and the institutions making contributions to CREF on behalf of the participant who would like to make the transfer. TIAA-CREF contends that this obstacle is insurmountable because the arrangement is, from the outset, an individual deferred annuity contract subject to insurance law. I already have argued that the CREF accumulation phase can at least as easily be considered a trust as insurance. If it is characterized as a trust, the transfer presents no legal obstacles. I also assume here the fairness of permitting CREF participants to transfer out while denying it to TIAA participants if the latter is impossible, thus making transfer from CREF a question independent of transfer from TIAA.

1.2.3.3.2 TIAA. At first look, it is plausible to consider the TIAA accumulation phase to be so closely linked to the payout phase by their operational unity within a system designed under insurance law that accumulation can best be treated as part of a deferred individual annuity contract. The accumulation phase would then be treated as the premium-paying period of the deferred annuity. While certainly possible, this is neither necessary nor desirable, for until retirement, the similarity of the accumulation phase of TIAA to an insurance policy is no greater than it is to a trust. If, however, the accumulation phase of TIAA is considered to be insurance, the obstacles of the insurance law do remain a problem.[71]

If book value must be used to determine the amount to be transferred, a major difficulty arises. The reasons for valuing TIAA assets at book rather than at market lie in the history of insurance regulation; for our purposes, we can assume the system makes good sense for a conventional annuity during the payout phase. No such concession need be made for the accumulation phase.

Dewey suggested a number of complicated possible ways to value a participant's interests for purposes of making transfers from TIAA;[72] but they seem to have been suggested in jest. The fair measure is the market value of the accumulations to date, including not only the accumulations in the individual participant's account but also an appropriate share of assets corresponding to the contingency reserves attributable to that participant — inasmuch as the need for a contingency reserve applicable to that participant's interests will have ended. Liquidation and administrative charges would be proper, at a reasonable approximation of the small actual cost.

Market valuation of transfers out may run into obstacles from insurance law, if insurance law applies. Dewey relies heavily on the provision of the New York Insurance Law that any modification of "a contract of annuity" must be in writing and signed by the insurer.[73] This provision does not apply unless there is a contract of annuity, a question already discussed for both TIAA and CREF. Moreover, it seems clear from the general tenor of insurance law cases that a court will look carefully to ascertain the law's purpose before applying the rule at the instance of the insurer. The purpose is clearly not to protect ownership rights of the insurer. Is it to protect the interests of other participants in the plan — participants who do not choose to modify their plans? Certainly it is not in the case of the CREF accumulation phase, during which instant valuation of each interest is possible and during which other participants will almost surely not be prejudiced by excessively rapid liquidation of assets (an unlikely event since, as Dewey argues, the agreement to transfer could never be obtained from all contributors to and beneficiaries of the total CREF fund). There is no clear indication, in the documents or in the law, of the provision's purpose. A plausible speculation is that it has a purpose similar to that of the parol evidence rule — to preclude the modification of contractual agreements by informal evidence.[74] Reliance of Dewey on this boilerplate language is misplaced. It protects the company only against the contention that a contract provision has been informally changed, but it will not be interpreted to give the company substantive rights it would not otherwise have.

If the TIAA accumulation phase is considered to be the premium paying part of a deferred annuity contract, it would be subject to the following provision of the New York Insurance Law: "For contracts which provide cash surrender benefits, such cash surrender benefits available on or prior to maturity shall not be less than ninety-three per cent of the sum of (i) the actual accumulation amount and (ii) the amount of any indebtedness to the company; decreased by the amount of any such indebtedness. The death benefit under such contracts shall be at least equal to the cash surrender benefits."[75]

Read literally (and there is no reason it would not be so read), if transfer out of TIAA were permitted, this provision would preclude the market valuation technique for measuring transfers and avoiding substantial arbitrage profits to knowledgeable participants. The Model Law of the National Association of Insurance Commissioners,[76] adopted by a substantial number of states, is even more restrictive.[77] Either that method must be abandoned or a change must be sought in the governing law.

One suggestion for transfers in the face of this limitation on the surrender charge is to provide for transfer on a gradual basis over a number of years, with or without a surrender charge on each occasion. Inability to predict the course of the markets would discourage market timers by putting greater risks on them while still making it possible for participants to change managers or to diversify among fund types. The purpose of a surrender charge, if there were one, would be to discourage casual changes. Tax law constraints are likely to make this partial transfer device impracticable, however.[78]

An alternative suggestion is to permit transfer only during the window of opportunity that exists whenever the market value of the TIAA portfolio is 93 percent or more of the book value. There could then be a surrender charge of up to 7 percent to absorb the difference between book and market. One refinement might be possible. The contingency reserves of TIAA ought to be released *pro tanto* as transfers are made, inasmuch as no funds need be available to back the guarantees to the transferors. Those reserves could be drawn upon to pay the first part of the surrender fee or perhaps to enlarge the window of opportunity.

There is a serious legal obstacle to the use of the window of opportunity device, however. Under the New York nonforfeiture law for annuities, if the contract "provides for a lump sum settlement at maturity, or at any other time," then upon surrender of the contract at any other time prior to the commencement of annuity payments, the company must pay a cash surrender benefit as specified in the nonforfeiture law (not less than 93 percent of the accumulated amount, which would be calculated under insurance valuation rules).[79] This rule would preclude use of the window of opportunity solution to the valuation problem, unless the provision were interpreted as not applying to transfers, exchanges, or rollovers, but only to true cash surrender benefits. That flexible interpretation is not one I would expect, however.

One might reasonably conclude that if insurance law applies, there is no practicable way to provide for transfer out of TIAA short of amendments to the insurance statutes, which are possible but difficult. As a fiduciary, however, TIAA-CREF would have an obligation to make reasonable attempts to obtain passage of insurance law changes that would benefit the individuals and institutions it serves. Change in the statutes would be difficult against TIAA-CREF opposition, but the educational community is entitled to expect cooperation, not opposition. In the absence of such changes, there are other ways to achieve the same objective immediately for *new* accumulations.

The conclusion that insurance law applies and is a barrier depends, however, on a determination that the TIAA accumulation phase is part of an annuity contract, a determination that is by no means inevitable for reasons stated earlier.

It must be conceded out of hand, however, that the prospects of achieving the results I have suggested as desirable for TIAA accumulations may face daunting obstacles in the procedural delays characteristic of legal proceedings. TIAA-CREF management, despite its clear fiduciary obligations to its constituency, appears to have dug in its heels and to be unwilling to accede without compulsion. The New York Insurance Department, jealous of its prerogatives, may intervene. If the administrative processes of that department became involved and if they could not be bypassed, some years would be added to the delays normally attendant upon litigation.

Yet negotiation with TIAA-CREF could potentially be undertaken from a position of great strength; TIAA-CREF is vulnerable not only because of weaknesses in its legal position but even more because of the unconscionability of its position. Besides, requests (or demands) for change would come from the sources of its future funds, the educational institutions TIAA-CREF exists to serve. A group of major institutions might be able to achieve what they wish by hard-nosed negotiation.

1.2.4 Conclusions

To avoid any need to discuss the questions, let us assume that at most times in the past, though not necessarily always, TIAA-CREF has been well managed and that its continuation as an important vehicle for retirement annuities for higher education is desirable. It does not follow that its near monopoly of that field should continue nor that participants in the TIAA-CREF system should never be able to escape from it, no matter what the circumstances or the future course of events. Sound policy for the educational world would include provision for diversification of managers of retirement accumulations, as well as diversification of types of investments. The reluctance of TIAA-CREF to make salutary changes has shown its lack of subjection to the healthy stimulus of competition. Long delay in shifting to indexation in CREF after the theory of efficient markets became widely accepted and the extreme deliberation with which it has proceeded to create new types of investment vehicles within CREF illustrate the point.

Let us also assume that once annuity payments begin, the contract must remain in place until it runs out at death or on the expiration of the guaranteed payments period in the event of earlier death. That assumption reflects the necessities of the insurance institution after mortality risk has been transferred, but it does not mean that there is not great merit in having more than a single institution available to participants for purposes of annuitization. Having no commitment to annuitize with a particular institution would make all possible annuitizers more responsive to participant needs and desires.

All of this reform could be achieved for the future by changes in the practices of educational institutions, and indications are that it will eventually be achieved in that way. Can it now be achieved also for old funds?

As a matter of policy, greater freedom to transfer accumulated retirement funds from both TIAA and CREF to other approved fund managers or for annuitization by approved institutions would be desirable. If TIAA-CREF were to cooperate, no serious practical or legal difficulties appear likely in working out arrangements for such transferability. But it is possible that declaratory judgment proceedings would be necessary to eliminate legal risk in making the changes.

If TIAA-CREF were to resist and could not be persuaded to cooperate in such a proceeding by negotiation, the question would arise whether it could be compelled to accede. No final answer could be supplied in advance of at least some litigation. I have reached the conclusion, though with the recognition that there is some uncertainty, that transferability by institutional and individual participants working together can be achieved for CREF funds, for the accumulation phase of CREF should clearly be regarded as a trust. No practical difficulties exist. The legal case appears to be very strong. The case is more complex with TIAA but I believe the same result should be reached.

Taking TIAA and CREF together, the legal case is strong enough to create the possibility of a satisfactory resolution by agreement, which is much to be preferred to litigation. TIAA-CREF is vulnerable to pressure from the sources of new funds. In addition, the trustees who own the stock of TIAA and are the members of CREF have yet to be heard from. Serving as the ultimate conscience of TIAA-CREF, they could intervene with decisive results and help achieve a satisfactory resolution without confrontation.

If a court were to conclude that a trust relationship exists in the accumulation phase of TIAA, how should the valuation problem be solved? I submit that the answer is simple in principle. If the accumulation phase involves a trust relationship, the proper method of valuation for operational purposes is whatever is agreed upon in the trust instrument. That is now the insurance method, and TIAA is under no obligation to accept another — for operational purposes. But if the grantor and beneficiary agree to change the trustee, the true or market value of the beneficiary's interest would have to be ascertained to make transfer out equitable. That conclusion follows from the very determination that there is a trust relationship, for the insurance-type valuation is used for operational purposes only, just as long as and no longer than the insurance mechanism is appropriate. The assumption that it will continue to be used for the remainder of the accumulation period would be negated by the change in trustee or terms.

Whatever the outcome in principle, for old money, and even for the investment proceeds of old money, there would be few changes in trustee, for under trust law, both the educational institutions and the individual participants would have to agree. Yet the mere possibility of making the change would be salutary, through subjection of TIAA to a kind of competitive pressure it has never felt before.

One possible result of increased competition would be for TIAA to develop again the kind of innovative capacity it once exhibited when the system was first begun and when the variable annuity was developed. That innovativeness could usefully manifest itself, inter alia, in the development of a more varied portfolio of products within both TIAA and CREF.

The fear of wholesale abandonment of TIAA seems fanciful, for not all educational institutions would be prepared to join in asking that the trustee be changed at the option of its employee-participants, nor would most individual participants be interested in making the change even if permitted to do so, at least with old money. Most participants, both institutional and individual, would be content to leave existing accumulations as they are now. For all of those, the terms of the relationship would continue unchanged. For most of its clientele and much the greater part of its present assets, therefore, TIAA would surely continue intact, except for the new and desirable competitive pressures put upon it. But the competition for new money, the threat of drying up such funds (if used as a negotiating lever), the residual possibility of legal action, and a call upon the conscience of TIAA-CREF through its trustee-owners and members might together produce an acceptable accommodation and do wonders for the quality and image of TIAA-CREF. That would be the best of all reasonably possible worlds.

1.3

Applicability of New York Law to Transferability of Funds from TIAA and CREF: Opinion of Elias Clark

Following is the text of an opinion letter, dated April 24, 1986, from Elias Clark, Lafayette S. Foster Professor of Law, Yale University, to Oscar M. Ruebhausen, Chair of the Commission on College Retirement:

You have asked me the following question: Is the present relationship of TIAA and CREF to the fund that they are accumulating as fiduciaries on behalf of a teacher-participant a trust and, if so, are the teacher and college empowered by Section 7-1.9 of the New York Estates, Powers and Trusts Law to amend the terms of the trust by requiring TIAA and CREF to transfer the fund, in whole or in part, between TIAA and CREF or to third party investment managers to be held in trust to secure for the teacher a lifetime retirement income from an annuity issued either by TIAA or CREF or by a third party?

My conclusion is that the relationship of TIAA and CREF to the funds in their care has all the essential characteristics of a trust. TIAA and CREF are incorporated in New York and are therefore governed by the laws of that state. I further conclude that the college, which has, either alone or in conjunction with the teacher, contributed the fund, and the teacher, who is the beneficial owner of the fund, are authorized by EPTL Section 7-1.9 to require an amendment in the manner in which the fund is managed and to prescribe alternative means by which the objective of retirement income for the beneficiary may be secured. The reasons for my conclusion follow:

1.3.1. Elements of Trust Present in TIAA-CREF's Holding of Funds

EPTL Section 7-1.9(a) permits the creator of a trust with the written consent of the beneficiaries to revoke or amend the trust in whole or in part.[1] The statute does not recognize any role for the trustee in this process, and its consent to the revocation or amendment is not required.

TIAA and CREF collect and invest funds to provide lifetime income (or death benefits in the event of death before retirement) to retired personnel from the nation's colleges and universities. Although they are organized under a single governing body, they maintain separate boards and operating staffs and exist to implement different investment objectives: TIAA seeks a fixed return based mainly on bonds and mortgages and CREF a variable return based on common stocks. Both receive contributions which represent a percentage of each teacher's salary and are paid either by the institution alone or by the institution and the teacher jointly. These funds are invested with the principal and accumulated income providing the means for the purchase of an annuity contract at the time of the teacher's retirement. Thus, within the framework of EPTL Section 7-1.9, the college, either alone or in conjunction with the teacher, is the creator or settlor of the trust, the employee, the beneficiary, and TIAA-CREF, the trustees.

TIAA and CREF refrain from describing their relationship to the funds as one of trust or themselves as trustees. The two agencies are variously called in reports and brochures "vehicles for funding college retirement plans"[2] or a "form of organization"[3] to provide annuities, or "machinery under which the teacher may protect himself and his family from dependence, whether by his own death, or by old age, or by disability."[4] An inquiry into the origins of TIAA and CREF suggests that this is a case of the offspring turning their backs on the family name.

In 1905, Andrew Carnegie established the Carnegie Foundation for the Advancement of Teaching ("the Foundation"), and for ten years thereafter the trustees offered free pensions to senior professors who had retired or who would retire from a limited number of universities and colleges in the United States and Canada. When it became evident that the task of providing an adequate pension system for a nationwide academic community was too large for the Foundation to undertake, the trustees of the Foundation, following extensive study and consultation with educators and others, created TIAA to take over the expanded trust responsibilities. TIAA was created as an insurance company so that it would be subject to the regulation of the New York State Insurance Department. Carnegie Corporation of New York ("the Corporation"), established by Andrew Carnegie in 1911, donated $1,000,000 in capital to TIAA and held the non-dividend-paying stock. The trustees of the Corporation held the stock as fiduciaries for the college community as a whole, and arranged for the election of representatives from that community to the Board of TIAA.

The trustees of the Foundation and the Corporation continued for a number of years to grant funds to TIAA to help defray operating expenses and meet pension obligations, but in 1937, the Corporations transferred the stock to a group which was to be representative of the college community, the Trustees of TIAA Stock. By 1957, contributions from the colleges and their personnel became the sole source of funds for staff pensions.

In 1952, CREF was founded by and in the image of TIAA to offer an alternative investment strategy. Thus both organizations were created by the trustees of a charitable trust to carry on the work of that trust. It is as true today as it was then that both organizations remain dedicated to the trust purposes for which they were created, namely, service to the academic community in a specialized way. Or, as this history was once described, TIAA was created "at the request of educators, with the assistance of educators and for educators."[5]

The law is clear that it is not necessary to use the words "trust" or "trustee" in order to create a trust.[6] "It is immaterial whether or not the settlor knows that the intended relationship is called a trust, and whether or not he knows the precise characteristics of the relationship which is called a trust."[7] What is required is that the settlor conveys property to another with the intention of imposing enforceable duties on the use of that property. The Court of Appeals for the Second Circuit in applying New York law to declare that an instrument labeled a Nominee Agreement created a trust said: "The three elements necessary to the existence of a trust were present, i.e., a designated beneficiary, a designated trustee, and an identifiable property. No particular words are required."[8]

These elements of trust are readily identifiable here. TIAA-CREF are trustees, the employee of the college the beneficiary, the contributions the property, and the college the settlor. In substance as well as form the characteristics of a trust are present. The Restatement of the Law of Trusts sets out the essence of the trust relationship by listing other legal relationships that a trust is not. Thus a trust is not a bailment, an executorship, an agency, a mortgage, an equitable charge, a debt, or a contract for the benefit of a third party. To the extent the label is determinative of the result, it would appear that the TIAA-CREF obligations to the teacher, if not a trust, must be classified as a contract for the benefit of a third party. Two cases, of the many available, make clear the distinction between a trust and a third party beneficiary contract.

The plaintiff in *Community Services, Incorporated* v. *United States*,[9] was an eleemosynary corporation that had set up a profit-sharing retirement plan in 1962 for its employees. By the terms of the plan, plaintiff contributed 25 percent of its net income each year to the Life Insurance Company of Virginia to manage and disburse the funds. The Insurance Company allocated the contributions to the individual accounts of eligible employees on the basis of years in service and rate of salary. Benefits were normally paid through the purchase of an annuity for life upon the employee's retirement at age sixty-five, although the plan and the contract between plaintiff and the insurance company authorized other modes of payment and provided for benefits on death or disability. The Internal Revenue Service ruled that plaintiff's contributions to the retirement plan were not deductible under IRC Section 501(a) because they were not paid to a "trust" as required by Section 401(a) of the 1954 Code.

The Claims Court held the contributions to be deductible, describing the question of whether a trust actually existed in this case "to be relatively easy to decide."

In the case at hand, it is clear that plaintiff established the
Life Insurance Company of Virginia as the trustee or guar-
dian of the contributions which plaintiff was to make under
the plan. The money contributed by plaintiff was the trust
res, and the plaintiff's employees were the beneficiaries of
the trust. It is also clear that the Life Insurance Company
of Virginia was holding the funds for the benefit of plaintiff's employees since it had certain duties and obligations
in respect to these funds, such as setting up employees' accounts and providing for the purchase of retirement annuities. Consequently, it would appear obvious that the
insurance company was in the position of a fiduciary in
regard to both the trust property and plaintiff's employees.[10]

The Court denied the Service's argument that the arrangement could not constitute a trust because the Insurance Company commingled the contributions with its own corporate funds.
To the contrary, the fact that the Company credited the contributions to the individual accounts of the employees was a
crucial element in the proof that a trust was intended. Furthermore, although the plan stated that the benefits did not vest until
retirement, the funds were dedicated to the exclusive use of the
employees, and the plaintiff and insurance company could not
modify or terminate the plan in a manner that would defeat the
ultimate application of the funds for the benefit of the employees.

By way of contrast, the case of *Christiansen* v. *National Savings and Trust Co.,*[11] highlights the characteristics of a third party
beneficiary contract. The plaintiffs brought a class action on
behalf of all federal employees who were Blue Cross and Blue
Shield subscribers. In 1960, the Civil Service Commission, pursuant to the authorization contained in the Federal Employees
Health Benefits Act of 1959, contracted with Blue Cross, Blue
Shield and Group Hospitalization, Inc. (the local Blue Cross
agency for the District of Columbia) to create a nation-wide indemnity plan to reimburse federal employees for specified medical expenses. The cost of coverage was contributed in part by
the United States and in part by deduction from the employees'
wages. The plaintiffs alleged that the relationship between the
health maintenance organizations and the contributed funds was

one of trust, creating fiduciary duties which the subscribers could enforce. Specifically, the plaintiffs claimed breaches of trust in that the health organizations retained more funds uninvested in bank checking accounts than was necessary to meet claims and that members of the Group Hospitalization board also served on the boards of the banks in which the checking accounts were maintained. The Court refused to rule as a general matter that the mere existence of an insurance contract precluded the trust relationship, and at a number of points in the decision intimated that on the facts alleged here an accounting to the federal government might be in order. The contract between the government and the health associations did not, however, create fiduciary obligations enforceable by the subscribers. The contract created no res in which the subscribers had any beneficial interest. Instead, the health associations had undertaken a personal liability to reimburse subscribers for expenses incurred for hospital and physician services, which, if any shortfall developed, were recoverable from the associations' own funds. The Court concluded:

> In summary we hold that Judge Greene's conclusion that the Federal Contract does "not fit the traditional trust category" is correct. If the Federal Contract is a third party beneficiary contract, the subscribers have enforceable rights to payment of their covered physician and hospital bills without limitation according to the terms of the plan they subscribed to — and, in fact, that is exactly what the parties bargained for and what the contract provides. On the other hand, if the contract were a trust, the obligation of the insurers to pay health benefits to subscribers would naturally be limited to the sum of the premiums paid and any earnings thereon — a limitation which no one bargained for and which is not present in the Federal Contract.[12]

It is apparent from these two cases (and many more making the same point in a variety of contexts) that the parties intend a trust, irrespective of what they call it, when the beneficiary owns the transferred property and a contract when the holder owns the property. The provisions in the agreements between TIAA-CREF and every participating teacher leave no doubt that the teacher is the owner of the property contributed in his or her behalf.

The contributions are individualized from the outset inasmuch as they vary in amount depending on the teacher's current salary level. The agreements speak of the contributions as "premiums," but they are not premiums in any conventional sense. They do not purchase from TIAA-CREF a promise to pay a sum certain on the occurrence of a future event, nor do they impress upon the corporate funds of either organization a personal liability that must be paid regardless of whether the premiums received are adequate to meet the obligation. To the contrary, CREF and TIAA continue to recognize that the funds belong to the individual, as each contribution is credited to the separate account of the teacher for whom the contribution was made. The CREF agreeement states that each contribution "purchases a number of Accumulation Units representing [the teacher's] share in CREF."[13] In practical effect, the teacher possesses a participation in a pooled investment fund similar to a beneficiary of a trust held by a corporate trustee in a common trust fund. The TIAA agreement employs somewhat different language, but it too makes each teacher a participant in a pooled fund.[14]

The teacher's ownership of his or her account is recognized throughout the agreements. CREF and TIAA invest the funds; if the investments prosper, the earnings and appreciation are credited to each owner's account; in the reverse situation, losses are charged against each account. In short, the funds are managed for the exclusive benefit of and at the exclusive risk of the beneficial owners. Continued ownership is guaranteed even if the contributions cease or the owner changes jobs. The only limitation on the beneficiary's rights appears in the spendthrift provisions, not unusual in a trust, found in both agreements, stating that the agreement "cannot be assigned nor does it provide for cash surrender or loans."

1.3.2 Section 513(a) of the Not-for-Profit
Corporation Law Is Not Applicable

The antecedents of TIAA and CREF are rooted in trust, and today CREF in all respects and TIAA in most respects operate in the manner of trustees of common trust funds. If, however, the availability of EPTL Section 7-1.9 is to be determined by the label put on the relationship rather than its substance, Section 513(a) of the New York Not-for-Profit Corporation Law appears at first reading to present a complication. CREF is a Type B corporation as defined in Section 201 of that Law. Section 513(a) states that a Type B corporation has "full ownership rights" in any assets transferred to it "in trust for, or with a direction to apply the same, to any purpose specified in its certificate of incorporation" and is not to "be deemed a trustee of an express trust of such assets." A brief recital of the legislative history makes clear that Section 513(a) was intended to define the relationship of a non-profit corporation to funds which had been given to it subject to limitations imposed by the donor on their use and to grant the corporation greater flexibility in the management of those funds. The statute is not applicable when, as in the case of CREF, the funds are transferred to the corporation for the benefit of named persons rather than specified causes.

The Revisers' Notes state: "The section codifies *St. Joseph's Hospital* v. *Bennett,* 281 NY 115, 22 NE2d 305 (1939), . . . "[15] In that case, testator bequeathed a share of his residuary estate to the hospital "to be held as an endowment fund and the income used for the ordinary expenses of maintenance." The hospital brought a declaratory judgment action, seeking permission to use the funds in payment of a mortgage or in furtherance of its general corporate purposes. The lower courts held for the hospital, relying on a general principle used primarily in the administration of the rule against perpetuities to the effect that a gift to a charitable corporation is absolute even though the donor imposed limitations on its use. The Court of Appeals reversed. It is true, the court said, that in these circumstances there can be no trust because the "trustee and beneficiary are one." The corporation is therefore free in the management of funds given to it of "the limitations and rules which apply to a technical trustee." It must nonetheless honor the donor's restrictions.

St. Joseph's Hospital v. *Bennett* is recognized as a leading case delineating the rights and obligations of a charitable corporation in the management and disposition of special purpose funds. Section 513(a), entitled "Administration of assets received for specific purposes," is a codification of these principles and no more. Neither the case nor the statute say anything about the regulation of the corporation when it acts as a true trustee. If, for instance, a hospital today receives a split interest gift (i.e., income to my spouse for life, remainder to the hospital), trust, not corporate, law will define the hospital's obligations to the spouse.

Section 513(a) and related sections are enabling acts, designed to make management of special purpose funds more flexible. Freed of restrictive trust rules, the directors of the corporation may invest more speculatively, delegate management to others, commingle funds, and treat realized appreciation as income.[16] Section 514 specifically authorizes the transfer of funds to outside investment managers.[17] The assumption underpinning these statutes is that greater flexibility will bring improved management to the end that the funds will appreciate and the purposes of the corporation will be better served. Section 513(a) would be misused if invoked as a bar to a petition that seeks to compel a corporation to make use of the management techniques authorized by the statutes.[18]

1.3.3. Applicability of EPTL Section 7-1.9

The label alone need not be controlling. The law of trusts is not confined to the definition of a single form of property holding. Rather, it establishes a broad set of equitable principles for the governance of any arrangement, whatever technical name it bears, whereby one entity is holding property for someone else's benefit.[19] EPTL Section 7-1.9 represents a codification of just such an equitable principle.[20]

The statute is designed to permit the parties to a consensual relationship involving the use of property to join together and make new provisions for its management and/or disposition. Consent of the trustee is not required. Thus the statute makes irrelevant such objections as might be raised by a trustee to protect its own interests or to preserve the intent of the settlor as originally expressed. Further, the parties are allowed to define for themselves what uses of the property are in their best interests. The issue here is whether the statute is available to a teacher and his or her college to implement their joint decision that increased investment opportunities will produce improved benefits for the teacher at retirement or death. It is difficult to imagine a more appropriate application of the statute or one more in harmony with its purposes.

The only question that remains is whether the interests of others are or might be adversely affected by the use of the statute in this context. An Ad Hoc Committee to the Joint Boards of Trustees of TIAA-CREF in its report dated December 31, 1984, rejected a proposal that funds be retroactively rolled over to another carrier.[21] The report gives no explanation that applies to this decision alone. Rather, it states that the transfer of existing funds to other investment vehicles will be used by beneficiaries to obtain a lump sum cashout of the funds and then proceeds to give reasons why cashouts are not permitted under the agreements.[22] This analysis creates and destroys a strawman but leaves the initial question unanswered. A beneficiary might want to live for the moment and to convert his accumulation units into cash. He can use EPTL Section 7-1.9 to further his purpose only to the extent that the college consents. As is noted frequently in the reports that set out the early history of the college pension program, the colleges are just as dedicated to the principle of annuitization as are TIAA and CREF and will not permit their employees to remove funds during the accumulation phase that might leave them impoverished after retirement. Thus there is no justification for the assumption made in the report that the funds when transferred to a new trustee will not be subject to a binding contract requiring annuitization at retirement.

The mechanics of transferring funds to a new trustee pose no problems. On the death of a teacher before retirement, both funds now offer as an option to the person entitled to succeed to the interest full payment of the amount accumulated in the account, and CREF permits transfer of funds in its care to TIAA. Funds may move in and out of CREF with the same ease as they do in and out of a common trust fund or any other pooled investment fund. This traffic in no way affects the interests of the beneficiaries who remain in the fund. The value of their shares remains the same, although their percentage participation fluctuates with the size of the pool and the number of participants in it. The situation as regards TIAA is slightly more complicated because it uses different valuation methods. The difficulties are not, however, insurmountable and ways can be devised for the transfer of TIAA funds without adversely affecting other beneficial owners.

I conclude that if a teacher and college were to petition a court, in the form prescribed by statute, for a transfer of funds to a new trustee in order to obtain improved benefits for the teacher at retirement, the court would so order under the mandate of EPTL Section 7-1.9.

1.4

Transfers of
TIAA and CREF Annuity Contract Interests:
Opinion of Dewey, Ballantine,
Bushby, Palmer, and Wood

Following is the text of an opinion letter, dated June 24, 1986, signed by David E. Watts, J. Paul McGrath, Charles A. Severs III, Carol Trencher Ivanick, and William K. Bortz of the New York law firm of Dewey, Ballantine, Bushby, Palmer & Wood to Francis P. Gunning, then executive vice president and general counsel, TIAA-CREF, on the subject of transfers of TIAA and CREF annuity contract interests:

You have provided to us a copy of an opinion [see Section 1.3 of this volume] by Professor Elias Clark dated April 24, 1986 ("the Clark Opinion"), and have asked for our views on the matters therein discussed. The Clark Opinion concludes that the retirement annuity contracts of TIAA and CREF each create a trust entity, and that a "teacher beneficiary" and an employer educational institution by joint action are empowered by Section 7-1.9 of the New York Estates, Powers and Trusts Law to require TIAA and CREF to transfer "the fund" under such contract to third party investment managers, without regard to any consent of TIAA and CREF or to the contrary terms of the retirement annuity contracts.

For the reasons discussed below, we strongly disagree with the novel conclusions and analysis of the Clark Opinion, and we are confident that they would not be supported by the New York courts. In our opinion, (i) there not only is no statutory or judicial support for the conclusions stated in the Opinion, but they are in fact contrary to express statutory provisions and decisions, (ii) the interest of a participant in a retirement annuity contract issued by TIAA or CREF does not constitute an interest in a trust, (iii) Section 7-1.9 of the New York Estates, Powers and Trusts Law has no application to such retirement annuity contracts, and (iv) the payment and other terms of such contracts cannot be altered unilaterally by the joint action of an employer institution and a participant without the consent of TIAA or CREF.[1]

1.4.1 The Retirement Annuity Contracts Do Not Create or Constitute a Trust Entity

The relationship arising from contributions paid by participating colleges and universities to TIAA and CREF for the purpose of providing annuities for the retired personnel of such institutions is intended by the parties to be, and is in fact, a contractual one, governed by the principles applicable to debts, third-party beneficiary contracts, and insurance law.

As the Clark Opinion acknowledges (page A-7) [Section 1.3, p. 72 of this volume], CREF is a Type B not-for-profit corporation subject to Section 513 of the New York Not-for-Profit Corporation Law. Section 513(a) provides:

A corporation which is, or would be if formed under this chapter, classified as a Type B corporation *shall hold full ownership rights in any assets* consisting of funds or other real or personal property of any kind, that may be given, granted, bequeathed or devised to or otherwise *vested in such corporation in trust for, or with a direction to apply the same to, any purpose specified in its certificate of incorporation, and shall not be deemed a trustee of an express trust of such assets.* . . . [McKinney 1970; emphasis supplied.]

The Clark Opinion also quotes (p. A-7 and p. A-8 footnote) [Section 1.3 of this volume, and note 16, p. 79] the Revisers' Notes, which state that the "section codifies *St. Joseph's Hospital* v. *Bennet* [sic] 281 N.Y. 115, 22 N.E.2d 305 (1939)," and further states: "As compared with trust law, the section gives the directors greater freedom of investment, including the pooling of two or more funds." No such freedom of investment would exist if directors are subject to the laws governing express trusts, or if they are precluded from longer-term investments by subjection to discretionary demands at any time for transfers requiring liquidated funds. Moreover, the *St. Joseph's Hospital* case on which the statute is largely based is in itself direct authority for the principle that a technical trust does not arise merely because of the imposition of contractual or other restrictions on a transfer of funds to a corporation.

The statute in express terms states that organizations like CREF "shall not be deemed a trustee of an express trust" of assets vested in it "for any purpose specified in its certificate of incorporation." All of CREF's assets are indeed held exclusively and uniformly for the purposes specified in its governing special act and constitution. Yet the Clark Opinion attempts to dismiss this statute as a "first reading" "complication" to the trust theory, declaring that the statute says nothing about action "as a true trustee," thus impliedly begging the question at issue as to whether CREF can be deemed to hold its assets on an express trust. Contrary to the conclusion of the Clark Opinion, in our view Section 513 was intended to preclude and would preclude the application of the restrictive rules of express trusts to the assets of nonprofit corporations such as CREF.

Four elements are necessary to the creation of a trust: (1) the intention of the transferor to convey only a legal interest in property and to impose upon the transferee certain fiduciary obligations with respect to the property conveyed; (2) an identifiable property or trust res in which the beneficiary has a beneficial interest; (3) a designated trustee; and (4) a designated beneficiary. Restatement, Second, Trusts, Section 2 (1959); A. W. Scott, *The Law of Trusts,* Section 2.3 (3d ed. 1967). Neither of the first two required elements exists with respect to any retirement annuity contract issued by either TIAA or CREF, and, of course, neither TIAA nor CREF is designated either expressly or impliedly as a trustee.

With respect to the first requirement, no institutional transferor could conceivably intend that the cash paid to TIAA or CREF for the issuance of a retirement annuity contract for a particular participant would be held in a separate trust for that participant, in view of the inconsistency of such intention with the specific terms of the contracts (see contract forms enclosed), the impracticality of tracing each particular monthly contribution to specified identifiable assets held over the years intervening between such contribution and the final annuity payments to the participant, and the absence in the retirement annuity contract terms of any language of trust or of requirements for such identification of separate property and of the gains, losses and income attributable thereto. Similarly, the second requirement for a trust that there be an identifiable property or trust res cannot be met since at no time is any specific property owned by either TIAA or CREF in fact held, or contemplated to be held under the annuity contract terms or otherwise, for any specific participant, nor is it possible as a practical matter to trace contributions and their proceeds into more than one million separate express trusts.

The existence of a trust for the benefit of a third party depends upon whether there is property held by one person for the benefit of a third party, or merely a personal obligation to make payments to a third party. If A pays money to B with the understanding that the money is to be kept in a separate fund and ultimately to be paid to C, B holds the money in trust for C. In such a case the beneficial interest in the money passes immediately to C, and never passes to B. The situation is different from that in which B is permitted to use the money for his own purposes, undertaking merely to pay a similar sum to C, in which case a trust is not created but there is a contract for the benefit of C. A. W. Scott, *The Law of Trusts,* Section 14.1 (3d ed. 1967).

The participating colleges and universities which make payments to TIAA and CREF for the benefit of their respective employees do not require or expect any segregation from TIAA and CREF's other assets of the monies conveyed or the investment proceeds thereof. See *Christiansen* v. *National Savings and Trust Co.,* 683 F.2d 520 (D.C. Cir. 1982). "Annuity agreements create only the relation of debtor and creditor, not a trust." *Chatham County Hospital Authority* v. *John Hancock Mutual Life Insurance Co.,* 325 F. Supp. 614 (S.D. Ga. 1971).

TIAA was formed under the New York Insurance Law and it and its obligations are governed thereunder. By Special Act of the New York Legislature, CREF is similarly subject to specified provisions of such Insurance Law and to regulation by the New York Department of Insurance. The relationship between an insurer and its policyholders is that of debtor and creditor and not one of trustee and *cestui que trust:*

> If, as is almost universally the case, the insurance company *is not required to and does not segregate the proceeds* but merely undertakes to make the required payments out of its general funds, *the company is not a trustee.* There is certainly no trust in the technical sense of the term, for nothing is held by one person for another. It is immaterial that the agreement between the company and the insured person is called a trust agreement, or that it is provided that the proceeds are to be paid by the insurance company to itself as trustee, or even that it agrees to hold the proceeds in trust, if it is also agreed that the proceeds shall not be segregated from the other assets of the company. There is no trust in the technical sense of the term even though it is provided by statute that the proceeds may be retained "under a trust or other agreement," as long as the proceeds are not segregated. [Footnotes omitted; emphasis supplied.]
> A. W. Scott, *The Law of Trusts,* Section 87.1 (3d ed. 1967).

In *Uhlman* v. *New York Life Insurance Co.,* 109 N.Y. 421 (1888), plaintiff purchased from defendant insurance company a "ten-year dividend system" policy. Under the terms of the policy, if plaintiff's policy was in full force at the expiration of ten years from the date of issuance, plaintiff became entitled to an equitable apportionment of the surplus and profits derived from the premiums paid on the policies of the class to which plaintiff's policy belonged. Upon expiration of the ten-year period, plaintiff brought an action for an accounting in order to determine whether defendant had, in fact, apportioned the surplus and profits in an equitable manner. Plaintiff predicated his right to an accounting on the theory that defendant's relationship to plaintiff was that of a trustee to his *cestui que trust.* The Court held:

[A]fter a careful examination of the character of the relations existing between these parties, . . . it cannot be said that the defendant is in any sense a trustee of any particular fund for the plaintiff, or that it acts as to him and in relation to any such fund in a fiduciary capacity. It has been held that the holder of a policy of insurance, even in a mutual company, was in no sense a partner of the corporation which issued the policy, and that the relation between the policyholder and the company was one of contract, measured by the terms of the policy. [Citations omitted.]

The Court's holding was premised on the fact that, upon payment of the premiums by various policyholders, the money immediately became the property of the company. The company had no obligation to keep the premiums separate and apart from its other funds nor any obligation to invest such funds in any particular manner. Its only obligation was to apportion equitably any surplus or profits.

Compare *Holmes* v. *John Hancock Mutual Life Insurance Co.*, 288 N.Y. 106 (1942) (no trust fund is created where proceeds of insurance policies are left on deposit with an insurance company, to be paid out in stipulated installments to insured's beneficiary; accordingly, the state statute regarding the rule against perpetuities is inapplicable); *In re Nires*, 290 N.Y. 78 (1943) (mother's petition to obtain allowance for support and education of minor children from accumulated interest on the proceeds of a life insurance policy left on deposit with an insurance company denied on the ground that the statute authorizing such distribution is only applicable to trust funds; the insurance company did not hold proceeds as a trust fund but as a debt owing to the beneficiaries).

1.4.2 TIAA-CREF's Retirement Annuity Contracts Are Subject to the Provisions of New York Insurance Law

Except as otherwise provided by statute, annuity or other insurance contracts are construed according to the rules governing the construction of contracts. *Green Bus Lines, Inc.* v. *Con-*

solidated Mutual Insurance Co., 426 N.Y.S.2d 981 (1980); *Michigan Millers Mutual Insurance Co.* v. *Christopher,* 413 N.Y.S.2d 264 (1979); *Charles, Henry & Crowley Co.* v. *Home Insurance Company,* 349 Mass. 723, 212 N.E.2d 240 (1965). Insurance contracts are mutual agreements and both parties are bound by the provisions unless waived or annulled for lawful reasons. 12 J. Appleman, Insurance Law and Practice Section 7004 (1981). The recent case of *Connick* v. *Teachers Insurance and Annuity Association & College Retirement Equities Fund,* 784 F.2d 1018 (9th Cir. 1986), applied these principles in determining that a holder of TIAA and CREF's retirement annuity contracts was bound by their terms and could not require premature distributions. *Accord, Alexandre* v. *Chase Manhattan Bank,* 61 A.D.2d 537, 403 N.Y.S.2d 21 (1st Dep't 1978).

Both TIAA and CREF contracts explicitly provide, in accordance with New York Insurance Law, that any amendment "will be valid only if in writing and signed by an Executive Officer or Registrar" of TIAA or CREF, respectively. See paragraph 9 of the enclosed TIAA contract and paragraph 11 of the enclosed CREF contract[2] [enclosures omitted, but see Appendix A to this opinion].

Section 1113 of the New York Insurance Law defines annuities to mean "all agreements to make periodical payments where the making or continuance of all or some of a series of such payments, or the amount of any such payment, depends upon the continuance of human life, except payments made under the authority of paragraph one hereof [i.e. life insurance]." Section 3204(a)(3) provides that, "*Such policy or contract* [referring to 'every policy of life, accident or health insurance, or contract of annuity, delivered or issued for delivery in this state'] *cannot be modified, nor can any rights or requirements be waived, except in a writing signed by a person specified by the insurer in such policy or contract*" (McKinney 1985; emphasis supplied.) This provision was added at the time of the recodification of the insurance law in 1984. It is derived from Section 164 paragraph 3.(1) of the prior law, which required that accident and sickness policies contain a provision that no change would be valid unless approved by an executive officer of the insurer and attached to the policy. New Section 3204(a)(3) expands the prior law to include life insurance policies and annuity contracts and establishes as a matter of law the requirement, for any change in an annuity contract, that there be a writing signed by a person specified by the insurer in the contract, as well as continuing the requirement that such a provision be included in an insurance contract.

The conclusion of the Clark Opinion that TIAA and CREF can be required by an educational institution and its employee participant to transfer funds without TIAA or CREF's consent is of course in direct conflict with this statutory requirement.

1.4.3 Section 7-1.9 of the New York Estates, Powers and Trusts Law Has No Application to TIAA-CREF's Retirement Annuity Contracts

Section 7-1.9 of the New York Estates, Powers and Trusts Law ("EPTL Section 7-1.9") applies only to a trust entity, and therefore, as discussed above, can have no application to TIAA or CREF's contractual commitments. However, even if a trust were to be assumed (contrary to the established authority and the retirement annuity contract terms), the statute would not aply to require TIAA or CREF to transfer property to a third party investment manager. EPTL Section 7-1.9, in pertinent part, provides:

(a) Upon the written consent, acknowledged or proved in the manner required by the laws of this state for the recording of a conveyance of real property, of all the persons beneficially interested in a trust of property, heretofore or hereafter created, the creator of such trust may revoke or amend the whole or any part thereof by an instrument in writing acknowledged or proved in like manner, and thereupon the estate of the trustee ceases with respect to any part of such trust property, the disposition of which has been revoked. If the conveyance or other instrument creating a trust of property was recorded in the office of the clerk or register of any county of this state, the instrument revoking or amending such trust, together with the consents thereto, shall be recorded in the same office of every county. [McKinney 1967.]

Although the statute itself does not distinguish between revocable and irrevocable trusts, EPTL Section 7-1.9 has been construed to apply only to those trusts wherein no power of revocation or amendment has been reserved, or which by their own terms are irrevocable. The procedure provided by the statute is not applicable to trusts where a specific method of revocation or amendment is set forth in the instrument. *Rosner* v. *Caplow,* 90 A.D.2d 44, 456 N.Y.S.2d 50 (1982), *aff'd,* 60 N.Y.2d 880, 470 N.Y.S.2d 367 (1983); *In Matter of Landau,* N.Y.L.J., March 3, 1981, at 6, col. 1, *rev'd on other grounds,* 87 A.D.2d 755, 449 N.Y.S.2d 2 (1982).

As discussed above and as shown by the enclosed contract forms, both TIAA and CREF retirement annuity contracts include explicit amendment provisions requiring the written consent of an Executive Officer or Registrar. Thus, under established New York law, EPTL Section 7-1.9 could not in any event apply in the face of the specific amendment provisions.

Since the consent of TIAA or CREF is expressly required by the terms of their retirement annuity contracts, the creators and beneficiaries of any contract interest cannot sidestep this requirement and resort to EPTL Section 7-1.9 as an alternative means to amend or revoke the agreement, whether or not consent was properly withheld. In *In re Dodge's Trust,* 25 N.Y.2d 273, 303 N.Y.S.2d 847 (1969), the settlor's inter-vivos trust instrument provided that the settlor could alter or modify or amend the trust at any time and from time to time, but only with the written consent of the trustee. The settlor had obtained the trustee's consent to modify the trust on three separate occasions, but when the settlor decided to revoke the trust in its entirety, the trustee refused to consent. As a result, the settlor sought relief under EPTL Section 7-1.9, contending that the statute provided him with a method of revocation which did not require the consent of the trustee. After a lengthy discussion of the requirements of the statute, the court held that EPTL Section 7-1.9 was inapplicable in this case, stating that "the settlor could not invoke the provisions of the statute in any event because the terms of the trust setting forth the procedure for revocation must be complied with . . . and here the trust instrument implicitly, if not expressly, requires the trustee's consent to a revocation." 25 N.Y.2d 273, 285, 303 N.Y.S.2d 847, 857. Similarly, in *In Re Mordecai's Trust*, 24 Misc.2d 668, 201 N.Y.S.2d 899 (1960), *aff'd*, 12 A.D.2d 449, 210 N.Y.S.2d 478 (1960), where settlor's revocation of a trust was subject to the consent of her trustees who withheld their consent, the settlor could not resort to EPTL Section 7-1.9 to override the provisions of the trust instrument. Although a settlor may have a cause of action if a trustee's consent is unreasonably withheld, the settlor's remedy does not arise under EPTL Section 7-1.9.

Even if (contrary to the extensive statutory and judicial authority discussed herein) there were a deemed express trust of TIAA and CREF's assets to which EPTL Section 7-1.9 could apply, and even if the specific amendment provisions had been omitted, the terms of the statute could not be met. Under those terms, the creator and all persons beneficially interested in the trust must consent to revocation or modification. Notwithstanding the statute's use of "creator" in the singular, the consent of *all* creators or settlors is required. *Rosner* v. *Caplow*, 90 A.D.2d 44, 456 N.Y.S.2d 50 (1982). Each of TIAA and CREF, if deemed a trust at all, would have to be considered a single trust, the res of which is composed of the contributions of numerous settlors (that is, of all 3,700 currently participating institutions as well as other institutions that may have contributed to current participants at any time over the past sixty-eight years) and the aggregate investment proceeds thereof, since there is no way that any asset held by TIAA or CREF can be regarded as constituting (or as intended by any party to constitute) a separate property or res held with respect to the contributions of a single institution for a single contractholder.[4] Neither TIAA nor CREF segregates assets arising from the contributions of one educational institution from those of another. Accordingly, *every* contributor to TIAA or CREF must *jointly* consent to any revocation or amendment under the statute. Similarly, every employee-participant who has contributed to TIAA or CREF must also be considered a creator. It has been held that the death of any one of a number of settlors permits no further change and renders a trust immutable. *Rosner* v. *Caplow*, 105 Misc.2d 592, 432

N.Y.S.2d 577 (1980). Thus, the application of EPTL Section 7-1.9 would be absolutely precluded because now-deceased employees who made contributions have surviving spouses or other beneficiaries that continue to have an interest in a TIAA or CREF annuity contract.

Still more formidable are the requirements of the statute that "all the persons beneficially interested in a trust of property" must give written consent to an amendment or revocation. TIAA and CREF have approximately one million participants, and other persons beneficially interested include spousal interests required by the Employee Retirement Income Security Act of 1974, as amended, and designated beneficiaries. See *Application of Roth,* 73 A.D.2d 560, 423 N.Y.S.2d 25 (1979). No such universal consents could conceivably be obtained.

Even if one could find that some one or more of the hundreds of properties held by each of TIAA and CREF should be treated as a separate trust property contributed by one institution to provide a retirement benefit for one participant, and even if the express requirement of TIAA and CREF's consent to any amendment is disregarded, then, at least in the case of TIAA's contracts, TIAA's consent would still be required for EPTL Section 7-1.9 to apply because it holds a proprietary interest in every asset held by it. It is evident that TIAA's ability to discharge its contractual obligations is contingent upon the successful investment and management of its assets. Moreover, TIAA is legally required to establish and maintain various contingency reserves (including the Mandatory Securities Valuation Reserve) and must look to excess earnings — earnings in excess of contractually guaranteed interest rates — to meet these requirements. Accordingly, TIAA has a material proprietary interest in the investment of its assets and its consent would be required under the statute.

Interestingly, if assertions of the Clark Opinion that "CREF in all respects and TIAA in most respects operate in the manner of trustees of common trust funds" (p. A-7) [Section 1.3, p. 78 of this volume] were a valid comparison, EPTL Section 7-1.9 could not in fact be applied. A common trust fund is a single express trust embracing in one entity all settlors and all beneficiaries (who are typically the settlors) for all substantive law and tax purposes. Under such a concept, every institutional contributor and every participant and other beneficiary of TIAA or CREF would be required to provide a written consent before EPTL Section 7-1.9 could apply—an obvious impossibility.

Finally, even if it could be determined under New York law that EPTL Section 7-1.9 could somehow apply to these annuity contracts, such application would be precluded under the preemptive provisions of federal law, discussed below.

1.4.4 Errors, Omissions, and Other Aberrations of the Clark Opinion

1.4.4.1 Errors Regarding Contract Terms

In attempting to support its analysis, the Clark Opinion disregards and misstates the terms of TIAA and CREF's retirement annuity contracts and their substantive effects. Indeed, the opinion evidences no understanding of the fundamental risks and guarantees associated with deferred annuity contracts. It apparently substantially equates the interests of participants under TIAA and under CREF contracts, although such interests are quite different in both form and substance. It states (at p. A-6) [Section 1.3, p. 77 of this volume] that "The provisions in agreements between TIAA-CREF and every participating teacher leave no doubt that the teacher is the owner of the property contributed in his or her behalf." "[The premiums] do not purchase from TIAA-CREF a promise to pay a sum certain on the occurrence of a future event, nor do they impress upon the corporate funds of either organization a personal liability that must be paid regardless of whether the premiums received are adequate to meet the obligation." "The TIAA agreement . . . makes each teacher a participant in a pooled fund." "CREF and TIAA invest the funds; if the investments prosper, the earnings and appreciation are credited to each owner's account; in the reverse situation, losses are charged against each account. In short, the funds are managed for the exclusive benefit of and at the exclusive risk of the beneficial owners."

All of these statements are completely erroneous with respect to TIAA contracts, and they are in part inaccurate and misleading to the extent they concern CREF contracts. No provision in the TIAA or CREF agreements supports the concept that the teacher is the owner of the institution's contributions (see the contract forms attached). Contrary to the unsupported and unsupportable assertions of the Opinion, TIAA's contracts *do* constitute a promise to pay sums certain as annuities at future dates, with the amounts initially promised increased by periodic dividends, and these promises *do* constitute a personal liability that must be paid regardless of whether the premiums received are adequate. TIAA's earnings and appreciation are *not* credited, and losses are *not* charged, to the participant's account, although TIAA may reflect gains by declaring dividends that are so credited if TIAA determines that its mandatory securities valuation reserve and its other contingency reserves will remain adequate to support its contractual guaranties.

The Opinion's footnote (p. A-6) [Section 1.3, note 14, of this volume] totally misunderstands the nature and extent of TIAA's guarantees. It states that the guarantee of 2.5 percent interest (actually now 3 percent prior to the annuity starting date — see paragraph 38 of the enclosed contract)* has no practical effect because TIAA's assets currently pay substantially more than this. However, TIAA's guarantees are not merely for an income return of 3 percent, but, much more importantly, involve guarantees of the payment of annuities based upon *the aggregate amount* of all contributions made under the contract, a minimum 3 percent annual income return, and the amount of all dividends credited to the participant's account.[5] Also, TIAA guarantees conversion of the guaranteed account under the deferred annuity contract to an immediate annuity at rates based upon a specified interest rate (in most cases 2.5 percent) and mortality table (see paragraph 38 of the enclosed annuity contract). The Clark Opinion further states that, if "TIAA could not earn this rate of return, it would have no source of corporate funds, other than the funds supplied to it by its participants, to

*Note: The contract is not included in this volume.

meet those obligations." If this statement were true, no insurance department would permit TIAA to issue an annuity contract. Even a cursory glance at any of TIAA's annual reports would disclose large mandatory securities valuation and other contingency reserves as required under applicable insurance laws and regulations (amounting to over one billion dollars at the end of 1985) that are available to meet such obligations.

1.4.4.2 Confusion of Fiduciary Obligations and "Elements of Trust" with Creation of Express Trusts

The Clark Opinion apparently tries to create a separate express trust entity for each of the nearly one million annuity contractholders of each of TIAA and CREF (and apparently also multiple separate trusts for each participant who has earned retirement benefits from more than one educational institution). There are of course "elements of trust" in many situations, such as the fiduciary obligations imposed on every corporate board of directors, on partners, on joint venturers, on agents, and imposed by the trust obligations explicitly stated by the Employee Retirement Income Security Act. However, the rights and remedies of the parties to relationships of this kind are not subject to the law of express trusts but to the substantive law which governs the particular relationship. Thus, the duties of an agent to his principal are defined by the law of agency, and the duties owed by corporate officers and directors are the exclusive province of substantive corporate law. A. W. Scott, *The Law of Trusts,* Section 495 (3d ed. 1967). Although the acts of the parties to such relationships may give rise to equitable remedies, such as constructive trusts, such "trusts" are not express trusts since the requisite intention of the parties to create a trust is lacking. These relationships are governed by common law equitable principles and not by the statutory provisions of the New York Estates, Powers and Trusts Laws. *Accord, Johnston* v. *Spicer,* 107 N.Y. 185, 13 N.E. 753 (1887); *Simonds* v. *Simonds,* 45 N.Y.2d 233, 408 N.Y.S.2d 359 (1978).

Similarly, the charitable grants made to found TIAA and to establish and strengthen its contingency reserves, and the restrictions on TIAA and CREF under their governing instruments to nonprofit educational purposes, make applicable to them certain charitable trust principles. But whatever their significance for some purposes, none of these elements, or other principles developed by the equity courts, are sufficient by themselves to establish an express trust for purposes of EPTL. Compare *St. Joseph's Hospital* v. *Bennett*, 281 N.Y. 115 (1939). The requirements for an express trust, as discussed above, require an intention to create an interest in an identifiable separate property or res, and the actual existence of such a separate property or res, neither of which requirements can be found under TIAA or CREF's retirement annuity contracts.

1.4.4.3 Improper Reliance on Community Services, Incorporated v. United States

The only judicial authority cited by the Clark Opinion to support its contention that an annuity contract issued by an insurance company creates an express trust is *Community Services, Incorporated* (422 F.2d 1353 [Ct. Cl. 1970]). Although the reasoning of that case involved the application of a trust concept, it has no relevance to the contention that express trusts arise under individual retirement annuity contracts. The issue in the case was whether an employer would be entitled to a Federal income tax deduction for amounts paid to an insurance company with respect to retirement benefits for its employees. The question of deductibility was believed largely to turn on whether the employer could terminate the insurance contract and recover the funds for its own use. The application of the trust concept was primarily of significance in the case, not to suggest the consequences of an express trust or to affect the insurance company's obligations and its right to preclude any change therein without its consent, but rather to provide assurance that the *employer* would be bound to use for the stated retirement purposes any funds so recovered pursuant to the terms of the insurance company contract. On the substantive law question, the New York Supreme Court, in *Mundell* v. *Gibbs*, 70 Misc.2d 174, 332 N.Y.S.2d 364 (1970), held that the contractual obligation of an insurer under a group annuity contract to pay out of its general funds all amounts required under the terms of the contract is not a trust agreement. Even in the income tax area, *Community Services* is a sport decision that dealt with a position briefly held by the Internal Revenue Service that has no continuing applicability, and that is believed to have never had any applicability outside this limited tax area. Moreover, *Community Services* involved a deposit administration group annuity contract, in contrast to the individual deferred annuity contracts of TIAA and CREF. The temporary litigation position taken by the Service, prior to ERISA, and reflected by the Government's position in this case, solely applied to profit sharing plans invested in deposit administration contracts.[6] The TIAA-CREF individual retirement annuity contracts are not deposit administration contracts. Moreover, the court's opinion appears to assume the validity of the provisions of the deposit administration contract providing for amendment or change by the mutual agreement of the employer *and the insurance company.*

Further, even if *Community Services* were regarded as currently applicable and as establishing a precedent for substantive law purposes, and even if the distinction between deposit administration contracts and individual deferred annuity contracts were disregarded, it would not support the conclusions of the Clark Opinion. The trust concept referred to in that case clearly refers to a unitary trust for all of the assets so held by the insurer. Thus, it affords no precedent for treatment of each participant's TIAA or CREF contract as a separate express trust, which, as discussed above, would be required for any practical applicability of EPTL Section 7-1.9.

1.4.4.4 Failure to Consider Controlling Statutes and Numerous Judicial Authorities

The conclusions of the Clark Opinion are inconsistent with the explicit statutory insurance provisions concerning amendment of annuity contracts and the extensive judicial authorities, discussed above. None of these statutory provisions or cases are even referred to in the opinion.

1.4.4.5 Failure to Identify What Property or Amounts Would Be Subject to the Proposed Requirement for Premature Transfers, or to Discuss the Enormous Problems Relating Thereto

The Clark Opinion does not state the amounts that CREF or TIAA should be required by a court to transfer to a third party investment manager under the proposal for compelled transfers prior to the contract maturities, nor does it discuss any of the difficult problems that would arise in attempting to quantify such amounts.[7] Indeed, the Clark Opinion lightly dismisses any consideration of such problems as follows (p. A-10) [Section 1.3, p. 63 of this volume]:

> The mechanics of transferring funds to a new trustee pose no problems. . . . Funds may move in and out of CREF with the same ease as they do in and out of a common trust fund or any other pooled investment fund. This traffic in no way affects the interests of the beneficiaries who remain in the fund. . . . The situation as regards TIAA is slightly more complicated because it uses different valuation methods. The difficulties are not, however, insurmountable and ways can be devised for the transfer of TIAA funds without adversely affecting other beneficial owners.

The view of the opinion that ways can be devised for such transfers without adversely affecting other participants might be more persuasive if evidence were provided that the question had been explored and if specific suggestions supporting such view were offered for consideration.

Since CREF holds only marketable securities that can be readily valued and CREF's obligations to participants are based on such values, there is at least a current market valuation that can be taken into account in determining the amount that might be transferred with respect to a CREF contract. Even in CREF's case, however, other considerations are involved. Such transfers would involve some liquidating and administrative costs. Since the amount of the annuities payable to participants during the payout period depends upon the mortality experience of all of CREF's annuitants, adverse selection prior to the annuity starting date could be expected to affect adversely other participants. In part because of these considerations, CREF's supplemental retirement annuities impose a front-end loading charge on contributions, which can be kept low because it is paid at the outset and involves a predictably limited amount of cash surrenders. However, there is no clear formula for determining an equivalent charge for the proposed transfers to reflect a deferral in the time of payment of the charge, the possibility of adverse selection based on circumstances at the time of transfer, and the unpredictable and potentially much larger amounts to be transferred. Also, in the case of the many participants who have been employed by more than one institutional contributor, difficulties may arise in determining the amounts allocable to the contributions of a particular institution if all such contributing institutions have not joined in the request for transfer.

The determination of a current valuation for interests in a TIAA retirement annuity contract involves all of the considerations applicable to CREF, but is greatly more complicated because the stated accumulation under such contracts is not determined by reference to current market values of any assets held by TIAA.

The determination by a court of a valuation of an annuity interest required to be transferred by TIAA to a new investment manager under the proposal of the Clark Opinion might in theory be made by reference to one or more of the valuation standards referred to below. However, each of such standards involves substantial practical problems, and none offers a precise method for taking account of the fact that all of TIAA's assets, including its contingency reserves, are dedicated by charter and charitable trust concepts to such retirement and related benefits. Since there is no separately identifiable property attributable to any particular retirement annuity contract, how could a court determine an amount that it would require to be transferred?

Various valuation theories that might be considered include the following, none of which could precisely take account of all of the relevant factors; therefore, each would present major difficulties to a court that was asked to require transfers:

1. The stated accumulation value at the time of transfer, with or without some arbitrary charge to reflect the costs of administration and liquidity and the risks of disintermediation and other elections against the interests of continuing participants.

2. The current market value of the projected deferred annuity payments provided by the contract, reflecting the 3 percent interest guarantees and possibly, but not necessarily, some assumption of dividend additions, such projected future payments to be discounted to the date of transfer in accordance with current market interest rates, and with or without further charges for administrative and liquidating expenses.

3. The market value of the annuity contract determined by comparing the market interest rates at the time of each contribution under the contract (including assumed rollovers of investments for contracts that have been outstanding over long periods) with the market interest rates at the time of the transfer of funds, on the assumption that the market values of assets held by TIAA will reflect the timing of TIAA's investments therein.

4. The current market value of the annuity contracts determined by reference to the aggregate current market value of TIAA's assets, which assets establish the amounts available to meet TIAA's obligations to all participants. (Since TIAA holds literally hundreds of assets which have no established market, any appraisal of those assets, particularly if kept up to date on a continuing basis, would be expensive and imprecise.) The aggregate values thus determined might then be allocated among the annuity contract obligations on the basis, for example, of one or more of the stated accumulation values, vintage account adjustments to the stated accumulation values, or discounted values of the projected future annuity payments provided by each such contract.

Unless a precise market valuation adjustment to the determination of amounts to be transferred by TIAA to new investment managers could be determined and imposed, it seems probable that, whenever current interest rates are higher than historical interest rates, all informed participants would wish to transfer their interests, to the great detriment to remaining participants, including those who are later in attempting to effect such transfers. Depending on the method and accuracy of the determination of the value of participants' accounts that would be subject to the proposed transfers, under particular economic conditions any large numbers of transfers could threaten TIAA's solvency.

1.4.4.6 Confusion of a Statutory Grant of Authority to Delegate Responsibility with an Assumed Requirement So to Delegate

The Clark Opinion states (p. A-8, footnote) [Section 1.3, p. 79, note 18, of this volume]:

> Were a court to hold that Section 513(a) makes EPTL Section 7-1.9 unavailable to the parties, they, either as individuals or in conjunction with the Attorney General, might then bring an action to compel TIAA-CREF to take the steps authorized in Not-for-Profit Corporation law Section 513 and 514 for the improved management of the funds. . . .

This is an astonishing statement and appears clearly wrong. Section 514 provides that "the governing board may (1) delegate . . . the authority to act in place of the governing board in investment and reinvestment of institutional funds, (2) contract with independent investment advisors, . . . and (3) authorize the payment of compensation for investment advisory or management services. . . . " (McKinney 1970.) This statutory provision simply permits a board that wishes to do so to delegate investment authority, and relieves such a board from responsibility for such investments if the delegation is in accordance with the terms of the statute. The statute cannot be construed *to compel* the delegation of investment authority if the board is willing to continue the responsibility therefor. To whom would a court require that the investment authority be delegated? Further, the statute requires that each contract so delegating such authority "shall provide that it may be terminated by the governing board at any time, without penalty, upon not more than sixty days' notice." How can the statute contemplate that the governing board can be compelled to delegate investment authority, and at the same time require that the board retain discretion to terminate such delegation?

1.4.4.7 Omission of Any Consideration of ERISA Problems

The Employee Retirement Income Security Act of 1974 ("ERISA"), 29 U.S.C. Section 1001 et seq., was enacted in 1974 as comprehensive federal legislation designed to regulate employee pension and welfare benefit plans. Except for retirement annuity contributions from state institutions, TIAA and CREF contracts are issued under pension plans that are subject to ERISA. The Clark Opinion does not deal with the problems raised by it under ERISA, or even refer to the existence or applicability of ERISA. This omission is critical, because in our opinion the preemption provisions of ERISA preclude the applicability of EPTL Section 7-1.9 on which the Clark Opinion relies.

Section 514(a) of ERISA states that the substantive provisions of ERISA (including ERISA provisions relating to the requirement that plan assets be held in trust and imposing fiduciary obligations on persons who hold or control plan assets) "shall supersede any and all State laws insofar as they may now or hereafter relate to any employee benefit plan. . . ." Subsection (b)(2) of Section 514 of ERISA includes the following relevant exception:[8]

(2)(A) Except as provided in sub-paragraph (B), nothing in this title shall be construed to exempt or relieve any person from any law of any State which regulates insurance, banking, or securities.

(B) Neither an employee benefit plan described in

section 4(a), which is not exempt under section 4(b) (other than a plan established primarily for the purpose of providing death benefits), nor any trust established under such a plan, shall be deemed to be an insurance company or other insurer, bank, trust company, or investment company or to be engaged in the business of insurance or banking for purposes of any law of any State purporting to regulate insurance companies, insurance contracts, banks, trust companies, or investment companies.

It appears quite clear that EPTL Section 7-1.9 cannot be considered a law which regulates insurance, banking or securities. Consequently, EPTL Section 7-1.9 would be preempted insofar as it "relate[s] to" an employee benefit plan.

As applied to the assets of an employee benefit plan, EPTL Section 7-1.9 clearly would "relate to" an employee benefit plan within the meaning of ERISA's general preemption rule. The basic issue involved is whether TIAA and CREF, or some other entity, will manage the assets of employee pension benefit plans established by participating institutions. Such asset management questions are considered in detail in Sections 402 and 403 of ERISA and are clearly questions of federal law since the enactment of ERISA. See, for example, *Marshall* v. *Chase Manhattan Bank,* 558 F.2d 680 (2nd Cir. 1977), which reversed the lower court's dismissal of a suit by the Department of Labor to enjoin a New York State court from approving liquidation of a pension plan on the grounds (inter alia) that state law concerning fiduciary conduct is preempted; and *O'Neil* v. *Marriott Corp.,* 538 F. Supp. 1026 (D. Md. 1982), which, in connection with an action alleging fraud, self dealing and imprudent investment of profit sharing plan assets, notes (at 1034) that state fiduciary laws are preempted with respect to ERISA plans.

In addition, EPTL Section 7-1.9 would "relate to" ERISA plans because its requirements would directly affect the rights of plan participants. In *Metropolitan Life Insurance Co.* v. *Massachusetts,* 105 S.Ct. 2380 (1985), the Supreme Court concluded (at 2389) that a state requirement that health plans provide certain mental health care coverage was a law that "relate[s] to" plans covered by ERISA for purposes of ERISA's preemption provision. The Court indicated (at 2390) that state laws "that regulate only the insurer or the way in which it may sell insurance" are not preempted by ERISA, but that content-related requirements of state law are laws that "relate to" an employee benefit plan for purposes of the preemption provision. The Court also cited (footnote 2 at 2383) grace period and conversion requirements as additional examples of content-related requirements. See also *Eversole* v. *Metropolitan Life Ins. Co.,* 500 F. Supp. 1162 (D. Cal. 1980), which in connection with state insurance laws concerning fraud against policyholders holds (at 1167) that state laws "which indirectly regulate the terms and conditions of the plan as a result of direct regulation" of the funding agent "relate to" the plan for purposes of ERISA preemption.[9] Since application of EPTL Section 7-1.9 would provide substantive rights to beneficiaries and settlors and impose obligations on funding agents such as TIAA and CREF, in our view, EPTL Section 7-1.9 is preempted to any extent that it would otherwise be applicable to an ERISA plan.[10]

The fiduciary requirements of ERISA are set forth in Part 4 of Title I of ERISA and do not include requirements comparable to EPTL Section 7-1.9. These requirements include (i) prohibitions concerning the investment of assets and self dealing (Sections 406 through 408), and (ii) basic fiduciary rules (relating to prudence and diversification and the exclusive purpose rule discussed further below).

Section 403 of ERISA also requires that all plan assets be held in trust, subject to an exception (inter alia) for "any assets of [an insurance company qualified to do business in a State] or any assets of a plan which are held by such an insurance company." Section 403(b)(2) of ERISA; see also the Regulations of the Department of Labor, 29 C.F.R. Section 2550.403b-1, and pages 298 and 299 of the Conference Report for ERISA (House Conference Rep. No. 93-1280, 93d Cong., 2d Sess. 298–299 (1974)). It is thus quite clear that ERISA provides specific trust requirements that are not applicable to an insurance carrier.

It is also clear under ERISA that an insurance carrier is a fiduciary with respect to assets held in a separate account with respect to which benefits are not guaranteed (for example, CREF), and in some cases may be a fiduciary with respect to a policy or contract under which benefits are guaranteed (for example, TIAA), but these fiduciary obligations do not import an express trust, or obviate the applicability of the insurance exemption to the specific trust requirement. Sections 3(21)(A) and 401(b)(2) of ERISA and the Conference Report for ERISA (at pages 296 and 297). For citations concerning whether an insurer is a fiduciary for guaranteed benefits, see 67 ALR Fed. 186, at 197 to 199. See also *Chicago Bd of Options Exchange, Inc.* v. *Connecticut General Life Ins. Co.,* 713 F.2d 254 (7th Cir. 1983), and footnote 13 in the preamble to Prohibited Transaction Exemption 81-82 (issued by the Department of Labor on September 15, 1981).

We believe that an insurance carrier is not acting in an ERISA fiduciary capacity in establishing (and deciding whether to amend) the terms of its contractual commitments with respect to a plan. The Department of Labor has indicated that, to the contrary, the contractholder " . . . has an obligation to fully inform himself regarding the relevant terms of the contract, including any charges that may be made in the event amounts deposited with the insurance company are withdrawn, and to take the anticipated liquidity needs of the plan into account in determining whether to enter into the contract."[11] Even assuming that TIAA and CREF are to be considered as fiduciaries with respect to their power to agree to amendments to TIAA and CREF contracts, each would be required under Section 404(a) of ERISA to take into account any adverse impact such amendment may have on the benefits for other contractholders, as well as on the benefits of the holder of the contract being amended.

ERISA also imposes special vesting requirements on employee pension benefit plans which are interpreted under Treasury Regulations Section 1.411(a)-7(1) to require that any optional form of payment under a defined benefit plan not be less valuable than the normal form. A reduction in the amount payable in connection with a single sum cash payment transfer option might therefore be considered a penalty that is not permissible under the vesting rules imposed by ERISA or under Code sections 403(b)(1)(C) and 411. While this risk would generally seem remote given the widespread practice of certain commercial insurance carriers of imposing a "market value adjustment" in certain cases where a cash withdrawal is made at a time when "book value" exceeds "market value," any amendment which allowed an impermissible penalty in violation of these vesting requirements would clearly cause any plan so amended to fail to qualify under Section 401(a), 403(a) or 403(b) of the Code, as well as subjecting the fiduciary to suit for violation of ERISA's vesting requirements. Moreover, the Department of Labor in Prohibited Transaction Exemption 81–82, above, has stated that the imposition of such a penalty could violate other ERISA requirements:

> . . . the Department [of Labor] is concerned with the effect of such [market value] adjustments on employee pension plans as well as with the potential that the fiduciary responsibility provisions of ERISA may be violated in connection with arrangements that involve the imposition of such charges.

Thus, even assuming that TIAA and CREF determined that a cash transfer would not adversely affect other contractholders, it would be inadvisable to determine the amounts payable on account of such a cash transfer option without further clarifications under ERISA and the Code. Also, since TIAA's contingency reserves are dedicated by charter and procedures to the provision of benefits for college employees, a determination that a premature settlement will not adversely affect other contractholders is much more difficult than in the case of a commercial company where reserves support the fixed contract obligations but otherwise may ultimately inure to the benefit of stockholders rather than the contractholders.

As indicated by the foregoing discussion, we consider the Clark Opinion to be superficial, factually erroneous, analytically unsound, contrary to express New York statutory provisions and to the explicit TIAA and CREF contract terms, contrary to well-established judicial authority, and in total disregard of the preemptive provisions of applicable federal law.

Appendix

Paragraph 9 of the TIAA
Contract (Form #1000.23)

"9. The Contract. This document is the entire contract between you and TIAA. We have issued it in return for your completed application and the first premium. Any endorsement or amendment of this contract, waiver of any of its provisions, or change in Rate Schedule will be valid only if in writing and signed by an Executive Officer or Registrar of TIAA. All premiums and benefits are payable at TIAA's home office in New York, NY."

Paragraph 11 of the CREF
Contract (Form #C1000.10)

"11. The Certificate. We have issued this certificate in return for your completed application and the first premium. Any endorsement or amendment of this certificate or waiver of any of its provisions will be valid only if in writing and signed by an Executive Officer or Registrar of CREF. All premiums and benefits are payable at CREF's home office in New York, NY."

1.5

Additional Opinion

Elias Clark

Following is the text of an opinion letter, dated February 10, 1987, from Elias Clark, Lafayette S. Foster Professor of Law, Yale University, to Oscar M. Ruebhausen, Chair of the Commission on College Retirement:

The commission's report, dated May, 1986, recommended that TIAA-CREF establish an orderly procedure for the optional transfer of a teacher-beneficiary's account, during the accumulation stage, to other investment managers, subject to annuitization at retirement. My opinion, which was attached to the report as an appendix, was concerned with the legal right under New York law of the college-employer and the teacher-employee, acting together to effect such a transfer as a last resort if TIAA-CREF are recalcitrant.

Subsequent to the publication of the commission report, you received a letter from Mr. James G. MacDonald, Chairman and Chief Executive Officer of TIAA-CREF, and an opinion letter from the law firm, Dewey, Ballantine, Bushby, Palmer and Wood, copies of which you sent to me. I have previously shared with you my views about the MacDonald letter and the Dewey opinion and am now responding to your request that I incorporate those views into a more formal opinion.

At the outset, it should be noted that neither the Mac-Donald letter nor the Dewey opinion respond to the commission's recommendation. No claim is made in the letter that the superiority of the TIAA-CREF stewardship renders unnecessary discussion of transferring funds to other managers. Nor is there any clear assertion in the opinion of a legal barrier prohibiting TIAA-CREF from initiating a policy of optional transferability on their own. Indeed, any such assertion, at least as to CREF, would be a contradiction of the specific authorization, permitting a fiduciary to transfer funds to outside investment managers, contained in the two statutes upon which CREF places heavy reliance in its claim that it cannot be compelled to make such transfers.[1] CREF has, of course, for some years recognized that it has this authority by permitting transfers of funds from CREF to TIAA.

Rather than the substantive response that might have been expected, the MacDonald letter relies exclusively on the assertion in the Dewey opinion that my findings are not supported by the law. In short, TIAA-CREF may ignore the commission's concerns (and presumably those expressed by other individuals and universities) because its legal counsel has advised them that dissatisfied teachers and colleges have no legal means to change the status quo. Throughout its analysis, the Dewey opinion consistently places the interests of TIAA-CREF above those of the academic community which they serve, a position at odds with the time-honored tradition that the function of fiduciaries is not to perpetuate their status or to generate fees but to serve the interests of the settlor and the beneficiary.

1.5.1. Assumptions in the Dewey Opinion That Are Either Erroneous or Inconsistent with Positions Taken by TIAA-CREF in the Past

Central to the Dewey analysis are two assumptions of fact, the first of which is based on a misrepresentation of the commission's recommendation and my conclusions and the second of which rests on a claim that TIAA is an insurance company, a position that TIAA has itself renounced in the past. The discussion that follows examines separately these two assumptions.

1.5.1.1. The Commission's Recommendation
Concerned the Investment of Contributions Prior
to the Teacher's Retirement, Not to the Pay Out
of an Annuity Purchased Upon Retirement

The relationship between a teacher and TIAA-CREF spans two separate periods of time. Period one occurs prior to the teacher's retirement when contributions are paid to the companies which they invest and accumulate on the teacher's behalf. The second starts after the teacher's retirement when he or she uses the accumulated funds to purchase one of the annuities offered by the companies. The accumulation of funds and the pay out of an annuity are two distinct activities which may proceed independently of each other. A teacher, for example, may use some other method of setting aside funds during his or her productive years and be in a position at retirement to purchase the same amount in annuity benefits from TIAA-CREF or another company.[2]

The Dewey opinion sets as its first objective proof that a "retirement annuity contract" is not a trust. It cites on that point a series of cases involving a wide assortment of insurance contracts, including, among others, a jeweler's block policy, an employer's indemnification policy and a homeowner's policy, to prove that obligations under an insurance policy are governed by contract rather than trust law.[3] Its point and the cases it cites are irrelevant because they seek to refute an argument that was never made.

The commission expressly states, first in the title and then throughout the text, that its recommendation is aimed at the management of the teacher's funds during the accumulation period, prior to retirement. A restatement of my conclusions further contradicts the representation that we were discussing the annuity or pay out phase. I concluded then and continue to hold to the view that TIAA-CREF manage the funds, which are being invested on behalf of a teacher-beneficiary prior to conversion into an annuity upon the teacher's retirement, essentially as trustees and that the teacher as beneficiary and his or her college as settlor, acting in unison, are entitled to invoke traditional trust remedies, of which N.Y. EPTL Section 7-1.9 is one, to obtain an improved return on investments. I did not contend that these trust remedies were available to the parties during the annuity or pay out phase. After a teacher retires and uses his or her accumulation units to purchase an annuity, the relationship becomes one of contract, involving a fixed obligation to make specific payments over a period of years based on life expectancies. Such a contract is not amendable without the concurrence of the company issuing the policy.

1.5.1.2 TIAA-CREF Operates During the Accumulation Phase in the Manner of a Trust; Previous Recognition of the Trust Analogy by TIAA-CREF

The Dewey opinion makes much of the fact that TIAA is incorporated under the New York Insurance Law and that its obligations include a guaranteed minimum return. It concludes that TIAA's responsibilities are to be defined by the laws governing insurance and goes on to suggest that, although CREF is organized under the New York Not-for-Profit Corporation Law, its operation and obligations are sufficiently similar to those of TIAA to require that it be answerable to the same laws as TIAA.

The Dewey statement is given to dismissing contrary arguments with expressions suggesting shock and outrage that anyone has the temerity to raise them. Such expressions seem misplaced in light of the fact that TIAA-CREF have eagerly sought to be described as trustees when that label was perceived to be to their advantage. The Tax Reform Act of 1986, as originally passed by the House, would have denied tax-exempt status to TIAA-CREF on the grounds that it is a business enterprise and "commercial-type insurance is a substantial part of its activities."[4] Mr. Donald S. Willard, Executive Vice President of TIAA-CREF, countered in a statement on the companies' behalf that TIAA must be distinguished from a commercial insurer because it is analogous to a "pooled pension trust" and entitled to the tax-exempt status of such a trust.[5]

Mr. Willard's statement did not include CREF in the

defense because of the general recognition that CREF is not
organized under the insurance law and operates as a segregated
asset account rather than a mutual life insurance company. Mr.
Willard's conclusion as to TIAA is correct and his omission of
CREF appropriate. I would contend further, reversing the
Dewey position, that the CREF stewardship during the accumulation phase is for all practical purposes indistinguishable
from a trust and that the TIAA operations are so similar to those
of CREF as to justify viewing its management of the contributed
funds as also the functional equivalent of a trust.

CREF invests the contributions received on the teacher's
behalf, crediting to the teacher in the form of accumulation units
his or her percentage share in the overall investment pool. Prior
to the conversion of the units into an annuity at retirement, the
teacher, like a trust beneficiary, bears the risks and benefits of
the investments and, as the owner of the units, is informed
periodically of their market value. Under TIAA, the teacher
is in many ways also a participant in a pooled fund. The relationship is not, however, described in that manner, and TIAA's
obligations to its participants differ from CREF's in several
respects. TIAA guarantees a minimum 3 percent return on contributed funds and on any additional funds that have been
credited to the participant's account. The company maintains
out of these funds a contingency reserve in the unlikely event
that it has to meet a shortfall between the amount the funds have
earned and the 3 percent guarantee. Excess earnings from the
reserves are credited to the participants' accounts periodically.
The teacher's interest is computed at book rather than market
value.

Those features do not transform TIAA into an insurer
nor do they destroy the analogy to CREF. Typically, an insurer
contracts to make fixed payments and stands to lose if the event
being insured occurs prematurely or the investment of premiums
fails to produce a sufficient return to meet the company's obligations. Unlike this model, TIAA during the accumulation phase
does not bear any risk of mortality or premature retirement,
nor, when all is said and done, does it have to cover the investment risk out of funds belonging to the corporation.

It is difficult to imagine a set of future circumstances that will make it necessary to use the 3 percent guarantee to define TIAA's obligations to its participants. As of now, TIAA has in its portfolio long-term assets paying substantially more than 3 percent, and all the indicators foretell an economy that will continue to make a larger return a virtual certainty. It is, however, to be emphasized that if in some distant future, TIAA does not earn the 3 percent rate of return it will have to make up the deficiency out of the contingency reserves that come from the participants' contributions and that are dedicated to be used exclusively for pension fund purposes. Indeed, Mr. Willard made the fact that the reserves belong to the pension funds and not to the corporation the cornerstone of his argument that TIAA is not a mutual insurance company.[6] Thus the reality is that the teachers and not the company bear the investment risk, making their relationship to the funds invested on their behalf similar to that of trust beneficiaries to a trust corpus.

The Dewey opinion foresees "enormous" problems in identifying and valuing the teacher's interest to be transferred. There may be some small administrative costs in making a transfer that are properly billed to the teacher. Beyond these minor expenses, there does not seem to be any problem in identifying or valuing the teacher's CREF accumulation units which represent a known percentage participation in a pooled fund for which there is always a current market value. The "problems" cited in the Dewey opinion pertain to the transfer of a teacher's interest after retirement when the units have been converted into an annuity. Inasmuch, as the commission did not recommend the transfer of annuitized funds, the Dewey contention is a nonissue.

The commission report recognizes that complications may arise because a teacher's participation in TIAA is determined by book rather than market value. An analysis of these complications is beyond the scope of this memorandum. That TIAA has developed a method of identifying and valuing a teacher's account that treats fairly the teacher who wishes to make a transfer and the participants who remain in the program is demonstrated by the fact that TIAA now offers a 10 percent cashout privilege on retirement and a 100 percent withdrawal option to the estate of a participant who dies before retirement, and a privilege to remove funds if they are below a certain amount at the termination of employment.

I continue to believe that in the relationship of TIAA to the funds which it is accumulating for its participants elements of trust predominate, and I think it likely if the issue were litigated that a court would agree. A cautious strategist might not wish, however, to risk an unfavorable decision and thus might prefer to concentrate the argument on CREF alone. If such litigation were to develop and the issue was narrowed to the elements of trust that exist in CREF's stewardship of a teacher's funds during the accumulation period, many of the practical and legal issues raised in the Dewey opinion would disappear. The balance of this letter addresses its remaining arguments.

1.5.2. Reaffirmation of the Argument That CREF Operates in the Manner of a Trust and That N.Y. EPTL Section 7–1.9 Is Available to Obtain a Transfer of Funds

The Dewey opinion disputes the trust concept as applied to the CREF stewardship during the accumulation phase on general law grounds and on the language of Section 513(a) of the New York Not-for-Profit Corporation Law. It argues that there is neither an intent to create a trust nor an identifiable trust res. I believe to the contrary that the parties intended to create the relationship that they did create and that it makes no difference at law whether or not they call it a trust, if in substance it is a trust.[7] Furthermore, a modern trust res can be and frequently is identified as a percentage participation in a pooled fund and need not be physically segregated from all other trust funds.[8]

I cited two cases, *Community Services, Incorporated* v. *United States*[9] and *Christiansen* v. *National Savings and Trust Co.*,[10] to illustrate traditional analysis of the difference between a trust and a contract.[11] I made no claim, as the Dewey opinion implies, that these cases constituted binding precedent on the facts here nor is the outcome in terms of who won or lost relevant. They make the point that a trust exists when the beneficiary owns the fund being held for him or her (because the beneficiary does not have physical possession of the property, ownership is equitable in nature), whereas a contract arises when the beneficiary has no property interest but possesses only a claim against the company's general funds. Instead of disputing this analysis, the Dewey opinion responds that the CREF accumulation units do not belong to the teacher but do belong to CREF and are properly includible in CREF's general funds.

This assertion of fact contradicts both CREF's representations and reality. Paragraph 13 of the CREF certificate promises "you continue to own all your Accumulation Units." There are numerous other instances where the CREF statements either recognize or imply the teacher's ownership.[12] These representations accurately describe the facts. CREF treats the teacher exactly as if he or she is a trust beneficiary in that the contributions made by the college and teacher are invested for the exclusive benefit of and at the exclusive risk of the teacher.

The Dewey opinion states that Section 513(a) of the Not-for-Profit Corporation Law mandates full ownership rights to contributed funds and earnings on those funds in CREF.[13] I stand by my original analysis of the origins and scope of this provision. The Court of Appeals in *St. Joseph's Hospital* v. *Bennett* held that the gift to the hospital, limited by the donor to several specific uses, did not create a trust because there was no beneficiary, implying that had a beneficiary been named, his or her interests would have been protected.[14] It continues to be the New York law that funds solicited by universities, hospitals, museums and similar not-for-profit institutions in the form of split interest gifts create trust obligations which the private beneficiary can enforce by invoking the whole range of equitable trust remedies such as a petition for an accounting, actions for specific performance and injunctions, and the like.[15] The contrary view would limit the beneficiary to an action in damages for breach of contract payable out of the corporation's general funds and would treat the beneficiary no better than a general creditor in the event of insolvency.

The Dewey opinion argues that even if the relationship is described as a trust, N.Y. EPTL Section 7-1.9 does not apply. It claims that paragraphs 9 and 11 of the TIAA-CREF certificates set out the exclusive procedure for amending the obligations of the parties. The clauses upon which this reliance is placed are boilerplate provisions frequently used in documents of this kind to protect the company from excessive statements or misrepresentations made by salespersons or other minor representatives of the company.[16] They in no way establish a procedure for the amendment of a trust by the joint action of the settlor and beneficiary to supersede the procedure set out in EPTL Section 7-1.9.

The opinion next states without the citation of authority that the consent of all the settlors and all the beneficiaries is required to any modification requested by an individual teacher and college. This proposition is defensible only to the extent that other settlors and beneficiaries are negatively affected by the action of a single settlor and beneficiary. Even now CREF and TIAA offer participants or their estates opportunities under certain circumstances to cashout their accumulation units in whole or in part. This process goes on without any financial loss to the participants who remain in the program, and no one would contend that CREF and TIAA, absent authorization in the certificates, would be violating their fiduciary duties when they make these cashouts without first obtaining the consent of all the other settlors and beneficiaries.

1.5.3. Transferability of Funds Is Not Barred by the Preemption Provisions of ERISA

The final argument in the Dewey opinion states that "the preemption provisions [Section 514(a)] of ERISA preclude the applicability of EPTL Section 7-1.9." It does not claim that the commission's recommendations violate the provisions of ERISA; rather it contends that the use of state law to implement those recommendations is proscribed. TIAA-CREF could, if they wished, take constructive action toward attaining the commission's objections by expanding in-house the range of investment

opportunities available to their participants. In adopting the
fiduciary standards sections of ERISA (primarily Sections 404
and 409), "Congress invoked the common law of trusts to define
the general scope of their [trustees and other fiduciaries] authority and responsibility."[17] Section 404 instructs the fiduciary to
discharge its duties "solely in the interest of the participants and
beneficiaries" and to administer the funds with the "care, skill,
prudence, and diligence" of a prudent person. An enlightened
policy that is approved by a college for its employees and that
offers an individual employee the option to select from a diversity of investment strategies is wholly compatible with the twin
charges of Section 404 and the general tenets of trust law. The
act seems to encourage innovation in funding arrangements by
authorizing in Sections 402(c)(2) and (3) and 405(d) the parties
to seek outside investment advice or to appoint outside investment managers.

Thus it is process, not substance, that is at issue. The commission's recommendation for an option allowing the transfer
of funds to third party investment managers is conditioned on
the new manager being subject to the same commitment to annuitization as in the existing plan. Accordingly, if a teacher and
college joined together to petition a state court for such a transfer
of funds to a third party investment manager, they would invoke the authority of EPTL Section 7-1.9 for that limited purpose only and not to alter any of the terms or conditions of the
pension plan. A denial of their petition would constitute in practical effect a grant of permanent tenure to the original investment manager. There is nothing in ERISA to suggest that Congress intended to confer any such tenure.

Congress enacted ERISA in 1974 to secure federal supervision of the terms and conditions of employee benefit plans in
place of piecemeal federal labor laws and conflicting state laws
and regulations.[18] This policy finds expression in Section 514
of the act (the "preemption" section), which reads in part:

> **(a) Supersedure; effective date.** Except as provided
> in subsection (b) of this section, the provisions of this title
> and title IV shall supersede any and all State laws insofar

as they may now or hereafter relate to any employee benefit plan described in section 4(a) and not exempt under section 4(b). This section shall take effect on January 1, 1975.

(b) **Construction and application.** . . .

(c) **Definitions.** For purposes of this section: (1) The term "State law" includes all laws, decisions, rules, regulations, or other State action having the effect of law, of any State. A law of the United States applicable only to the District of Columbia shall be treated as a State law rather than a law of the United States.

(2) The term "State" includes a State, any political subdivisions thereof, or any agency or instrumentality of either, which purports to regulate, directly or indirectly, the terms and conditions of employee benefit plans covered by this title.

(d) **Alteration, amendment, modification, invalidation, impairment, or supersedure of any law of the United States prohibited.** Nothing in this title shall be construed to alter, amend, modify, invalidate, impair, or supersede any law of the United States . . . or any rule or regulation issued under any such law.

A number of Circuit Courts have observed that, while Section 514 is comprehensive, Congress did not intend for it to preempt every state law that has a discernible impact on pension plans. So it has been recognized that, over and above the specific exceptions set out in the statute, the preemptive scope of 514 is not "all-encompassing"[19] and is subject to "necessary limits."[20] In declaring that New York's right to set hospital rates chargeable to employee benefit plans was not preempted, Judge Van Graafeiland refused to construe Section 514 as creating "a fully insulated legal world," holding instead that:

Where, as here, a *State statute of general application* does not affect the structure, the administration, or the type of benefits provided by an ERISA plan, the mere fact that the statute has some economic impact on the plan does not require that the statute be invalidated [emphasis added].[21]

Paragraph (c) of Section 514 defines the type of "State laws" that are preempted because they "relate to" an employee benefit plan as any state action "which purports to regulate, directly or indirectly, the terms and conditions of employee benefit plans." The cases, including those cited in the preceding paragraph, make clear that this definition of "State" either modifies the meaning of "relate to" or imposes independent requirements of its own.[22] See, for example, the statement in *Lane* v. *Goren,* supra, at page 1339:

> Congress further limited the preemptive effect of ERISA in the definitional section, [Section 514(c)(2)], wherein it is established that the term "State" for preemption purposes included a state or its political subdivisions or agencies of either, "which purports to regulate, directly or indirectly, the terms and conditions of employee benefits plans covered by this subchapter."

Thus, under the statute, a state court order, issued at the joint request of the employer and employee, transferring the employee's accumulation units to a new investment manager for administratiuon during the period prior to retirement, is not preempted unless it purports to regulate the terms and conditions of the employee's benefit plan. The stipulation that the funds are to be annuitized at the employee's retirement is proof that it is neither the purpose nor effect of the order to alter the substance of the pension plan. Furthermore, preemption of state action is not required by ERISA unless there is persuasive evidence of its necessity.[23]

Section 502(a)(1)(B) of the act authorizes the beneficiary to bring a civil action to "enforce" or "clarify" his or her rights, and Section 502 (e)(1) provides that this civil action may be brought in either the federal or state court. These provisions explicitly recognize that there is a state role in the process so long as it does not regulate the terms or conditions of the pension plan nor contravene any other provision of the act.

Aside from Section 411(a), which makes a person convicted of a serious crime ineligible for appointment, ERISA is neutral about the identity, numbers and qualifications of persons or entities who serve as fiduciaries. Once named, the fiduciary is responsible to federal standards for the conduct of its office, but there is nothing in the text establishing those standards that gives tenure in office to any particular fiduciary. Indeed, common sense tells us that Congress did not intend to prohibit an employer and a union representing the employees from taking joint action to name a new fiduciary.

There are a number of cases holding that a beneficiary cannot invoke state common law trust or contract remedies against a fiduciary because an expansion of the fiduciary's liability may cause an indirect regulation of the pension plan. In many of these cases the employee was opposed to the employer. In the situation posed by the commission the employer and the employee are by hypothesis in full agreement and have joined together to take action against the fiduciary, who by the terms of the act exists only to provide service to the employer and the employees.

These cases do, however, make it necessary to ask whether either CREF or TIAA offer during the accumulation period unique services such that their removal would effect an alteration of the pension plan. CREF provides traditional investment and bookkeeping services that could be replicated by a wide variety of financial institutions. It is perhaps arguable that the TIAA guarantee of a minimum return on investments and its use of book rather than market value might be made the basis of a finding that its stewardship of the funds during the accumulation phase is essential to the preservation of the "terms and conditions" of the plan. More likely, however, a court would conclude that the likelihood of the guaranteed return becoming operative is remote, that adjustments can be made in valuation so that participants are not financially disadvantaged by the transfer of funds, and that TIAA, like CREF, can be replaced without alteration of the pension plan.

As suggested by the note of uncertainty in the preceding paragraph, the scope of Section 514 continues to be the subject of debate, and the outcome of future litigation is not certain. The issues here are not, however, closed out by a holding that a *New York court* is preempted from ordering a transfer of funds to new investment managers. The teacher as a participant in the plan may under the provisions of Section 502(a)(1)(B) bring an action in the *federal court* to enforce or clarify his or her rights and may seek appropriate equitable relief to that end. In order to ensure national uniformity in the oversight of pension plans, federal law must be applied in such an action. Both the legislative history and subsequent judicial decisions make clear that the federal law includes general common law trust and contract principles. The following statement appears in H.R. Rep. No. 93–533, p. 11 (1973):

> The fiduciary responsibility section [404], in essence, codifies and makes applicable to these fiduciaries certain principles developed in the evolution of the law of trusts.

This statement has been cited with approval and the common law has been incorporated into the federal law to define the scope of the fiduciary's authority and responsibility in a number of cases.[24]

The Supreme Court in *Shaw* v. *Delta Air Lines, Inc.,*[25] had occasion to examine the application of the preemption provision to state law that has been incorporated into the federal law. It concluded that the state law is not preempted, indeed, that it is entitled to the protection guaranteed to federal law against impairment or invalidation set out in Section 514(d), so long as it does not permit practices that are prohibited by federal law.

The substance and procedure set out in EPTL 7-1.9 whereby the settlor and beneficiary of a trust may take joint action to modify the trust's terms are not unique to New York. The enactment of the statute broke no new ground nor does its provisions represent a social policy significant only in New York. The Restatement recognizes it as a general principle of trust law.[26] Statutory codification is the exception rather than the rule. Most jurisdictions treat the doctrine as an extension of the overriding principle that a trust exists for the benefit of the settlor and beneficiary and that their intent about how the trust is to be administered is paramount.[27] It follows that the substance of EPTL 7-1.9 is available to the parties in the federal courts as a part of the common law of trusts and, because it does not contravene any other federal statute or principle, may be invoked as appropriate equitable relief.

The case for preemption is not compelling. By hypothesis here the college and the teacher wish to take steps to obtain an improved administration of their funds during the accumulation phase in order to have greater resources with which to purchase an annuity at the teacher's retirement. To deny them this right would be wholly at odds with the spirit and purposes of the federal legislation. ERISA was enacted to enlarge, not diminish, the beneficiaries' rights, and its preemption section should not be read to undercut that policy by subordinating the interests of the settlors and beneficiaries to those of the trustee. The preemption principle was inserted into the statute to insure national uniformity in the administration of pension plans. That principle is not at risk here. The goal of the parties is to increase the value of future benefits, not to change the terms or conditions under which those benefits are received.

Epilogue

In May 1987, when the Commission on College Retirement reissued its Policy Statement on Transferability of Funds, TIAA-CREF had recently come under new executive leadership, a leadership that desired, in its own words, "to pursue new goals."

In pursuit of these goals, a Special Trustee Joint Committee of TIAA-CREF was created and charged, among other things, "to review recommendations made in recent years" by groups such as the Commission on College Retirement. The special trustee committee began its work in late June 1987 and submitted its final report, "TIAA-CREF: The Future Agenda," for Board approval on November 18, 1987.

That report signaled a sharp break with the past TIAA-CREF policies that rigidly limited investment choice and precluded fund transferability (with very minor exceptions) to other investment managers. That signal of a policy reversal with respect to transferability became a TIAA-CREF commitment on April 28, 1988, when, in a press release, TIAA-CREF announced the following:

> Meeting in joint session Thursday, the TIAA and CREF trustees approved a proposal that would accommodate greater policyholder and institutional discretion in

Note: The quotations ascribed to Dr. Wharton are found in his preface to *TIAA-CREF: The Future Agenda,* a TIAA-CREF publication issued in November 1987.

105

transferring funds, now in individual pension annuities, between TIAA and CREF or to employer-approved alternative funds.

In announcing the action, Dr. Clifton R. Wharton, Jr., TIAA-CREF chairman and chief executive officer, said steps to gain necessary regulatory approvals would begin immediately.

"We believe that TIAA-CREF has responded positively and responsibly to approve the larger degree of pension flexibility that some employing institutions and policyholders desire in today's financial marketplace," Dr. Wharton said.

When the new TIAA-CREF policies for investment choice and fund transferability are fully and effectively implemented, they should not only carry out the recommendation of the Commission on College Retirement but also, in Dr. Wharton's phrase, transform TIAA-CREF "into a more dynamic, responsive organization."

Part Two

Retirement Ages
for College and University Personnel

The concept of retirement from paid employment is central to pension policy. Employees who continue in paid employment for life would, normally, have no need for a pension to maintain their standards of living. Thus, it is the retirement from paid employment that triggers the need for, and the social desirability of, pensions.

Planning for pensions is based, accordingly, on the assumption that employees will retire at some point in the life cycle. Sound pension planning, moreover, requires a furthur assumption that there is an anticipatable time in the life cycle of employees at which the need for pension payments will arise. Since, however, there is no predictable date on which any particular individual will retire from paid employment, and no ideal date for retirement that would be applicable to all persons, some reasonable retirement date is selected for pension planning purposes. Thus, the criterion of a chronological age, at which it would be reasonable for pensions to become payable, has come to be adopted for pension planning purposes.

The use of chronological age as a criterion for purposes of pension planning has produced little controversy. Controversy ultimately came, however, when age was used for purposes of triggering retirement as well as pensions. This controversy intensified after the enactment in 1967 of the federal age discrimination laws with respect to employment.

107

Thereafter, if chonological age were perceived as the basis for employee dismissal or for forcing an employee to retire involuntarily, a question would arise as to whether there had been a violation of federal or state age discrimination laws.

The issues involved in the age discrimination controversy over retirement ages relate primarily to whether employees who retire are, in fact, being dismissed because of age, involuntarily and without their consent. Such dismissals could violate the law. Colleges and universities and their faculties have not been exempted from these issues.

In short, although under age discrimination laws, employees may not be terminated, dismissed, or forced to retire without their consent, solely by reason of their chonological age, it is permissible (1) for employees to retire at a time, and for a reason, of their own choice, including their chonological age, (2) for employees to agree with their employers to retire on a fixed date, or at a specified chronological age, or upon specified event, and (3) for employees to be terminated, with due process, for reasonable cause. The Commission on College Retirement in its Policy Statement on Retirement Ages reflected these basic principles. The thrust of its policy statement was to enable college and university faculties and their institutitions to realize their proper personal and institutional objectives, and to do so in a way that would not be open to question under age discrimination laws. Its recommendations were as follows:

- A fixed retirement date is essential to a sound and workable retirement system for colleges and universities, and, furthermore, a preselected and agreed-upon chronological age is the most suitable such date.
- A fixed retirement date should not preclude early retirement arrangements, phased retirement programs, or post-retirement employment, as may be needed and agreed upon to meet individual and institutional goals.
- The selection of the precise chonological age that should be the pivotal fixed retirement date is ideally a matter for decision by each college and university after an institution-wide review.

- Such a decision so reached can then be incorporated in the controlling contracts between each institution and its faculty.
- Colleges and universities that have not already done so should, with the concurrence of their faculty, explicitly make the desired retirement age an integral part of the tenure contract.
- Government intervention in the retirement age consensually so arrived at, and contractually so expressed, is neither necessary nor desirable.

The commission's Policy on Retirement Ages, as well as related documents, follows.

2.1

Policy Statement on Retirement Ages for College and University Personnel

The objectives of a retirement program for academic institutions and their personnel are essentially the same as those of other institutions and individuals in our society. They include:

For the Institutions: orderly self-renewal, flexibility to meet emerging opportunities, the maintenance of vitality through infusions of fresh energy and ideas, and a workable system to reward personal growth, to cushion any decline, and to plan transitions — all of this to be achieved while preserving morale, momentum, and academic freedom; and

For the Individuals: basic economic independence, reasonable personal autonomy, continuing good health, a sense of productivity and a continuing opportunity to do things of personal and social significance after retirement.

A sound and sensible retirement program for colleges and universities must seek to fulfill these legitimate personal and institutional aspirations. Indeed, it should be an essential goal of any retirement program that an adequate pension system be in place, that retirees have rewarding continuing activity available to them, and that necessary health care be affordable in retirement.

In separate reports, this commission will have specific suggestions for better meeting the objectives of (1) an adequate income stream for retirees, (2) facilitating continuing activity after retirement, (3) financial planning assistance (both for active)

faculty and for those who have retired), and (4) available as well as affordable long term care when it is needed by retirees.

A workable retirement program, however, must not be uncertain. It should have predictability, stability and coherence. It should not hinge on adventitious events or on difficult and subjective judgments of continuing competence.

A fixed retirement date is essential to a sound and workable retirement system for colleges and universities, and, furthermore, a preselected and agreed-upon chonological age is the most suitable such date. In reaching this conclusion the commission fully recognizes that there is no point in time that marks the ideal retirement date for all persons, or even for any particular individual. Yet, a judgment as to what would be a reasonable retirement date for a given activity, or institution or group of individuals can be fairly and rationally made.

Although the commission is satisfied that it is essential for academia that there be a fixed retirement date as the pivot around which a fair and effective retirement system can be constructed, the commission does not conclude that all persons should in fact retire from full-time employment at academic institutions at such a fixed date. The commission believes that flexibility should be built into academic retirement programs.

A fixed retirement date should not preclude early retirement arrangements, or phased retirement programs or post-retirement employment, all as may be needed and agreed upon to meet invidividual and institutional goals.

Variable career incentives and compensation plans can be hinged on the pivot of a fixed retirement date so as to meet emerging educational objectives as well as individual and institutional needs.

Accordingly, there can and should be flexibility among colleges and universities in fixing the retirement date that best serves the requirements of their own institution and their own personnel. There should also be flexibility in devising individual retirement arrangements. There is enormous variety in the missions pursued by different colleges and universities and in the policies and programs to fulfill those missions. There is equal variation in the longevity, motivation, productivity and needs of different individuals.

Flexibility and innovation should, however, be built around a fixed retirement date. A fixed retirement date is a central pillar of the tenure system for faculty at colleges and universities. Neither the job security of continued employment, nor academic freedom — both made possible by the tenure system — would be achievable without the assurance that such a retirement date exists and is effective. In turn, without job security and academic freedom for faculty, academic institutions would falter in discharging their responsibilities not alone for education, but also for the development of new knowledge and understanding.

In addition, without a fixed retirement date, serious questions would arise as to the amount of the pensions that are needed for academic personnel, and the development of a reasonable pension system could be frustrated. Moreover, institutional planning for the maintenance of educational standards could be thwarted and a troubling level of uncertainty would be introduced into the academic career path.

2.1.1 Chronological Age as a Criterion for Faculty

Chronological age is not a perfect criterion for a fixed retirement date. Individuals of the same chronological age vary widely in their capacities, interests and motivations. Aging is a process not fixed by time or chronology.

Yet, chronological age is the most suitable retirement criterion available for tenured faculty. (For a fuller exposition, see Section 2.2.) Age is also an excellent proxy for a diverse number of considerations relevant to the selection of a retirement date that will well serve the many complex, and often subtle, individual and institutional objectives in higher education.

The selection of the precise chronological age that should be the pivotal fixed retirement date is ideally a matter for decision by each college and university after an institution-wide review. A decision so reached can reflect not only special campus considerations but also societal changes such as the lengthening of the human lifetime or the predictable future reduction in the proportion of young people entering the labor force. A decision so reached would not be imposed by boards of trustees or administrators. It should reflect the institutional democracy characteristic of the campus.

Such a decision so reached can then be incorporated in the controlling contracts between each institution and its faculty.

A contract system is already in place for faculty at virtually all American colleges and universities. The present contract system for faculty in institutions of higher education is of two types: (1) a contract for a term of years which is usually, but not always, restricted to the first probationary years of teaching, and (2) the tenure contract which terminates with retirement.

2.1.2 The Tenure System

Colleges and universities that have not already done so should with the concurrence of their faculty, explicitly make the desired retirement age an integral part of the tenure contract.

The tenure system of contracting is almost universally in use in this country. It provides a mechanism for fixing a faculty retirement age by voluntary agreement. Such a consensual determination of the operative retirement date is very desirable.

The standard retirement age of seventy, permitted by the federal Age Discrimination in Employment Act, as amended, for involuntary retirement, has been widely adopted by colleges and universities as the agreed retirement date for tenured faculty.

The tenure system, and the tenure contract, as used in American colleges and universities today, was developed and given its meaning primarily through the joint efforts of representatives of faculty and their institutions. This process should continue.

The faculty contracts in use today at institutions of higher education vary widely in form. With that diversity in form, ambiguity as to substance can readily arise. Contractual diversity is not undesirable. What is undesirable, however, is any ambiguity in the form of faculty contracts that creates questions as to their intended substance.

The commission believes that greater clarity can be brought to the retirement arrangements embodied in the faculty contracts now in use.

Government intervention in the retirement ages consensually so arrived at, and contractually so expressed, is neither necessary nor desirable.

The commission accordingly opposes legislation that would prevent colleges and universities either from agreeing with their faculty on a fixed chronological age for retirement or from expressing that agreement in the tenure contract. [For a discussion of current legislation, see Section 2.3 of this volume.]

The special educational considerations that sparked the tenure system, the tenure contract and a fixed chronological age for the retirement of faculty do not necessarily apply to other college and university personnel, such as the administrative, clerical and operational staff. The terms of employment for these non-faculty personnel, however, may also be embodied in contracts. If so, then retirement provisions can also be made part of these consensual arrangements. To the extent that the non-faculty staff are employees-at-will, however, their retirement arrangements are governed by custom, special agreements, and applicable law.

Staff employees, unlike faculty, do not have the job security conferred by tenure until the date of retirement. Also, unlike faculty they are not partners sharing in the governance of the college or university. Important as staff personnel clearly are to educational institutions, the success of the educational mission is not as uniquely and inextricably linked with, dependent upon, and controlled by staff as it is with, upon, and by faculty.

The uniqueness of the tenure contract, and the shared governance enjoyed by faculty, make it essential that there be a fixed retirement date for faculty at institutions of higher education and that such a date explicitly be made a part of the tenure bargain agreed upon by both the faculty members and their institution.

2.2

Age as a Criterion
for the Retirement of Tenured Faculty

Oscar M. Ruebhausen

Retirement from full-time paid employment at a fixed chronological age became, in this century, a socially worthy objective.[1] This objective is expressed in a substantial body of law, custom and contract. Although retirement at a prearranged age worked imperfectly, it became widely accepted as a sound and sensible system.

A similar observation can be made about academic tenure for the faculty at institutions of higher education. Faculty tenure has long historic roots; yet faculty tenure, as we know it, is a product of this century.[2] Nearly 95 percent of all faculty members in American colleges and universities, public and private, two-year and four-year, are believed to be employed in institutions that award tenure. Tenure for faculty has also worked imperfectly, but it too has been widely accepted as a sound and sensible system.

These two separate concepts were linked in this century at colleges and universities when retirement at an agreed age became one of the central features of the tenure system.[3]

There are three central features of the tenure system: (1) probationary period (normally six years) of careful appraisal by faculty colleagues before the grant of faculty tenure, (2) job

Note: Reprinted with permission from Oscar M. Ruebhausen, "Age as a Criterion for the Retirement of Tenured Faculty," *The Record* of the Association of the Bar of the City of New York, Vol. 41, No. 1, 1986.

security until retirement at a fixed chronological age (normally seventy), except for institutional financial exigency or change of program, or for grave cause given by the faculty member, and (3) effective control by the faculty members over the nature and conduct of their own teaching, scholarship and research.

Implicit in the tenure bargain is the expectation that faculty members on retirement will, through social security, pension and health plans and supplemental savings, enjoy an adequate income stream and access to affordable health care. Equally important, but thus far less well provided for, is some continuing role and activity for retired faculty essential to the maintenance of their self-esteem.

Implicit also in the tenure bargain is the understanding that tenured faculty have, and in fact do exercise, increasing responsibility for the governance of their institutions. Tenured faculty are, in reality, normally partners sharing control of a common enterprise. This relationship is far removed from the standard employer-employee relationship in corporate America.

Further, unlike most other employees in America, the continuation of tenured faculty in their jobs is not contingent upon regular and repeated performance appraisals.[4] Tenured faculty are, in this way, given protection in their work from the reach of people in power.

The job security created by the tenure contract, and the autonomy over one's own work conferred by it, supply the framework for the academic freedom in higher education which is so prized a part of our culture.

The employment bargain encompassed in the tenure contract is, accordingly, a unique arrangement between employer and employee in our society. The bargain has a powerful internal coherence. It foregoes the use of performance appraisals both as a test of faculty capacity to continue in their jobs until the agreed termination date and as a test of faculty capacity to continue in those jobs beyond the agreed date for retirement.[5]

No society is static however. Our own is witness to profound changes. Among them are the dramatically increasing longevity of the population, the absolute and relative growth in the size of the older population that has left the work force, and an awareness that aging is a highly individualized process, not a fixed and standard event, or a series of them, at any predictable age. These and other changes in recent decades have fueled concern over the possibly arbitrary use of chronological age to discriminate against the employment of older workers. Thus, there is growing tension today between the concern about age discrimination and the use of chronological age as the criterion both for the termination of tenure and for the retirement of tenured faculty.

This tension impels a reexamination of the appropriateness of using chronological age as the criterion for retirement of tenured faculty at institutions of higher education.

2.2.1 The Retirement Arrangement

The retirement which we address is the retirement of faculty called for under their tenure agreement. It is retirement at a prearranged date. That date is fixed by the tenure contract. It is a date known in advance to, and concurred in by, both the faculty member and the institution. The criterion used for ascertaining the date of retirement is chronological age.

Chronological age is not a subjective fact. It is easy to determine. It is uniform and neutral in its application. The same criterion governs all of a faculty member's tenured colleagues. Indeed, it has come to be relied on by them, as well as by their institutions, as providing a nonstigmatizing arrangement in their mutual interest.

Retirement pursuant to the bargain involved in the tenure system, accordingly, is an agreed retirement pursuant to an established program.[6] It is to be distinguished from dismissal. In dismissal the retirement is involuntary.

This distinction tends to be blurred when retirement under the tenure system is referred to, as it frequently is, as "mandatory." The distinction is further obscured when, as often occurs, the agreed upon retirement is characterized as "forced" retirement. The word *forced* tends to imply duress, not agreement.

The retirement we are considering is "forced" only in the sense it is required by the tenure contract. It is the keeping of a promise. In no other sense is it forced or involuntary.

There are many advantages to a retirement system under which the retirement date is fixed by an operative fact that is known well in advance, is readily ascertainable, is uniform and objective in operation, is not based on invidious judgments or comparisons, and is neither costly nor cumbersome to administer. There are also further advantages when the operative fact of age facilitates the coordination of retirement with the age-based Social Security and Medicare Systems, with the age-related payments under private pension programs and with the payouts of Individual Retirement Accounts required by law at age seventy. Chronological age, when used as the determinative criterion for programmed retirement, enjoys all of these advantages.

In addition, programmed retirement at a date known in advance is important, and often crucial, for institutional planning and for orderly transitions. The individual faculty member, the college or university, and the system of higher education in this country, all of them have a vital interest in the ability to plan ahead for orderly transitions.

Planning is vital to the faculty member in order to prepare for the post-retirement years, to organize a life of reduced stress, to launch a new career or to take advantage of other opportunities for personal growth and enjoyment. With planning, for example, faculty members can maximize their post-retirement income stream, arrange for available and affordable health care, and fully develop opportunities for desired continuing activity, paid or unpaid. With planning, moreover, the college or university can assist faculty members to achieve each of these three important objectives. Only with planning can there be reasonable assurance that retirement will, in fact, be a career change and not simply a cessation of activity.

The importance of these faculty objectives lies in the fact that, taken together, they define the retiree's ability to maintain self-esteem and lead a rewarding life. It is not part of the ethos of our nation that people should work for a living until they die.

Colleges and universities also have a vital stake in planning for faculty retirement. With planning they can better discharge their educational mission. Thus, with orderly planning, colleges and universities can meet emerging needs for talent; they can phase-out the specialties perceived as having become less useful or less relevant to a changing society; they can reward and advance junior faculty with predictable opportunities; they can maintain and preserve a range and balance of the diverse faculty interests and enthusiasms they perceive are required; and they can open the way for the intellectual surge that comes with the fresh energies and new perspectives of recently trained scholars and teachers who reflect the current state of knowledge and have benefited from modern advances in academic training.

Without such planning, and without fixed retirement dates to build around, orderly academic change and renewal could readily be overwhelmed by adventitious circumstance.

Without programmed retirement, accordingly, a college or university might find itself unable to maintain its educational effectiveness, particularly in a time of declining student enrollment. If so, it would not adequately meet its responsibilities either to the nation or to its own students.

It is true that some faculty members may, when the time comes, wish never to retire from their then-held positions, whether or not retirement and a career change might be in their own best interest as well as that of their institution. Conversely, it is true that some faculty members would wish to — and in fact do — retire earlier than any date that could reasonably be fixed under any uniform system. It is also true that some faculty members will be fully capable of genuinely valuable educational services beyond any agreed-upon chronological age.

A sensible system must, however, be certain to meet general concerns and normal situations rather than try to cover every variation. A sensible system must also balance the individual, institutional and societal goals. And it must recognize reasonable norms of experience.

The fact that there are variances from any agreed-upon norm is not so much an argument for abandoning the advantages of a uniform system as it is a powerful argument for endeavoring to accommodate special situations when they appear. Colleges and universities can be much more vigorous and affirmative than they have been to date in meeting the needs and desires of retired faculty for continuing, rewarding activity.

Three points have been made thus far. One: Programmed retirement pursuant to the contract of tenure is not a retirement imposed by force; it is consensual. Two: Chronological age is not the *reason* for the retirement, it is simply the criterion used to construct a fair and feasible program of retirement at a predetermined date. Three: The retirement program so constructed seeks by contract to carry out institutional, educational and social as well as faculty objectives.

2.2.2 The Fairness of Age as a Criterion

The foregoing discussion supports the fairness of a system of programmed retirement at an agreed-upon date. The next issue is to examine whether the use of chronological age for such a purpose is, itself, fair and reasonable.

Chronological age is familiar and widely accepted in our society as a reasonable criterion for public policy decisions and distinctions. It is embedded in our Constitution. Age is the criterion of eligibility for the House of Representatives (twenty-five years), the Senate (thirty years) and the Presidency (thirty-five years).[7] Chronological age is the operative fact used in the Constitution to confer the right to vote (eighteen years).[8]

The Congress of the United States repeatedly uses chronological age as a criterion to delineate the boundaries of social policy. Thus, age rather than a pragmatic, but demeaning, "means test" is the determinant of eligibility for benefits under our federal Social Security laws.[9]. Similarly, the benefits of a qualified pension plan under the Internal Revenue Code are not available to a person over age seventy and distributions under such plans must be made in the calendar year in which an employee reaches the age of seventy years and six months. Congress has also determined both that age sixty is the age at which a worker may withdraw earnings from an Individual Retirement Account without penalty, and that age seventy is the age at which such sheltering of earnings for retirement must cease.[10] Indeed, seventy is the age at which earnings accumulated in an IRA must be paid out. There are, in addition, several dozen major federal programs that benefit the elderly and many of these, by statute or regulation, use chronological age as a criterion for eligibility.[11]

Similarly, age twenty-six has been fixed by the Congress as the criterion for the cut-off in required registration for the military draft.[12]

Chronological age is also the criterion used by state legislatures to determine who may lawfully drink or drive, be employed or be married. Further, more than half of our states, by statute, require or authorize the retirement from state employment of persons over a fixed age (usually age seventy).[13]

The acceptability of the criterion of chronological age as a proxy to carry out social policy is not confined to its use in constitutions, statutes, ordinances and regulations.[14] The acceptability of this criterion is repeatedly confirmed by its use in a wide variety of private arrangements. Chronological age, for example, is universally used as a criterion for triggering benefits under private pension plans. Employment contracts also use age as a criterion for measuring the employment period, or shifting to a new relationship or responsibility, or fixing the duration of deferred payments to be made.

Similarly chronological age is a criterion used in many insurance contracts to measure the amount and duration of premium payments, or to fix the date when the face amount of the policy will become payable to the insured. Widespread also is the use of chronological age as a criterion in the management of personal assets: trusts, for example, often use chronological age to fix the date or dates when income or principal become payable to a beneficiary.

The use of chronological age as a proxy to carry out social policy determinations is clearly not novel. It is, also, clearly not offensive either to public policy or to societal standards of fairness.[15] The use of age as a criterion by academic institutions for programmed retirement under a tenure system is, accordingly, fair and reasonable.

It is undeniable that aging is a process which is experienced differently by different people and at differing chronological ages. Aging is also experienced differently not only in different societies but in the same society in different decades.

Chronological age, as such, is not a *cause* of infirmity. Yet, there is a close *correlation* between both age and health and age and performance.[16] It is not unreasonable, accordingly, for society, from time to time, to determine that, as a group, those under sixteen, or eighteen, or twenty-one, are not yet ready for mature responsibilities. Or that those over age twenty-six are not the most suitable for the military draft. Similarly with the elderly.

The elderly are a vulnerable group in our society.[17] It is generally accepted, moreover, that chronological age is accompanied by an increasing burden of chronic disease, functional disabilities, acute illness and injuries.[18] It is also judicially recognized that such a burden can erode and impair effective performance.[19]

The risk of such impairment increases as the years advance. Actuaries build their mortality and morbidity tables upon this reality. Although the increased risk is statistically accurate for a group, there is no precise correlation, for any particular individual, between chronological age and impaired performance.

The risk of impaired functioning, however, is greater at age seventy-five than at sixty-five, and at age eighty as compared with seventy. And, further, for the population aged eighty-five and over, an estimated two-thirds are either institutionalized or need the help of another to function in daily life.[20] These percentages will grow in the decades ahead.[21] Yet there will be many individual exceptions.

At some point in the aging process, impaired functioning becomes so great a risk that it is reasonable for an employer to be unwilling to assume it; and unreasonable for a society to insist that employers be subjected to it.

The thrust of this discussion leads to the conclusion that the use of chronological age as a criterion for the retirement of tenured faculty is fair and reasonable.[22] It might be added that the reasonableness of age as a criterion for faculty employment has also been judicially supported.[23]

The fact, however, that chronological age tells us so little about the performance capability of particular individuals is a troubling one. It warrants a further question: Is there some other criterion, that would be better than chronological age as the agreed-upon criterion for retirement?

2.2.3 Is There Another Criterion Better Than Age?

If there is no criterion better than age to achieve the objectives of the retirement arrangement in the tenure system, as previously described, then the use of chronological age as the criterion for the retirement of tenured faculty is not only reasonable, it tends to become essential.

One possible alternative that clearly merits examination would be to substitute regular individual performance appraisals for chronological age as the criterion for the retirement of tenured faculty.

The concept of individual performance appraisals is simple. Yet, performance appraisals have so many variations that it is crucial to examine what the concept involves in different contexts. Thus, performance appraisals differ greatly in quality, character and utility when made for different purposes or in differing circumstances.

Some performance appraisals may be directed only to a specific skill or capacity. Even then they can become subtle and complex as the skills and capacities being tested become less tangible and more difficult to measure. Some appraisals may also involve no more than a relatively simple ranking or comparison of one individual with another. Often, however, the actual level of performance to be appraised is itself nebulous, and hard to identify with precision.

In academia, performance appraisals of many kinds are very familiar. Students are regularly subject to them. So, too, are faculty. Faculty are evaluated when they are initially hired, and appraised even more rigorously before a tenure contract is extended. In addition, performance is a consideration in the grant of salary increases or promotions for tenured faculty. Perhaps the most continuous appraisal of faculty is that engaged in by their students, sometimes formally, always informally.

Yet, none of these appraisals of performance either achieves the gravity, or enjoys the constitutional due process protection, that would characterize the "stay-or-go" evaluation of performance capacity if it is used for purposes of the retirement decision. In the "stay-or-go" evaluation of a faculty member, unlike many other appraisals, continuing and future capacity to meet expected levels of performance would be more than the central issue, it would tend to be the only issue. In an appraisal focussed on performance capability, other important criteria such as the needs of a department, or of the institution, or of the students, would tend to become irrelevant. Yet, all of these considerations were material to the hiring, the grant of tenure, salary increases, and the promotion of such a faculty member.

Accordingly, if performance appraisals were to be used, in lieu of chronological age, as the criterion for retirement of tenured faculty the appraisal would be of a singular kind. It would be concentrated upon the capacity of the faculty member to continue to perform in the future, and the difficult burden of proof would be placed upon the academic institution affirmatively to establish a lack of capacity as the basis for retirement.

Performance appraisals as the governing criterion for retirement seem reasonable for jobs which are directly dependent on readily measurable capacities such as eyesight, hearing, muscle strength, physical stamina, eye-hand coordination, or mobility. Firefighters, police and sanitation workers illustrate this category. Individualized performance evaluations also seem feasible for jobs where the adequacy of performance is fairly judged by a readily measurable output over a given period of time. Production or assembly line employees are illustrative of this category.

Tenured faculty do not fit into either of these two categories. Indeed, the performance capability required in academia is not a static one. In many disciplines, advances in knowledge pose a challenge to their mastery. Such advances are unpredictable, but when they do emerge prior academic expertise may no longer be truly relevant.

A major problem with performance appraisals as a criterion for faculty retirement lies in the difficulty of identifying, and quantifying, the data needed to establish the requisite performance capability.[24] The weight to be attached to any one characteristic in any one person, moreover, is far from clear. So subjective is the evaluation of what makes for excellence (or even adequacy) in scholarship, research and teaching, that there is little likelihood of consensus on the data that would be conclusive for any particular individual. Without clear criteria that can be agreed upon, evaluation of performance for a purpose as crucial as the "stay-or-go" determination is likely to be unrealistic and unfair.

The difficulty of identifying the characteristics that should be measured to determine the performance capability of tenured faculty would be compounded by the difficulty of measuring in any persuasive way the possession of such characteristics by any particular individual. The reason is that the crucial key to human functioning may often lie in the unquantifiable domain of the personality, cultural background, pride and spirit of the individual. These in turn may depend on the social, family and personal experience of the individual. Thus, even with a complete physical examination, together with an in-depth psychological appraisal and a review of an individual's family and social environment, conclusive judgments will be hard to make.[25] So complex an exercise of judgment must inevitably be controversial.

The complexity and nature of the inquiry that would have to be conducted in any meaningful performance evaluation of tenured faculty suggests why it would not be a practical or reasonable alternative to chronological age as a criterion for retirement. But these are not the only objections to such an evaluation. Thus, for example, the effort to acquire the relevant family life history and the physical, mental and emotional profile needed for the estimation of future performance by a particular individual would be invasive of privacy and personally obnoxious to the individual faculty member; the complexity of the process and the difficulty of the evaluation will clearly tend to shift the ultimate determinations of faculty competence to the courts for a case by case factual review and decision — thus adding heavy expense to an already chilling burden and further threatening the case handling capacity of our judicial system;[26] and junior faculty will be inhibited and can be expected to resist evaluating senior faculty for whom they once were proteges. Thus, the sorting out process, individual by individual, to achieve a reliable system of performance appraisals would be time consuming, expensive, difficult, and unpleasant.

These difficulties are not peculiar to the use of age as a criterion for retirement. Thus, if individual performance appraisals were to replace age as the criterion of fitness for responsibility generally, not only for the elderly, but for the young, the consequences could be staggering. If would mean, for example, that the state would have to substitute for chronological age a system of individual appraisals of fitness for responsibility to marry, or to hold office, to vote, contract, drink or drive, or register for the draft.[27]

Even if we assume that this thicket of difficulties can be fairly overcome, a performance appraisal as part of a "stay-or-go" evaluation, leading to retirement, would of necessity formalize a finding of lack of fitness. Simple civility, however, commands that we find some criterion for retirement that does not place upon a colleague the stigma of unfitness.

Finally, one other important factor must be taken into account. It is this: Could systematic performance appraisals be introduced into higher education as a condition of continued employment of tenured faculty without crippling the tenure system and jeopardizing academic freedom? Regular performance evaluations as a condition of continued employment are in conflict with a central feature of the tenure system.[28] And to modify the tenure system so as to permit appraisals only for faculty who are, say, over sixty or sixty-five, would risk violating the age discrimination statutes.[29]

The issues posed by tenure and academic freedom, and their importance to our educational system, are issues in which the public has a stake. They must be resolved before regular performance evaluation can be accepted, in lieu of chronological age, as the criterion for the retirement of tenured faculty. This essay does not examine these issues both because they form a separate subject and because chronological age is, in any event, a more feasible and humane criterion for the retirement of tenured faculty.

In summary, there is a persuasive surface appeal to the use of individualized performance appraisals as the criterion for retirement. It avoids the individual errors that will always occur when a standard index, such as age, statistically valid for a group, is applied to specific individuals. Yet, the magnitude of the difficulties surrounding the use of performance evaluations as a criterion for the retirement of tenured faculty are so daunting they are tantamount to making sound evaluations for that purpose not only impractical but in reality impossible.

2.2.4 Who Should Determine the Criterion to Use?

The employer and the employee have the most at stake in the retirement process. There are risks for both, and advantages for both. They would also seem to be in the best position to assess those risks and advantages. They, along with their associations and their unions, should, accordingly, have a powerful voice in the development of retirement policies and in determining the criteria to be used to carry them out.

The employment decision is one that is mutually arrived at between employer and employee at colleges and universities, as in other enterprises. Under American common law, in the absence of contract, employees are generally employees at will. Their employment, under the often criticized and now eroding American rule, is terminable at their option, and at the option of their employer, for any reason or for no reason.[30]

For tenured faculty, however, the employment is governed by the tenure contract. The terms of the tenure contract have evolved over decades. It is part of the bargain made in the contract that the tenured faculty will, for some three decades, have job security not conditioned upon performance appraisals. It is also part of that bargain, as was discussed at the beginning of this essay, that retirement from full-time paid employment take place at a fixed chronological age and without a performance appraisal.[31]

Although tenured faculty have essential job security, they may of course resign or retire at any time. It is the college or university that, in the tenure contract, has yielded up what would have been its normal right under common law to appraise performance and terminate at will. The gains to the institution from this concession are far from trivial. They include academic freedom and the sense of being partners in, and sharing responsibility for, the academic enterprise. What is lost by the institution in the exchange is the ability to manage its faculty most efficiently for increased effectiveness. The gains were believed to be worth the cost, at least as long as planning could be based on a tenure contract provision for retirement at a fixed chronological age.

The tenure system is a response to perceived needs of higher education. Under that system the use of age as a criterion for retirement is only one aspect of the full contractual package. The use of age in this context is empirically derived.[32]

The precise age at which tenured faculty should retire is, of course, a matter of judgment. There is clearly much justification for using any age between sixty-five and seventy-five as the retirement age for tenured faculty. There is also much justification for using a series of ages as the criteria for a phasing of retirement from a full time tenured faculty role to part time faculty responsibility and ultimately to other activity either within the academic institution or elsewhere. A phased system of retirement can facilitate the redeployment of faculty energies and skills in a constructive fashion both for the institution and for the faculty member.

Any age or ages that are selected for retirement, however, will, as is true of all classification systems, have imperfections, particularly at the dividing lines. It is reasonable to leave the decision on these matters for negotiation and decision by the academic and administrative actors in the educational community.

There is reason, also, for diversity among academic institutions in the selection of the appropriate age or ages to use for retirement or phased retirement. Faculty may wish to retire for reasons quite unrelated to their continuing fitness for responsibility. Similarly, academic institutions may wish a faculty member to retire for reasons not directly related to fitness to function.

Thus, faculty members may yearn for new challenges, a new career, a new climate or, even, new colleagues. Often, they may wish to retire not because they think they have lost competence, but because they have achieved that measure of psychological security, economic independence and personal dignity that enables them to say, "I do not wish to be bossed any more." The "bossing" they seek to avoid is not just that by their employer. It includes the pressures brought to bear by deans, students, colleagues and staff.

So, too, with academic institutions. There are factors unrelated to faculty competence that point to retirement as the way to increase educational effectiveness. For example, students may cease to sign up for a faculty member's courses, or student enrollment at an institution may decline; or places must be found for new areas of scholarship or research; or existing areas of faculty expertise may decline in relevance; or scholars of greater academic potential than a tenured faculty member may become available for recruitment; or a static or declining financial condition (which falls short of the harsh test of "exigency") may cry out for faculty reductions; or room should be made for more women or minorities on the faculty roster. But, most important, continuous renewal of the vitality, the interests and the perceptions of the faculty is essential if educational quality is to be sustained.

Accordingly, the judgment reached by institutions and their faculty, in conjunction with their relevant representatives and associations, as to what is the appropriate chronological age to use as a criterion for retirement policy, and whether such retirement should be phased over a period of time, is a judgment that merits great respect.

There is no evidence that institutions of higher education or their faculty have abused their responsibility to devise a reasonable policy for tenured faculty.

2.2.5 Should Government
Intervene in This Determination

Great deference is paid in American law and values to the contractual promise. Courts and legislators are traditionally reluctant to intervene in the contractual bargain. There are grave occasions, however, where the claims of public policy will clearly outweigh the terms of a private contract. Much of the New Deal legislation of the 1930s illustrates the subordination of private contracts to considerations of public policy.

The Norris-LaGuardia Act enacted in the depression year of 1932 is an early example.[33] There, the Congress found "under prevailing economic conditions . . . the individual unorganized worker is commonly helpless to exercise actual liberty of contract and to protect his freedom of labor and thereby to obtain acceptable terms and conditions of employment." The Congress, accordingly, declared that such a worker "shall be free from the interference, restraint or coercion of employers of labor" in the designation of agents or in concerted activity for the purpose, among others, of collective bargaining. Any contract in conflict with this public policy was declared unenforceable. The target was the "yellow dog" contract which precluded employees from joining a union.

No comparable policy issues surround the faculty contract for tenure. The terms of the tenure contract are essentially those developed by faculty for educational purposes.[34] They are not imposed by an exploitive employer in disregard of employee desires.

The terms of tenure are known to beginning faculty and the tenure contract is keenly sought by them. The status of a tenured faculty member is one that is highly prized among academics. Job security and the control over one's own career provided by the tenure contract are greatly valued. The retirement feature of the tenure contract is one of which young faculty are fully aware since, without the planned retirement of tenured faculty members, tenured positions would not open in an orderly way for the new generation aspiring to tenured status.

The tenure contract, rather than being assailed as unconscionable or exploitive, is widely approved by academics. Nor do we know of any serious argument that the well-educated, mature academic who agrees to a tenure contract, is helpless.

College and university faculty are not unskilled labor trapped by poverty into a single geographical location. Indeed, there is considerable mobility in higher education — not only within it but between it and the world of business, commerce, banking, insurance, law, public service and the nonprofit institutions. Many leaders in these fields have been academics at one or more stages of their careers. Nor do academics lack organizations to represent them in refining the tenure contract, when and if refinement is believed desirable.[35]

It is frequently proposed, nevertheless, that legislatures should intervene, that colleges and universities, among others, should be compelled by law to continue to employ faculty until incompetence can be clearly established after hearings and due process, and that such employment should continue whether or not the continuing services of a faculty member are needed and without recognizing that the tenured faculty member may have agreed to a specific retirement date.[36]

Many who urge congressional intervention cite the waste and unhappiness that can characterize the retirement years. These are real and important concerns. They merit creative attention. But, continuing to work full time in your previous paid employment is not necessarily the best answer. Surely, higher education requires something more of its senior faculty than a finding of "not incompetent."

Most who argue for legislative intervention invoke the language of civil rights. It is frequently claimed that chronological age should not be a basis for differentiation any more than sex, race, creed or color.

A claim to a right, however, cannot prevail simply by virtue of its naked assertion. A claim has to be weighed in its context of fact and experience.

Civil rights are the product of history. They are recognized to deal with pervasive and systematic unfairness or oppression. There is no such history of the aged being denied any fundamental human or civil status. The aged have not been systematically barred from public accommodations, thrust into slavery, refused access to the polls, precluded from owning property, treated as chattels, or denied separate legal status because they were aged. The elderly have not, in the language of the United States Supreme Court, been "subjected to such a history of purposeful unequal treatment, or relegated to such a position of political powerlessness as to command extraordinary protection from the majoritarian political process."[37]

Indeed, the evidence runs to the contrary. Age has been more a basis for systematic benefits, not systematic barriers, in our society. Our laws tend consistently to recognize the infirmities accompanying age and seek to ameliorate them.

The issue really, then, is whether Congress should intervene and grant by statute an additional benefit to tenured faculty who are over seventy—namely the privilege of continuing in current employment until unfitness can be clearly proven and regardless of institutional needs.[38] Viewed in this perspective the questions become: Why should such a benefit be given? Is it needed because pensions are inadequate? Is it fair to subject higher education, and faculty colleagues, to such a burden? Is it desirable to override the terms of the tenure contract? Should colleges and universities be forced by law to continue to employ faculty members for life, if they do not resign? Is the benefit worth the social and educational cost?

Conferring this legislative benefit on the over-seventy faculty member seems unnecessary. There is no contractual or other bar that prevents a tenured faculty member, after retirement, from undertaking other work, either paid or unpaid. And with the current decline in the number of young entrants into the labor force, an increase in the demand for older workers can be expected. Accordingly, if there is a bar to other employment after seventy, it could lie in the motivation or infirmity or personality or lack of skill of the faculty member, not in age. Some retired faculty may, however, need help to secure other employment or rewarding activity. The colleges and universities, the academic associations and unions, can and should take the lead to make certain that such help is available when needed.

Even worse than being unnecessary, such a statutory benefit to tenured faculty after age seventy could jeopardize academic quality and the educational mission of colleges and universities. The threat lies in the direct conflict between the tenure system that, after an extended period of job security, there be faculty rotation through retirement without a performance review and at an agreed-upon age.

The extent to which age is to be used as a criterion for the retirement of tenured faculty should be determined by the principal academic and administrative actors in a college or university. It is neither necessary nor desirable that this determination be made by government intervention, or that contractual freedom to bargain in these matters be inhibited.

2.2.6 Is the Use of Age as a Criterion Barred by Federal Law?

There is ample evidence that differentiations based on age are acceptable. Classifications based on age are a familiar part of our culture and of the legal fabric of our society. They are thought to be reasonable and protective of the individuals within the classification and of society in general.

Nevertheless, these differentiations exist alongside, and must be harmonized with, the federal Age Discrimination in Employment Act (ADEA) which became law in 1967.[39] That law had its origins in the civil rights movement of the 1960s. Yet the impact of the law on tenured faculty is far from clear. We know of no definitive judicial opinion on the impact of the ADEA upon the tenure contract or the tenure system.[40]

ADEA is popularly thought of as protecting the elderly, yet it was limited by its terms initially to the middle aged, namely those between forty and sixty-five. Although amendments in 1978 extended the middle-aged protected group to age seventy, the ADEA still implicitly recognizes the reasonableness of classification by age for the young and the old.

Several features of the ADEA are crucial to an analysis of its impact on the tenure contract.

Most important is that the ADEA is not an absolute ban against all discrimination in employment. It does not ban discrimination by *all* employers, only by some.[41] It does not extend protection to *all* employees, but only to those between the ages of forty and seventy.[42] Its goal is not to prohibit *all* discrimination but only "arbitrary age discrimination in employment."[43] Thus, ADEA explicitly permits age discrimination in a substantial number of employment situations.

Viewed from this perspective, it would not seem that the ADEA prohibits the reasoned classification of tenured faculty by age to achieve educational objectives. The use of chronological age in the tenure contract as a criterion for the retirement of tenured faculty is a rational exercise of discretion for a sensible purpose.[45] As such, it should not fall in the category of the "arbitrary age discrimination" that was ADEA's stated concern.

It is, moreover, not the intent of the ADEA to prohibit employees from entering voluntarily into contracts, such as the tenure contract, with their employers to retire at an agreed date or age. Nor does the language of the ADEA ban a system of such agreements, such as the tenure system, using age as a criterion for retirement pursuant to a program designed to serve educational, institutional, social and faculty objectives.

One must not overlook, however, the language of Section 623(a) of the ADEA. There it says, *inter alia,* that

It shall be lawful for an employer . . . to . . . *classify* his employees in any way which would deprive *or tend to deprive* any individual of employment opportunities or otherwise *adversely affect his status* as an employee, *because* of such individual's age (*Italics* supplied).[46]

That language is sweeping, but the sweep is not as broad as it sounds. The sweep is limited by the fact that the ADEA sought to prohibit only "arbitrary" age discrimination. There is also a limit in the phrase, "because of such individual's age." The fair intent of that phrase in this context is "solely" or, at least, "primarily" because of age. Thus, classification is prohibited only where age is the cause and not a criterion being used as a proxy to achieve reasonable educational objectives.[47]

The limited scope of this sweeping language is further confirmed by Section 623(f) where it is expressly provided that

It shall not be unlawful for an employer . . . to take any action otherwise prohibited under subsection (a) . . . [either] (1) where age is a bona fide occupational qualification reasonably necessary to the normal operation of the particular business [or] (2) [where] the differentiation is based on reasonable factors other than age.

This brings us to the fundamental questions: (1) Is the use of chronological age in the tenure contract as a criterion for retirement "reasonably necessary to the normal operation of the particular business" of a college or university? (2) Is the differentiation, which uses age as a criterion in the tenure contract, "based on reasonable factors other than age."

The answer to both of these questions is in the affirmative if the analysis in the preceding sections of this essay is valid.

One need not agree with that answer, however, to agree that these are the central questions that need to be examined in analyzing the impact of the ADEA upon the use of chronological age as a criterion for the retirement of tenured faculty. Both of these questions are responsive to factual proof. It is to these factual issues that the debate should be addressed.

2.2.7 Is the Use of Age as a Criterion Barred by State Law?

At least forty-three of our fifty states have enacted age discrimination laws. Many of these state statutes follow the model of the federal ADEA. To the extent that they do follow the federal model, the comments in the preceding section are applicable to the state legislation.

Although it is beyond the objective of this essay to analyze each of the statutes in our fifty states, some aspects of those statutes merit comment in the context of the use of age as a criterion for the retirement of tenured faculty.

State legislatures have, in general, been quite hospitable to the use of chronological age as a criterion for the retirement of tenured faculty. Thus, six states lack any statutes prohibiting age discrimination in the employment of the elderly.[48] Three additional states limit their statutory age discrimination restrictions to public employment.[49]

The attitude of the states is underscored by the fact that the statutes of twenty-six states — or more than half of the states — expressly authorize or require the use of chronological age as a criterion for the retirement of faculty at state colleges and universities.[50] It would be inconsistent, or worse unfair, if the law of these twenty-six states were interpreted so as to deny to private academic institutions the use of age as a criterion for retirement when precisely that use is authorized for public institutions of higher education. None of the statutes in these twenty-six states expressly bars the use of chronological age as a criterion for the retirement of tenured faculty in private colleges or universities.

The favorable view of the states toward the use of chronological age as a criterion for the retirement of tenured faculty is demonstrated in other ways. For example, four states exclude non-profit educational institutions from the reach of age discrimination statutes.[51] Five additional states, similarly, expressly exempt from their age discrimination statutes those faculty members serving under tenure contracts, sometimes with the proviso that an opportunity be afforded the faculty member to continue thereafter on a year-to-year contract.[52]

In summary, over two-thirds of the states,[53] either by the absence of age discrimination laws or through supportive legislation, have accepted the use of chronological age as a criterion for the retirement of tenured faculty at institutions of higher education.

The statutes of only five states — Florida, Hawaii, Maine, Utah, and Wisconsin — broadly prohibit age-based mandatory retirement from all public and private employment. And the statutes of four of these states contain the familiar exemption of the ADEA permitting age classification when it is reasonably necessary to the normal operation of the enterprise.

Thus there is only one state, Wisconsin, which seems to bar age-based mandatory retirement at any age over forty and does not appear either to exempt educational institutions or tenured faculty or to exclude from the bar the use of age as a criterion when it is a "bona fide occupational qualification reasonably necessary to the normal operation" of the enterprise, or based on factors other than age. The declaration of policy in Wisconsin, however, is, understandably, directed only at "unfair discrimination" against "properly qualified individuals" and it is only "involuntary retirement", not consensual retirement, that receives the statutory condemnation.

The general thrust of state legislative policy throughout the nation, accordingly, is clear: the use of age as a criterion for a program of agreed-upon retirement of tenured faculty is either acceptable or deemed desirable.

2.2.8 Conclusion

The purpose of this essay is two-fold: *first,* to reframe the questions on retirement policy for tenured faculty, and, *second,* to point out a path for the retirement of tenured faculty which lies outside the ambit of the statutes on age discrimination in employment.

The focus of this essay is on the tenure contract, and on whether it is reasonable and enforceable in accordance with its terms. Those terms, among others, include an agreement to use chronological age as a criterion for fixing the retirement date of tenured faculty. The criterion, in turn, is a proxy to carry out social and educational objectives.

The contractual approach puts emphasis on the bargain that the parties have made. It also underscores the unique nature of the bargain agreed upon in the tenure contract.

The analysis differs, accordingly, from that prompted when the question is posed differently, as, for example, "Is mandatory retirement desirable?"

The latter question tends to be pejorative. The word *mandatory* implies something that is forced or involuntary, or even inequitable. Unless there is a reasonable basis for mandatory retirement, it is difficult to justify.

The question so framed, moreover, lacks precision: it ignores the reason for the retirement and the circumstances under which retirement occurs. Most people would concur in the desirability of "mandatory retirement" if it is occasioned by mental incapacity, or physical inability to perform. Similarly most people would concur in "mandatory retirements" in the presence of the extreme financial exigency of the employer. "Mandatory retirement" is also accepted when it is voluntarily agreed upon by the employer and the employee.

The issue, accordingly, is not whether retirement is "mandatory" or not. The real issue is whether the reason for the retirement is an acceptable one.

The age discrimination laws, within the limited scope of their coverage, establish that retirement *arbitrarily* required because of chronological age, without other supporting justification or relevant purpose, is not acceptable policy.[54] This essay does not debate that proposition.

Age classifications, made without supporting justification, can constitute age discrimination. On the other hand, all age classifications are not necessarily age discrimination. Age classification, when used as a proxy for desirable social objectives, is not, *per se,* age discrimination. The purpose for, and the setting in, which the age criterion is employed must, therefore, be examined to determine the reasonableness of its use.

The tenure contract, and the educational purposes for which the tenure system was devised, provide ample justification for the use of chronological age as a criterion for the retirement of tenured faculty in colleges and universities.

A contract which is voluntarily entered into between an employer and employee, a contract which is designed to achieve sensible objectives, and which includes, as part of the bargain, that the employee will retire at a certain age, is generally viewed as reasonable. All agreements for so-called early retirement come in this category. Moreover, such a contract is enforceable, in the absence of duress, unless it violates some law or otherwise offends public policy.

The use of chronological age as a criterion, and a proxy to express a complex series of factors that are difficult to identify or measure with precision, is not offensive to public policy. If it were, it would not be so widely accepted, and so well embedded, as a standard in our laws, our contracts and our culture.

Nor is the tenure system a subterfuge for systematic discrimination.[55] The system has evolved, with decades of faculty involvement, to reflect a *bona fide* conviction of how best to respond to faculty aspirations, to preserve academic freedom and, at the same time, to enable institutions of higher education, in an orderly way, to renew their intellectual vigor and efficiently meet their educational objectives.

It also follows that it is not reasonable to view the tenure contract, a consensual arrangement, as imposed upon academics under duress.

There remains the question of whether the retirement provision of the tenure contract, were it not now in compliance with the ADEA, would violate the federal law. The question is not yet judicially settled; but the arguments are compelling that the federal statute should not be construed to invalidate the tenure contract or jeopardize the tenure system. And state laws by their terms are generally hospitable to the retirement provisions of the tenure contract.

A final question is whether the federal law should be amended — either to invalidate the retirement feature of the tenure contract or to preclude the agreed-upon retirement at age seventy.

Although the tenure contract now generally uses the age of seventy as the criterion for retirement, there is no magic about that particular age. Institutional and individual needs are not static. Nor is the aging process fixed for all time. The operative age can be changed when the principal actors in the academic community — faculty, their institutions, professional associations and unions — believe that another age is more suitable. Or such a change can come, institution by institution, over time as conditions change.

Similarly with the tenure system itself. It too may be modified, or even abandoned, in favor of other alternatives as new conditions emerge. All healthy institutions respond in this way to change and new experience.

Whatever the perceived merits of, or objections to, the tenure contract or the tenure system may be, the people and the institutions involved are fully capable of working out their different viewpoints. Thus, it would seem that the tenure contract should be left to the members of the academic community to shape in the future as they have in the past.

In any event, the case has not yet been made that the intervention of the state or federal governments is needed. To the contrary, government intervention to "uncap" the retirement age would imperil academic freedom since regular performance evaluations of all tenured faculty would become inevitable.

"Uncapping," imposed by government, moreover, is a flawed response to a perceived need. The response has a false premise, namely, that there is *no* chronological age which may reasonably be agreed upon as a criterion for retirement.

Perhaps most serious for society as a whole, however, is that an "uncapping" amendment by its focus on the single solution of preserving an existing job until unfitness can be proven, diverts the nation from an affirmative strategy for meeting the real needs of people over seventy. Those needs are for an adequate income, affordable health care, rewarding activity and a continuing network of supportive associations. These are four essential elements of human self-esteem. It is to the realization of these four essentials for the elderly that the attention of our legislators should be directed. If these essential elements of sound social policy for the elderly are present for faculty retirees, it will be clear that there is no need for government intervention to pressure the academic community to a lifestyle in which people work full time for their living until death.

2.3

Laws Governing Involuntary Retirement of Tenured College and University Faculty by Reason of Age

Joan Ehrenworth Erdman

At one time, retirement at age sixty-five was an integral part of the tenure system at colleges and universities in the United States. In response to changing demographics and federal laws, age seventy has been substituted. There is a need for a clear understanding of federal and state laws that affect retirement of tenured faculty. The first step in assessing those laws is to find out what the laws say.

The Federal Age Discrimination in Employment Act, as amended in 1978, prohibits, with a number of exceptions, age discrimination against employees between the ages of forty and seventy. A special provision was included in the 1978 amendment, dealing with tenured college and university faculty. That provision, which expired by its own terms on July 1, 1982, allowed mandatory retirement of tenured faculty at the age of sixty-five.[1] It was included in the 1978 amendments in response to expressed concerns that raising the age at which involuntary retirement is permitted from sixty-five to seventy would, at least in the first few years, have serious adverse consequences for the college and university community.

The issue, however, is by no means settled. As advocates for the elderly continue to press for total uncapping of the retirement age at the federal level, the question remains as to the applicability of uncapping to tenured college and university faculty.[2]

141

The United States Congress is not the only source of law in this area. Forty-three states now have age discrimination statutes of their own, all of which deal either explicitly or implicitly with the question of mandatory retirement.

An examination of state law is in order for a variety of reasons. It would identify those states, if any, in which involuntary retirement by reason of age of tenured faculty has been completely eliminated.[3] A review of the state laws also gives us some indication of the extent to which total uncapping at the federal level would conflict with the legislative judgments of state lawmakers. We learned, for example, that approximately half the states have statutes that authorize mandatory retirement ages for faculty at public institutions of higher education. We also learned that eight states expressly exempt institutions of higher education or tenured faculty from their age discrimination statutes. Such statutes could, however, be preempted by federal law to the contrary.

Another, perhaps more subtle, question addressed by a review of state law is whether the important issues are receiving adequate attention at the state level. As previously mentioned, forty-three states now have age discrimination statutes, and many states have focused on mandatory retirement in particular. If additional federal restrictions are warranted, therefore, they must be justifiable as an implementation of overriding federal policy and not as a remedy for neglect by the states.

2.3.1 Federal Age Discrimination Law

The federal Age Discrimination in Employment Act (hereafter, ADEA or act), 29 U.S.C. Sec. 621 et. seq. (1976 and Supp. 1984), protects individuals who are at least forty but less than seventy, from age discrimination in employment (Secs. 623(a) and 631(a)). The act applies to employers who are engaged in an industry affecting commerce and who have twenty or more employees (Sec. 630 (b)). The ADEA also applies to state and local governments and to instrumentalities thereof (id.).[4]

With certain exceptions, the ADEA prohibits involuntary retirement by reason of age of certain employees between the ages of forty and seventy (Sec. 623(f)(2)). The act does not prohibit such retirement where it has a reasonable basis other than age or where age is a "bona fide occupational qualification reasonably related to the normal operation of the particular business" (hereafter, BFOQ) (Sec. 623(f)(1)).[5] The ADEA also contains a provision (hereafter referred to as a BFE/HPP) that permits involuntary retirement at age sixty-five of bona fide executives and others in high policy-making positions who meet the requirements of Section 631(c)(1) of the act.[6]

Prior to 1978, the ADEA protected only employees between the ages of forty and sixty-five. At that time, Section 623(f)(2) provided that it was not unlawful for an employer "to observe the terms of . . . any bona fide employee benefit plan such as a retirement, pension, or insurance plan which is not a subterfuge to evade the purposes of this chapter, except that no such . . . plan shall excuse the failure to hire any individual." In *United Air Lines* v. *McCann,* 434 U.S. 192, 98 S. Ct. 444, 54 L. Ed. 2d 402 (1977), the question was whether an employee could be forced to retire at age sixty in accordance with the terms of a preexisting retirement plan that called for retirement at that earlier age. In essence, the issue was whether Congress had intended to outlaw mandatory retirement of those under sixty-five. After consideration of the legislative history, which was by no means clear, the Court held that mandatory retirement at an age under sixty-five in accordance with a bona fide retirement plan was not prohibited by the ADEA.[7]

Even before the decision was rendered in *United Air Lines* v. *McCann,* efforts were underway in Congress to clarify the ADEA. (See 434 U.S. 192, 218.) The Age Discrimination in Employment Act Amendments of 1978 (hereafter, ADEAA), Pub. L. 95–256, 92 Stat. 189, were approved by the president on April 6, 1978. As amended by Section 2(a) of the ADEAA, Section 623(f)(2) now provides that an employer may observe the terms of a bona fide employee benefit plan, "except that no such . . . plan shall excuse the failure to hire any individual, and no such plan shall require or permit the *involuntary retirement* of any individual [covered by the act] *because of the age* of such individual" (emphasis supplied). At the same time, Congress extended the protections of the act to individuals who are at least forty but not yet seventy years of age (29 U.S.C. Sec. 631(a), as amended by Pub. L. 95–256, Sec. 3(a)).

The ADEAA did, however, include certain exceptions to its ban on involuntary retirement by reason of age. The ADEAA left intact the BFOQ exception in Section 623(f)(1) of the act. In addition, Section 12(c) of Pub. L. 95–256 added the previously mentioned provision allowing involuntary retirement at age sixty-five of certain bona fide executives and others in high policy-making positions. Section 2(b) of Pub. L. 95–256 contained a grace period, which expired on January 1, 1980, for mandatory retirement provisions in existing collective bargaining agreements. In addition, the ADEAA (Section 12(d)) included the following provision regarding tenured college and university faculty:

> Nothing in this Act shall be construed to prohibit compulsory retirement of any employee who has attained 65 years of age but not 70 years of age, and who is serving under a contract of unlimited tenure (or similar arrangement providing for unlimited tenure) at an institution of higher education (as defined by section 1201(a) of the Higher Education Act of 1965).

As provided for in Section 12(b)(3) of the ADEAA, the exemption for tenured faculty expired on July 1, 1982. Consequently, tenured faculty at colleges and universities are no longer specifically exempted from the federal ban on age discrimination between ages sixty-five and seventy.

The relationship between the federal ADEA and state laws can be characterized as one of partial preemption. The federal statute supersedes less protective state laws. See *Orzel* v. *City of Wauwatosa Fire Dept.*, 697 F.2d 743 (7th Cir. 1983); see also *E.E.O.C.* v. *Wyoming* (note 4, above). However, to the extent that state age discrimination statutes provide additional protection, and are not otherwise in conflict with federal legislation, they will be given effect.[8] See *Simpson* v. *Alaska State Commission for Human Rights*, 423 F. Supp. 552, aff'd. 608 F.2d 1171 (9th

Cir. 1979). Consequently, it is necessary to examine both state and federal statutes to determine what the restrictions are on mandatory retirement of tenured faculty in each state.

It is essential to keep in mind, however, that no matter what state law may provide, federal law, with a number of exceptions, prohibits involuntary retirement by reason of age between ages forty and seventy, with the BFE/HPP and BFOQ exemptions mentioned above. Some state age discrimination statutes, for example, allow an employer to observe the terms of a bona fide retirement plan but do not include the language prohibiting involuntary retirement by reason of age that was added to federal law by the 1978 ADEAA. (Such a provision will hereafter be referred to as a BFRP.) This does not mean that employers in that state may require employees to retire by reason of age in accordance with the terms of a bona fide retirement plan. To the extent that federal law would prohibit such retirement, the state BFRP is an exemption only from the state age discrimination law.

To the extent that state statutes extend protection from age discrimination to persons older than seventy, a BFRP exemption may render what appears to be a stricter state statute ultimately no more restrictive than the ADEA on the question of mandatory retirement. A BFRP that does not expressly prohibit mandatory retirement ordinarily allows it at any age in accordance with a bona fide retirement plan. (See *United Air Lines v. McCann.*) However, a state statutory provision allowing mandatory retirement before age seventy would be preempted by the federal act.

It is also worthwhile to note that the state plays a variety of roles in the area of age discrimination and mandatory retirement. In its role as protector of the public interest, the state may have enacted legislation against age discrimination. The state is also an employer, and state age discrimination statutes may or may not apply to the state and units thereof. The terms and conditions of public employment are a matter of state concern, and some states have enacted statutes that require mandatory retirement of faculty at public colleges and universities.[9] Since, as previously noted, the ADEA applies to the state in its role as employer, federal law would preempt any state statute that attempted to impose an involuntary retirement age between forty and seventy for public college and university employees, unless the state could establish that its law fell within an exception to the federal act. (See *E.E.O.C.* v. *Wyoming,* notes 4 and 5.)

2.3.2 State Age Discrimination Laws

Forty-three states have statutes prohibiting discrimination in employment on the basis of age.[10] In forty-one of these states, age discrimination is prohibited in both the public and private sectors.[11] In Arkansas and North Carolina, the restrictions apply only to public employment.[12] Seven states do not prohibit age discrimination by statute.[13]

Of the forty-one states that prohibit age discrimination in employment in the private sector, thirty-seven have BFOQs, and eighteen have BFE/HPP provisions in their statutes applicable to private employment.[14]

Of these forty-one states, twenty-two have in their statutes upper age limits of seventy or lower.[15] No state has an upper limit higher than seventy. Thus, the effect of an upper limit is that state law does not, in this respect, provide tenured faculty with protection from mandatory retirement beyond that offered by federal law.[16]

Most state laws, as does the ADEA, use age forty as the lower protected age, although a number of states protect against age discrimination beginning at age eighteen. Nineteen of the forty-one state statutes that prohibit age discrimination in the private sector do not have upper age limits.[17] Absent some provision to the contrary, an age discrimination statute without an upper age limit is likely to be held to prohibit mandatory retirement at any age (See *Simpson* v. *Alaska Human Rights Commission.*)

In addition to the forty-one states where age discrimination statutes reach both public and private employment, Arkansas and North Carolina prohibit age discrimination in the public sector alone.[18] Of these forty-three states, thirty-seven have BFOQs in their statutes applicable to public employment, and seventeen have BFE/HPP exemptions.[19] Further, of these forty-three states, twenty-three have upper age limits of seventy or lower and thus do not provide protection from involuntary retirement by reason of age beyond that offered by federal law.[20] Twenty of these forty-three states have no upper age limits.[21]

Frequent mention is made of states that have uncapped their age discrimination statutes. This term can be somewhat misleading. If uncapping refers simply to the elimination, or lack, of upper age limits, nineteen of the forty-one states that prohibit age discrimination in the private sector, and twenty of the forty-three states that prohibit age discrimination in the public sector, have uncapped. However, uncapping in that sense is not the same thing as eliminating mandatory retirement. As shown below, many state laws without upper age limits contain BFOQs or BFRPs, or other provisions, which have the effect of allowing involuntary retirement at a fixed age for at least some individuals.

As previously stated, the effect of an upper age limit of seventy or lower is that state law does not in this respect provide tenured faculty with protection from mandatory retirement beyond that offered by federal law.[22] In those states that do not have upper age limits in their age discrimination statutes, a BFRP exemption can have the same limiting effect.

Of the nineteen state age discrimination statutes that have no upper age limit and are applicable to private sector employment, five include a BFRP exemption that does not prohibit mandatory retirement.[23] Of the twenty statutes that prohibit age discrimination in the public sector and have no upper limits, these same five states have such a BFRP exemption. A BFRP exemption that does not expressly prohibit involuntary retirement (by reason of age) ordinarily has the effect of permitting such retirement at any age in accordance with the terms of a bona fide retirement plan.[24] However, this is not always the case. In three additional states where the age discrimination statutes do not have age limits but do include BFRP exemptions, mandatory retirement may nonetheless be prohibited.[25]

Of the remaining state statutes that do not have age limits (eleven applicable to the private sector, twelve applicable to public employment), seven have BFRP exemptions that follow the federal model and prohibit involuntary retirement by reason of age in such plans.[26] Obviously, this kind of BFRP does not serve to permit such mandatory retirement.

The remaining states that have statutes without age limits (four applicable to the private sector,[27] five reaching public employment[28]) do not include any sort of BFRP exemption.

Thus, there is no BFRP exemption that would permit mandatory retirement in public employment in twelve states[29] and in private employment in eleven states.[30] However, eight of the states expressly exempt tenured faculty. Thus, the age discrminination statutes of Alaska and New Hampshire are not applicable to nonprofit educational corporations and associations.[31] Connecticut law allows mandatory retirement of any person who has attained the age of seventy and is entitled to benefits under a pension or retirement plan provided for employees of an institution of higher learning.[32] The statutes in California, Massachusetts, New Jersey, New York, and Vermont expressly permit mandatory retirement of tenured faculty.[33]

Accordingly, of the states that have uncapped their upper age limits and have a BFRP exemption that bars involuntary retirement by reason of age, only four states (Hawaii, Maine, Nevada, and Wisconsin) bar such retirement and do not specifically exempt tenured faculty at public colleges and universities from the uncapping. In the private sector, only Hawaii, Maine, and Wisconsin are in this category. However, the statutes of each of these states, except Wisconsin, contain a BFOQ exemption.

The BFRP exemption is not the only way in which states can extend the protection of their age discrimination laws beyond that of the ADEA. Thus, the age discrimination statutes in Montana and Utah have been construed so as to preclude mandatory retirement at any age, notwithstanding the existence of statutory language allowing compliance with the terms of a bona fide retirement plan.[34] Further, one of the two age discrimination statutes in Florida has a BFRP that does not prohibit mandatory retirement, but the two have been reconciled to prohibit mandatory retirement, in both employment sectors, at any age.[35] Also, Georgia law includes a provision that may allow a private sector employee to waive retirement benefits to avoid mandatory retirement, and there is no indication that this option, however unattractive, would not be available to tenured faculty at private colleges and universities.[36]

None of these states has a specific statutory exemption for institutions of higher learning or tenured faculty. Thus, eight states in all (Florida, Georgia, Montana, Utah, Hawaii, Maine, Wisconsin, and Nevada) may be said to provide tenured faculty with some protection from mandatory retirement beyond that offered by federal law.[37]

2.3.2.1 State Laws Requiring Retirement of Faculty at Colleges and Universities

As previously mentioned, the state as an employer has the power to enact legislation setting the terms and conditions of public employment. The federal ADEA applies to the states and, with certain exceptions, prohibits age discrimination against employees between the ages of forty and seventy. To the extent not prohibited by applicable state and federal laws, however, the state may, by statute, set mandatory retirement ages for state employees.[38] At least twenty-six states have passed laws authorizing or requiring mandatory retirement ages for at least some college and university faculty.[39]

Thirteen states have absolute maximum age limits beyond which some or all public college and university professors may not continue to work.[40] Eleven others have a mandatory retirement age but allow employees to continue indefinitely, with the requisite approval, usually on a year-to-year basis.[41] Two additional states do not require mandatory retirement but specifically authorize it by statute for public college and university faculty.[42]

2.3.2.2 State-by-State Analysis

Alabama: Alabama has no statute prohibiting age discrimination in employment. Therefore, involuntary retirement is prohibited only to the extent it is reached by the federal ADEA (*Adams* v. *James*, 526 F. Supp. 80 (M.D. Ala. 1981). Faculty at public colleges and universities are required to retire at age seventy but may continue from year to year, with approval, if evidence of physical and mental fitness is furnished (Ala. Code Sec. 16-25-14(a)(3), as amended by Act 85-208 (signed March 25, 1985).

Alaska: Alaska law prohibits age discrimination in employment (Alaska Stat. Ann. Sec. 18.80.220(a)(1)). The statute has a BFOQ exemption, and it applies to the public and private sectors (Sec. 18.80.300(1) and (3)). The law does not, however, apply to nonprofit educational corporations and associations (Sec. 18.80.300(3)).[43] The statute has no upper age limit and was held to prohibit mandatory retirement at any age (*Simpson* v. *Alaska State Commission for Human Rights,* 423 F. Supp. 552 (D. Alaska 1976), aff'd., 608 F.2d 1171 (9th Cir. 1979)).

Arizona: Arizona law prohibits age discrimination in employment (Ariz. Rev. Stat. Ann. Sec. 41-1463B.1). The law applies to both public and private employment (Sec. 41-1461.1,2, and 5) and reaches individuals forty to seventy (Sec. 41-1465). The statute has a BFOQ exemption (Sec. 41-1463F.4(a)) and allows compliance with the terms of a BFRP, except that no such plan may require or permit involuntary retirement (Sec. 41-1463F.4(b)). There is also a BFE/HPP exemption (Sec. 41-1463K)).[44]

Faculty at Arizona state colleges and universities must retire at age seventy but, with approval, may continue on a year-to-year basis (Secs. 38-759; 38-759.01B; 38-781.07; 38-781.36B; and 15-1628).

Arkansas: Arkansas law prohibits age discrimination in public employment only (Ark. Stat. Ann. Secs. 12-3501 and 12-3502(a)). The law protects individuals from forty to seventy (Sec. 12-3505(a)) and has a BFOQ (Sec. 12-3503(a)) and a BFE/HPP (Sec. 12-3505(b)). The law is expressly applicable to public institutions of higher learning (Sec. 12-3505(c)).

California: California law prohibits age discrimination in employment in the public and private sectors and protects individuals forty and over (Cal. Gov't. Code Secs. 12941; 12926; and 12926(a)). The law expressly prohibits mandatory retirement (Sec. 129422), but has a BFE/HPP exemption (Sec. 12942(c)). There is also a specific provision that allows mandatory retirement of tenured faculty at institutions of higher learning, provided the institution has a policy allowing continued employment in a nontenured status (Sec. 12942(a)).

Colorado: Colorado has a statute that prohibits discharge on account of age of anyone between the ages of eighteen and sixty. The statute does not expressly apply to the public sector.[45]

Connecticut: The Connecticut age discrimination statute applies to public and private sector employment and has no age limits (Conn. Gen. Stat. Ann. Secs. 46a-60(a)(1) and 46(a)-51(10)). The law includes a BFOQ exemption (Sec. 46a-60(b)(1)(C)). It allows compliance with the terms of a BFRP, provided no such plan calls for mandatory retirement and provided there is a BFE/HPP exemption (Sec. 46a-60(b)(1)(E) and (B)). The law also specifically allows termination of any person who has attained the age of seventy and is entitled to benefits under a pension or retirement plan provided for state employees or for teachers in the public schools or under a pension or retirement plan provided for employees of an institution of higher learning (Sec. 46a-60(b)(1)(A)).

Public college and university faculty in Connecticut who are members of the state employees' retirement system must retire at seventy with the opportunity to continue year to year with approval (Secs. 5-164(b) and 5-160(g)). However, many are eligible for an alternate retirement plan that does not impose mandatory retirement. (See Secs. 5-160(g); 5-154(u) and (v); 5-158f; and 5-156.)

Delaware: Delaware prohibits age discrimination in the public and private sectors and covers individuals forty to seventy (Del. Stat. Ann. tit. 19, Secs. 711(a)(1); 710(2); and 710(7)). The statute has a BFOQ (Sec. 711(e)(1)), a BFRP (Sec. 711(h)), and a BFE/HPP exemption (Sec. 711(i)).

Faculty at public colleges and universities in Delaware, except certain employees of the University of Delaware, must retire on the last day of the contract year in which they attain the age of seventy (Del. Stat. Ann. tit. 29, Secs. 5501(a)(1)(b); 5505; and 5521).

Florida: Florida law prohibits age discrimination in employment in the public and private sectors and has no age limits (Fla. Stat. Ann. Secs. 760.10(1)(a) and 760.02(5) and (6)). The statute has a BFOQ (Sec. 760.10(8)(a)) and a BFRP, except that no such plan shall excuse involuntary retirement on the basis of any factor not related to ability (Sec. 760.10(8)(b)). Florida has another statute that prohibits age discrimination in the public sector (Secs. 112.043 and 112.044(3)(a)1 (1982)). This statute has a BFOQ (Sec. 112.044(3)(f)1) and a BFRP that does not preclude involuntary retirement (Sec. 112.044(3)(f)2). In a recent opinion, the state attorney general considered the two statutes and concluded that, notwithstanding the BFRP in one of the laws, mandatory retirement is unlawful in the public sector in Florida (Op. Att'y. Gen. 84-60, June 26, 1984).

Georgia: One age discrimination statute in Georgia does not expressly apply to public employment. That law prohibits age discrimination against any individual between forty and seventy and has a BFOQ (Ga. Code Ann. Sec. 34-1-2(a)). The statute has a BFRP, except that when a plan prohibits employment for excessive age, an individual may waive the right to participate in the plan as a condition of employment. There is, in the statute, an exemption for bona fide executives and others in high policy-making positions.

Another Georgia law prohibits age discrimination in public employment (Ga. Code Ann. Secs. 45-19-21 and 45-19-29(1)). Its age limits are forty and seventy, and the statute includes a BFRP (Secs. 45-19-28 and 45-19-35(d)(5)). The public sector BFRP does not have the provision allowing waiver of benefits that is available in the private sector.

Faculty in the Georgia state university system must retire at the close of the school year in which they attain age seventy (Secs. 47-3-1(128)(k); 47-3-60; and 47-3-101(b)).

Hawaii: The Hawaii statute prohibits age discrimination in public and private employment and has no age limits (Hawaii Rev. Stat. Secs. 378-2(1) and 378-1). The statute has a BFOQ (Sec. 378-3(2)) and a BFRP, but the exception shall not be construed to permit mandatory retirement (Sec. 378-3(4)). Hawaii law does include, however, a grace period for mandatory retirement provisions in existing bona fide plans until April 30, 1986.

A recent opinion of the attorney general of Hawaii held that the board of regents of the University of Hawaii is precluded from applying a policy of mandatory retirement to faculty and other university personnel (Op. Att'y. Gen. 84-6, August 23, 1984).

Idaho: The Idaho law against age discrimination appears to apply to the public sector as well as to private employment (Idaho Code Secs. 67-5909(1) and 67-5901). The law applies to individuals between forty and seventy (Sec. 67-5910(7)). The statute contains BFOQ (Sec. 67-5910(2)(a)) and a BFRP, but no such plan shall require or permit mandatory retirement, except of certain bona fide executives and others in high policy-making positions (Sec. 67-5910(2)(b)).

Illinois: Illinois law prohibits age discrimination in public and private employment and applies to individuals forty to seventy (Ill. Rev. Stat. ch. 68, Secs. 2-102(A); 2-101(B)(1); and 1-103(A)). The law has a BFOQ (Sec. 2-104(A)), a BFE/HPP (Sec. 2-104(E)(2)), and a BFRP, provided that the plan does not have the effect of unlawful discrimination (Sec. 2-104(E)(1)). The language of Section 2-104(E)(1) was held to preclude involuntary retirement of tenured faculty before seventy (*Board of Trustees of Community College District No. 508* v. *Human Rights Commission*, 88 Ill. 2d 22, 429 N.E.2d 1207 (1981)). The case was decided during the period when federal law contained an exemption allowing mandatory retirement of tenured faculty at sixty-five.

Indiana: The Indiana age discrimination statute applies to the public and private sectors and to individuals between forty and seventy, but excluded from the definition of employers are nonprofit educational corporations or associations and any person or governmental entity subject to the federal ADEA (Ind. Code Ann. Secs. 22-9-2-2; 22-9-2-1; 22-9-2-1(1); and 22-9-2-1(2)). The law also does not apply to anyone who is qualified or benefits under the terms of a retirement plan (Sec. 22-9-2-10), and the law specifically provides that it shall not be construed to affect the freedom of any employer to provide for mandatory retirement for any class of employees at an age less than seventy (Sec. 22-9-2-11).

In Indiana, members of the teachers' retirement fund, including some college and university faculty, must retire at the end of the school year in which they attain age seventy-one, but they may continue year to year on the basis of a physician's certificate of mental and physical ability to teach (Sec. 21-6.1-1-1-1, et seq.).

Iowa: Iowa law prohibits age discrimination in public and private employment (Iowa Code Ann. Secs. 601A.6.1.a and 601A.2.5). (See also Iowa Admin. Code 240-5.1, et seq., prohibiting age discrimination in public employment.) The Iowa age discrimination statute has a BFOQ (Sec. 601A.6.1.a) and applies to individuals eighteen and over (Sec. 601A.6.2). The statute allows an employer to comply with the terms of a BFRP, provided that no such plan may require involuntary retirement of anyone under seventy (Sec. 601A.13.1). There is a BFE/HPP exemption (Sec. 601A.13.1.a).

Kansas: Kansas law prohibits age discrimination in employment in the public and private sectors and protects individuals from forty to seventy (Kan. Stat. Ann. Secs. 44-1111 and 44-1112(a) and (d)). The statute has a BFOQ (Sec. 44-1113(b)(2)) and a BFRP (Sec. 44-1113(b)(3)), and it expressly permits mandatory retirement at age seventy or above (Sec. 44-1113(b)(4)). There is also a provision allowing compliance with the terms of a retirement plan permitted by state or federal law or by municipal ordinance (Sec. 44-1113(b)(5)).

Faculty at state colleges and universities in Kansas must retire no later than the academic year following their seventieth birthday (Sec. 74-4925(1)(d)).

Kentucky: Kentucky prohibits age discrimination in public and private employment (Ky. Rev. Stat. Secs. 344.040(1); 344.010(1); and 344.030(1)). The age limits of the law are forty and seventy (Sec. 344.010(4)). The only express BFOQ in the law is in a provision dealing with employment advertisements and applications. (See Sec. 344.080.) The law does include a BFRP. State college and university faculty covered by the teachers' retirement system must retire as of July 1 following their seventieth birthday (Sec. 161.600). The board of trustees at the University of Kentucky is expressly authorized to set a mandatory retirement age for faculty at that institution (Sec. 164.220(3)).

Louisiana: Louisiana law prohibits age discrimination in public and private employment and protects individuals from forty to seventy (La. Rev. Stat. Secs. 23:972A(1); 23:971(1);

and 23:972G). The statute has a BFOQ (Sec. 23:972F(1)) and a BFRP (Sec. 23:972F(2)), and it expressly provides that it does not repeal or invalidate any mandatory retirement age provided in any other statute or ordinance (Sec. 23:975).

All state employees in Louisiana, including college and university faculty, must retire at seventy; however, employment may continue year to year when continuation is advantageous to the public service because of expert knowledge and qualifications (Sec. 42-691).

Maine: Maine law prohibits age discrimination in public and private employment (Me. Rev. Stat. Ann. tit. 5, Secs. 4572.1.A; 4553.4; and 4553.7). The Maine age discrimination statute has a BFOQ (Sec. 4572(1)) and a BFRP, except that no plan may require or permit mandatory retirement of anyone, including those exempted from the coverage of the federal ADEA (Sec. 4573.1-A.B). The statute has no age limits, and it expressly prohibits mandatory retirement in the private sector (Sec. 4574.3.B). Another Maine statute prohibits mandatory retirement of public employees (Secs. 1006-2 and 1001-01).

Maryland: Maryland law prohibits age discrimination in public and private employment (Md. Ann. Code art. 49B, Secs. 16(a) and 15(b)). The statute includes a BFOQ (Sec. 16(g)(1)) and BFRP (Sec. 16(g)(4)).

Faculty at public colleges and universities in Maryland must retire at seventy but, with approval, may continue to work on a year-to-year basis (Md. Ann. Code art. 73B, Secs. 11(1)(b); 86(1)(b) and (c); 110(k)(1)-(3); 117(1)(b); and 145(1)(b) and (c)).

Massachusetts: The Massachusetts age discrimination statute applies to individuals forty and above (Mass. Gen. Laws Ann. ch. 151B, Sec. 1-8). It prohibits age discrimination in private sector employment, except where age is a BFOQ (Sec. 4-1B). It prohibits age discrimination in public employment, unless pursuant to a general or special law (Sec. 4-1C). The statute includes a BFRP, except that no plan may require or permit involuntary retirement (Sec. 4-17(a)). There is a BFE/HPP exemption (Sec. 4-17(b)) as well as a special provision permitting mandatory retirement at age seventy of tenured faculty at independent institutions of higher learning (Sec. 4-17(c)).

Another Massachusetts statute prohibits, in the private sector, discharge on the basis of age of anyone forty or above (Mass. Gen. Laws Ann. ch. 149, Sec. 24A). That statute allows discharges that are permitted by the provisions of Chapter 151B, Section 4-17.

Public college and university faculty who are members of the Massachusetts public employees' retirement system must retire on the last day of the month in which they attain age seventy (Mass. Gen. Laws Ann. Secs. 1; 3(2)(g); and 5(1)(a)) but may continue if mentally and physically capable of performing their duties (Sec. 90F). An employee who wishes to continue beyond age seventy "shall annually, at his own expense, be examined by an impartial physician designated by the retirement authority to determine such capability" (Sec. 90F).

Michigan: Michigan law prohibits age discrimination in employment in the public and private sectors (Mich. Comp. Laws Ann. Secs. 37.2202(1)(a); 37.2201(a) and 37.2103(f)). The law has no age limits (Sec. 37.2103(a)), a BFOQ (Sec. 37.2208), and a BFRP (Sec. 37.2202(2)).

Minnesota: Minnesota prohibits discrimination in employment on the basis of age in the public and private sectors (Minn. Stat. Ann. Secs. 363.03 subd. 1(2) and 363.01 subd. 7 and 15). The statute has no upper age limit (Sec. 363.01 subd. 28) and includes a BFOQ exemption (Sec. 363.03 subd. 1). Minnesota prohibits mandatory retirement before age seventy, except where compelled or specifically authorized by law, with a BFE/HPP exemption (Sec. 181.81). State law also expressly permits a mandatory retirement age of seventy or above, if established by law or in a published retirement policy (Sec. 363.02 subd. 6; see also Sec. 181.81 subd. 1(a)).

Faculty at public colleges and universities in Minnesota, not including the University of Minnesota, must retire at age seventy, but retirees may be employed as substitutes or on a part-time basis (Sec. 354.44 subd. 1a).

Mississippi: Mississippi law does not prohibit age discrimination in employment. Public college and university faculty in the state, except those excluded by the federal ADEA, must be retired at the age of seventy (Miss. Code Ann. Secs. 25-9-103(e); 25-11-101 et seq.; and 25-11-111(f)).

Missouri: Missouri does not have a state statute that prohibits age discrimination in employment.[46] Public college and university faculty in the state, but not those employed by the University of Missouri, are required by law to retire on July 1 following the school year in which they attain age seventy (Mo. Rev. Stat. Sec. 169.060).

Montana: Montana has statutory provisions dealing with age discrimination in public and private employment. Mont. Code Ann. Sec. 49-2-303(1)(a) prohibits age discrimination in the private sector. (See Secs. 49-2-101(8) and (15) and 49-2-308.) The prohibition has a BFOQ exemption (Sec. 49-2-303(1) and (2)) and no age limits (Sec. 49-2-101(1)). Age discrimination in public employment is prohibited by Section 49-3-201. That provision, like the one applicable to the private sector, has a BFOQ exemption (Sec. 49-3-103(1)), but no age limits (Sec. 49-3-101).

A BFRP in Section 49-3-103(2) is expressly applicable to both public and private employers. Nevertheless, the Montana law prohibiting age discrimination in public employment has been held to supersede, or to repeal by implication, state statutes setting mandatory retirement ages for public employees (*Taylor v. Department of Fish, Wildlife, and Parks,* 666 P.2d 1228 (1983); *Dolan* v. *School Dist. No. 10, Deer Lodge Cty.,* 195 Mont. 340 636 P.2d 825 (1981)).[47]

Nebraska: Nebraska law prohibits age discrimination in public and private employment (Neb. Rev. Stat. Secs. 48-1004 (1)(a) and 48-1002). The age limits of the law are forty and seventy (Sec. 48-1003(2)).

State college and university faculty in Nebraska must retire at the age of seventy but are allowed to continue if the requisite approval is obtained (Sec. 85-606).

Nevada: Like Georgia and Montana, Nevada has separate age discrimination statutes dealing with public and private employment. Nev. Rev. Stat. Ann. Sec. 281.370 prohibits age discrimination in public employment. The statute has no age limits and has been held to prohibit mandatory retirement of public university faculty at any age (*Board of Regents* v. *Oakley,* 97 Nev. 605, 637 P.2d 1199 (1981)).

Another statute prohibits age discrimination and applies to public and private sector employers (Nev. Rev. Stat. Ann. Secs. 613.330-1(a); 613.310-1; and 613.310-4). The age limits of this statute are forty and sixty-nine (Sec. 613.350-3). The law has a BFOQ (Sec. 613-350-1) and a BFRP (Sec. 613-350-5).[48]

New Hampshire: New Hampshire law prohibits age discrimination in the public and private sectors but does not apply to private nonprofit educational corporations or associations (N.H. Rev. Stat. Ann. Secs. 354-A:8I and 354-A:3(5)).[49] The statute has a BFOQ and expressly prohibits mandatory retirement (Sec. 354-A:8VIII). New Hampshire law specifies no age limits.

New Jersey: New Jersey law prohibits age discrimination in public and private employment and applies to individuals eighteen and over (N.J. Stat. Ann. Secs. 10:5-12(a); 10:5-2.1; and 10:5-5e). The statute includes a BFOQ (Sec. 10:5-2.1). As recently amended by *L.* 1985, *c.* 73, signed March 11, 1985 (effective January 1, 1984, for public employees and October 1, 1985, for private sector employees), Section 10:5-2.1 allows compliance with the terms of a BFRP, provided that the provisions of the plan are not used to establish an age for mandatory retirement.

Another New Jersey statute prohibits age discrimination in public employment (N.J. Stat. Ann. Sec. 10:3-1). It protects individuals forty and over. That section was also amended by *L.* 1985, *c.* 73, and it now expressly prohibits mandatory retirement. However, *L.* 1985, *c.* 73 contains an exception that permits mandatory retirement of tenured faculty at both public and private institutions of higher learning.

New Mexico: The New Mexico age discrimination statute has no age limits and applies to the public and private sectors (N.M. Stat. Ann. Secs. 28-1-7A and 28-1-2A and B). However, the law expressly permits mandatory retirement at age sixty-five or over in accordance with a bona fide retirement plan that meets the requirements of ERISA (Sec. 28-1-9).[50] The statute also includes a BFOQ and a BFE/HPP (Sec. 28-1-7A).

New York: New York prohibits age discrimination in

public and private employment (N.Y. Exec. Law Sec. 296 subd. 3-a(a)). As of January 1, 1985, the age discrimination provisions applicable to public employment protect individuals eighteen and over (Sec. 296 subd. 3-a(a), as amended by 1984 N.Y. Laws Ch. 296, Secs. 1 and 12). In the private sector, the law currently protects only individuals between eighteen and sixty-five, but as of January 1, 1986, the upper age limit will be removed from the private sector restrictions as well. The age discrimination statute, as amended, has a BFOQ (Sec. 296 subd. 3-a(d)) and a BFE/HPP for the private sector only (Sec. 296 subd. 3-a(e)). The statute expressly allows mandatory retirement of tenured faculty, in both the public and private sectors, at age seventy or older (Sec. 296 subd. 3-a(f)).

North Carolina: North Carolina law prohibits age discrimination in employment in the public sector only (N.C. Gen. Stat. Sec. 126-16). The statute has a BFOQ and applies to individuals from forty to seventy.

A new statute in North Carolina has eliminated mandatory retirement of public employees but expressly allows mandatory retirement of faculty in the University of North Carolina system until July 1, 1998 (1984 N.C. Sess. Laws Ch. 1019, Sec. 2).

North Dakota: North Dakota prohibits age discrimination in employment in the public and private sectors (N.D. Cent. Code Sec. 14-02.4-03; see also Sec. 34-01-17). The age limits of the statute are forty and seventy (Sec. 14-02.4-02-1). The statute has a BFE/HPP (Sec. 14-02.4-02-1) and a BFOQ (id.; see also Sec. 34-01-17).

Ohio: The Ohio age discrimination statute prohibits age discrimination in public and private employment (Ohio Rev. Code Ann. Secs. 4112.02(A) and 4112.01(A)(2); see also Sec. 4101.177(A)). The statute protects individuals from forty to seventy (Sec. 4112.01(A)(14); see also Sec. 4101.17). The law contains a BFOQ (Sec. 4112.02(O)(1)) and a BFRP, but no plan may require or permit involuntary retirement, except as provided for in the federal ADEA (Sec. 4112.02(O)(2)). The statute also includes a BFE/HPP (Sec. 4112.02(O)(3)).

Ohio law expressly authorizes involuntary retirement of public college and university faculty at age seventy (Secs.

3307.01(A) and (B) and 3307.37). These statutory provisions were held to preclude mandatory retirement of faculty before age seventy in *Spinak* v. *University of Akron* (3 O. App. 3d 388, 445 N.E.2d 692 (Ct. App. Ohio 1981)). This decision was rendered during the period when federal law authorized mandatory retirement of tenured faculty at age sixty-five.

Oklahoma: Oklahoma does not have a statute prohibiting age discrimination in employment.[51] Nor does state law impose a mandatory retirement age on public college and university faculty.

Oregon: Oregon prohibits age discrimination in public and private employment (Or. Rev. Stat. Secs. 659.030(1)(a) and (b) and 659.010(6)). The law includes a BFOQ (Sec. 659.030(1)(a)) and applies to individuals between eighteen and seventy (Sec. 659.030(1)(a) and (b)). The statute allows compliance with a BFRP, provided that no such plan may require mandatory retirement of anyone between eighteen and seventy because of age (Sec. 659.028). There is, however, an exception for mandatory retirement under the age of seventy if required by law (Sec. 659.030(3)).

Faculty at public colleges and universities in Oregon must retire at age seventy but, with approval, may be continued until age seventy-five (Secs. 237.129(2) and 237.133(1)(a)). A special statutory provision authorizes the state board of higher education to seek approval to employ individuals beyond the mandatory retirement age (Sec. 237.139).

Pennsylvania: Pennsylvania prohibits age discrimination in employment in both the public sector and the private sector (Pa. Stat. Ann. tit. 43, Secs. 955(a) and 954(b)). The law protects individuals between the ages of forty and seventy and anyone else who may be protected by subsequent amendment of the federal ADEA (Sec. 954(h)). The law includes a BFOQ (Sec. 955) and a BFRP (Sec. 955(a)(1)).

Rhode Island: Under Rhode Island law, age discrimination is prohibited against any individual between forty and seventy, in both public and private sector employment (R.I. Gen. Laws Secs. 28-5-7(A); 28-5-6(B); and 28-55-6(I)). The statute allows actions on the basis of a BFOQ with the approval of the state Human Rights Commission (Sec. 28-5-7(D)).

State college and university faculty in Rhode Island must retire on the first day of the next calendar month succeeding their seventieth birthday (Secs. 36-10-9 and 16-17-1).

South Carolina: South Carolina prohibits age discrimination in public and private employment (S.C. Code Ann. Secs. 1-13-80(a)(1) and 1-13-30(d) and (e)). The law protects individuals from forty to seventy (Sec. 1-13-30(c)), and it includes a BFOQ (Sec. 1-13-80(h)(7)(i)). Compliance with the terms of a BFRP is allowed, provided that the plan does not call for mandatory retirement (Sec. 1-13-80(h)(7)(ii) and (iii)). There is a BFE/HPP exemption (Sec. 1-13-80(h)(8) and (9)). In addition, the law specifically provides that it shall not be construed to override South Carolina Code Section 9-1-1530, which requires public employees to retire at the age of seventy (Sec. 1-13-80(h)(11)).

State college and university faculty in South Carolina must retire at the age of seventy but, with the requisite approval, may continue working until age seventy-two (Secs. 9-1-1530 and 9-1-10(4)). Under state law, tenured faculty at public colleges and universities may not be forced to retire before reaching age seventy (*University of South Carolina* v. *Batson,* 271 S.C. 242, 246 S.E.2d 882 (1978)). University of South Carolina could not take advantage of federal law permitting involuntary retirement of tenured faculty at sixty-five, as state law precluded involuntary retirement before age seventy.

South Dakota: South Dakota Codified Laws Annotated Section 3-6A-15 prohibits discrimination on the basis of age, between the ages of eighteen and seventy (except where age is a BFOQ), in the South Dakota Career Service Personnel Management System. That section does not apply to faculty under the jurisdiction of the state board of regents (S.D. Codified Laws Ann. Sec. 3-6A-13(5)).

Most state employees, including college and university faculty, must retire at the age of seventy (S.D. Codified Laws Ann. Secs. 3-6A-36.1 and 3-6-28).

Tennessee: Tennessee prohibits age discrimination in public and private employment (Tenn. Code Ann. Secs. 4-21-105(a)(1) and 4-21-102(4)). The age limits in the statute are forty and seventy (Secs. 4-21-101(b) and 4-21-126(a)). The law contains a BFOQ (Sec. 4–21–125(1)) and a BFRP, except that no plan may impose mandatory retirement unless otherwise provided by law (Sec. 4–21–125(2); see also Sec. 4–21–126(b)). There is a BFE/HPP exemption (Sec. 4–21–126(c)).

Under Tennessee law, faculty at public colleges and universities may be involuntarily retired at age sixty-five and must be retired at age seventy, except that they may, with approval, complete the school year (Sec. 8–36–205(4) and (5)).[52]

Texas: Texas prohibits age discrimination in employment in the public and private sectors (Texas. Rev. Civ. Stat. Ann. art. 522lk, Secs. 5.01(1) and 2.01(5)). The law applies to individuals from forty to seventy (Sec. 1.04(a)) and includes a BFOQ (Sec. 5.07(a)(1)) and a BFE/HPP (Sec. 1.04(a)). The law allows compliance with a BFRP, except that no plan may require or permit mandatory retirement by reason of age (Sec. 5.07(a)(3)).

Utah: Utah prohibits age discrimination in public and private employment (Utah Code Ann. Secs. 34–35–6(1)(a) and 34–35–2(5); see also Sec. 67–19–4). The new law protects individuals forty and over (Sec. 34–35–6(1)(a)) and includes a BFOQ (Sec. 34–35–6(2)(a)). This statute contains a BFRP (Sec. 34–35–6(3)), but it also expressly prohibits mandatory retirement, notwithstanding any statutory provision to the contrary (Sec. 34–35–6(1)(f)(iii)). In a recent opinion, the attorney general of Utah concluded that the Utah age discrimination statute prohibits mandatory retirement based on age even when done pursuant to a BFRP (Informal Opinion No. 84-62, November 1, 1984).

Vermont: The Vermont age discrimination statute applies to public and private sector employment and protects individuals eighteen and older (Vt. Stat. Ann. tit. 21, Secs. 495(a)(1); 495d(1); and 495(c)). The law contains a BFOQ (Sec. 495(a)) and allows compliance with the terms of a BFRP, provided that such plan does not impose mandatory retirement (Sec. 495f). Vermont law specifically allows the termination of tenured faculty at age seventy and provides that anyone so terminated may, at the discretion of the institution, be allowed to continue in a nontenured status (Sec. 495g).

Virginia: Virginia does not have a statute prohibiting age

discrimination in employment.[53] Faculty at public colleges and universities in Virginia must retire at the age of seventy but, with approval, may continue until the last day of the fiscal year (Va. Code Sec. 51-111.54).

Washington: The state of Washington has two statutes that prohibit age discrimination in employment (Wash. Rev. Code Ann. Secs. 49.60.180 and 49.44.090). The two must be construed together (*Saruf* v. *Miller*, 90 Wash. 2d 880, 586 P.2d 466 (1978); *Gross* v. *Lynnwood*, 90 Wash. 2d 395, 583 P.2d 1197 (1978)). Age discrimination is prohibited in both public and private employment (Sec. 49.60.040). The law includes a BFOQ (Sec. 49.60.180) and a BFRP (Sec. 49.44.090), and it protects individuals from forty to seventy (Sec. 49.44.090; see also *Saruf* v. *Miller* and *Gross* v. *Lynnwood*). Age limits in one statute are applicable to the other.

Washington law expressly prohibits mandatory retirement of public employees before the age of seventy (Sec. 41.04.350(1)). It also allows public employers to waive mandatory retirement requirements that exist for employees seventy and over (Sec. 41.04.350(2)). Faculty at public colleges and universities in Washington must retire at the age of seventy but may be reemployed, because of outstanding qualifications, on a part-time basis (Sec. 28B.10.420).

West Virginia: West Virginia law prohibits age discrimination in public and private employment (W. Va. Code Secs. 5-11-9(a) and 5-11-3(d)). The law has a BFOQ (Sec. 5-11-9(a)), a BFRP (id.), and applies to individuals between forty and sixty-five (Sec. 5-11-3(d)).

West Virginia prohibits mandatory retirement of public college and university faculty before age seventy or before the end of the fiscal year or semester in which they attain age seventy (Sec. 18-7A-25a). However, retirement may not be extended for more than six months (id.).

Wisconsin: Wisconsin law prohibits age discrimination in public and private employment and protects individuals forty and older (Wis. Stat. Ann. Secs. 111.321; 111.322(1); and 111.33(1)). The statute allows compliance with a BFRP, provided that no such plan may require or permit mandatory retirement (Sec. 111.33(2)(b)).[54]

Wyoming: Wyoming prohibits age discrimination in public and private employment (Wyo. Stat. Secs. 27–9–105(a) and 27–9–102). The law protects individuals between forty and seventy (Sec. 27–9–105(b)) and allows compliance with a BFRP, provided that it does not call for mandatory retirement (Sec. 27–9–105(c)).

Current Wyoming law provides for mandatory retirement of all state employees, including college and university faculty, at age sixty-five (Secs. 9–3–414 and 9–3–402(a)(v); (xviii); (xix); and (xxi)).[55]

Epilogue

Part Two included a review of federal and state laws affecting the faculty retirement policies of colleges and universities. It should be noted that such laws are subject to continual change. On October 31, 1986, some months after the commission's policy on retirement ages and its related documents were issued, the federal Age Discrimination in Employment Act of 1967 was amended. Prior to these amendments, the protection of the federal age discrimination laws was limited to employees between the ages of forty and seventy. The 1986 amendments eliminated the upper age limit and are often referred to as "uncapping" the protected retirement ages. Thus, after January 1, 1987, protection was extended by the 1986 amendments to employees over the age of forty. The 1986 amendments also contained a "Special Rule for Tenured Faculty."

These 1986 amendments did not alter any of the basic principles reflected in the commission's policy statement. The amendments, in fact, tended to confirm the analysis on which the commission's recommendations were based. The 1986 amendments, and their "Special Rule for Tenured Faculty," nonetheless have important implications for the tenure and retirement policies of academic institutions. These implications were addressed by the chair of the Commission on College Retirement in a published commentary. The thrust of that commentary was summarized in the *Journal of College and University Law* in these words:

The potential for conflict between the duration of faculty tenure arrangements and the age discrimination laws poses a latent threat to the system of tenure itself. This threat, while real, is avoidable. Such is the thesis of this commentary by the former Chair of the Commission on College Retirement whose reports were issued in 1986 and 1987. This commentary first analyzes, and brings fresh insights to, the nature of the tenure arrangement, the distinction between retirement and the termination of tenure, and the recent amendments to the federal Age Discrimination in Employment Act, particularly the "special rule" for tenured faculty. The commentary then explores steps that could avoid potential conflict between the tenure arrangements and the age discrimination laws. Specific suggestions are made for arrangements for the termination of tenure contracts between faculty and their colleges and universities.

Uncertainty still surrounds the interface between tenure, retirement, the use of chronological age as a criterion either for the end of tenure or for the beginning of retirement, and the impact of the age discrimination laws. Colleges and universities and their faculties, by their own actions, can do much to dispel this uncertainty. If they fail to do so, however, that opportunity will shift to the Congress or the courts.

Note: See Oscar M. Ruebhausen, "The Age Discrimination in Employment Act Amendment of 1986: Implications for Tenure and Retirement." *Journal of College and University Law,* 1988, *14,* 561.

Part Three

A Pension Program for College and University Personnel

The commission finds that over the years, great progress has been made toward the goal of providing adequate pensions for college and university personnel. Almost all now have protection under social security and a high proportion are covered also by either a defined contribution plan, primarily TIAA-CREF, or a defined benefit plan such as those provided for the employees of many public institutions. By and large, these are good plans. And TIAA-CREF, the most common plan for protecting personnel in private institutions, has shown in several ways that it is capable of adapting imaginatively to emerging problems.

Academic institutions and their personnel share the same pension program goal: the assurance that employees of colleges and universities will have a reasonable opportunity to maintain the quality of their lives throughout their retirement years.

There can be no guarantee, obviously, that any particular pension program will achieve the desired goal for all retirees or for the entire retirement period. Life's uncertainties, the unpredictability of the future, and the infinite variety of the human condition preclude the possibility of a foolproof plan.

The commission believes, nevertheless, that existing pension plans can be modified to respond to the shared pension goal of institutions of higher education and their personnel.

A pension plan, however, is but one significant part of a retirement program. The overall effectiveness of any pension plan, accordingly, will depend on the complete retirement program of which it is a part. Among the essential elements of an effective retirement program are the following:

- an agreed upon but flexibly administered retirement date (the commission's report on "Retirement Ages for College and University Personnel" (Part Two of this volume) sets out its recommendations on this issue);
- an adequate income stream for retirees throughout the entire period of their retirement (the subject of this report);
- opportunities for appropriate continuing activities that can play a role in sustaining the effective functioning of the retiree;
- financial planning assistance; and
- protection against the cost of health care and long-term care services when needed by retirees.

The last three of these issues are addressed in Parts Four, Five, and Six of this volume.

Principles

There is, of course, no precise income stream that will uniformly meet the desired goal for all people. There are, however, some principles that the commission concludes are basic to the achievement of the pension goal.

First, a pension plan should provide income for the lifetimes of the retirees and their spouses. The lifetime annuity has long been a central feature of pension planning for higher education. It is basic to the pension system administered by TIAA since 1918 and its affiliate, CREF, since 1952. More than $44 billion have been entrusted to TIAA-CREF to provide annuities for participants.

Second, a pension plan should provide income that, when added to other sources of support available to the family, can be expected to maintain throughout retirement a standard of living comparable to that enjoyed immediately prior to retirement. Social security benefits, spousal earnings, savings, and income from other assets are all important contributors to retirement income security.

Third, a pension plan for college and university personnel, particularly faculty, should be portable so that, notwithstanding job changes, the existing pension plan of which such personnel are the beneficiaries will follow them in their new positions.

Finally, the commission believes that academic defined contribution pension plans should provide their beneficiaries with reasonable flexibility in the selection (1) of the investment managers to whom their funds are entrusted for investment, (2) of the investment objectives for which such funds are invested and (3) of the institution(s) that will provide the retirees' lifetime annuities. While such flexibility must have limits, for reasons both of prudence and of administrative cost, flexibility greater than that now afforded by the traditional TIAA-CREF arrangement is not only desirable but also may be legally required if requested by the college or university and the participant.

Findings

The conclusion that emerges from a survey of pension provisions is that, despite great progress, many employees of colleges and universities fail to achieve the commission's goal of maintaining preretirement living standards throughout their retirement. Some people who work for state or local institutions still lack the basic protection offered through a fully indexed and portable retirement plan such as social security. Others, primarily clerical and service employees, have social security coverage but are not in any kind of employer pension plan. Those who participate in defined contribution plans may expose themselves to unnecessary risk through poor choice of investments as they approach retirement and end up with inadequate initial benefits. College and university employees and their spouses who are beneficiaries of the TIAA-CREF program, while bearing the risk of investment returns on their accumulations, are not now given the right to transfer their accumulated funds freely within TIAA-CREF and cannot transfer their funds to another custodian. In the case of those covered by public sector defined benefit plans, employees who change jobs frequently see their accrued pension benefits eroded by inflation. Finally, even those people who do arrive at retirement with an adequate initial benefit, whether from a defined benefit or a defined contribution plan, are likely to see the purchasing power of that benefit decline over time in the face of rising prices.

Based on these findings, the commission makes the following recommendations.

Recommendations

1. *All employees of colleges and universities should be participants in a minimum or core pension plan whose accumulations should be invested prudently and whose benefits should be paid out in the form of an annuity for the lifetime of the participant and spouse.*

2. *Equally important to setting the initial pension benefit is establishing a mechanism to offset the effect of inflation in eroding the purchasing power of benefits over the period of retirement. Several partial solutions are available for inflation-adjusting benefits, and one of these should be used by all providers of core pension benefits. Full indexing, which would guarantee inflation protection, would require that the government issue index bonds, an option that merits further study.*

3. *In addition to the core pension, supplementary pension plans of maximum flexibility should be offered to all employees to enable them to meet and sustain their target retirement benefit, such as the benefit, which when combined with other sources of retirement income, will allow them to maintain their pre-retirement standards of living.*

4. *The accumulated core pension money should be transferable between alternative funds offered by a given vendor and across vendors at the request of both the participant and the college or university. Transfer and payout of supplementary funds should be made at the sole option of the participant. These recommendations require that TIAA-CREF alter its policy regarding transferability of cash accumulations between its two funds and to other vendors.*

5. *Financial information and planning services should be made available to employees to enable them to make better decisions regarding the level, composition, investment and payout of their pension accumula-*

*tions. Services should also be made available to institutions to help them
select the most appropriate pension program for their campuses.*

6. *College and university employees who are covered by defined benefit
plans and who leave their jobs should receive a severance benefit based
on expected salary at retirement rather than on salary at the time of termination of employment.*

7. *For defined benefit plans, standards should be established for
pension funding, reporting, and disclosure.*

8. *Social security coverage should be extended to those currently
not participating in the system.*

3.1

Current Retirement Plans
for College and University Employees

In evaluating the existing array of public and private pensions in the academic community, the commission first identified the characteristics of a desirable retirement system. The commission concluded that pension arrangements should be designed so as to allow individuals to continue the same standard of living in retirement that they enjoyed while working, and that the pension schemes should fulfill this goal without interfering with job mobility or creating strong incentives to postpone retirement. The existing combination of social security and employer pension plans has gone a long way toward ensuring a continued stream of retirement income for most college and university employees, but some serious gaps in protection still exist, and the pension plans currently offered can impede mobility or encourage delayed retirement.

This chapter documents the current status of retirement provisions for members of the college and university community as background for the commission's specific recommendations presented in Section 3.2.

3.1.1 Retirement Income Goals

Maintaining preretirement living standards throughout retirement requires not only establishing an appropriate initial level of retirement income but also constructing mechanisms that provide protection against inflation. In addition, to protect against the risk of large financial outlays that could wipe out accumulated resources, individuals need health insurance to cover part of the costs of chronic and long-term care. (The commission's recommendations for long-term care insurance are presented in Part Four of this volume.)

3.1.1.1 Establishing the Initial Benefit

Retirees require considerably less than 100 percent of their preretirement income to maintain their standard of living. Whereas preretirement earnings are subject to the federal income tax, the social security payroll tax, and state and municipal taxes, a large portion of retirement income is not taxed. For example, at the present time, up to specified income levels, social security benefits are not included in taxable income and above these levels, only one-half of social security benefits are taxable.

Second, work-related expenses, such as transportation, clothing, and meals purchased away from home, are reduced during retirement. Pension contributions and other saving can also cease in retirement. As a result of these factors, retirees require approximately 60 to 80 percent of preretirement earnings to maintain their living standards (see Table 3.1). The range in this table is attributable to variations in tax rates for different income levels and marital status.

Even though the income replacement rates shown in Table 3.1 may serve as general planning guides, college and university employees face circumstances that may make their needs different from these rule-of-thumb replacement needs. For example, individual and family variations in savings rates, child-rearing expenses, mortgage expenses, and other life-style-related expenditures may make their needs in retirement different from the average for their income level. This heterogeneity of needs was found in a commission-sponsored financial planning pilot conducted in 1985. While the *average* retirement income needs did not differ significantly from those shown in Table 3.1, the variation from the average (as measured by the standard deviation) was very large.

Table 3.1. Retirement Income Needed to Maintain Preretirement
Standard of Living for Persons Retiring in January 1985, Selected Income Levels.

Gross pre-retirement income	Preretirement taxes		Disposable preretirement Income	Reduction in expenses at retirement			Net pre-retirement Income	Postretirement taxes		Equivalent retirement income	
	Federal[a]	State and local[b]		Work-related expenses[c]	Savings and investments			Federal Income[a]	State and local[b]	Amount	Ratio
					Amount	Percent					
Single person											
$7,000	$ 1,110	$ 110	$ 5,790	$ 342	$ 0	0.0%	$ 5,448	$ 0	$ 0	$ 5,448	0.77
10,000	1,775	194	8,031	474	237	3.0	7,320	0	0	7,320	0.73
16,000	3,351	402	12,247	735	808	6.6	10,704	208	37	10,949	0.68
20,000	4,605	577	16,218	973	1,459	9.0	13,786	574	103	14,463	0.72
30,000	6,006	703	23,291	1,397	2,794	12.0	19,100	1,273	229	20,602	0.68
37,800	8,743	1,097	27,960	1,678	3,691	13.2	22,591	1,798	324	24,713	0.65
50,000	11,836	1,654	36,510	2,191	5,477	15.0	28,842	3,266	588	32,696	0.65
70,000	19,482	3,030	47,488	2,849	8,548	18.0	36,091	6,412	1,154	43,657	0.62
Married couple (filing jointly)											
7,000	901	74	6,025	362	0	0.0	5,663	0	0	5,663	0.80
10,000	1,519	147	8,334	500	250	3.0	7,584	0	0	7,584	0.75
16,000	2,861	313	12,826	770	847	6.6	11,209	0	0	11,209	0.70
20,000	3,861	443	15,696	942	1,413	9.0	13,341	0	0	13,341	0.66
30,000	5,147	548	24,305	1,458	2,917	12.0	19,930	547	99	20,576	0.68
37,800	7,451	865	29,484	1,769	3,892	13.2	23,823	947	170	24,940	0.66
50,000	10,018	1,327	38,655	2,319	5,798	15.0	30,538	2,034	366	32,938	0.65
70,000	16,599	2,512	50,889	3,053	9,160	18.0	38,676	3,812	686	43,174	0.61

[a]1984 federal income and social security taxes. Changes to the tax laws may significantly alter the calculations in this table.

[b]Based on state and local income tax receipts, which were 18 percent of federal income tax receipts from 1973 to 1983. Does not include property tax.

[c]Estimated as 6 percent of disposable income.

[d]Postretirement federal income taxes are levied on adjusted gross income plus the lesser of one-half of social security benefits received or one-half of the excess of adjusted gross income plus one-half of social security benefits over $25,000 for a single person or $32,000 for a married couple filing jointly.

Source: Calculations based on President's Commission on Pension Policy, Coming of Age: Toward a National Retirement Income Policy (GPO, February

3.1.1.1.1 Social Security. For most employees in the college and university community, a significant portion of their retirement needs will be met through the social security system. Since social security coverage is nearly universal, workers can move from job to job and continue to accrue benefits that keep pace with the growth in their earnings. After retirement, a progressive benefit formula provides relatively larger benefits to lower-paid workers, and annual cost-of-living adjustments ensure that benefits keep pace with prices.

For people in the middle of the income distribution, social security benefits replace about 30 percent of preretirement earnings (see Table 3.2). Replacement rates for married couples in this middle range average roughly 38 percent. Due to the progressivity of the benefit formula, the level of replacement is greater for low-income retirees than for people at the high end of the income distribution. In all cases, however, social security provides less than the amount needed to maintain preretirement living standards, so employer-based public and private pensions have an important role to play in assuring economic security in retirement.

3.1.1.1.2 Employer Pension Plans. Although all college personnel, including both faculty and staff, should have employer pensions, these pensions need not be designed to fill the entire gap between the income required to maintain preretirement living standards and the income provided by social security. Somewhat less than full replacement is appropriate since most retirees have access to additional resources through the equity in their homes and through other saving.

For example, consider the case of the couple in the middle of the income distribution who require roughly 70 percent of preretirement income to maintain their living standard and who will receive 38 percent from social security. Conservatively assuming that housing and financial assets would produce income equal to 12 percent of preretirement earnings, a pension benefit should be set at roughly 20 percent of preretirement earnings. Under the simplest assumptions of a forty-year worklife, a twenty-year retirement span, and a zero real rate of return,

Table 3.2. Median Social Security Replacement
Rates for Men, Nonmarried Women, and Married
Couples, by Preretirement Earnings Levels.ᵃ

Preretirement earnings quintilesᵇ	Median social security replacement rate		
	All men	Nonmarried women	Married couples
Lowest	50	57	56
Second	34	42	45
Third	30	40	38
Fourth	25	35	31
Highest	17	27	23
Total	28	38	37

ᵃSocial security benefits as a percentage of estimated total price-indexed earnings in the highest three of the last ten years.

ᵇQuintiles computed separately for each group. The differences in replacement rates between nonmarried women and others is because they, on average, earned less than the other groups.

Source: Alan Fox, "Earnings Replacement Rates and Total Income: Findings from the Retirement History Study." Social Security Bulletin, Vol. 45, No. 10 (October 1982), Tables 8 and 10, pp. 14 and 20.

these indexed benefits for the average couple could be financed by an annual contribution of 10 percent of gross earnings under a defined contribution plan or an accrual rate of approximately 1 percent of final salary under a defined benefit plan. Higher-income people will need somewhat greater benefits; individuals at the low end may require somewhat less. In addition, a shorter contribution period would increase the required annual cost, while a positive rate of return would lower it.

The preceding analysis should not be imbued with unwarranted precision, but it does highlight the commission's main conclusion that the maintenance of preretirement living standards through a combination of social security, pensions, and individual saving is a reasonable goal.

For employees in higher education, the two major types of plans used to complement social security are defined benefit plans, offered primarily by public sector employers, and defined contribution plans, provided primarily through TIAA-CREF for employees of both private and public institutions. Although TIAA-CREF remains by far the largest defined contribution

---

system, over fifty employers are offering a choice of vendors, such as the Fidelity, Scudder, and Vanguard mutual fund families for employer and employee pension plan contributions.

Each type of pension plan has its own advantages and disadvantages. Under defined contribution plans, individuals or their employers put aside a certain percentage of earnings each year, and the ultimate benefit depends on the investment performance of accumulated assets. The key advantages of these plans are that they are fully portable, often immediately vested, and relatively simple to administer and understand. The biggest shortcoming of a defined contribution retirement plan is that the participant assumes the investment risk. This risk, in turn, places information and investment allocating demands on participants. In addition, the plans provide significant incentives for individuals to continue working beyond their normal retirement age.

Under a defined benefit plan, the employer guarantees a retirement benefit that usually amounts to a certain percentage of final or average pay for each year of service. These plans have two very attractive features: the predictability of the benefit as one nears the normal retirement age and the possibility of building early retirement incentives into the structure.

The major disadvantage of defined benefit plans is the lack of portability. People who change jobs frequently suffer serious losses under defined benefit plans. Even if benefits are fully and immediately vested, individuals receive significantly lower pensions as a result of moving among plans — even if they are all identical — than they would receive from continuous coverage in a single plan. This difference arises because pension benefits for nonmobile employees are generally related to earnings just before retirement, while the benefits of the mobile employees will be based on earnings at the time they terminate employment from each employer.

3.1.1.2 Maintaining the Value of Benefits After Retirement

Maintaining living standards over the entire period of retirement requires not only establishing an adequate initial benefit but also protecting the benefit from the effects of inflation.

In an inflationary environment, the purchasing power of benefits fixed in nominal terms will deteriorate and retirees' standards of living will decline. When high rates of inflation are combined with earlier retirement and increased longevity, the value of unindexed pension benefits falls drastically. Even a relatively mild rate of inflation, such as 4 percent, will cut the purchasing power nearly in half over a fifteen-year period.

Theoretically, providing indexed pensions should be possible if earnings on pension assets follow inflation. But if real rates of return (earnings above the rate of inflation) on stocks and bonds decline in response to unanticipated inflation, as they did during the 1970s, nominal yields will not fully reflect the rate of price increases. Therefore, pension and annuity programs cannot offer fully indexed benefits without requiring higher levels of funding.

Several approaches toward maintaining the value of benefits after retirement have been tried in the United States and in other countries. The ideal investment instrument for pension funds is an index bond of the type that has been issued in Great Britain during the last few years. These bonds are not available in the United States, but recent studies have shown that annuities tied to Treasury bills or short-term bonds can produce streams of benefits that are quite stable in real terms. The problem with this approach is that investing in these short-term securities involves a substantial tradeoff of return for their high correlation with inflation. For example, over the period 1926–1984, the real return on U.S. Treasury bills was 0.2 percent, while the inflation-adjusted return on common stocks averaged 6.2 percent (see Table 3.3).

The second method of inflation protection that can be utilized is some form of performance indexing, under which inflation-augmented or "excess" investment earnings would be used to escalate the value of pensions in retirement. Even if equities and fixed-income securities fail to incorporate a full inflation premium, returns usually tend to be higher in periods of rapidly rising prices. Full performance indexing requires that the pension or annuity plan's liability for benefits in force be valued at a real rate of return of 2 or 3 percent, and that any

Table 3.3. Inflation-Adjusted Total Returns on
Various Asset Types, Summary Statistics, 1926–1984.

Asset type	Geometric mean	Arithmetic mean	Standard Deviation
Common stocks	6.2	8.5	21.4
Small stocks	9.2	14.8	35.7
Long-term corporate bonds	1.1	1.5	9.5
Long-term government bonds	0.6	1.0	9.4
U.S. Treasury bills	0.2	0.3	4.5

excess of the actual return over this amount be used to increase pension income. CREF, by setting an initial assumed earnings rate of 4 percent, utilizes a form of performance indexing. From the perspective of beneficiaries, performance indexing provides at least as much inflation protection as they can secure on their own, but benefits are not fully indexed and benefit amounts can be quite volatile without the imposition of floors and ceilings in the indexing provisions. Utilizing low assumed earnings rates also means that the initial benefit payment is lower than that which can be achieved by a fixed or level payment annuity method.

A third method of dealing with the erosion of the value of benefits is to offer a graduated benefit that grows by a fixed amount every year. For example, benefits may grow at 3 percent or 5 percent per annum. While this does not protect the participant against unexpected inflation, it does pattern the payout in a manner more in accord with inflationary expectations. The advantage of this approach, although only a partial solution, is that it leaves the annuity provider with a nominal rather than a real obligation, which may be funded with a higher yield portfolio of assets. Instead of using short-term Treasury bills, for example, it is more appropriate to fund a long-term nominal liability with bonds of a similar long-term duration. With normal yield curves, the expected rate of return would be higher, although Table 3.3 indicates that historically this difference has not been as great as commonly perceived.

3.1.2 Retirement Plans in Higher Education

The college and university community consists of slightly over 1.5 million employees: 56 percent faculty and administrative personnel, and 44 percent clerical and service workers. These people work in roughly 2,000 two- and four-year institutions of significant size operating under both public and private auspices. Although the nature of the retirement provisions depends crucially on the status of the institution and the employee, some generalizations are possible.

3.1.2.1. Social Security

Almost all members of the college and university community are covered by social security. This means that they can move from job to job and continue to build up benefits that keep pace with the growth in their earnings. After retirement, a progressive benefit formula provides relatively larger benefits to lower paid workers and annual cost-of-living adjustments ensure that benefits keep pace with prices. Married couples with a nonworking spouse will receive additional benefits and surviving spouses will be assured a continued stream of retirement income. Social security coverage also offers valuable protection in the event that a breadwinner suffers a long-term disability.

The only exception to the nearly universal coverage is a small group of college and university employees who are part of the 30 percent of state and local employees not currently participating in the system. This lack of coverage creates two types of problems. First, no other existing pension plans offer the broad protection provided under social security. Most state and local defined benefit plans have either five- or ten-year vesting requirements, so mobile employees with less than this amount of service must forfeit all rights to earned pension credits. Moreover, since employer-sponsored plans usually have strictly wage-related benefit formulas, low-wage employees receive no special subsidies to retirement income. Since state and local plans provide only limited cost-of-living increases, retirees are exposed to the risk of declining real benefits in the face of inflation. Finally, employees not covered by social security are exposed to a variety of gaps in basic protection — most notably in the areas of survivor, disability, and postretirement medical insurance.

The lack of universal coverage also creates an equity problem. State and local employees can sometimes gain social security coverage as a result of a second career and be in a position to profit from the weighting in the social security benefit formula designed for low-wage earners. Since a worker's monthly earnings are calculated by averaging covered earnings over a typical working lifetime rather than over the actual years of covered employment, a high-wage earner with a short period of time in covered employment is not distinguished from an individual who worked a lifetime in covered employment at exceptionally low wages. Hence, a worker who achieves insured status under social security through moonlighting or a second career can qualify for heavily subsidized benefits.

Many of the state and local pension plans not participating in the social security program are located in New England. Public employees in Maine and Massachusetts are not covered by social security, while participants in Connecticut's Teachers' Retirement System also lack social security protection. Other states where employees in public colleges and universities lack coverage include Colorado, Illinois, Louisiana, Nevada, and Ohio.

3.1.2.2 Pension Benefits at Private Institutions

Approximately 30 percent of the 1.5 million employees in higher education work in private institutions. These private universities and, primarily four-year, colleges employ a somewhat greater number of faculty and administrators than clerical and service personnel. For both groups of employees, defined contribution pension plans provided through TIAA-CREF are by far the largest source of pension benefits (see Table 3.4).

3.1.2.2.1 Coverage. Coverage under TIAA-CREF is considerably more prevalent among the professional staff than among clerical and service workers, since nearly half the institu-

Table 3.4. Percentage of Employees in Higher
Education Covered by Various Types of Retirement Plans.

	Private Institutions		Public Institutions	
Type of Plan	Faculty and Administrative	Clerical and Service	Faculty and Administrative	Clerical and Service
State and Local Plans				
Teachers	6%	—	54%	30%
Public employees	—	—	35	61
TIAA-CREF	89	55	58	22
Self-funded or trusteed plan	7	36	6	13
Insurance company plan	5	18	10	7
Church pension plan	12	4	—	—
Addenda:				
Number of employees	247,000	191,000	618,000	480,000
Number of institutions	1,078		1,014	
Four-year	478		929	
Two-year	600		85	

Note: Percentages add to more than 100 because more than one plan may be reported by an institution for concurrent or alternative coverage.

Source: Estimates based on data provided by Francis P. King and Thomas J. Cook, Benefit Plans in Higher Education (New York: Columbia University Press, 1980), Tables 2A and 2B, pp. 276–277 and subsequent data. Used by permission.

tions restrict the participation in TIAA-CREF retirement plans to certain employee subgroups. For instance, 36 percent permit just faculty and administrative officers to participate, 8 percent cover only faculty members, and 5 percent provide coverage for all employees except the service staff. Moreover, even when clerical and service workers are covered, their participation is less likely to be required or automatic than is the case for faculty and administrators (see Table 3.5).

Table 3.5. Required Participation in TIAA-CREF by Class of Employee, 1984.

Class of Employee	Number of TIAA-CREF Plans	Percentage with Required Participation
Faculty	1,447	68%
Administrative	1,348	65
Clerical	822	45
Service	747	45

Source: TIAA-CREF, *Summary of Retirement Plan Provisions,* July 1, 1984, Tables B-1 and B-2. Used by permission.

Faculty members and administrative staff may join the TIAA-CREF retirement plan immediately upon employment under roughly half the plans, the rest report a waiting period that depends on age or years of service or both. The situation is different for clerical and service workers, who face age and service requirements for participation under most TIAA-CREF plans. Only 18 percent of the plans that cover these workers offer immediate participation (see Table 3.6).

3.1.2.2.2 Contributions. Institutions using TIAA-CREF plans usually adopt one of two approaches when establishing contribution rates: the level percentage approach in which the contribution rate is a uniform percent of salary, or, the step-rate approach in which a higher contribution rate is applied to the portion of salary above the social security wage base than below. The level percentage approach is the most popular (being used by 81 percent of the plans covering 70 percent of the

Table 3.6. Waiting Period for Participation in TIAA-CREF Plans, 1984.

	Number of TIAA-CREF Plans	Immediate Participation	Percentage of Plans with				
			Years of Service Without Age Requirements			Age 25 and/or 1 or more Years of Service	Other[a]
			1	2	3		
Faculty	1,447	52%	15%	6%	4%	14%	10%
Administrative	1,348	48	16	6	4	15	10
Clerical	822	18	21	8	9	28	14
Service	747	18	21	7	12	28	14

[a]Primarily age thirty or one year of service or both; ERISA amendments now require the age to be no later than twenty-six.

Source: TIAA-CREF, Summary of Retirement Plan Provisions, Tables C-1, C-2, C-3, and C-4 (July 1, 1984). Used by permission.

participants), and among institutions using this approach the most common combined contribution rate is 10 percent (see Table 3.7). In terms of numbers of participants, however, contribution rates of 12 percent and 15 percent are either equally or more prevalent. This discrepancy suggests that the 10 percent plans must be more common at smaller colleges and universities with fewer plan participants.

Table 3.7. Contribution Rates in TIAA Plans — Level Percentage Approach.

Level Contribution Rate	Percentage of	
	Level Plans	Participants in Level Plans
Under 10 percent	8.9%	6.4%
10 percent	34.4	17.8
10.1–11.9 percent	5.1	3.7
12–12.9 percent	17.6	16.3
13–13.9 percent	6.2	9.3
14–14.9 percent	4.9	9.9
15 percent	14.0	29.6
Above 15 percent	8.9	7.1
Addenda:		
Level plans as percentage of total plans — 81.2 percent		
Participants in level plans as percentage of total participants — 70.0 percent		

Source: *TIAA-CREF College and University Retirement Plan Provisions, 1984,* Table E-1, p. vii. Used by permission.

For the majority of plans and participants, contributions are paid jointly by the institutions and the employees. Data for faculty indicate that the most common arrangement under both level and step-rate plans is for the employer to pay a larger share. On the other hand, 20 percent of participants are covered by plans in which the employer pays the entire cost and another 20 percent belong to plans in which the contributions are shared equally.

3.1.2.2.3 Assessment of TIAA-CREF Plans. Vesting: A particular advantage of the TIAA-CREF plans is that they are vested quickly, since even in those instances when participation is contingent upon age or service requirements, the delay is never more than three years. In addition, as with any defined contribution plan, the covered employee can move from one job to another without suffering any loss in the value of accrued benefits; hence, the mobility of faculty and staff covered by these plans is in no way impaired.

Limited coverage: One concern with existing TIAA-CREF arrangements is that many participating institutions have elected not to extend coverage automatically to clerical and service workers, and often when the institutions do cover these workers, they make participation optional rather than mandatory. Since many individuals are reluctant to plan ahead for retirement, many may well choose not to participate in a pension program that requires them to contribute some of their current income; the lack of universal and mandatory coverage may leave many clerical and service workers with inadequate retirement benefits.

Risk: The second concern with TIAA-CREF plans, which is typical of any defined contribution pension, is that the individual rather than the employer bears the entire risk associated with poor investment performance. This risk is accompanied by the responsibility to make major decisions concerning the allocation of accumulated funds. These decisions represent a considerable burden for plan participants, who are often unaware of the basic risk and return characteristics associated with different types of financial assets. Moreover, the burden is excacerbated by the relatively little information on investment risk provided by TIAA-CREF.

Limited transfer of funds: A third concern, unique to TIAA-CREF, is that although individuals bear the risk of their investment decisions, they do not have the right to transfer their accumulated funds freely among investment vehicles within TIAA-CREF and are prohibited from transferring their funds to another custodian. This lack of flexibility severely limits the amount of competition among custodians, which may result in less than maximum possible returns on invested assets or in adequate reporting and other ancillary services. At the same time, the participants' inability to transfer money from TIAA to

CREF, the result, in part, of the nonmarketable character of much of the TIAA-CREF portfolio, prevents investors from making major changes in the allocation of their assets.

Disincentive to retire: A fourth concern is that TIAA-CREF plans, like all defined contribution plans, create strong incentives to postpone retirement. Since additional investment income and contributions can substantially increase the value of accumulated pension "wealth" and the amount of the annuity payment is actuarially adjusted for the age of retirement, participants can often double their monthly benefit by working an additional five years. Given recent demographic pressures, this incentive to postpone retirement could have an adverse impact on the age profile of college and university faculty.

In the late 1960s and 1970s, higher education faculties expanded to accommodate the needs of the baby-boom generation. However, the 1980s have witnessed a decreasing population of eighteen to twenty-one year olds, and at the same time an increased number of Ph.D.s entering the job market. Since tenured faculty rarely leave their positions, the decrease in the required number of academic slots to educate the declining college-age population precludes opportunities for many young professors. If tenured faculty should be induced through the provisions of defined contribution pension plans to postpone retirement to an even later date, little opportunity will be preserved to take advantage of a new generation of ideas associated with young professors.

As a result, a number of early retirement incentive plans have been developed to encourage older faculty to retire. These plans can be either *ad hoc* or formula arrangements by which a college and a faculty member agree on an earlier-than-normal retirement. Both the *ad hoc* and formula plans usually make financial arrangements in one of four ways: lump-sum payments, increased pension contributions, phased retirement, or bridge plans.

Under a lump-sum arrangement, the faculty member accepts a bonus for retiring early, usually some percentage of base pay. Under an increased pension contribution plan, the college or university makes up for all or a portion of pension contributions that are lost because of early retirement by increasing the institution's pension contribution over several years prior to retirement. A phased retirement plan allows faculty members to reduce their responsibilities to part-time, often without a proportional reduction in salary. A bridge plan differs from the above three in that it attempts to replace much of the retiree's after-tax income in the period between early and normal retirement, at which time the retiree begins to collect his or her normal pension annuity. Employers are finding that these types of early retirement incentive plans, if properly structured and tailored to the institution's individual needs, can be an effective method of dealing with the age composition of the faculty.

Vulnerability to inflation: The final issue is the amount of the benefit provided under the TIAA-CREF plans and its ability to keep pace with inflation over the period of retirement. The typical contribution rate (10 percent to 15 percent) at participating institutions should provide an initial benefit, which, when combined with social security and individual saving, will enable full career employees to continue the same living standard in retirement as they enjoyed while working. Indeed, results of a survey of faculty and administrators conducted by the commission confirms that most people will begin retirement with enough income to satisfy their retirement goals (see Table 3.8). (Of course, clerical and service employees who do not have a lifetime of pension contributions will not be able to achieve the goal of maintaining preretirement living standards.)

TIAA-CREF has been an innovator in annuity design through its introduction of the TIAA graded benefit payment method annuity and the CREF variable annuity. In establishing CREF in 1952, TIAA responded imaginatively to the emerging concern about future inflation. CREF was the first institution to provide a variable annuity, which, through investing in common stocks, was designed to provide some protection against inflation and the opportunity for higher yields than the more conservative investments typical of pension plans and insurance companies at that time. The current offer by TIAA of the graded benefit payment method annuity and the opportunity to start portions of an annuity at different dates are also important options for meeting part of the threat of future inflation.

Table 3.8. Percentage of Survey Participants Who
Will Achieve Retirement Goals, by Year of
Retirement, with 4 Percent Postretirement Inflation Rate.

Percentage of Retirement Goal Achieved	Year of Retirement				
	1st year	5th year	10th year	15th year	20th year
0–50	6.4%	3.5%	4.0%	10.6%	19.3%
50–60	1.9	2.0	2.8	3.8	4.8
60–70	2.6	2.7	4.7	5.8	6.0
70–80	3.1	3.9	5.9	6.5	7.1
80–90	2.8	5.4	5.3	8.2	8.0
90–100	5.1	6.4	8.8	7.4	7.8
100 +	78.2	76.1	68.7	57.7	47.1

Source: Commission survey.

However, unlike social security, TIAA-CREF and most other private pension plans do not provide fully indexed annuities. Also, few TIAA annuities choose the graded benefit payment option. Therefore, even those who start retirement with adequate income are likely to see the purchasing power of that money eroded over the years by inflation. The magnitude of this erosion will relate directly to how well the financial instruments in which a given plan has invested have kept up with the rate of inflation. As shown in the exercise presented in Table 3.8, even though 78 percent of those persons included in the commission survey are projected to meet their retirement goals in the first year of retirement, this figure would drop to 58 percent after fifteen years in retirement even if prices increase only at the moderate rate of 4 percent.

3.1.2.2.4 Summary of Defined Contribution Plans. In short, while many employees in private colleges and universities are able to accumulate a substantial supplementary benefit through TIAA-CREF, several problems remain. First, many clerical and service personnel are not covered automatically under these plans. Second, participants bear considerable financial risk, and the amount of the initial benefit can vary considerably depending on the investment performance of the portfolio. Third, although the risk is borne by individuals, they are severely constrained in their ability to move funds within TIAA-CREF and to shift funds among custodians. Finally, even those participants who receive an adequate initial benefit face the specter of a serious decline in purchasing power as inflation erodes the real value of the unindexed annuity payment. Another potential problem that could arise under a defined contribution plan is the incentive to postpone retirement, since it is possible by working a few extra years dramatically to increase monthly benefits. This problem, however, seems to be countered by the early retirement incentive programs that have been introduced at a number of institutions.

3.1.2.3 Pension Benefits at Public Institutions

Roughly 70 percent of employees in higher education work at public colleges and universities. As in the private sector, over half of the total are faculty or administrative officers. While public and private institutions are roughly equal in number, they differ sharply in character. Public institutions tend to consist of many more two-year colleges and on average tend to be considerably larger than private institutions.

3.1.2.3.1 Coverage and Benefits Under Public Defined Benefit Plans. The majority of employees in public colleges and universities are covered by pension plans sponsored by state or local governments. Faculty and administrative officers tend to belong to systems designed specifically for teachers, while clerical and service workers generally belong to plans for all public employees (see Table 3.4).

Most public retirement systems are of the defined benefit type. Benefits are usually determined by three factors — a percentage factor, a final average salary, and years of credited service — which, when multiplied together, yield the monthly benefit amount. A survey by TIAA-CREF of the sixty-five major defined benefit plans covering public colleges and universities showed that benefits were usually based on the highest three years (forty systems) or the highest five years (twenty systems) of earnings. The most common percentage factor used by these systems was

2 percent per year of service (twenty-two systems). Hence, under the typical plan, an employee with thirty years of service would receive benefits equal to 60 percent of final pay.

The variety of percentage factors used by other plans range from 1.1 percent to 2.5 percent. In addition, fifteen plans apply different factors to different salary levels and to different periods of service, generally giving greater value to later years of employment. As a result, replacement rates for the major public defined benefit plans range from a low of 26 percent in the Maryland state pension system to a high of 74 percent in the Louisiana state systems for a person with an average final salary of $15,000. The two Louisiana systems do not, however, participate in social security. Of those that do participate, the Wyoming Retirement, the Texas Teachers' Retirement System, and the New York systems provide the largest replacement rates with no offset for social security benefits.

Almost all the public retirement systems covering employees in public institutions of higher education are financed jointly by the employer and the employee. The most common employee contribution is 3 percent of pay, with some systems requiring contributions as high as 9.5 percent. In the latter cases, the systems do not participate in social security so that a portion of the contribution could be thought of as a substitute for the employee's social security tax.

3.1.2.3.2 Assessment of Public Defined Benefit Plans.

Assurance of benefits: The most obvious advantage of public retirement systems is that for the long-term employee, they guarantee a substantial and predictable benefit. Since benefits are expressed as a percentage of earnings just prior to retirement, employees have a clear idea of the contribution that their public pension benefit will make toward maintaining their preretirement standard of living. In contrast to defined contribution plans, the investment risk under defined benefit plans is borne by the plan sponsor, who is responsible for all investment decisions.

From the perspective of public policy, some might argue that benefits by some public retirement systems for full-career employees are excessive; occasionally they allow participants to enter retirement with incomes which, when combined with social security and individual saving, exceed those enjoyed while working. This concern, however, must be weighed against the likely decline in purchasing power over the retirement period as inflation erodes the value of nominal benefits that, at best, are only partially indexed for inflation. Roughly half of the state and local plans that cover employees in public institutions of higher education adjust benefits automatically for changes in the consumer price index, but these adjustments are usually subject to a cap, typically of 3 percent (see Table 3.9). The rest of the public plans provide either occasional cost-of-living increases or none at all. Hence, the erosion of the value of benefits after retirement continues to be a problem under most public defined benefit plans. The problems can be particularly severe for those participants not covered by social security, since they will not have even a portion of their retirement income fully protected against inflation.

Lack of portability: In contrast to full-career employees who may fare well under public retirement plans, those who change jobs usually forfeit substantial benefit claims under defined benefit plans. Most of the public systems that cover employees have either a five- or ten-year vesting provision, so that participants who leave before this requirement has been satisfied lose all rights to benefits. These delayed vesting provisions not only undermine the financial security of public employees but also serve to impede labor mobility.

While vested employees have less to lose from changing jobs than do those who are not vested, they will still receive a lower benefit as a result of moving than they would have received from continuous coverage in a single plan. This difference arises because pension benefits are based on final earnings levels. Thus, employees who remain with the plan will receive benefits related to earnings just before retirement, while benefits for mobile employees will be based on their earnings each time they terminated employment. The magnitude of this effect depends on the rate at which earnings rise over the course of the employee's work life. If wages rise 4 percent, the pension received by workers who held four jobs during their lives would equal 61 percent of the pension received by workers continuously employed by one firm (see Table 3.10). If wages increase by 8 percent annually, the relative position of mobile employees would deteriorate further, so that their benefit would be worth only 44 percent of that awarded to the one-job employee. Thus, the higher the wage growth, the more discontinuous employment reduces the real value of benefits. This erosion occurs because benefits are not indexed between termination of employment and retirement. This lack of indexing, like delayed vesting, impedes the ability of faculty and other employees to move freely from job to job.

Inadequate funding: One last problem that can arise in connection with defined benefit plans is lack of adequate funding. Although most public pension plans are responsibly financed, several major plans have accumulated large unfunded liabilities. In Massachusetts, for example, these liabilities exceed $10 billion and represent a significant claim on future tax resources. With the enormous projected increase in pension costs, continued underfunding could lead to situations in which legislators may have to choose between raising taxes to confiscatory limits or reneging on benefit commitments to public employees.

Moreover, with such large pension burdens in the offing, one would think that states and localities could not afford either benefit increases without price tags or assets that are not invested at maximum returns. However, current reporting, disclosure, and fiduciary standards do not insure against either outcome. The actuarial reports for many of the individual systems are so complicated, the use of terms so ambiguous, and the assumptions so variable, that it is impossible to discern the cost impact of a change in benefit provisions. Similarly, none of the financial reports provide the market value data for the accumulated pension assets with historical information that would allow officials to evaluate the effectiveness of the financial managers.

3.1.2.3.3 Summary of Public Defined Benefit Plans. The defined benefit plans in the public sector, which serve as the major source of pensions for employees at public colleges and universities, provide full-career employees with generous and

Table 3.9. Cost-of-living Adjustment Provisions for State and Local Pension Plans.

Name of System	Frequency of increase	Based On	Maximum increase	Remarks
Alaska Public Employees Retirement System	Annual	CPI	4.0% or actual CPI if less	Contingent on financial experience of the fund
Alaska Teachers' Retirement System ...	Annual	CPI	4.0% or actual CPI if less	Contingent on financial experience of the fund
California Public Employees' Retirement System	Annual	CPI	2.0%	Automatic
University of California Retirement System ...	Annual	CPI	Matches CPI to 2.0%; 1/3 of increase between 4.0% and 8.5%	Automatic
Colorado Public Employees' Retirement Association	Annual	CPI	3.0%	Automatic; CPI increase over 3% accumulated for following years
Connecticut Teachers' Retirement System	Annual	CPI	5.0%	Automatic

System	Frequency	Index	Limit	Type
Florida Retirement System	Annual	CPI	3.0%	Automatic
Georgia Teachers' Retirement System ...	Every 6 months	CPI	1.5%	Automatic
Idaho Public Employees' Retirement System ...	Annual	CPI	6.0%	1.0% automatic, remaining increase contingent on experience of the fund
Louisiana State Employees' Retirement System	Annual	Difference between current CPI and that of two years earlier	3.0%	Automatic
Maine State Retirement System	Annual	CPI	4.0%	Automatic
Maryland State Pension System	Annual	CPI	3.0% for regular plan	Automatic
Massachusetts State Board of Retirement ..	Annual, contingent on a CPI increase of at least 3.0%	CPI	Determined by legislature	Contingent on financial experience of the fund

Table 3.9. Cost-of-living Adjustment Provisions for State and Local Pension Plans, Cont'd.

Name of System	Frequency of increase	Based On	Maximum increase	Remarks
Mississippi Public Employees' Retirement System	Annual	CPI	2.5%	Automatic
Missouri Public School Retirement System	Annual	CPI	4.0%	Automatic; total increase limited to 32% of original benefit
Missouri State Employees' Retirement System	Annual	CPI	5.0%	Automatic; total increase limited to 50% of total benefit
New Jersey Public Employees' Retirement System	Annual	CPI	⅔ of CPI	Automatic
New Mexico Educational Retirement System	Annual	⅔ of CPI	2.0%	Automatic
North Carolina Teachers' and State Employees' Retirement System	Annual	CPI	Determined by legislature	Contingent on financial experience of the fund

System	Frequency	Basis	Cap	Type
Ohio Public Employees' Retirement System	Annual, contingent on a CPI increase of at least 3.0%	CPI	3.0%	Automatic; CPI increase over 3% accumulated for following years
Ohio State Teachers' Retirement System	Annual, contingent on a CPI increase of at least 3.0%	CPI	3.0%	Automatic; CPI increase over 3% accumulated for following years
Oregon Public Employees' Retirement System	Annual	CPI	2.0%	Automatic
South Carolina Retirement System	Annual, contingent on a CPI increase of at least 3.0%	CPI	4.0%	Automatic
South Dakota Retirement System	Annual	CPI	3.0%	Automatic
Tennessee Consolidated Retirement System	Annual, contingent on a CPI increase of at least 1.0%	CPI	3.0%	Automatic

Table 3.9. Cost-of-living Adjustment Provisions for State and Local Pension Plans, Cont'd.

Name of System	Frequency of increase	Based On	Maximum increase	Remarks
United States Civil Service System	Annual	CPI	CPI	Automatic
Utah State Retirement System	Annual, contingent on a CPI increase of at least 4.0%	CPI	4.0%	Automatic, CPI increase over 4% accumulated for following years
Virginia Supplemental Retirement System	Annual	CPI	Matches CPI to 3.0%; half of increase between 3.0% and 7.0%	Automatic
Washington Public Employees' Retirement System	Annual	CPI	3.0%	Automatic

Source: Public Retirement Systems, TIAA-CREF, 1985. Used by permission.

Table 3.10. Comparison of Benefits for a Four-Job Worker and a One-Job Worker.

Item	Compensation base: final pay[a]	Compensation rule (percent of salary)[b]	Benefits	Ratio of benefits: four-job/one-job worker
Wage Growth: 0 percent				
Four-job worker[c]				
Job 1	$ 10,000	10%	$ 1,000	—
Job 2	10,000	10	1,000	—
Job 3	10,000	10	1,000	—
Job 4	10,000	10	1,000	—
Total	—	40	4,000	—
One-job worker	10,000	40	4,000	1.00
Wage Growth: 4 percent				
Four-job worker[c]				
Job 1	14,802	10	1,480	—
Job 2	21,911	10	2,191	—
Job 3	32,434	10	3,243	—
Job 4	48,010	10	4,801	—
Total	—	40	11,715	—
One-job worker	48,010	40	19,204	.61
Wage Growth: 8 percent				
Four-job worker[c]				
Job 1	21,589	10	2,159	—
Job 2	46,609	10	4,661	—
Job 3	100,626	10	10,063	—
Job 4	217,243	10	21,724	—
Total	—	40	38,607	—
One-job worker	217,243	40	86,897	0.44

[a]Base salary is $10,000 and benefit is calculated on earnings in last year of employment.
[b]Assumes annual benefit accrual of 1 percent a year.
[c]Assumes worker stays at each job for ten years.

Source: Alicia H. Munnell, *The Economics of Private Pensions* (The Brookings Institution, 1982), Table 7-2, p. 176. Used by permission.

predictable retirement benefits that are frequently at least partially indexed for inflation after retirement. On the other hand, employees who change jobs several times are forced to forfeit accrued pension credits either because of delayed vesting requirements or because inflation erodes the value of terminated vested benefits. The potential loss facing a person thinking of shifting jobs can only serve to impede mobility and leaves those who do move with inadequate retirement incomes. A final element of uncertainty is introduced by a handful of public pension plans that are seriously underfunded, yet little information is provided on a regular basis to monitor the status of these funds.

3.1.2.4 TIAA-CREF for Employees at Public Institutions

In addition to publicly sponsored defined benefit plans, 385 institutions also permit concurrent or alternative participation in TIAA-CREF, and at 171 public institutions TIAA-CREF is the only plan offered (see Table 3.11). As a result, 58 percent of faculty and administrative officers and 22 percent of the clerical and service personnel at public colleges and universities are covered by TIAA-CREF.

3.1.3 Conclusion

The conclusion that emerges from this brief survey of pension provisions is that, despite great progress, many employees of colleges and universities fail to achieve the commission's goal of maintaining preretirement living standards throughout their retirement. Some people who work for state or local institutions still lack the basic protection offered through a fully indexed and portable retirement plan such as social security. Others, primarily clerical and service employees, have social security coverage but are not participants in any kind of employer pension plan. Those who participate in defined contribution plans may expose themselves to unnecessary risk through poor choice of investments as they approach retirement and end up with an inadequate initial benefit. College and university employees

Table 3.11. Public Institutions with TIAA-CREF Plans, 1985.

State	TIAA-CREF Supplements Public Plan	TIAA-CREF Is Alternative to Public Plan	TIAA-CREF Is the Single Plan
Alabama	7		
Arizona		3	
Arkansas		17	
Colorado			5
Connecticut		25	
Delaware			1
District of Columbia			4
Florida	1	11	
Indiana		3	3
Iowa			3
Kansas			10
Kentucky			3
Maine			9
Maryland		36	
Michigan		7	6
Minnesota		6	
Nebraska			15
Nevada			8
New Hampshire			4
New Jersey			33
New York		88	
North Carolina	1	17	
North Dakota			12
Oklahoma	4		
Oregon		9	
Pennsylvania		30	3
Rhode Island			3
Tennessee		27	
Texas		66	
Utah			8
Vermont			6
Virginia		1	
Washington			35
West Virginia		17	
Wyoming		9	
Total	13	372	171

Source: Summaries of TIAA-CREF Retirement Plan Provisions at Public Colleges and Universities, July 1985, Page IV. Used by permission.

and their spouses who are beneficiaries of the TIAA-CREF program, while bearing the risk of investment returns on their accumulations, are not now given the right to transfer their accumulated funds freely within TIAA-CREF and are prohibited from transferring their funds to another custodian. In the case of those covered by public sector defined benefit plans, employees who switch jobs frequently see their accrued pension benefits eroded by inflation. Finally, even those people who do arrive at retirement with an adequate initial benefit, whether from a defined benefit or a defined contribution plan, are likely to see the purchasing power of that benefit decline over time in the face of rising prices.

In Section 3.2, the commission puts forth several recommendations aimed at closing some of the major gaps in protection. These proposals take the form of modifying the plans already in place rather than advocating the establishment of a new pension system. The commission's recommendations are designed to ensure an adequate retirement income, a goal consistent with the interests of both the institution and the employees, without unduly interfering with the freedoms of the individual participants or unduly burdening the colleges and universities.

3.2

The Recommendations

The commission has developed several recommendations designed to enable the retirement systems of colleges and universities better to meet the goals outlined in the previous sections. Existing institutional arrangements for providing pensions have been taken into account in these recommendations. The commission has not attempted to choose between defined benefit and defined contribution approaches, both of which cover hundreds of thousands of college and university personnel and both of which have advantages and disadvantages. Rather, the commission has taken the continued existence of both as a given and has made suggestions to improve both types of pension plans.

It is in the collective interest of the faculty, staff, and administration to have former employees live in dignity and with at least minimum resources. Almost all college and university employees will receive social security benefits, and that income will serve as a base of support during retirement.

Since individual circumstances and financial needs differ, there should be allowance for flexibility in designing pension plans. For this reason, the commission believes that the optimum pension should be divided into two parts. The first is a core pension (Recommendation 1), compulsory, prudently invested, and restricted to payout in annuitized form. It also should be at least partially indexed for inflation (Recommendation 2). The second part, which we call the supplementary pension (Recommendation 3), should allow additional choice of investment and payout options (Recommendation 4), a subject that has been addressed in an earlier commission report. In addition, better financial planning and information services are called for (Recommendation 5) to assist individuals and families in better meeting their specific retirement income needs. With these first five recommendations, the commission presents a new approach to pension planning for college and university employees: an *individualized, flexible, target benefit approach.* Greater flexibility and improved information combine to assist employees better to meet their goals in retirement.

The remaining recommendations address the need for improved portability and standards for funding, reporting, and disclosure for defined benefit plans (Recommendations 6 and 7). The need to extend social security coverage is addressed in the last recommendation.

1. *All employees of colleges and universities should be participants in a minimum or core pension plan whose accumulations should be invested prudently and whose benefits should be paid out in the form of a lifetime annuity.*

The fraction of income contributed to the core pension in defined contribution plans or the formula relating benefit to income and years of service in defined benefit plans will and should vary from institution to institution. Although each institution and its staff should determine appropriate levels, some rules of thumb may be useful.

For most defined contribution plans, the current contribution rate is 10 percent or more of pay. This level of contribution, when combined with social security, could yield a substantially inflation-protected benefit equal to about 55 to 60 percent of final pay, although the calculation is sensitive to the length of the career and the real rate of return on investment. A ten-percent-of-pay plan can probably meet the *minimum* standards for a core pension plan for many institutions. While the commission recommends that greater choice of investment vehicles than now offered through TIAA-CREF be made available for core pension contributions, it would be appropriate for institutions to require that contributed funds be invested prudently. Institutions could use criteria such as fund size, type of fund, performance record of fund managers and volatility of returns to determine the appropriateness of various funds for core pension contributions.

For individuals in defined benefit plans, the relationship between benefits and final pay depends crucially on their career paths. For guideline purposes, however, a formula that provided an initial benefit equal to 1 percent of final pay per year of service would provide an initial salary replacement rate of 25 to 35 percent for long-service staff. This initial benefit, however, would be an adequate core benefit only if it were substantially indexed for inflation. Without such indexation, an initial benefit of at least 1.5 percent of final pay per year would be necessary, in addition to full social security benefits.

The commission feels that the adequacy of the core pension benefit is the joint interest of the college or university and the participant. We, therefore, recommend that the payout at retirement be limited to lifetime annuities with the exception of a small amount (TIAA-CREF allows 10 percent of accumulated funds) that could be available as a cash settlement at retirement. The *Joint Statement of Principles on Academic Retirement* of the American Association of University Professors (AAUP) and the Association of American Colleges (AAC) states a retirement plan "should be such that participants may receive the accumulated funds only in the form of an annuity. Exceptions might be made for (i) small proportions of the accumulations of retiring participants or (ii) small accumulations in inactive accounts." The commission concurs with the AAUP-AAC statement of principles for *core pension plan amounts*.

2. *Equally important to setting the initial pension benefit is establishing a mechanism to offset the effect of inflation in eroding the purchasing power of benefits over the period of retirement. Several partial solutions are available for adjusting benefits to inflation, and one of these should be used by all providers of core pension benefits. Full indexing would require that the government issue index bonds, an option that merits further study.*

The high initial income levels that can be offered with

fixed nominal annuities such as those offered by commercial insurance companies or the so-called level-payment method annuity offered by TIAA-CREF are misleading, since the value of the benefits is likely to be eroded by inflation. Inflation can cause the value of the pension to shrink dramatically over the period of retirement. Even with a relatively modest inflation rate of 4 percent, the value of the pension fifteen years into retirement is worth only half what it was at the beginning. Thus, inflation protection is very important to the security of the retired individual, yet complete protection against inflation is difficult to attain in a private plan. The trade-off is of the likelihood of much lower average yields under an inflation-protected plan. For example, Treasury bills have tracked inflation better than common stocks, but the real return has been close to zero, whereas over a long period of time, common stock returns have averaged the rate of inflation plus 6 percent. A zero percent interest rate for an annuity invested in Treasury bills would require the participant to start with an income reduced from the CREF rate by about 30 percent, although this income would follow the cost of living much more closely. For some, full cost-of-living protection may not be worth such a penalty.

The only way to insure full protection against inflation would be for the United States government to offer index bonds as is done in the United Kingdom. This possibility should be studied further, although, as in the case of Treasury bills, the return would likely be less than the long-term average yield for common stocks.

Alternatives for *partial* indexing currently available to defined contribution plans include the graded benefit annuity offered by TIAA. Under this annuity, initial payments are lower but payments increase during the retirement years. This option is imperfect, because it is little more than a method of deferring initial payments, but it is a useful way of patterning the benefits to reflect expected inflation. Fewer than 2 percent of new annuitants, however, choose this option each year.

TIAA-CREF also offers participants the option to annuitize portions of their accumulated assets at different dates.

For example, one could annuitize one-third of accumulations at age sixty-five, another one-third at sixty-eight, and the final one-third at age seventy. The nonannuitized portion of the portfolio is implicitly performance indexed until it is converted to an annuity. This option of multiple settlement dates allows the participant substantial flexibility in patterning the payout in retirement. Unfortunately, as with the graded benefit option, multiple settlement dates are underutilized, possibly because of a lack of publicity and understanding of the option.

TIAA-CREF has clearly been a leader in offering flexible forms of annuities. The CREF variable annuity, the graded benefit payment annuity plans, and the multiple settlement date options are all useful and partially overcome the inflation protection problem. To encourage greater utilization of these approaches, TIAA-CREF beneficiaries and those in other pension plans should receive annual illustrations showing both graded payment annuity projections and projections showing the declining purchasing power of fixed or level-payment method annuities during their anticipated retirement years. Further, TIAA and other annuity providers should offer graded payment options or an annuity with a similar purpose as the standard option — the option that would be used in the absence of a specific decision by the retiree to choose another payment method. None of them offers complete protection, however. Given the magnitude of the sacrifice in expected return necessary to gain almost complete inflation protection, many people may choose one of these partial solutions. Individuals differ in their tolerance of risk, and there may be merit in offering a low-yield, highly inflation-protected alternative. Even the standard option should either have a graduated structure of benefits or be performance indexed.

Most defined benefit plans are in public institutions. Most states have only limited inflation indexing (usually with a ceiling of 3 percent) and should consider increasing protection. The contributions to and investment policies of state plans should be based on providing adequate inflation protection for the core pension.

3. *In addition to the core pension, supplementary pension plans*

*of maximum flexibility should be offered to all employees to enable them
to meet and sustain their target retirement benefit, such as the benefit, which
when combined with other sources of retirement income, will allow them
to maintain their preretirement standards of living.*

The core pension as envisioned in the first recommendation offers only the basic supplement to social security. Together they are not seen as being sufficient, in most cases, to provide for full replacement of the preretirement standard of living of the employee. Many institutions and most individuals will find it desirable to supplement the core portion of the plan with additional contributions and benefits.

The delineation of core and supplementary pensions is based on the commission's view of the collective interest of the institution to insure at least a minimally adequate retirement income supplement to social security. Some institutions may wish to do more than provide this minimum supplement. They may wish to contribute 15 percent of pay to a defined contribution plan such as TIAA-CREF, an amount that would provide a nearly complete maintenance of preretirement living standards for the average, full-career employee. Other institutions may wish to have an employer contribution of 10 percent matched by an employee contribution of 5 percent to reach this goal.

The initial setting of the supplementary contribution rate should be based on a target earning replacement rate and retirement date. Because of the variation in investment results, it is impossible to set the contribution rate necessary to achieve individual targets with much precision.

Since a contribution of approximately 10 percent of pay will likely provide a minimally adequate retirement income for the average full-career employee, institutions should permit greater flexibility in the investment and payout options on funds resulting from contributions above this amount. Employees should be permitted the maximum amount of discretion permitted by law for investment and payout flexibility for this part of the retirement benefit as long as reasonable administrative arrangements can be made.

For participants in defined contribution plans, for whom the ratio of retirement income to final pay (the "replacement rate") is heavily dependent on investment return, the supplemental part offers an opportunity to provide more carefully for retirement. During the accumulation phase, if it appears that the core plan will not meet retirement goals, the participant can increase the amount in the supplementary plan. If, on the other hand, it appears that income from the plans will be more than sufficient to meet the goals, then the employee can reduce or eliminate the supplementary plan contribution, or even turn some of the assets into cash.

Although supplementary pensions are most valuable to people in defined contribution plans, they can also be very useful for people in defined benefit plans, particularly for those who move among institutions. They can be helpful to those whose circumstances are such that the basic plan does not meet their retirement needs.

4. *The accumulated core pension money should be transferable between alternative funds offered by a given vendor and across vendors at the request of both the participant and the college or university. Transfer and payment of supplementary funds should be made at the sole option of the participant. These recommendations require that TIAA-CREF alter its policy regarding transferability of cash accumulations between its two funds and to other vendors.*

The advantages of transferability are several. First, it permits the participant and the college or university to alter investments as circumstances change. Second, it puts constructive competitive pressure on each vendor if all accumulated funds are at all times subject to transfer. Moreover, if both the college or university and the participant request a transfer of the funds, the relevant trust law appears to require that such a transfer be accomplished. These issues are discussed in Part One of this volume.

5. *Financial information and planning services should be made available to employees to enable them to make better decisions regarding the level, composition, investment, and payout of their pension accumulations. Services should also be made available to institutions to help them select the most appropriate pension program for their campuses.*

A shortcoming of defined contribution plans is that the participant is uncertain about the amount of money that will be available in retirement. This problem is seriously exacerbated by the paucity of information exchanged between the participant and the trustee of the plan. In addition to increasing exchange of information between the pension plan and the beneficiary, third party financial planning information should prove useful for many employees.

Periodically (with increasing frequency as retirement approaches), the participants should receive a statement that compares actual investment performance with that necessary to achieve the target. The statement would project outcomes based on assumed yields and on an unchanged supplementary contribution rate. The statement should also project social security benefits giving the participant a better idea of combined resources in retirement. This would alert participants as to whether they are undershooting or overshooting their target levels of benefits.

A new calculation of contribution rates necessary to reach the target should be issued with each statement, again with no guarantees made and some explicit discussion of yield variance. With these periodic progress reports, the participants would be given information on both the projected consequences of not altering their contribution rates and on the rate change necessary to match the projections with the target replacement rates.

The projections could be more accurate and the resources in retirement more predictable if the participant gradually shifts to a less risky portfolio as retirement approaches. This would normally involve a reduction in the fraction of the portfolio invested in common stocks. The benefit of such a decreased reliance on stocks is the reduced portfolio risk, while the cost is the lower expected return of the alternative assets. It is a trade-off that may be worthwhile for many, but not all, of those approaching retirement. Discussion of these issues would be one of the functions of the financial planning and information service.

In addition, participants should be provided illustrations showing the initial value of an annuity that is designed to maintain purchasing power throughout the retirement years. All projections could be stated in terms of reasonable ranges instead of point estimates in order to emphasize the uncertainty in future circumstances. The ranges on the projections could be narrower for those who are nearer retirement.

These statements could be provided by the sponsor of the pension plan or by a third party. They also could be part of a more comprehensive financial planning profile provided as an employee benefit by the institution. How best to provide these services is discussed more fully in a forthcoming commission report on implementing financial planning and information services.

6. *College and university employees covered by defined benefit plans who leave their jobs should receive a severance benefit based on expected salary at retirement rather than on salary at the time of termination of employment.*

People who change jobs frequently suffer serious losses under defined benefit plans. Even if benefits are fully and immediately vested, individuals receive significantly lower pensions as a result of moving among plans — even if they all are identical — than they would receive from continuous coverage in a single plan. This difference arises because pension benefits for a nonmobile employee are generally related to earnings just before retirement, while the mobile employee's benefits will be based on earnings each time he or she terminates employment.

There are a number of ways to eliminate the discrimination of defined benefit plans against mobile employees. All of them are costly. However, the commission feels that portability and mobility are important and that pension severance arrangements should not discourage job transfers. If job switching is not to be penalized, then either the pension received in retirement should be based on a salary projected to the time of retirement (rather than the salary at the time of job severance) or an amount of cash necessary to fund such a benefit should be rolled over into the new employer's retirement plan. Such cash rollovers would amount to a sum similar to what would have accumulated in an equivalent defined contribution plan.

7. *For defined benefit plans, standards should be established for pension funding, reporting, and disclosure.*

While all of the pension plans of college and university employees do not necessarily have to be subject to funding, reporting, and disclosure of requirements of the Employee Retirement Income Security Act of 1974, prudent standards should be set either by the federal government, by the states, or by an organization designated by institutions of higher education.

The promise of future pension benefits may prove of little value to participants if the plan is inadequately funded. Poor funding may lead to future benefit decreases or pension plan amendments that decrease the value of future benefit accruals or inadequate protection for inflation. This has happened in many public pension plans. Good reporting and disclosure requirements can insure that plan participants, their employers, and the public are aware of potential funding problems before such drastic measures are necessary.

8. *Social security coverage should be extended to those currently not participating in the system.*

As previously noted, since social security coverage is nearly universal, workers can move from job to job and continue to accrue benefits that keep pace with the growth in their earnings. After retirement, a progressive benefit formula provides relatively larger benefits to lower paid workers, and annual cost-of-living adjustments ensure that benefits keep pace with prices.

Extending social security coverage to those college and university employees who are among those state and local workers remaining outside the system would significantly enhance their level of benefit protection. Social security offers benefits that are fully adjusted for wage increases over the individual's work life and fully indexed for inflation after retirement. The complete indexing and portability of this system make it extremely valuable for mobile employees. Moreover, full survivor and disability protection is more quickly achieved under social security than under most public plans.

Part Four

A Plan to Create Comprehensive Group Long-Term Care Insurance for College and University Personnel

Security in retirement is more than a recurring monthly income; it is also the ability to meet highly unpredictable costs associated with illness and the need for long-term care. Medicare and Medicare supplements cover a large proportion of acute care expenses for older people. But because of the lack of public and private long-term insurance coverage, people who become disabled can experience great difficulty in paying for extended care. Most public funding of long-term care has come from state Medicaid programs, part of the welfare system.

Although many individuals use nursing home services at some time during their lives, the lifetime risk of suffering chronic functional disabilities requiring costly personal care of long duration is small. The cost can be devastating, however, for those who require such care. Disability replacement income does not go very far if it must be used for disability-related, long-term care.

Major long-term-care expenses are the most serious threat to the standard of living that employer pensions are designed to achieve for retirees. Long-term care is covered to only a limited extent by private health insurance for people under sixty-five, and by Medicare or private Medicare supplements for those sixty-five and over. Some private long-term-care insurance on an individual, voluntary basis is available, but it has met with low market reponse. The policies now on the market cover little of the home-delivered care that many people would prefer and limit nursing home coverage so that enrollees with the longest stays and highest costs are not fully protected. Those policies that do offer extended home-care benefits require prior nursing home care.

Recognizing the inadequacy of the existing methods that college retirees might use to finance long-term care, the commission supported the design and development of a new approach to this problem and contracted with the Brandeis University Health Policy Center to assist it. Under the direction of the commission, and to develop concepts put forward by the commission, the Health Policy Center's Long-Term-Care Group prepared the framework of a comprehensive long-term-care insurance plan.

The comprehensive long-term-care insurance plan outlined by the commission would protect against large long-term-care expenses for participants with substantial needs for disability-related services. Such long-term-care insurance would provide a means for employers to protect the value of the disability income and pension benefits they provide to employees and so would be a desirable addition to benefits for college employees and retirees. Lifetime coverage for long-duration home and nursing home care, purchased on a group basis during working years, could overcome many of the problems of current private insurance approaches.

Group coverage would drastically reduce sales and marketing costs, as well as the risk of adverse selection — the over-enrollment of individuals most likely to use insured services. Because of the large number of persons who would eventually be enrolled under such a group plan, it would be feasible to pay organizations to provide needed home and community-based services on a prospective basis. These providers, called *managed care organizations,* would supply patients with the home-delivered services they need, and with nursing home care if required. Through such a managed care approach, long-term home-care costs are most controllable; organizations liable for both nursing home and home-care use, and subject to cost constraints, can control the cost of home-delivered services and can keep costs below the cost of nursing home care. Finally, paying for long-term-care insurance as an employee benefit during working years could make insurance protection feasible during higher-risk retirement years.

The value of an employer-sponsored, prefunded, group approach to long-term-care insurance is put into perspective by considering the possibility of developing a publicly financed long-term-care insurance plan. The Brandeis Long-Term-Care Group, several of the commissioners, and many of the plan's reviewers and consultants would have preferred such a universal, publicly financed program — a program that might be implemented as an expansion of the Medicare program, for example. A universal pay-as-you-go public program could be more equitable and more efficient, and it could obviate a number of technical problems of the group insurance approach — problems such as portability, coverage of older persons during the transition phase, estimation of premiums needed to cover expenses subject to many future uncertainties, and vesting. However, no policy consensus for such a public program existed in 1986, and it was not clear when and if such a consensus might come about.

Therefore, the commission favored further development of this private group approach, and they hoped the detailed specification and cost estimates for a long-term-care insurance program (with desirable features such as coverage of comprehensive services at home, coverage of long-duration needs for nursing home and home care) could promote the evolution of a public plan — when and if such a plan received the necessary public support. The commission's proposed plan provided a model for colleges and universities seeking to protect their employees and retirees from an important uncovered risk.

The commission's approach to comprehensive group long-term-care insurance for college and university faculty and staff was conservative in its provisions and allowed considerable flexibility. A plan was designed to protect participants against the relatively small risk of becoming severely disabled and having to make large expenditures; they did not design it to purchase services that beneficiaries could finance themselves. Beneficiaries would have acccess to regular pension and social security income, so that they could be expected to pay a significant share of the cost. Thus, benefits would be allocated to participants who met stringent disability criteria, but only after the recipient had been disabled for a period of time.

Preliminary estimates of the present value of expected lifetime long-term-care expenses indicate that such a plan is affordable with monthly premiums, stated in real terms, falling into the range of ten to twenty dollars per month per participant enrolling at thirty-five years of age. According to commission estimates, such premiums would currently be less than 1 percent of payroll for eligible employees and should not exceed this as they are adjusted upward for inflation. Although many uncertainties surround projections of the cost of benefits to be paid far in the future, the long time span between initial participation and actual service delivery provides time to adjust to changing situations.

The Commission on College Retirement sought comments on the issues and opportunities presented in its proposed plan. The commission believed that only after further careful discussion and analysis by the colleges and universities and insurance experts could an improved version of its plan be developed and introduced.

4.1

Findings of the Commission

The long-term-care needs and expenses of college and university retirees must be viewed in the context of the existing system of providing and financing long-term care in this country. The following is a brief summary of the findings from the commission's review of the current long-term-care system and the system's impact on the well-being of college retirees.

Long-term care provides compensation for chronic functional disability through a broad spectrum of medical and support services. In 1983, approximately eight million Americans experienced some limitations in functional ability.[1] The vast majority (88 percent) needed assistance only with personal-care activities such as eating, dressing, bathing, or moving about and with household tasks such as cooking, cleaning, and shopping; they did not require skilled nursing care on an ongoing basis. About one-third needed help with household tasks only.[2]

The oldest members of our population have the greatest need for long-term care, but even among the very old, the majority remain functionally able. Among those age eighty-five and older, only 31.6 percent need personal care assistance.[3]

Most long-term care is provided by family and friends. Over 70 percent of people with long-term-care needs live in private residences, and about three-quarters of the noninstitutionalized disabled population receive all needed assistance from family and friends.[4] Another 20 percent receive assistance from these informal care givers and from professional service agencies.[5] Evidence suggests that Americans are, by-and-large, committed to assisting disabled family members. However, this commitment is frequently a heavy burden that can put families under great stress.

Medicare and private Medicare supplements provide little coverage for long-term-care services. Although Medicare covers services from providers who supply both acute and long-term care, the program actively distinguishes between the two types of care. Medicare covers inpatient hospital services and all physician services, except physician visits for preventive care. However, coverage of nursing home care is limited to short-term, skilled-nursing, or rehabilitative care received subsequent to an inpatient hospital stay. Coverage of home care is limited to skilled-nursing care and physical or speech therapy provided on a part-time or intermittent basis to homebound individuals — except that other home-care services may be paid for if provided to a person receiving one of the services mentioned above. Thus, Medicare frequently does not cover the basic services most needed by people with long-term functional disabilities. Seventy percent of the elderly hold private insurance policies that supplement Medicare, but these policies are similarly limited.[6] Given these limitations, it is not surprising that in 1984, less than 2 percent of nursing home care was paid for by Medicare and less than 1 percent by private insurance. Nearly 50 percent was paid directly as an out-of-pocket expense, and about 44 percent was paid for by Medicaid, a means-tested public program.[7]

Medicaid covers some long-term-care expenses under certain circumstances but, because of its limits on eligibility, services, quality, and access, does not provide satisfactory protection. Medicaid coverage is limited to people who are poor, who become poor due to catastrophic expense, or who divest their wealth to become eligible for Medicaid. The amount and type of home care covered is extremely limited; in most states, Medicaid-covered long-term care is almost entirely in nursing homes. Because Medicaid payment for services is usually below private market rates, Medicaid patients' access to services is reduced, and, in some circumstances, quality of care is jeopardized.

Most people incorrectly believe that Medicare and supplemental insurance will cover most long-term-care expenses. A national survey conducted in 1985 by the American Association of Retired Persons (AARP) revealed that 79 percent of the population at large and 70 percent of the population over age sixty-five erroneously believed that Medicare would cover a long nursing home stay regardless of type of care required. Half of those with Medicare-supplemental insurance policies believed that they were covered for long-term-care expenditures. As noted above, neither belief is correct.

Individuals face a relatively small probability of needing a large, costly amount of long-term care. A sixty-five-year-old person faces a significant chance, about two in five, of ever needing nursing home care during the remainder of his or her lifetime. Nursing home stays are brief for most individuals, but about 10 percent of the elderly will stay for over a year. These individuals make use of about 90 percent of nursing home resources. The average expected nursing home cost for persons with stays of one year or greater is almost $100,000.[8]

Individual savings is not an efficient means of preparing for long-term-care needs. Although estimates of lifetime liability indicate that 97 percent of sixty-five-year-old people could meet all nursing home expenses with savings of $80,000 (current dollars) each, a large proportion of this group will never need nursing home care.[9] An individual saving such a large sum earmarked for this specific use is denied the additional goods and services such assets could buy. In addition, it is virtually impossible for most people to save enough to cover the small chance of extremely large expenditure needs.

The skewed distribution of long-term-care expense suggests that some form of risk pooling might be appropriate. If each individual contributed the relatively small average value of expected use, the group as a whole could be insured for these expenditures.

Private insurance covering some long-term care is now available in some regions of the country, but it is a long way from providing needed coverage. The market penetration of these policies has been minimal, with only about 125,000 policies sold to date.[10] Most policies are sold to older people on an individual basis. The result is high marketing costs and a high risk of use because policyholders are already elderly and because there is a significant likelihood of adverse selection. For these reasons, insurance companies set high premiums and limit their liabilities by limiting coverage. Plans almost always cover primarily nursing home care, which most people seek only when the need is very great. Even this is covered on an indemnity basis (a fixed dollar amount per day of stay), with coverage limits that preclude payment for very long, expensive stays. Few policies cover stays for skilled-nursing care beyond three years, and even fewer cover stays greater than two years if the need is for personal care only. The severe limits on coverage of home-delivered care, or the complete lack of coverage, is an important drawback for these policies, because care at home is what a majority of people would prefer. A few policies do offer substantial home-care benefits, but they require prior nursing home care.

College retirees are more secure financially than the general population, but their security is threatened by the possibility of incurring large, long-term-care expenses. Initial estimates suggest that almost two-thirds of college retirees could not meet, with disposable retirement income, the costs of a one-year nursing home stay.[11] They would have to draw down assets if they needed large amounts of long-term care. Although many retirees would be able to cover costs from their assets, it is not pleasant to contemplate exhausting one's life savings because of the mischance of disability needs. This problem is particularly acute when one member of a couple needs nursing home care and the spouse must maintain a home in the community.

Financing long-term care is expected to be even more difficult for future college retirees. Longer life spans, the increased labor force participation of women, who have traditionally supplied a majority of in-home care, and a continued high divorce rate are expected to cause an increase in the population needing formal, long-term care, and an increase in the care needed. Any improvements in morbidity (reductions in the proportions of disabled people in each age group) are unlikely to outweigh the combined effects of these other factors.

4.2

Goals of a College and University Sponsored Long-Term-Care Insurance Plan

Although examination of the current long-term-care situation suggests the desirability of college- and university-sponsored long-term-care insurance plans, it does not provide the guidance needed to shape the specifics of a program. In order to construct such a plan, the principles or goals of a new program must be made explicit. The commission has adopted six goals that guided the development of the proposed plan.

1. Neither employers, retirees, nor their spouses should suffer a substantial loss in standard of living as a result of requiring long-term care. At the same time, it is not a goal of the program to build estates by protecting people from spending their social security and pension benefits to meet substantial parts of long-term-care costs if admitted to a nursing home, when admission means no longer having to maintain a home.

The insurance program should insure against the relatively small chance of a large expense depleting an individual's or couple's resources, resulting in a reduced standard of living. Retirees will have regular, recurring pension income; and in most cases, disabled people of working age will have income support from social security and, in many cases, private disability insurance, so they can afford to share in the cost burden of long-term care. Institutional long-term care includes basic expenses such as room and board, which insurance should not be expected to subsidize. For married persons, it is the standard of living of the couple that is to be protected. Therefore, spouses should

221

be insured and the cost of maintaining a home for a spouse should be considered in the determination of cost sharing.

2. The insurance program should be designed to support maximum individual independence and social, physical, and mental functioning. Whenever possible, it should provide the individual with a choice of services and settings.

Insured services should be directed toward active support to compensate for functional deficits and prevention of further functional loss. Decisions regarding type and location of care should not be solely professional judgments but should also be consistent with the life-style choices of the individual and his or her family. Thus, within cost and other constraints, individuals should be able to receive services outside of traditional nursing homes if they so choose.

3. Insured services should be of good quality and available within a reasonable distance of the plan members' homes.

An insurance program will not be effective if desired services that meet minimum standards of quality are not available. Given the current shortage of nursing home beds and the lack of coordinated home- and community-based care in many areas, as well as the variable quality of long-term-care services, it is advisable for the insurance program to develop special arrangements with local service providers and to establish quality standards.

4. The insurance program must recognize the important role of family and friends in the provision of services. By filling gaps and relieving family care givers, insured services should foster and enhance family care for patients at home.

An effective long-term-care delivery system must consider the costs to, and the desires of, the individual's family, as well as program costs and individual needs. There will be times when formal, paid care should be used to relieve the family of some or all care-giving responsibilities and times when patients cannot be maintained at home without such care.

5. The plan should have objective criteria for distributing benefits — criteria that are understandable to the enrollees.

Insofar as possible, the program should distribute its benefits according to objective criteria. Enrollees of the plan should be presented with clear, understandable explanations of which services are covered and under what circumstances they are covered. Explanations should also address other aspects of the program, such as copayments, deductibles, and portability.

6. *The insurance program must remain affordable and thus, should provide incentives for cost containment to enrollees, providers, and plan management.*

4.3

The Proposed Plan

In collaboration with Brandeis University, the Commission on College Retirement has developed a comprehensive long-term-care insurance plan to protect college and university employees and retirees against large long-term-care expenses. It is designed to respond to current difficulties in the finance and delivery of long-term care and to support the commission's goals for such a program. After a brief overview of the plan, the following topics are presented in more detail: program administration, employer participation, employee eligibility, spouse coverage, premiums, portability, criteria for benefit eligibility, benefits, system management, reimbursement of providers, financing, adjustment for inflation, adjustment for unexpected developments, preliminary cost estimates, transition issues, employer-sponsored plans, and other considerations. More fully detailed plan specifications would have added depth to this report. However, both the commission and Brandeis realize that a plan such as this will best be developed with the input from the colleges and universities that it is hoped will participate in this plan and from the many experts in the fields of long-term care, insurance, and employee benefits. The plan is thus presented as a draft, with the knowledge that it will be modified and further developed in response to the anticipated input.

4.3.1 The Plan in Brief

The program would be administered by a nonprofit organization called the Consortium of Long-Term-Care Plans. Necessary administrative functions would include setting and collecting premiums, managing reserve fund investments, assessing eligibility for benefit receipt, and negotiating agreements with provider organizations. If desirable, the consortium would contract for such services. Payments made on behalf of eligible employees and their spouses during working and retirement years would accumulate to provide lifetime coverage for nursing home and home-delivered services to meet major, long-term-care needs. Two levels of coverage would be available: a basic plan covering only the most catastrophic long-term-care situations, and a full plan covering a higher proportion of long-term-care expenses. Employers would pay for the basic plan for all eligible employees. Employers, employees, or both could contribute further payments to bring coverage up to the full plan, which is the main focus of this report.

4.3.1.1 Full Plan

Under the full plan, benefits would be provided to participants assessed as being severely disabled under plan disability criteria — but only after a deductible period of six months. Disability criteria would be set to identify participants most likely to experience major long-term-care expenses — those assessed on scales of physical and mental functioning as needing significant amounts of personal care or supervision. Such severely disabled persons are often cared for in nursing homes, but under the plan, they could receive insured care at home as well, as long as insured costs were lower. The assessment function would be performed by assessors independent of any care providers. Their independence would eliminate financial incentives to certify plan members, who were less severely disabled, for benefits.

Beneficiaries would be expected to pay for their own care during the deductible period and to pay a share (20 percent) of the cost of disability-related services thereafter. The program should not make beneficiaries better off financially if they enter a nursing home, so beneficiaries entering a nursing home would also pay an additional copayment (25 percent) in recognition of the costs of food and shelter that are included in nursing home rates. Program participants with regular pension income should be able to continue responsibility for these ongoing living expenses. This living expense copayment would be waived if the beneficiary's spouse maintained a community residence. Eligible beneficiaries who chose home-delivered services would receive care from managed care organizations paid on a per-patient-month basis. These organizations would also be responsible for nursing home care for plan members enrolled with them. Providers would thus have incentives to control home-care costs, and bias toward nursing home care for difficult patients would be averted.

Premiums would be set so that expected payments over a participant's lifetime would cover expected lifetime long-term-care use under the plan. The real dollar lifetime premium for each individual would vary by age at first enrollment in the plan and would be adjusted annually for general inflation. Accumulations under the plan would be vested and portable. Premiums could be increased within limits if plan experience exceeded expected cost; other adjustments, including curtailment of benefits, would have to be undertaken if use far exceeded expectations.

4.3.1.2 Basic Plan

Because some employees might not wish to pay for full coverage, the consortium would also offer a basic plan. This plan could be useful during the transition period, as a less costly means of extending its benefits to older employees. Benefits under this plan would be similar but would be available only after a longer deductible period (nine months to a year) and would cover only a basic share of the cost of care (for example, 50 percent for home care, 25 percent for nursing home care, 50 percent for nursing home care when a spouse maintains a community residence). The basic plan could be provided to all eligible employees on an automatic basis, and employees who wished could pay supplementary premiums to reach full coverage. Because of the automatic nature of basic coverage, the impact of adverse self-selection among those choosing full coverage would be reduced.

4.3.2 Program Administration

The mechanism for implementing the proposed plan is a Consortium of Long-Term-Care Plans (the consortium). This umbrella organization would carry out needed functions or contract with other entities to perform some or all of them. It would be responsible for setting and collecting premiums from participating employers, investing reserves, assessing disability level of participants, requesting benefits, and negotiating agreements with providers to supply care. The consortium mechanism would allow vesting of entitlement to insurance for individuals, portability of benefits across institutions, application of uniform benefit criteria across geographically dispersed beneficiaries, and control of the cost of benefits through agreements with service providers.

A long-term-care insurance program, even if offered by only one employer, must handle a number of administrative functions, some specific to the program itself, some nationwide in scope, and others relating to local service delivery. The commission's proposed program is designed with the idea that a number of colleges and universities would offer long-term-care insurance as an employee benefit. Given many participating employers, it would be worthwhile to consolidate needed functions in an umbrella organization or entity in order to realize economies of scale and to allow portability across employers. An insurance company, by offering such a program to employers on the open market, could fill this role. The commission believes, however, that in the absence of private carriers, the college and university community may wish to establish a consortium, directed by the participating colleges and universities, that could set broad policies, contract with insurance companies and other organizations, and provide some administrative services itself if needed.

The consortium would be a nonprofit organization directed by the employers participating in the insurance program and would be responsible to them. As described in the sections below, the consortium would have responsibility for a number of functions that must be consistently applied across employers and across geographical areas if entitlement to coverage is to be portable for employees and if eligibility and benefits are to be uniformly available no matter where retirees reside. For example, the consortium or its designee would develop the information needed to set actuarially fair premiums for all employees and would adjust those premiums for inflation, plan experience, and other developments. It would establish and maintain the accounts for vesting program entitlement of individual enrollees, thereby allowing the insurance to be portable across employers. And it would be responsible for investing reserves, although it could delegate this responsibility to a financial institution.

Retirees, the major users of long-term care, may move away from the community in which they were employed, so a dispersed network for assessing beneficiaries and controlling the cost of benefits must be established. This approach would be more efficient if carried out on behalf of all participating employers, through the consortium, as opposed to being duplicated by many individual employer or insurance company programs. Wherever possible, the consortium or its agent would designate managed care organizations to enroll beneficiaries who initially choose to receive care at home and would designate preferred nursing homes to provide institutional care. The consortium or its agent would negotiate agreements with local providers (nursing homes and managed care organizations) and could assist the development of managed care organizations in new markets; it would negotiate payment rates for providers under the program. The consortium could delegate any or all of these functions to other organizations under contract — for example, to insurance companies, money managers, and assessment organizations — but would retain overall responsibility for the program.[1]

The consortium mechanism could also support colleges and universities in setting up individual employer-sponsored long-term-care insurance plans. These employers could arrange to make use of the consortium's nationwide network of assessment teams and provider relationships. Such employers would be considered consortium members even though they would not participate in the consortium insurance plans and would not rely on the consortium to collect premiums and invest reserves. The consortium could also sell its services on a contract basis to other organizations — to insurance companies or non-university employers, for example.

4.3.3 Employer Participation

Colleges and universities would participate in the long-term-care insurance program by joining the Consortium of Long-Term-Care Plans (the consortium). The college or university could offer the consortium full long-term-care plan, to be discussed below. A basic coverage plan with a higher copayment rate and a longer deductible period would also be available through the consortium. As an alternative to the consortium plans, an institution could offer its own plan, using consortium-designated agencies to carry out administrative functions [see Employer-Sponsored Plans, Section 4.3.17].

The consortium could be flexible in enrolling participating colleges and universities. First, it is likely that more employers would offer long-term-care insurance and participate in the consortium if they could offer either standard consortium insurance plans or a tailored, employer-specific plan using the administrative structure of the consortium for implementation and management. In addition to averting a monopoly position for any one insuring entity, including the consortium itself, this latter option would allow program features to be adjusted to individual employer situations. Unlike the commission plan, however, such employer-sponsored programs could not be vested or portable across employers. Nevertheless, given the early stage of development of group long-term-care insurance and the very different situations that various colleges and universities face, it is desirable to be as flexible as possible in beginning a new system. Furthermore, the time it takes to develop and implement this new system of protection will be greatly reduced if decisions that require consensus across all participating institutions can be kept to a minimum; by supporting employer-sponsored plans, the con-sortium can realize economies of scale in its activities while allowing employers to offer insurance with higher or lower coinsurance, longer or shorter deductible periods, and different eligibility rules. During the initial stages of the program, an employer might find it preferable to purchase the basic or full portable plans for younger employers and to finance less expensive, more limited employer-sponsored coverage for older employees and, possibly, current retirees (see Transition Issues, Section 4.3.16). The current discussion focuses on the full consortium-based insurance program, but plans operated by particular employers for the benefit of their own employees and retirees only are compatible with the consortium approach[2] (see Employer-Sponsored Plans, Section 4.3.17).

4.3.4 Employee Participation

The long-term-care insurance program would be part of the college retirement plan. All full-time and permanent part-time faculty and staff who are covered for regular retirement benefits would automatically be covered in the institution's plan.

The program should be automatic for all eligible employees. Three related factors led to the recommendation that these plans be provided through automatic coverage rather than through voluntary participation. First, through a combination of misinformation, refusal to consider unpleasant future possibilities, and individual preferences, people tend to undervalue long-term-care insurance. This is especially true of younger employees. Therefore, the number of employees who would voluntarily enroll might initially be small. Second, individuals who show the most interest in purchasing such insurance would tend to be older; the result would be a less affordable average premium for lifetime coverage. Finally, if the plan allowed persons to choose or reject coverage at will, it would open itself to adverse selection, that is, overrepresentation of persons most likely to need care. The risk of adverse selection increases as potential applicants approach high-risk brackets.

Long-term-care insurance for retirees would protect the standard of living established in retirement by pension income.

Therefore, the coverage for this new benefit should be concurrent with eligibility for cash retirement benefits. (The commission has recommended elsewhere that retirement benefits be extended to all college and university employees.)

When the program matures, many employees and retirees would have joined during their early working lives, and long-term-care insurance funds would have accumulated for them during that time. Because there would be no accumulation at the start of the plan for older employees and currently retired persons, full eligibility would be expensive for them. Special consideration must be given to participation in the new system by these older persons (see Transition Issues, Section 4.3.16).

4.3.5 Spouse Coverage

The consortium's plan should automatically cover spouses of covered employees. To avert adverse selection in employment by people with disabled spouses, spouses in need of long-term care prior to plan enrollment would not be covered; the same restrictions would apply to new spouses.

Long-term-care spending on behalf of a spouse can leave the employee or retiree in poverty and can be a major threat to the security of a retiree's surviving spouse. These possibilities suggest that both members of a married couple should be insured.

However, if spouses were to be covered without restriction, people with disabled spouses could seek employment with participating employers in order to obtain long-term-care coverage. Marriage or remarriage by participating employees might make the plan liable for care for new spouses who are disabled. Because of these possibilities for adverse selection, spouses in need of long-term care prior to participation in the plan should not be covered.

Dependent children would not be covered during the initial phase of the program, but they might be added later.

4.3.6 Premiums

The dollar amount of the monthly premiums should be set so that inflow of premiums matches lifetime liability for insured care and administrative costs. Therefore, the premium set for each individual would vary

232 Pension and Retirement Policies in Universities

with issue age. The issue age is the age at which the individual begins participating in the plan. Premiums would be paid at the same base rate, with adjustments for inflation and other developments, throughout the participant's lifetime or until eligible for benefit receipt. Employers would pay the portion of the premium that covers the basic consortium plan for all their eligible employees and spouses. The additional premium needed to finance the full-coverage plan described here could also be paid by employers or could be paid by employees as an optional additional benefit. Premiums would continue into retirement unless the participant had already been certified to receive benefits. Premiums in retirement would typically be paid in full by retirees, but employers could offer partial or full premium payment as a retirement benefit.

Premiums, paid to the consortium by or on behalf of participating individuals and couples, would be computed to cover expected lifetime insured long-term-care costs of plan enrollees. The premium for an individual enrolling at a given age should be set in real terms, with the same real amount due monthly until benefits are required. In other words, the premium would increase in line with inflation but would not rise as individual risk increased with age; other adjustments could be made within strict limits, as described below (see Adjustments for Unexpected Developments, Section 4.3.14). In effect, insured persons would accumulate and pool funds at interest over a lifetime to finance their own lifetime cost of insured long-term care. This prefunding of the expected cost of future needs would be vested on an individual (as opposed to a couple) basis and so could survive termination of employment or marriage.

Because long-term-care use varies by age, the consortium should base premiums on the expected future discounted cost of long-term care for each enrolled employee and spouse according to age at initial enrollment. Initial premiums would be computed using the best available utilization and cost predictions. National and special utilization studies would be the source for initial estimates.

It could be difficult for an automatic, mandatory program to require premium contributions from participating employees. Indeed, under current law, this would be illegal in some states. Yet the program should not be optional for employees because of the risk of adverse selection. One way to reduce the cost burden for employers would be for them to provide mandatory coverage at a basic level, for example, with larger copayments and longer deductible periods than in the full plan described here. Employees could then supplement this basic coverage by paying additional premiums or by making lump-sum contributions to bring coverage up to the full level. To limit the possibility of adverse selection, such a decision to supplement would be required before a given age, such as fifty-five.

Premium payments should continue in retirement so that the plan could maintain the actuarial soundness of the risk pool in response to inflation and unpredicted use. The commission recommends that any premium payments made by individuals be stopped when the participant begins receiving benefits. After retirement, individuals would be responsible for paying their own premiums unless continued premium payment was made a retirement benefit by employers. Individuals whose premiums had been paid in full by their employers during active employment would find their premiums increasing. However, this premium obligation, adjusted only within strict limits for inflation and other developments, should not be a serious burden to college retirees who, by and large, have secure and reasonably adequate pension incomes and whose social security payments are indexed for inflation. This premium is expected to be substantially less than that for similar individual coverage purchased after retirement because of the large prepayment of future costs during working years and because of the many cost-lowering advantages of group insurance.

The prepayment to cover future risks entails a pricing method that contrasts with the method used for long-term-care insurance now on the market. Current policies charge premiums that increase with age, because risk increases with age. Premiums are adjusted periodically to reflect unpredicted use of insured services. Indemnity plans, which offer a dollar amount per unit of service, need not adjust for changes in long-term-care prices, but service-based plans — for example, those covering a percentage of the cost of nursing home charges — must adjust premiums to reflect increasing prices. The long-term-care service coverage described here could be purchased by accumulating funds during employment for a specially designed annuity, with payments increasing directly in line with the age-related premium of an equivalent long-term-care insurance policy. But such an annuity would not be able to adjust for increases in premiums over time, so inflation and other risks would be borne completely by the insured individual, who must make up the difference between the annuity payment and the actual premium. In constrast to such a savings plan linked to "term" long-term-care insurance, the program proposed here both allows and limits inflation and other adjustments in premiums and thus opens the potential for cohorts of individuals, and their employers, to share these risks.

4.3.7 Portability

If an employee transferred between participating institutions without a break in service, coverage under the plan would continue automatically. If the individual accepted employment at an institution that did not participate in the plan, that individual would be responsible for the entire premium if he or she chose to remain in the plan. The employee could also arrange to have a new employer pay all or part of the premium as an employee benefit. Administrative mechanisms should be developed so that individuals leaving the plan who had built up partial entitlement to long-term-care coverage could eventually receive alternative coverage, rollovers into pension benefits, or refunds of supplementary premiums they may have contributed.

Spousal coverage would be portable on the same basis as employee coverage: the spouse would continue to be covered when the employee transferred to another participating institution, or the principal policyholder could pay the spouse's premium into the plan, should the new employer not participate in the plan. In addition, if the marriage were terminated through death or divorce, the spouse would be able to continue coverage by continuing to pay full individual premiums into the plan.

The existence of a consortium would permit portability of benefits. Portability is especially important for this insurance program because premiums paid in over a lifetime are designed to use early contributions to finance later needs. Portability would be feasible only on a small scale at the beginning of the program because employment transfers among the handful of pioneering participating institutions would probably be few. However, it is critical that the program be developed to support future portability as more institutions participate.

Individuals who terminated covered employment and continued coverage on their own would assume responsibility for premium payments on an individual basis. A grace period of, for example, one year could be instituted so that such participants could make up missed premium payments with interest and not lose all accumulated entitlement to benefits. However, if this policy were adopted, the commission recommends that appropriate preexisting condition clauses be used to screen out reentrants in immediate need of benefits.

Employees who do not wish to continue coverage after leaving covered employment present a dilemma for the insurance program. Premiums paid by employers on behalf of these employees throughout their covered employment would not only already have covered the very small risk of long-term-care expense during working years but also would have accumulated interest to cover a portion of lifetime expected needs. For fairness, terminating employees should be able to benefit from this portion of their compensation package in some way. The accumulation against future needs could be rolled over into a pension account. Alternatively, even though partial accumulations would not buy the full consortium long-term-care coverage, they might still be used for long-term care. The commission therefore recommends that administrative mechanisms be designed so that accumulated partial coverage could be rolled over at a specific age (for example, at sixty-five) to pay for other, more limited long-term-care insurance packages or to supplement pension accumulation. The accumulated value of any supplementary contributions made directly by the employee, less amounts contributed to coverage of current long-term-care risk, could be made available as a lump-sum payment upon termination of covered employment to employees not selecting these other options.

4.3.8 Criteria for Benefit Eligibility

All plan members would be eligible to receive plan benefits six months after they were certified according to plan criteria, if upon recertification they still met those criteria. Individuals requesting continued benefits would be recertified every six months. All certifications and recertifications would be conducted by the staff of the consortium or by a designated subcontractor. However, certification could not be conducted by individuals or organizations that were consortium-approved providers [see System Management, Section 4.3.10].

The consortium long-term-care insurance program should be designed to meet major disability needs when the amount and duration of need for care can jeopardize financial security and personal well-being of individuals and couples. This design implies that benefits should be available to the relatively few participants who experience significant disability rather than to the larger number who have less severe needs for long-term-care services. Participants who become disabled would be assessed using standard assessment instruments (see Appendix A: Assessment of Eligibility for Benefits) with criteria for eligibility set to screen out all but those in greatest need of care. For example, participants might be certified as eligible for benefits if they were dependent on other people for assistance in two or more of the five activities of daily living (ADLs) used in long-term-care assessment (bathing, dressing, using the toilet, transferring from bed to chair, eating), or if they were assessed, using standard instruments, as severely cognitively impaired. Certification of eligibility for benefits should not be affected by family availability but should be based to the extent possible on objectively assessed disability—although the benefits sought by an individual would be likely to reflect the availability of family support.

For fairness and cost containment, assessment of eligibility for benefits must be carried out by organizations responsible to the consortium, not by providers of care (see System Management, Section 4.3.10). The assessment team would also provide information to all applicants for certification and to their families about local service providers holding agreements with the consortium—especially information about case management organizations.

These criteria would exclude many plan participants who have moderate to mild functional impairments. Although a plan that covers the care needs of less severely disabled people might be seen as more desirable from some viewpoints, it cannot be recommended at this time for three reasons. First, the severe levels of impairment that will be covered under this plan will be assessed using a scale of independence in the activities of daily living—eating, dressing, bathing, moving from bed to chair, using the toilet, and controlling bowel and bladder (see Appendix A). Lower levels of impairment are usually assessed by measures of independence in instrument activities of daily living such as cooking, cleaning, and managing financial affairs. These scales are not as objective as those that measure higher-level impairment. Failure to carry out instrumental activities may be due to lifetime habits and skills or to social and environmental situations, as well as to functional loss. Second, criteria are not as well established for translating moderate and mild loss of function into service needs. For example, the service need of a person who cannot do housecleaning is difficult to measure and depends on many external factors. Third, including the mildly impaired group is likely to increase dramatically both the cost of the program and the uncertainty of the cost estimates. It is preferable to start conservatively and to broaden eligibility over time, if that proves to be desirable.

In addition to physical impairment, functional loss associated with severe cognitive impairment would be covered. Individuals suffering from severe cognitive impairment may need two types of assistance. First, they may need assistance in the activities of daily living. Alzheimer's disease patients, for example, may forget how to dress themselves or may become incontinent. Second, some cognitively impaired persons may require near-constant supervision to prevent them from harming themselves or others. Some types of dementia, including Alzheimer's disease, may cause behavioral problems including wandering, abusive language, and assaultive behavior, although the affected individuals maintain physical functioning.

A deductible period (six months) is recommended in order to limit protection to individuals who need care over extended periods, thus keeping premiums affordable while still covering those most in need of protection. In addition, a deductible period rather than a dollar amount would prevent bias toward nursing home care and would be fair to insurance participants who prefer care at home: a deductible stated in dollar terms would be much more likely to be reached, and reached quickly, by a person in a nursing home in contrast to a similarly disabled person cared for at home. The promise of 80 percent coverage of cost after spending a dollar deductible on a short nursing home stay could encourage disabled beneficiaries to seek institutional care and to minimize the role of family and other informal care providers. Instead, the deductible-period feature combined with coinsurance should encourage individuals and families to arrange cost-conscious care at home, using informal (unpaid) care when possible.

An individual would pay the deductible only once. A beneficiary thus would be liable for no more than six months of care for severe disability, whether at home or in a nursing home. Once a participant was initially assessed as meeting plan criteria, reassessment would be carried out at three months and again at six months, so a participant with two nonconsecutive three-month spells of certifiable disability would be deemed to have met the deductible; assessment would be carried out every six months after the first benefit receipt to confirm that benefit recipients were truly in need of care and to monitor quality of care.

Because of the rare but financially devastating risk of uncovered personal care needs caused by the onset before retirement age of such diseases and conditions as multiple sclerosis, spinal cord injury, and Alzheimer's disease and related dementias, the commission recommends that the plan cover disability-related long-term care for all participants regardless of whether they are working or retired at the onset of disability. The availability of immediate coverage for this small but important risk would make the plan more desirable to younger employees than it would be if only retirees or persons over a certain age were covered.

4.3.9 Benefits

The benefit package would include services provided by licensed nursing homes and by a wide variety of home- and community-based long-term-care services provided by managed care organizations holding agreements with the consortium. Eligible beneficiaries, who would all meet plan eligibility criteria for severe functional disability, should have the option, within limits, of receiving care in a nursing home or at home. Those who chose home-based care would receive it through a managed care organization, paid on a per-patient-month basis. In areas where agreements had not been negotiated with managed care organizations, beneficiaries could receive care from other providers on a fee-for-service basis with a monthly dollar cap. As discussed below [see System Management, Section 4.3.10 and Reimbursement of Providers, Section 4.3.11], the benefit system would be set up so that the cost of insured benefits provided in the home setting would not exceed the cost of nursing home care. Beneficiaries would contribute copayments set at an estimated 20 percent of cost per unit of service they actually receive. In addition, beneficiaries who made a permanent move to nursing home care would make an additional payment of approximately 25 percent of costs as a room and board charge, because the insurance program should not cover these ongoing living expenses. To avoid hardship to a spouse, the room and board copayment would be waived for a nursing home resident whose spouse was maintaining a community residence. Medicare and any private insurance policies held by the enrollee would be specified as primary payors.

Need for nursing home care is the most important cause of devastating long-term-care expense. The plan would cover nursing home care after the six-month deductible period, but only up to per diem rates established by the consortium (see System Management, Section 4.3.10 and Reimbursement of Providers, Section 4.3.11). The plan offers a lifetime benefit to participants. Care is covered for eligible beneficiaries for as long as it is needed, without the length-of-stay limits found in the few long-term-care insurance policies now on the market. Beneficiaries would pay 20 percent of the cost of service, plus an additional 25 percent in recognition of the room and board services provided by the nursing home, unless a residence was being maintained for use by a spouse.

A goal of the consortium program is to provide enrollees with as broad a choice of service type and setting as is feasible. Because disabled people often prefer to receive care at home, with support from family and friends, it is undesirable to offer only nursing home benefits. Moreover, in many instances, such care at home will be more appropriate for the beneficiary and is likely to be less expensive. Given the current state of development of home- and community-based long-term care, home-care benefits are most insurable when offered through a managed care system with the provider at some financial risk. Strategies for developing arrangements with such providers, and methods of setting payment, are discussed below (see System Management, Section 4.3.10 and Reimbursement of Providers, Section 4.3.11). The community-based managed care organization would be responsible for a wide range of long-term-care services, including nursing home care if the patient required it later. This responsibility would give the managed care organization incentives to serve the beneficiary at home for as long as this was less expensive, thus ensuring that home-care costs did not exceed nursing home costs. The managed care organization would be responsible for allocating a comprehensive range of long-term-care services to enrolled home-care patients.

The program as a whole is designed to contain overall costs by restricting the patients enrolled with these organizations, and those receiving insured care in nursing homes, to the most severely disabled, rather than by restricting covered service type to nursing home care or skilled home care. Once enrolled with a managed care organization, beneficiaries would receive whatever disability-related services were needed, as long as monthly costs did not exceed insured nursing home costs.

The minimum set of services to be offered through managed care would be the following:

- Skilled nursing facility care
- Intermediate care facility care
- In-home skilled nursing care
- Home health aide services
- Respite care: short-term in-home and nursing home care to relieve family care givers

- Homemaker service
- Medical and social day care
- Transportation to approved services
- Physical, speech, and occupational therapy
- Counseling and psychological services

Competing managed care organizations could offer benefits in addition to those listed above, but they would receive the same capitation rate. Although the managed care organization would be paid on a per-patient-month basis, the individual beneficiary, through the copayment provision, would pay a portion of the cost of services. For consistency with the nursing home situation, the individual home-care patient should pay a fee per unit of service actually received, targeted at 20 percent of cost. This approach has a parallel in most health maintenance organizations, in which enrollees pay a small user fee per unit service received, per physician visit, or per prescription, for example. This user fee would encourage cost-effective use of care and continued participation of informal care givers. In general, the college and university employee and retiree population has sufficient assets and ongoing income to meet long-term-care costs during the deductible period and to pay copayments, even for those relieved of maintaining a community residence, at a 45 percent rate for nursing home care. Preliminary results from commission survey data imply that few if any covered individuals would spend down to Medicaid through the deductible and coinsurance payments.

4.3.10 System Management

In addition to a deductible period and copayments, the consortium would use uniform, independent certification of beneficiaries' levels of need, negotiated agreements with nursing homes and community-based providers, and per-patient payment of managed care organizations as methods to control costs and insure quality and access.

The long-term-care insurance program should do its best to avoid the problems of traditional fee-for-service health insurance, which tends to encourage beneficiaries to overuse services and providers to supply more care than is necessary. The requirement that participants be certified as being in need of care for six months before receiving any benefits would keep all but those most in need of long-term-care services from using insured care. To avoid incentives for certification of beneficiaries who do not meet standards, the organizations that certify individuals as eligible for benefits must be completely independent of the providers of care. Copayments should encourage beneficiaries to use insured care only when disability needs are serious. Beneficiaries would receive fully insured care only from nursing homes and home-care providers that had negotiated agreements with the consortium, except in areas where no such agreements exist; this preferred-provider approach would give the consortium added control over cost, quality, and access to care. The payment of managed, community-based care providers on a per-patient basis, covering expected cost of care, would keep providers from oversupplying home-care services and would give them incentives to keep beneficiaries out of nursing homes.

For fairness across beneficiaries and for control of costs, it is critical that the organization certifying individuals as disabled by plan definition be independent of service providers. The individuals who perform the assessment would be trained by consortium personnel using established training protocols (see Appendix A: Assessment of Eligibility for Benefits). The certifiers would be either consortium employees or local subcontractors. However, in no case would an individual or organizations be both a certifier and a provider. The certifiers would thus have no direct incentive to inflate the degree of disability they found. To assure a standard certification process across all beneficiaries, this system should be continually monitored and should include frequent retraining of assessors. The need for an independent, consistent, nationwide assessment network underlines the importance of the consortium mechanism, which could supply this function to independent university long-term-care plans and to other employers, as well as to colleges and universities participating in the standard consortium plans.

The consortium also would negotiate with and select appropriate providers in each long-term-care market area. Again, this function could be carried out much more efficiently by this national umbrella organization than would be possible if each employer or long-term-care plan had to certify providers in every local area where retirees reside. Where there are multiple providers, beneficiaries would be able to choose the nursing home or managed care organization they preferred from among consortium-designated providers and would be able to change providers if not satisfied with the service they received.

Every effort would be made to negotiate agreements with multiple providers. The consortium would designate nursing homes on the basis of cost and quality. These facilities would have negotiated agreements to provide care to certified beneficiaries who chose institutional care or who could be cared for effectively only in a nursing home. They would be paid at agreed upon per diem rates adjusted for patient care needs (see Reimbursement of Providers, Section 4.3.11).

Within limits, certified beneficiaries could also choose to receive insured care at home, again from an approved managed care organization under an agreement with the consortium. These managed care organizations would offer a full array of covered community-based services and nursing home care, if needed. Beneficiaries who did not initially enter a nursing home would enroll with these organizations, and the consortium would pay the managed care organization a fixed monthly amount per patient. The managed care organization would be responsible for developing and monitoring a plan of care for each enrollee, in addition to providing or contracting for all needed services specified in the benefit package. The role of family and friends in providing care would be recognized and supported by the plan of care as appropriate.

It is important that nursing home care be included in the managed care package. When the managed care organization is responsible for the cost of nursing home care, keeping beneficiaries out of nursing homes for as long as they and their families wish is to the organization's advantage — as long as the cost is less. If the managed care organization were not at risk for nursing home services, it would have a financial incentive to institutionalize beneficiaries who were difficult to serve, or who were more costly than average. In order to control home-care cost, the managed care organization would limit expenditure on home-delivered services to the insured cost of nursing home care. The beneficiary and his or her family and friends could supplement the insured care with paid and informal care, if required to keep the patient at home.

The consortium or its agents would negotiate agreements with institutional providers and managed care systems in local areas and would establish quality-assurance protocols. Types of organizations that could seek to qualify as managed care organizations include hospitals, nursing homes, health maintenance organizations (HMOs), Social/HMOs, continuing care retirement communities (CCRCs), Medicare-approved competitive medical plans (CMPs), and Medicare-certified home health agencies, which number almost 6000.[3] Alhough the managed care organization approach is not yet widespread, home health agencies and case management organizations are beginning to seek contracts with Medicaid programs for care paid on a per-patient basis rather than on a unit-of-service basis. The consortium could play a valuable role by identifying and developing managed care organizations in areas with college retiree populations.[4]

Initially, some plan members would likely reside in areas without an approved managed care system. The commission recommended that in these cases, the consortium pay 80 percent of claims for needed services within monthly cost limits (see Reimbursement of Providers, Section 4.3.11).

4.3.11 Reimbursement of Providers

The insurance program would pay designated nursing homes at negotiated per diem rates, with adjustment for patient status as assessed by the consortium's independent certification agents. If patients sought care in nondesignated facilities, the insurance program would pay an indemnity payment equal to the lowest per diem rate negotiated with local designated providers, less appropriate copayment. The insurance program would pay designated managed care organizations at negotiated rates per patient month, adjusted for patient status. Certified beneficiaries residing in areas without managed care organizations would be reimbursed for 80 percent

of charges for covered home-delivered services, up to a monthly cap set
for the local area and adjusted for patient status.

The insurance program must pay for nursing home care in a way that controls cost while encouraging area nursing homes to serve program beneficiaries. The prices that would meet these goals would probably be higher than Medicaid rates in most states and would possibly be below the prices paid by private patients. To encourage nursing homes to accept high-cost patients, the rates should be adjusted for several levels of need to reflect differences in the cost of care across patient types — for example, using factors based on the resource utilization groups being developed for nursing home patients in New York State. (Rewards for improvement or maintenance of patient functional level should eventually be incorporated in the negotiated rates, but nursing home reimbursement methods that provide such incentives are not yet well developed.) Nursing homes should be interested in seeking agreements with the consortium to care for program patients because of the eventual stream of patient referrals (including those referred at first assessment who would pay private rates during the six-month deductible period) and because of rates that would be higher than Medicaid rates for these long-stay patients. However, beneficiaries choosing nursing home care should be able to receive it from nondesignated facilities; for example, some beneficiaries might desire a higher amenity setting or care from a facility with a particular ethnic or religious orientation. The insurance program would pay a fixed per diem indemnity amount for such care, set at the lowest area-negotiated insured rate, less appropriate copayment, so care in designated facilities would remain financially advantageous to beneficiaries and nursing homes would be better off when they maintained consortium agreements.

The payment rates for the managed care organizations must be set to cover 80 percent of the expected cost of home-delivered services for these severely disabled beneficiaries and, because the managed care organizations would be at financial risk for nursing home care, must cover the possibility that the patient might have to be transferred to a nursing home. The payment rate per month would fall below the local insured cost of nursing home care for similarly disabled beneficiaries, so patients who were very costly to maintain at home would not be accepted by managed care organizations and would have to seek nursing home care. The managed care organization would not be obligated to supply services valued at more than the insured cost of nursing home care, and the beneficiary would be entitled to receive only needed home services up to this amount. If a beneficiary wished to remain at home despite need for care that exceeded this level, paid or informal services could be used to supplement insured care. In this way, the insurance program could assure that cost per month for beneficiaries cared for at home would not exceed the cost of similar care in an institution.

If there were managed care organizations in an area, and if the consortium could not develop them, the consortium would pay 80 percent of claims for home care on a fee-for-service basis, up to a monthly limit established for each patient based on comparable managed care costs.

4.3.12 Financing

Each year, the consortium would collect premiums that were actuarially computed estimates of the annualized cost of the lifetime long-term-care liability for covered persons. Benefits would be paid from this fund, which would be designed to grow until the program reached maturity.

Full prefunding of future liabilities is a necessary aspect of the consortium plan. It is the only way to provide full portability of coverage and individual vesting. Individual premiums, based on age at first enrollment, would allow accumulation of funds by low-risk younger persons to cover their later increased risk of needing long-term care. When inflation or unpredicted use rates altered liability predictions, adjustments would be made to maintain actuarial soundness of the fund (see Adjustment for Inflation, Section 4.3.13 and Adjustment for Unexpected Developments, Section 4.3.14).

4.3.13 Adjustment for Inflation

The premium required to cover each individual should be set in real terms and adjusted annually to keep up with economy-wide inflation.

Projections of any differential between general inflation and inflation in long-term-care prices must be included in premium computations.

The insurance program must be prepared to adjust for two types of inflation. To deal with economy-wide, general inflation, premiums should be adjusted upward each year to keep up with the general price level. Employers and employees contributing to the program should be able to afford premium increases in line with an appropriate national index — for example, the consumer price index (CPI); and because retirees' social security pension incomes are indexed to the CPI, the premium for retirees would remain a constant proportion of this part of retiree income. Premium estimates have been made with the assumption that, over the long run, reserve funds could be invested to keep up with inflation, that is, funds could earn real interest rates of zero or greater. Premiums cannot be adjusted for inflation once they are no longer charged, an important reason for recommending that premiums be paid by or for retirees as well as employees.

Inflation of long-term-care prices is likely to be greater than that of the general price level. Specifying the deductible in terms of time and the coinsurance as a percentage of costs implies that beneficiaries would be responsible for a portion of the cost of care that is constant in real terms. But special additional adjustments must be made to ensure that accumulated premiums would be able to cover the cost of insured care when it was needed, especially since there is no basis for assuming that investments will be able to keep up with long-term-care prices, as can be assumed over the long run for general inflation. The cost and premium estimates must be made assuming a higher rate of inflation for long-term care. These estimates would be revised annually and used to set the base premium structure for new enrollees each year. Deviations from the expected would justify premium adjustments within limits (see Adjustment for Unexpected Developments, Section 4.3.14).

4.3.14 Adjustment for Unexpected Developments

Strategies must be developed to maintain actuarial soundness of the plan in the face of developments that might increase plan liabilities above the accumulated funds. Premiums could be adjusted in light of new data and plan experience so that they would continue to target the best estimate of the full present value of insured long-term-care cost. But enrolled individuals and their employers should not face unlimited liability to fund unpredicted costs. It is recommended that real premium increases be permitted within narrow limits. If premium inflow is still inadequate to finance future plan benefits, other options must be considered. These include adjustments in benefits — for example, increasing the deductible period, increasing coinsurance, or increasing the level of disability required for benefit receipt.

Initial estimates of insured long-term-care use would be based on the best available data but would surely have to be modified to conform to later plan experience. It is impossible to guarantee that a specified set of service benefits would be available to beneficiaries in return for a lifetime stream of premiums even though, as discussed above, premiums would be adjusted for general inflation. The plan must offer a realistic guarantee to participating employers and enrollees. The commission recommended that this guarantee allow both limited real premium increases over the life of the contract with each enrollee and reduction of benefits if premiums proved inadequate to meet future needs.

Numerous uncertainties surround cost projections of benefits to be paid in the future. The liabilities expected to fall due in a particular year, two or three decades ahead, can be affected by changes in the mix of participants by marital status, sex, and physical and mental status; by shifts in the supply and relative price of long-term care; by delivery system developments in long-term and acute care; by advances in health care technology; by demographic shifts; by life-style changes; by biological events; and by environmental trends. Investment risk is also present. The premium estimates assume that funds accumulated by the plan are invested to keep up with general inflation or to earn a small real return. If this does not happen, funds will be inadequate to meet predicted liabilities. However, the long time span between initial participation and actual service delivery also provides time to adjust to changing situations. Information gathered in the first plan years can be used to adjust future expectations in light of experience. The insurance plan can and must have a built-in method for containing "midcourse correction" to reassess future liabilities and to meet them on a continuing basis.

Needed premium adjustments should be gradual and limited so that employers and contributing participants are not locked into large increases in real terms, either in any one year or during their participation in the program. The commission recommended that limits be established for premium increases over the life of the contract with each individual enrollee. If permissible premium increases still resulted in funding that was inadequate to meet future predicted liabilities, then benefits might have to be reduced. But individuals might be willing to pay supplemental assessments to maintain full coverage, and in a special situation, participating employers might assess themselves to meet unexpected costs; but this cannot be guaranteed to beneficiaries.

Future public policy regarding long-term care is another uncertainty the program must face. The directors of the consortium should be empowered to determine the program's response to enactment of a general, public long-term-care insurance program — for example, an expansion of Medicare. One approach would be to maintain the overall benefit structure, reducing coverage under the consortium plan to make the public program the primary payor for this care. Resulting accumulations would be returned to enrollees and employers as appropriate. If the long-term-care benefits of a future public insurance program equaled or exceeded the benefits specified here, the program could be terminated. Alternatively, accumulated funds could finance benefits more extensive than those of the public program — for example, by offering a more liberal definition of benefit eligibility. The plan could thus supplement and expand public coverage available to college and university employees and retirees.

4.3.15 Preliminary Cost Estimates

Considering only costs for persons sixty-five and older, the undiscounted cost of the full, lifetime long-term-care policy is estimated at approximately $9700 at age sixty-five, including administration costs of

10 percent of service costs. At a 2 percent real interest rate, this sum could be accumulated by a constant real premium of sixteen dollars per month starting at age thirty-five and continuing ten years into retirement. Refinements in these estimates and the addition of estimates for expected costs of long-term care for persons below age sixty-five are the focus of current research activity. Using a long-term-care simulation model, the cost estimates can be improved and placed in a more complete context. Until this resarch is completed, a monthly real premium range between ten and twenty dollars is recommended for planning purposes.

Preliminary cost estimates have been made for the full plan using current rates for nursing home care and assumptions about the order of magnitude of disability, home-care length of stay, and costs of home care and nursing home care. The estimates were made assuming that about one-quarter of covered nursing home days would be used by married beneficiaries paying only 20 percent copayments. This is a conservative estimate (based on 1977 National Nursing Home Survey data) and is likely to be revised downward by later simulation. The estimates are for coverage of 55 percent of nursing home costs for nonmarried beneficiaries and 80 percent of home-care costs, after a six-month deductible period. Costs of administration were estimated at 10 percent of service costs. The preliminary estimates reported here are limited to the liability for use by people sixty-five years of age and older, in part because the needed age-specific probabilities of use and distributions of length of stay in nursing homes and home care have not been as fully developed for the under-sixty-five population. The empirical work now being conducted is applying parallel methods of estimation to the under-sixty-five population to estimate liability for long-term-care services.

Preliminary premium estimates of $20.21 per month ($14.71 for nursing home and $5.50 for home care) at zero percent real rate of interest and $16.32 per month ($11.88 for nursing home and $4.44 for home care) at 2 percent real rate of interest would be adjusted upward annually to account for general inflation. They assume payments over a thirty-five year working life and ten years of payments during retirement. The premiums needed to fund basic coverage, with a longer deductible period and higher copayment rates, would be significantly lower. As a rough estimate, the premium inflow to cover two members of a married couple would be double the amount for individuals.

These estimates are sensitive to the many assumptions on which they are based. Current research includes efforts directed to improving the estimates. First, specific characteristics of the college retiree population, namely gender and marital status distributions and mortality, must be incorporated into the estimates. Second, alternative estimates change assumptions and allow evaluation of whether meaningful differences would result (sensitivity analysis). Various levels of responsiveness to insurance coverage (elasticity of demand) are incorporated, particularly for home-care use by those identified in the simulation as disabled. Third, specific forms of deductibles and coinsurance are tested to evaluate cost effects and distribution implications.

Costs must also be estimated for college employees under age sixty-five. Although this population has a lower risk of needing long-term care, they also have a longer expected life span; long-term-care costs for a person disabled at age forty-five, for example, may accumulate over many more years than for a person who becomes disabled at age seventy-five. Appropriate care is especially important for this group, because it may make the difference between the ability to continue in a productive work role and a life of dependency.

The present value of costs for eligibility at initial ages greater than sixty-five will also be estimated. This is critically important to employers' decisions about covering current retirees (see Transition Issues, Section 4.3.16). Depending in part on the discount rate, the present value of use may not, in fact, be much greater for an eighty-five-year-old person than for a sixty-five-year-old person. The former has a higher risk of nursing home entry during remaining years of life but also has a counterbalancing higher risk of death, so expected length of stay is shorter and the probability of surviving to the next year of risk is lower. The liability incurred by adding current retirees to the program will be estimated by computing present value of liability for older age brackets using the age distribution of current retirees.

4.3.16 Transition Issues

Although the steady state insurance program will cost a relatively small proportion of college payroll, an immediate transition to coverage of older employees and current retirees would be more expensive. It is recommended that all employees be included in basic coverage and that universities make participation and financing decisions about their current retirees based on their own circumstances.

An insurance program covering long-term-care costs on a lifetime basis would require a long time to reach a full steady state, defined as a situation in which all participants had joined as new college employees. In the steady state, many enrollees are likely to begin participating in the plan as a benefit of their first jobs, in their late twenties or early thirties, so actuarially fair premiums based on age at initial enrollment would be small. Young employees hired during the first year of the plan would be the first wave of the transition to this steady state. The cost of including current employees would be considerably higher than the steady state per-employee cost because annual premium payments based on age at initiation of the plan must cover an older individual's lifetime long-term-care liability over a shorter time period.

Some employers will be interested in covering current retirees and their spouses, because this group's need is most apparent. This coverage would also give the program valuable immediate experience with distributing benefits. To cover current retirees and their spouses, the employer and retiree must be willing to pay the actuarially fair annual value of lifetime coverage based on age at enrollment, or the employer may self-insure for actual use by its own retirees. The cost of this coverage would be even higher than that for older employees. Because of the expense, an employer might consider limiting eligibility to retirees who are not eligible for benefits when the plan begins.

4.3.17 Employer-Sponsored Plans

Employers could establish independent long-term-care insurance plans, using consortium administrative services. Employee participation, eligibility for benefits, benefits, and financing could all be tailored to the specific employer's needs, practices, and preferences. Because premiums would not be paid to the consortium by and on behalf of participating employees under the employer-sponsored plans, coverage would not be portable across employers.

An employer could choose to sponsor its own long-term-care plan, relying on the consortium for certification of disabled beneficiaries and selection of providers. An employer might wish to set different criteria for participation; for example, coverage might be provided as a retirement benefit to all those who were employed by the institution for ten or more years and who left its employ at age fifty-five or later.[5] The institution might specify a different deductible period (for example, one year instead of six months) and require higher or lower copayments.

Employer-sponsored plans can be financed as the employer sees fit, remembering that as the program continues, the employer will accumulate increasing obligations to specific cohorts of employees. These liabilities may be prefunded or dealt with on a pay-as-you-go basis. To prefund, the employer would immediately or gradually build an actuarially sound fund to cover liabilities. Future liabilities of current employees likely to become eligible for coverage would be computed, and a reserve fund would be established to meet them. It is unlikely that complete prefunding of such liabilities would be feasible immediately, but the employer could amortize the future expected liabilities that would result from promising coverage to current employees. The employer would then fund a proportion of these one-time increased obligations, as well as the obligations to new employees, each year until the steady-state fund was reached. Alternatively, under a pay-as-you-go approach, the employer could pay for benefits out of current income. The choice would depend on employer policies and circumstances.

4.3.18 Other Considerations

Wherever possible, the benefits of the consortium's long-term-care plan and the benefits of the long-term-care plans offered by member institutions should be integrated with other employee benefits, especially postretirement health benefits (including Medicare).

Long-term-care insurance provides a means for employers to protect the value of the disability income and pension benefits they provide to employees. Disability replacement income does not go very far if it must be used for disability-related long-term care, and major long-term-care expenses are the most serious threat to the standard of living that employer pensions achieve for retirees. It is appropriate to seek a balance between cash benefits and long-term-care insurance.

Integration of long-term-care benefits with postretirement health coverage has implications for predictability and control of both acute and long-term-care benefits. If long-term-care insurance is added as an independent, marginal piece of the retirement package, hospitals may reduce their costs by discharging disabled patients even more quickly to supportive nursing home and home care. Conversely, independent payment and management of nursing home care, while hospitals and physicians are still paid under Medicare, may encourage the nursing home and the long-term-care case manager to hospitalize patients for minor illnesses. If, however, long-term-care insurance is integrated with acute-care coverage, for example, on a capitation basis like that used by the Social Health Maintenance Organization (SHMO), managed care organizations would have incentives to use acute and long-term care appropriately and effectively. This integration could be accomplished by contracting for both long-term-care and acute-care benefits on a capitation basis.

Although it is not practical to mandate integration with acute coverage at this time, such integration should be strongly encouraged.

Epilogue

In a direct continuation of the work of the Commission on College Retirement, Harvard University initiated a study of long-term-care insurance. This study, supported financially by Carnegie Corporation of New York, had three objectives: to conduct detailed actuarial studies and further analysis required to design and evaluate a long-term-care insurance plan; to initiate discussions within Harvard University to determine whether such a long-term-care insurance plan was desirable, feasible, and timely for adoption; and to explore with other colleges and universities whether a consortium of colleges and universities would be a practical way to develop and implement a long-term-care insurance plan.

The Harvard study group, sometimes referred to as the Commission on Long-Term Care, issued three papers. The first, entitled "Long-Term Care: Three Approaches to University-Based Insurance," was issued in May 1987. The second paper, entitled "Understanding How to Evaluate the Structures and Administration of University- or College-Based Long-Term-Care Insurance," was issued in September 1987. A final paper followed, entitled "Retirement Benefits for University: Evaluating the Trade-Offs."

The Harvard study group's essential conclusion, as stated in its report to Carnegie Corporation in May 1988, was, "In sum, it appears that if long-term care insurance is to be a widely available benefit at colleges and universities it is going to be a long, slow process." This pessimistic conclusion underscores the seriousness of the continuing need for a solution to the problem of organizing and paying for long-term care for the disabled elderly.

This problem was directly addressed in a May 1988 publication by health care experts at the Brookings Institution. That publication, "Caring for the Disabled Elderly: Who Will Pay?" was authored by Alice M. Rivlin and Joshua M. Wiener. Their salient conclusion was that long-term care is a normal, insurable risk for the elderly and should be covered by a new publicly organized social insurance program to which everyone would contribute and from which all contributors could draw benefits when and if they needed them, without having to prove financial need.

Appendix

The proposed group long-term-care insurance is designed to provide benefits to plan members who are severely disabled and for whom the amount and duration of need for care may be financially catastrophic. In order to meet this goal, and to maintain plan solvency, it is critical that assessment tools measure as accurately as possible the relevant levels and types of functioning. Assessment measures should have a high degree of interrater reliability to assure equity and should be relatively inexpensive to administer. Such measures do currently exist and could be easily adopted by the consortium. This appendix briefly addresses the issue of appropriate eligibility criteria and discusses implementation of the assessment procedures with respect to staffing, training, and data reliability.

Criteria for Benefit Eligibility

Benefit criteria should be designed to target the long-term-care benefit for plan members who are severely disabled and for whom the amount and duration of need for care may seriously jeopardize financial security and resources, whether care is provided at home or in a nursing home. Those who are most at risk for substantial chronic care assistance of long duration may be characterized as either needing personal assistance in activities of daily living (ADL) or needing significant daily supervision due to mental impairment. Eligibility criteria should be designed to measure functioning along these two dimensions and to require meeting preset criteria in either of these two areas.

Criterion: Needs Personal Assistance in at Least Two ADLs

Activities of daily living (ADLs) are tasks that each individual must perform on a daily basis. These include bathing, dressing, going to the toilet, transferring from bed to chair, eating, and maintaining continence. Independent functioning in these activities tends to be lost in a consistent and predictable order. Individuals who are unable to perform these activities independently may use mechanical aids, assistance from another person, or both. Need for a mechanical aid only is considered indicative of a higher level of independence than is need for personal assistance. Some researchers and case managed clinical programs, including the Social/Health Maintenance Organization (Social/HMO) program, have considered the need for personal assistance in one or more ADLs as indicative of a severe level of need. Because the commission recommends that this plan start conservatively, the consortium should apply a criterion for eligibility of dependence in two or more ADLs, with the option to expand this criterion to dependence in one or more ADLs. Estimates of the proportion of the community resident elderly population needing personal assistance in two or more ADLs range from about 2.9 percent (NHIS, 1977) to about 3.7 percent (NLTCS, 1982); including people who need personal assistance in only one ADL brings the range up from 4.7 percent (NHIS, 1977) to 8.0 percent (NLTCS, 1982).

A number of well-validated scales can be used to measure the level of need for help in these activities. These scales have well-articulated definitions for each category which, with training, can be interpreted reliably by different assessors. The Katz Index of ADL is a well-known and well-defined scale that considers the same activities listed above. The scale is highly reliable, with coefficient of reproducibility as high as .948 and .976 (Sherwood and others, 1977). If continence is not included, the level of reliability increases. Independence, partial dependence, and dependence in each activity are well defined. The Barthel Self-Care Ratings consider a similar list of activities, in which the individual is scored as intact, limited, helper, or null (unable to perform even with assistance). Test-retest reliability is unknown, but high alpha reliabilities have been reported (Sherwood and others, 1977).

Criterion: Needs Significant Daily Supervision Due to Mental Impairment, as Indicated by Two of Three Measures

Clients who require daily supervision by another person due to mental impairment are likely to need substantial chronic care resources for a long duration. We suggest using a combination of measures to assess this dimension for two reasons. First, mental impairment is more difficult to measure reliably than is impairment in physical functioning. Second, the need for supervision may be due to cognitive impairment or to the severe behavior problems that can result from dementia. In order to capture both types of needs, and to ensure that only those with the most serious need receive benefits, we propose that eligibility be assessed on three scales: cognitive impairment, mental-behavior problems, and need for supervision. A plan member would have to meet the cutoff criterion on two of the three tests in order to be eligible for benefits.

In the discussion of measuring need for supervision, we have used extremely high thresholds for eligibility. This approach is in keeping with our belief that it is best to start with strictly limited benefits and to expand as possible, given improved data about prevalence of disability within the covered population and about use of benefits. This approach is especially important in discussion of cognitive impairment because no existing data suggest even a range of expected prevalence.

It will be a simple matter to expand benefits using the three assessment measures. In the case of the cognitive impairment scales, for example, it will be as simple as changing the cutoff point from two correct answers to three or four correct answers. The requirement that the client meet the eligibility criteria on two out of three assessment tools makes possible the incremental expansion of eligibility by changing the cutoff criteria on only one of the three instruments.

Cognitive Impairment Scales. The recommended criterion is the client's giving incorrect answers to eight or more items on a ten-item index. A number of cognitive impairment scales have shown good test-retest reliability — for example, the Mental Status Questionnaire (MSQ, Kahn and others) and the Short Portable Mental Status Questionnaire (SPMSQ, from the OARS instrument). Both of these tests are administered by interview. Questions measure orientation to time, place, and person; mathematical ability (SPMSQ only); recent memory; and remote memory. The SPMSQ is a more difficult test, but it offers the advantages of having norms adjusted for race and education and of correlating with clinical diagnosis of organic brain syndrome. Test-retest reliability is .8 or better for both tests. In either of these instruments, incorrect scores are aggregated to form a scale with cutoffs indicating no impairment, minimal, moderate, or severe impairment. A client with a score indicating severe cognitive impairment is severely disoriented to time, place, and person, and has poor memory recall (for example, does not know own address, day of week, month, year, or age). It is not enough to use this measure alone, since early Alzheimer's or dementia clients may exhibit defensive behaviors and may refuse to respond to the questions.

Mental-Behavior Problems List. The recommended criterion is the client's exhibiting any one of several behavior problems on a frequent basis. Behavior problems can require frequent supervision by nursing home staff or in-home care givers. Many state preadmission screening (PAS) forms used to determine need for nursing home placement consider a variety of behavior problems; wandering, verbal abuse, assaultive behavior, and regressive behavior are those problems most appropriate for screening a geriatric population. Usually, information on whether these problems are present never, sometimes, or frequently is elicited from care givers. Frequent presentation of any of these behaviors is suggestive of need for a high level of care.

Need for Supervision: Interviewer Assessment. The recommended criterion is the assessment of the client as being in need of constant supervision. This index, adapted from a PAS item used in Minnesota, has been used in the Social/HMO program and has been found to be a useful screening device. On the basis of interviewer probe questions to either the client or care giver, the client is assessed as being in need of no supervision, minimal, moderate, or constant supervision. These probe questions test for memory loss as exhibited by the need for assistance with activities such as taking medication, or managing finances. With training, assessors have achieved good inter-rater reliability on this index. The interview instrument currently being used by the Social/HMO demonstration has not been validated, although it appears to be quite effective.

Assessment Procedures: Staff, Training, Screening

Assessment of plan members to determine eligibility for the long-term-care benefit would be implemented by staff of the consortium, or, as the program developed, by staff of local agencies contracted by the consortium. These assessors would be independent of the provider organizations selected to deliver managed care benefits, and they would be trained in reliable implementation of the assessment instruments by a consortium trainer. Periodic checking of inter-rater reliability among all assessors would be implemented at least semianually. Refresher training programs would be conducted as necessary to introduce new eligibility criteria or assessment instruments, or to maintain high levels of inter-rater reliability as determined by the consortium trainer. Initial screening forms and telephone screening could be used to reduce the number of unnecessary, costly comprehensive assessments.

Assessor training and reliability checking are necessary to maintain equity in eligibility determination and to ensure adherence to the goals of the program. These activities would be conducted under the direction of the consortium trainer to ensure national comparability.

Assessment of plan members for benefit eligibility would

be conducted by trained consortium personnel or by local agencies under contract to and trained by the consortium. Assessors would be independent of provider organizations to prevent any direct incentive for overcertification, and they should have nursing or social work skills and experience in geriatric care.

Checking of all assessors at least semiannually would ensure a continuously high level of inter-rater reliability. Inter-rater reliability checks could be implemented in one of two ways: the consortium trainer could sit in on randomly selected assessment interviews with each assessor twice per year, or the trainer could audiotape and review a randomly selected number of assessment interviews. The latter method has been used effectively in the Social/HMO demonstration, which currently employs twenty assessors in four different sites, in four states from East Coast to West Coast. Reliability check results could be used in developing the ongoing refresher training program, implemented by the trainer, as required.

In order to reduce unnecessary comprehensive assessments, an initial screening form could be designed to accompany the client's application for benefits. This form would require client response to a number of questions concerning physical health, physical functioning, and mental status. Upon receipt of these forms, the consortium assessor or local assessment representative could conduct a telephone screening interview with the client to go over appropriate items in the initial screening form and to verify the need for a comprehensive assessment. Clearly defined indicators would be developed to determine the necessity for a comprehensive assessment based on responses to the initial screening form and telephone screening interview. This method has been used effectively in the Social/HMO program to identify clients likely to qualify for long-term-care services and to reduce the number of unnecessary comprehensive assessments. The Social/HMO experience has shown that client completion of the initial screening form is frequently inaccurate or incomplete. The telephone screening process has been effective as a verification procedure.

Part Five

Financial Planning

Financial planning is central to effective and efficient pension policy. Such planning is inherently exceedingly difficult for institutions seeking to devise workable and desirable pension programs, and it is at least as difficult for the individuals for whose benefit such programs are designed. The issues involved in financial planning have become steadily more complex, factually and legally. The choices involved increasingly call for sophisticated judgment; an especially difficult burden faces smaller institutions.

Much of the information crucial to financial planning lies in the future and must be estimated. Events that directly affect financial planning are subject to variables beyond the control of the institutions or the individuals involved. What constitutes a sound pension target, moreover, varies among individuals and with time, and diversity in the financial vehicles available to assist in meeting those targets is on the increase.

From the outset, the Commission on College Retirement recognized that some of the difficulty in financial planning could be eased if the institutions and individuals involved in pension planning had better access to better information on a more timely and continuing basis than is now available. The issue before the commission was how best to secure the desired availability of the revelant information. The commission proposed that a permanent, independent, unbiased organization be created to assist in achieving that goal. Currently, no such objective

263

organization exists to focus on the pension planning needs of higher education—or on the opportunities available.

The commission recognized that further discussion within the academic community of its proposal was a prerequisite to the development of a sound and successful solution and to the creation of the will to achieve it. The commission also recognized that the volume, variety, and fragmentation of the information relevant to individual employees' financial planning could be overwhelming unless efficiently assembled, recorded, and disseminated. The commission refrained from calling for the establishment of an organization to act as a central record keeper for individual, pension-related financial records and refrained from adding the record-keeping function to the organization that it proposed for financial planning assistance. The merit of such an organization, it believed, required further deliberation by and among all of the active participants in pension operations.

Thus, the commission cast its report on financial planning as a discussion paper on the informational and administrative services essential to a sensible planning process.

5.1

Implementing Financial Planning, Information, and Administrative Services

Academic institutions and their faculty and staff face many pension-related issues. While these issues steadily have become more complex, information that is relevant and crucial to policy decisions has not been easy to obtain.

Among the factors contributing to the complexities facing institutions and their personnel are the need for pension plan redesign due to changes in federal and state laws, increasing demand for other fringe benefits, the emergence of additional tax-efficient savings options, shifts in retirement age policies and the development of early retirement incentive programs, the introduction of increased investment options for pension plans, and the emergence of greater diversity of retirement needs among college personnel due to societal changes such as new marital and career patterns.

Moreover, the commission's recommendation concerning transferability of accumulations (see Part One of this volume) and its proposal for an individualized, target benefit approach toward retirement planning (see Part Three of this volume) add significant new dimensions to retirement planning. The TIAA-CREF system has offered important safeguards and services that may be lost if institutions expand investment options without insisting that pension assets be held for annuitization. Smaller institutions could find themselves without adequate service. Greater choice will inevitably lead to greater complexity and risk; institutions and their trustees must understand the implications of any changes they authorize.

In order to evaluate pension plan options and alternatives, individuals and institutions need reliable information on the past performance and experience of those who seek to invest their funds or to provide investment advice. But such performance data are often not comparable, and risk is seldom explicitly discussed in marketing literature. Past performance itself is not a reliable indicator of future performance, so institutions and their personnel will also need objective information on the advantages and disadvantages of transferring assets from one vehicle to another, on the advisability of offering multiple investment options, on the intricacies of plan design, and on modifications that might be necessitated by changes in legislation. No organization currently provides such information, except as part of its own marketing efforts. Consulting actuaries do offer objective advice on these matters, but many colleges and universities will be reluctant to incur such costs.

Individuals will also need to do more planning. Pension and annuity providers offer only some of the information needed to plan for retirement. TIAA-CREF makes an effort to provide projections of retirement benefits to its policyholders, but the projections are not easily understood. Moreover, the estimates are sensitive to the assumptions used and therefore have to be approached with caution and care. The current use of assumptions by TIAA-CREF in those projections can cause policyholders to underestimate the need for additional savings. Mutual fund companies, on the other hand, usually do not provide even limited projections. Furthermore, neither TIAA-CREF nor the mutual funds include information about social security in their statements. As a result, supplementary voluntary savings plans are more likely to be encouraged as tax avoidance schemes rather than as necessary components of a comprehensive retirement program.

Concern about such matters is hardly unique to higher education. Higher education has an important stake, however, in the portability of pensions and the maintenance of compatible pension systems. The sharing of information on retirement planning, the common development of financial planning programs, and the ability to learn from the mistakes and experience of others is therefore essential to effective transition to a system that includes transferability of assets, multiple choice of investment vehicles, and a wide variety of annuity options. Clear, unbiased, individualized information concerning the range of available programs is needed in the college and university community, particularly as addditional options beyond TIAA-CREF are added to benefit programs.

The Commission proposes the creation of an independent organization to assist colleges and universities (i) in evaluating financial planning organizations and available computer-based financial planning assistance (ii) by disseminating information on the programs available to colleges and universities, and (iii) by providing objective criteria, information, and advice on available investment and annuity options and alternative pension plan designs.

The commission identified three areas of special concern to faculty, staff, and institutions that such an organization could address: (1) individualized retirement and financial planning services, (2) institutional retirement planning and plan design, and (3) factual information about appropriate allocation of assets for investments during the accumulation phase, about capacity and performance of alternative investment managers for the accumulating funds, about insurance companies for the subsequent annuities, and about the pros and cons of available annuity options.

The proposed organization should address these concerns primarily by providing information rather than by marketing particular programs or products. Its purpose would be to encourage competition and new development in all these areas.

The commission has concluded that a new organization is probably the best means of integrating all of the needed services. Such an organization should also assist existing groups and consortia of colleges and universities in the development of new planning and advisory services. The commission seeks the advice of all segments of higher education in structuring such an organization to meet this critical need.

Initial funding for the organization might be provided by participating academic institutions, by the vendors whose marketing and support services would be enhanced by such an organization, by TIAA-CREF as part of its services, by members of the higher education community, and by interested foundations. Ultimately, the services of the organization should be self-sustaining.

Financial planning is a young and rapidly changing profession. The commission has found through pilot projects it sponsored on twenty-one campuses that faculty and staff have a strong interest in having computer-based financial planning assistance.

The computer-generated financial profiles produced by the commission's test programs covered the following areas: statement of financial objectives, cash flow and budgeting, risk management, investments, income taxes, estate planning, and retirement planning. Special emphasis was given in the profiles to retirement planning and to the process of meeting retirement income goals. All sources of retirement income for participants and their spouses, including social security and income from assets, were included. The potential effect of inflation on the purchasing power of retirement income was also shown. Eighty percent of the participants found that the process was useful and that it assisted them in planning for their retirements and other intermediate goals.

Although the commission has recommended that investment options in addition to those currently offered by TIAA and CREF should be made available to college and university personnel, it believes that offering unlimited choice to faculties and staffs would be a mistake. Each institution has an obligation to tailor the range of choice to a reasonable number of prudent alternatives.

The commission recognizes that many colleges and universities may not have the staffs or resources to gather sufficient information with which to make judgments concerning investment and payout alternatives on their campuses. The proposed organization could meet this need at a lower cost. Similarly, the proposed organization should prepare periodic reports on the alternative vendors, on investment performance of the alternative funds, and on insurance products and annuity options.

An additional issue that this proposed organization may need to address is how the administrative burdens and costs of providing greater choice and flexibility can be minimized. Individuals probably will invest in multiple vehicles during their preretirement years, and they will have to keep careful track of each investment in order to have information necessary for financial planning. Institutions will need to obtain information about the totality of each individual's investments for retirement to evaluate the effectiveness and adequacy of the institution's retirement plans.

The commission considered calling for the establishment of an organization to record and report an individual's total pension accumulations, thus enhancing services now available from TIAA-CREF for its own policyholders. It may be that TIAA-CREF would consider establishing a separate corporation to provide such services.

The advantages of such an organization would be considerable: the maintenance of basic pension principles, such as required annuitization of accumulations, could be more easily accomplished by a single organization; participants would have one organization to call upon for account balance and other benefit information; and administrative efficiencies would result from maintaining one set of records.

In its report on transferability, the commission endorsed TIAA-CREF's policy of requiring the purchase of a lifetime annuity with accumulated funds. Upon the request of colleges and universities, mutual fund companies and commercial insurance companies have made arrangements to limit the payout of accumulations to the purchase of lifetime annuities. The commission supports these arrangements and believes they are legally enforceable by the colleges. Such arrangements may, however, subject college administrators to additional duties related to their enforcement.

Institutions that currently offer choice in addition to TIAA-CREF must make arrangements with each of the alternative vendors for the remittance of contributions. Each vendor, in turn, creates separate account balance and remittance records for each individual participant, so participants receive account balance information from each vendor, and usually from each fund. This fragmentation of record keeping introduces new complexity and expense in providing consolidated benefit statements. In addition, fragmentation could make the implementation of the commission's proposal for an individualized target benefit approach to retirement planning somewhat more difficult to achieve. No national organization currently appears to have the capacity to provide the necessary administrative services for all colleges and universities.

A common record keeper for all Internal Revenue Code sections 403(b) and 403(b)(7) providers could ease administrative burdens on sponsoring institutions, could lower administrative fees charged to individual accounts, and could provide the resources necessary to improve information and planning services to college and university faculties and staffs.

The commission has not concluded who should perform these centralized administrative services. Given the complexities involved, it may ultimately not be feasible to accomplish the desired objective by means of a single organization. More deliberation is required on this question. Therefore, the commission recommends a joint effort by TIAA-CREF, other vendors, the colleges and universities, the educational associations, and the foundations to address the idea of creating an organization to provide needed record keeping and administrative services.

Epilogue

There was a prompt response to the recommendations made by the Commission on College Retirement with respect to financial planning. Leadership in that response was taken, principally, by the National Association of College and University Business Officers (NACUBO).

A national leadership conference was sponsored by NACUBO and the commission to discuss and plan the creation of an independent information service organization. NACUBO then created a task force, with the financial support of Carnegie Corporation of New York, to pursue the creation of such an organization. That task force held a series of meetings with interested individuals and organizations and prepared drafts of proposed position papers.

The NACUBO task force's conclusions and recommendations were submitted in June 1988. They call for the establishment of the Center for College Retirement Information.

Part Six

Encouraging Continued Activity After Retirement

Fruitful and rewarding retirement calls for more than a steady income stream—more even than the maintenance of physical health or the ability to meet the potentially catastrophic costs of long-term care. Essential to the individual retiree, and important for society, is the maintenance of the retiree's sense of identity and worth. Essential as is this sense of individual worth and dignity, it remains for many an elusive goal. It is also a challenge for society.

Throughout its deliberations, the Commission on College Retirement was alert to this challenge. It sought to formulate ways by which colleges and universities might assist in meeting it. The concept of continuing activity during retirement seemed promising to the commission because it offers one way in which identity can be maintained, and it offers a network of continued support for the retiree.

Explicit reference was made in several of its reports to the important role the commission assigned to continuing activity in the life of the retiree. In fact, the commission produced a "Working Paper on Continued Activity" and added to it throughout its discussions. That working paper was designed to put forward concrete suggestions regarding what colleges and universities might feasibly do to assure a greater opportunity for continuing involvement of retirees in activities they view as rewarding and worthy of their talent.

Although the commission's "Working Paper on Continued Activity" was never separately published, the commission adopted the paper's recommendations before concluding its work and intended them to be part of the public record of the commission's conclusions.

That working paper, in its final form, is presented here as part of this complete collection of the commission's work.

6.1

Working Paper on Continued Activity

Important considerations in retirement planning are (1) provision for continued activity, (2) preservation of the retiree's sense of status as an individual and with respect to the institution, and (3) opportunity for the institution and society at large to benefit from continuing contributions of outstanding retirees.

The commission surveyed institutions about concerns expressed by faculty approaching retirement; responses indicate that the prospect of the change in way of life that retirement represents is frightening to many. Just as important, the loss of retired faculty talent is something that institutions and society at large can ill afford. The commission has developed a series of recommendations directed at these complementary concerns.

The commission recommends that institutions consider the establishment of an office of retirement services.

Such an office might coordinate and encourage many of the activities designed to continue the involvement of retired faculty. The commission recognizes that establishing such an office may be difficult at small institutions if a sizeable expenditure is contemplated, but volunteer assistance from retired faculty, staff, and alumni, or from the pooling of resources among institutions, may make modest efforts possible. Alumni or other funding not likely to be given for other sorts of institutional functions may be available for this activity.

275

The commission recommends that institutions implement, insofar as they are able, policies that help retired faculty members retain their institutional identities — maintenance of library, computer, and parking privileges and continued access to other facilities and activities, particularly athletic facilities, fitness programs, lectures, sports, theater events, and faculty dining rooms. In view of the commission's concern for health care of retirees, it is recommended that wellness programs be established for retirees as well as for currently employed faculty and staff.

Key to some of these recommendations is regular communication with retired faculty, a function for an office of retirement services. Spouses of deceased retirees can easily lose their sense of identity if no effort is made to communicate with them; they should be included in many of the activities listed above.

The commission recommends that a variety of opportunities for continued professional activity beyond mere maintenance of institutional identity be provided.

The following categories of continued activity should be considered, not only as important for preserving the retirees' sense of worth, but as means to make use of the valuable resource retirees represent. Institutions, through an office of retirement services or by other means, should stand ready not only to provide information but also to facilitate these activities:

Teaching at the Same Institution, Full or Part Time

The commission recommends that all institutions consider developing plans for phased retirement.

The commission has recommended that although there should be a fixed retirement age, it should be possible for some faculty to continue beyond normal retirement age. The exact nature of the continued employment should be open to negotiation between the faculty member and the institution. However, to make effective a general policy of retiring at or before the "normal" retirement age, it has to be clear that there is no expectation of continued employment. Complementary to this notion is a phased retirement plan to open up options for faculty by reducing their commitments to the institution while they continue to contribute their talents and retain a sense of position and personal worth; many institutions have developed such plans.

Opportunities to Participate in Ongoing Research

The commission recommends that whatever assistance is possible should be provided to active researchers who want to continue their work.

The suggestion that emeritus faculty be able to pursue their research and to apply for research grants is, of course, problematical because of limited institutional space, facilities, and support services. Nonetheless, important societal, institutional, and individual goals can be served by facilitating the research of retirees. Several efforts have been initiated to provide opportunities for continued activity for retired scholars outside the usual academic channels — efforts such as the organizing of the Academy of Independent Scholars. Although the programs thus far have had limited impact, there may be potential for development.

Opportunities to Participate in Teaching-Related Activities, Including Teaching in Programs Different from Their Preretirement Career

The commission recommends that colleges and universities devote some thought to devising and implementing programs using retired faculty to serve the mission of the institution.

As an example of this sort of continued activity, the commission notes that some institutions, such as the University of Michigan, have special teaching programs for selected retirees — programs not within the schools in which they previously taught. The opportunity for contact with students is as important for some as library access or continued research is for others. The use of emeritus faculty for committees or other special educational activities can greatly benefit the college or university, since academe, like many institutions, seems destined constantly to reinvent the wheel. Southern Illinois University at Carbondale has established Emeritus College, whose members provide mentorship for students and assist in such activities as recruitment.

Considerable evidence indicates that older faculty members can often serve as counselors (paid or volunteer) to younger colleagues on problems of teaching and research.

Opportunities to Teach at Other Institutions

The commission recommends that more attention be given to making better use of retired faculty as a resource for other institutions.

One national faculty exchange program includes retirees, and some disciplinary organizations (for example, the American Mathematical Society) maintain rosters of retired faculty who are available for employment. An example of institutional initiative in this field is the Hastings College of Law, which formerly appointed only retirees to the faculty and still provides postretirement employment for many. Although some may object that the widespread reemployment of retired faculty by other colleges and universities will cut off opportunities for young scholars in those fields in which positions are scarce, the commission does not believe that such fears are realistic.

Opportunities to Teach in Special Programs of Various Sorts, such as Noncredit or Retiree Programs

The commission recommends that institutions encourage the development of a variety of vehicles for continued intellectual activity.

A number of institutions have established special programs in which emeritus faculty teach noncredit courses either to a general audience or to other retirees. For example, American University has a program called the Institute for Living in Retirement. Retirees, not only faculty and staff but also others in the community, can join for a modest fee; activities include courses and seminars on a wide range of subjects, from Shakespeare to opera to computer literacy to less academic topics. Many of these are conducted by retired faculty. The university subsidizes the program to some extent in the provision of facilities. A similar program, the Institute for Retired Professionals, has been set up at the New School in New York City. Such programs work best in areas such as Washington, D.C., or New York City, where there are large numbers of well-educated retirees.

Second Career Opportunities, Paid or Voluntary

The commission recommends that institutions encourage and facilitate volunteer and paid employment opportunities for retirees, in particular, exploring the possibilities of cooperating with local businesses and government agencies in establishing volunteer coordination programs for retirees.

With the attention currently focused on the need for qualified teachers in the public schools, volunteerism would seem to be an area in which retired faculty could be extremely useful. There is always a certain amount of understandable resistance to the use of volunteers to replace paid employees, but where the need is great enough, resistance may be overcome. Also, paid employment on a part-time basis would be a good use of resources and talent. It is conceivable that some federal or foundation support might be obtained for pilot projects, particularly for subjects in which the need is especially critical. Securing such support would be a way for colleges and universities to involve their retired faculty in continued activity while at the same time providing service to their communities. Provision of adult literacy programs is another area in which similar opportunities and challenges exist.

There are, of course, many other opportunities for volunteer work. Making the best possible use of retirees' talents may, however, require more extensive coordination than now exists in most communities. This is also true for employment of retirees, although there are public and private "over-sixty" employment centers in some areas. The University of California at Los Angeles Emeriti Center coordinates volunteer activities and employment in addition to performing many other retirement-related functions. Emeritus faculty from the nineteen California State University campuses have established an umbrella group to provide similar services. The specialized talents of retired faculty are a resource that deserves some creative effort to see that it is not wasted; colleges and universities are well suited to assist.

The American Association of Retired Persons has recently established a national program to utilize the volunteer services of its members. A number of businesses have developed programs that use the skills of their retirees in community service — for example, AT&T, Dow, the Equitable, Exxon, Honeywell, and John Hancock.

Some state and local governments have established offices that are much like the proposed campus offices of retirement services but that in addition coordinate volunteer and paid employment opportunities for retirees. The State of Kansas is one state that has such an agency. Colleges and universities too small to establish their own retirement offices might help to set up a community office under government auspices. Efforts should be made to coordinate and broaden the movement to organize such offices.

Postscript

Pension policy is an integral part of retirement programs. Were it not for retirement from paid employment, the need for pensions would be questionable, and the role of pensions would be vastly different. Thus, pension policies must be evaluated in the context of the retirement programs of which they are part. In turn, sound retirement programs must meet twin tests. They must be sound for the employing institution; and they must be sound for the retiree.

Such a prescription is not readily filled. The characteristics of employing institutions, and of their retirees, vary widely. Their needs and aspirations are equally varied. Thus, a retirement program that well serves a highly mechanized manufacturer or an employer with a high ratio of unskilled employees may not be the most suitable for the educational mission of a college or university and its core of professionals.

As a group, and at their best, colleges and universities play a critical, and probably unique, role in establishing the quality of American life.

Institutions of higher learning serve as one of the key storehouses of knowledge, understanding, and cultural values in our society, and they carry responsibility for transmitting information, perceptions, and values between generations. They also have responsibility for developing new knowledge and providing the intellectual leadership needed for the rigorous examination of existing learning so that even better understanding may be achieved.

Thus, contemporary higher education has at least two broad functions — teaching and research. The first provides students with knowledge and a set of skills, the most important of which are the ability to learn and the capacity to understand how the present relates to the past so that we can determine how to develop our human and physical assets for the future. The second is the pursuit of new knowledge and understanding, which provides the foundation for innovative approaches to meeting various challenges and opportunities. Teaching and research programs, therefore, serve society in several ways. In providing education (including advanced research training), they are society's servants. In continuously looking for new and better ways of doing things, they are society's critics. In addition to the dual tasks of educating and developing new knowledge, academic institutions also serve, with certain other institutions, as a "conscience" for society and as a stimulus for appropriate change.

The enormous variability in roles, missions, and performance among the institutions of higher education is often overlooked. A few examples make the point. Some institutions are tied to public employment practices (including provisions for retirement), others are not. Some faculty are represented by labor unions, others are not. Some institutions function on a merit-based system of faculty salaries, others do not. Some sustain a deep commitment to scholarship, while others see their primary mission as teaching. For some institutions, mobility of faculty is a constant consideration, for others it is less so. Some institutions are well endowed and rich in facilities, others are not. Some perform very well, others do not. Corresponding to these differences are important differences in the working conditions, aspirations, institutional and professional loyalties, and governance responsibilities of the faculty.

Retirement programs for colleges and universities should, accordingly, be flexible to meet the varying institutional needs. They should also be designed to support the institutions in carrying out their special role and responsibility in American society. At the very least, the retirement programs ought not to limit the ability of colleges and universities to fulfill their mission.

Notwithstanding the diversity, one compelling constant characterizes higher education in America — the maintenance of academic freedom and a system of academic tenure as the means to assure such freedom. It is believed that nearly 95 percent of all faculty members in American colleges and universities, public and private, two-year and four-year, are employed in institutions that award tenure.

The tenure system is a nearly unique employment relationship with faculty. In essence, the tenure arrangement is a long-term contract of employment, often as long as thirty-five years. It is an arrangement that provides job security for the faculty member without any regular performance appraisal as a condition of continued employment. Such a contract is far removed from the conventional employer-employee relationship in corporate America.

The job security provided by the tenure contract, and the accompanying autonomy over the nature of one's own work, confers on faculty academic freedom, which is the defining characteristic of the higher education desired by a free society.

The uniqueness of the tenure relationship between employer and employee in academia is further enhanced by the governance responsibilities exercised by faculty as an implicit part of the relationship. Tenured faculty function normally as partners sharing control of a common enterprise. This is vastly different from the hierarchical flow of power and control over employees in other work situations.

Most employers would consider a thirty-five year contract of employment to be irresponsible without a regular performance review as a condition of continuing employment. The contribution that academic freedom makes to the quality of higher education, and to American society, transforms such an arrangement into a sensible one for academic institutions. Even for academic institutions, such a contract might be questionable were it not for the termination date agreed upon as part of the initial tenure bargain.

Thus, it is of crucial importance to the mission of higher education not only that the tenure system be maintained but also that a date for the termination of individual contracts of tenured employment be agreed upon between academic institutions and their faculties; and lastly, it is crucial that such agreements be respected both by legislatures and by the courts.

Notes

Section 1.1

1. TIAA and CREF will differ in the timing and method of making such charges and credits because of their different objectives and procedures, but in either case, the economic risks and benefits are for the account of the beneficial owner. For example, TIAA marks its fixed income investments to their book values. CREF's equity investments are marked to their market values, and market value appreciation is a long-term objective.

2. "The contracts [under which contributions accumulate] are designed for use in pension plans with the specified purpose of ensuring that annuity funds accumulated over a lifetime of service in educational institutions will provide income for life during retirement" (Ad Hoc Committee Report, p. 65). Later on the same page, the report refers to the "absolute dedication to the support of life annuity payments of funds accumulated in TIAA-CREF." However, TIAA-CREF has recently offered a cashable Group Retirement Annuity option. See Ad Hoc Committee Report, p. 75.

3. For example, see Ad Hoc Committee Report, p. 66.

4. Such adverse effect might occur, for example, on a transfer of TIAA funds, either because of disintermediation (if the market

285

value of such funds were well below their TIAA book value) or through adverse selection (if the new provider of annuities did not provide spousal benefits or did not use unisex tables).

5. See 17b McKinney's *Consolidated Laws of N.Y., Estates Powers and Trusts Law,* Section 7–1.9(a).

6. There are a few significant exceptions, described by TIAA-CREF however, as *de minimis*. See Ad Hoc Committee Report, pp. 70 et seq. Further, when CREF was created in 1952, transfers from TIAA into CREF were broadly allowed for a limited time. See George E. Johnson, "An Experiment with the Variable Annuity," in Proceedings of the Association of Life Insurance Counsel, 1953, pp. 597, 616–17.

7. See, for example, Ad Hoc Committee Report, pp. 3, 65–73. Interestingly, however, the Ad Hoc Committee Report supports transferability of both CREF and TIAA funds accumulated through salary reduction agreements (so-called SRAs). See Ad Hoc Committee Report, p. 85.

8. It's only remaining argument is that "it would be unfair to TIAA policyholders to provide only for cashouts or transfers out of CREF when both TIAA and CREF policyholders were subject to the same contractual provisions when they entered the system" (Ad Hoc Committee Report, p. 70). Whether or not this argument is persuasive, such different treatment is now the policy for transfers from CREF of supplemental retirement income. See Ad Hoc Committee Report, p. 85. CREF also has, from time to time, unilaterally and significantly changed its policies — for example, (1) the fraction of funds that could be put into CREF, (2) the age at which transfers to TIAA could be made, and (3) the proposed offering of a new money market option — seemingly without concern that these changes might be "unfair to TIAA policyholders."

Section 1.2

1. TIAA-CREF, Report of the TIAA-CREF Ad Hoc Committee on Goals and Objectives to the Joint Boards of Trustees

of TIAA-CREF (hereafter, Ad Hoc Committee Report), Dec.
31, 1984, pp. 1, 11.

2. Ad Hoc Committee Report, note 1 above, pp. 11–12; *Laws
of New York 1952,* ch. 124.

3. For example, *The Wall Street Journal,* Sept. 29, 1986, p. 21D,
names TIAA as the thirteenth largest life insurer in the world
and the ninth largest in the United States, when measured by
assets. Listings based on premiums written in the most recent
year, on insurance in force, or on other measurement criteria
would place insurers in a somewhat different order. If CREF
and TIAA were considered a single life insurer, the two combined would rank perhaps fourth in the United States in assets.
Although combining them is not appropriate when comparing
life insurers, it does serve to underscore the enormous size and
importance of TIAA-CREF, especially in view of their clientele
being limited to a small segment of the public.

4. The word *owner* is not used here as a term of art. The true
relationship of the parties is part of the subject of this article.

5. "The commission *recommends that the funds held by CREF and
TIAA as fiduciaries during the accumulation phase should be transferable,
in whole or in part, not only between TIAA and CREF, but to third
party investment managers to be held in trust to secure for the beneficial
owners a lifetime retirement income from an annuity issued either by TIAA
or CREF or by a third party,"* (Commission on College Retirement, *Transferability of Funds Being Accumulated by TIAA-CREF
for the Benefit of College and University Personnel* (hereafter, *Transferability*), 1986, p. 7 (Section 1.1 of this volume, p. 12.) The
recommendation was qualified by several conditions, including one that any transfers should not be prejudicial to those
who do not transfer. The commission also recognized that meeting this condition would present more difficulties in the case
of TIAA than in the case of CREF. Those difficulties are dealt
with herein.

6. *Transferability,* note 5 above. I would have been more liberal than the commission in allowing accumulated funds not
to be annuitized after certain core requirements are met. That

allowance would add flexibility to the retirement planning of
the relatively more affluent faculty members; it would be advantageous mainly if the unannuitized portion could be dealt
with in ways that would not subject it to immediate taxation,
such as rolling it over into an IRA to be paid out in installments.
There might even be instances in which taxation would be an
acceptable price to pay for access to the funds. In the interest of
simplicity in and unanimity of the recommendations, however,
I do not dissent from the commission's formulation. Further,
I recognize that my preferred position might face additional
obstacles from rules of tax law.

7. Opinion letter from Dewey, Ballantine, Bushby, Palmer &
Wood addressed to Francis P. Gunning, Esq., executive vice
president and general counsel, TIAA-CREF, June 24, 1986
(Reprinted in Section 1.4 of this volume).

8. I use the word *understanding* to avoid characterizing the arrangement in technical legal terms.

9. For all of these purposes, the funds are valued differently
in TIAA and CREF, as discussed below.

10. "Benefit" is put in quotation marks because in the TIAA
case the privilege is harmful to the system and may be unfair
to other participants. The reasons for this appear below.

11. In a number of instances, individual participants have attempted to compel TIAA-CREF to make lump-sum payments;
they have failed in all the cases I have seen. In *Connick* v. *TIAA
& CREF,* 784 F.2d 1018 (9th Cir. 1986), an individual participant demanded a lump-sum payment, seeking reformation of
the contract for breach of contract, unconscionability, misrepresentation, and changed circumstances. *Yaker* v. *TIAA, CREF and
New York University,* S.D.N.Y., unpublished opinion (March 5,
1982); *Beers* v. *TIAA and CREF,* Iowa District Court for Boone
County, unpublished opinion (June 26, 1981); and *Abbett* v.
TIAA and CREF, N.Y. Sup. Ct., unpublished opinion (July 8,
1968) were all similar to *Connick.* In *Overman* v. *Overman,* 570
S.W.2d 857 (Tenn. 1978) and *Alexandre* v. *Chase Manhattan Bank
et al.,* 61 A.D.2d 537, 403 N.Y.S.2d 21 (1978), divorced wives
unsuccessfully sought access to accumulated funds for alimony

payments. In none of these cases did the institutional participant join the individual participant in seeking modification of the arrangement.

12. The first paragraph of the TIAA Retirement Annuity Contract says, "This is a contract between you, as its owner (Annuitant), and TEACHERS INSURANCE AND ANNUITY ASSOCIATION OF AMERICA ("TIAA"). No other person or institution is a party to this contract."

13. N.Y. Ins. Law Section 208-c 3(a), par. 2.

14. The beneficiary may take the accumulation as a life annuity instead.

15. A loss of funds due to investment risk occurs when the income of the portfolio is less than the guaranteed amount, or when overvalued assets must be sold at market to meet payment requirements. Mortality risk is the risk that the individual will die too soon or live too long. In life insurance it is the first risk that is transferred, in annuity contracts the second is transferred.

16. TIAA-CREF Annual Report 1986, p. 23, shows capital of $1.2 million, up from $1 million in 1985. The summary of operations, id., p. 24, shows a transfer to capital of $200,000 under the heading "Changes in Contingency Reserves for Policyholders." The capital of only $1.2 million is trivial for a company with assets over 20,000 times that large, underscoring the uniqueness of TIAA-CREF and its difference from commercial insurers. Half of the original $1 million Carnegie grant was for working capital and was presumably expended; it was replaced at some point, probably by a book entry much like that for 1986.

17. TIAA, *The Participant,* June 1986, p. 2. For the dimensions of such reserves, see TIAA-CREF Annual Report 1986.

18. The same is true of mutual life insurance companies, except in that case, undistributed surplus builds up over time; as a result, there may be intergenerational transfers, with previous generations of policyholders or annuitants providing investment risk backup to the current generation. TIAA claims that it has minimal or no such intergenerational transfers, the contingency reserves contributed by and for individual participants being

drawn down and paid out to those participants during the payout period to the extent practicable (TIAA, *The Participant,* June 1986, p. 2; TIAA-CREF Executive Vice President Donald S. Willard, *Tax Notes,* March 10, 1986, p. 1000). Whether that claim is completely accurate is not important for present purposes. It may be noted that the Section 38 guarantee of the mortality table will involve some (probably fairly small) intergenerational transfers.

19. See, for example, Alliance of American Insurers, *1986 Policy Kit for Students of Insurance,* pp. 320, 322.

20. It is tempting to call the TIAA annuity a fixed-dollar annuity, but, unlike the comparable product of many commercial companies, there is participation in excess earnings such that recently, the TIAA annuity payments have gone up even when CREF annuities, based on the state of the stock markets, were going down. This behavior is inconsistent with the common notion that the sole reason for creating CREF was to serve as a hedge against inflation. At least in the short run, it is an imperfect hedge; CREF annuities declined recently even while inflation soared, and then they increased as inflation came under control. But see Ad Hoc Committee Report, note 1 above, which states, "Changes in the value of common stocks and other equities are by no means perfectly correlated with cost of living changes, but they have provided a considerably better protection against inflation than have debt obligations" (p. 12).

21. The *New York Insurance Law* (McKinney's, 1984–85 Cumulative Annual Pocket Part) provides, in Section 91, that, "All bonds . . . having a fixed term and rate of interest . . . , if amply secured and if not in default as to principal or interest, shall be valued as follows: If purchased at par, at the par value; if purchased above or below par, on the basis of the purchase price adjusted so as to bring the value to par at maturity and so as to yield in the meantime the effective rate of interest at which the purchase was made."

22. Ad Hoc Committee Report, note 1 above, p. 69.

23. Ad Hoc Committee Report, note 1 above, p. 70, fn. 7.

24. Alliance of American Insurers, *1986 Policy Kit for Students of Insurance,* pp. 320, 322.

25. For example, see the Ad Hoc Committee Report, note 1 above, pp. 12, 83.

26. Schmitt and Hobbie, in "Teachers Insurance and Annuity Association-College Retirement Equity Fund (TIAA-CREF) and the Tax Bill (H.R. 3838): Issues and Analysis" (memorandum of Congressional Research Service, Library of Congress, Jan. 28, 1986, revised Mar. 13, 1986), say that TIAA-CREF "views itself as a 'pooled pension trust,' and says it should have the tax-exempt treatment of such a trust" (p. 11). That statement is not strictly accurate. TIAA-CREF emphasized its differences from commercial insurers and insisted that it should not be subject to any greater tax burden than is applicable to pension trusts (which is zero). See, for example, a statement of Donald S. Willard, executive vice president of TIAA-CREF, in an exchange in *Tax Notes* (p. 999) of Mar. 10, 1986, that to compare "TIAA with stock and mutual commercial insurance companies may have some validity as to form, but certainly not as to substance. Although TIAA was technically formed as a New York stock insurance company in 1918 before *pension trust* provisions were added to the Code, it was and is quite unlike a commercial insurance company since by charter *and charitable trust law* it can operate only for exclusively educational purposes" (emphasis added). In testimony before congressional committees, James G. MacDonald, chairman and chief executive officer of TIAA-CREF, urged the existing subjection of both TIAA and CREF to the "charitable trust principles of common law and New York statutes which are enforced by the Attorney General and courts of New York State" as a reason for such favorable treatment (statement before the Senate Finance Committee, hearings on H.R. 3838, Washington, D.C., Feb. 4, 1986, p. 5).

27. Dewey, Ballantine opinion, note 7 above (Section 1.4 of this volume).

28. Dewey, Ballantine opinion, note 7 above, pp. 18–19 (Section 1.4, pp. 101–102 of this volume).

29. See, for example, p. 6, where *Chatham County Hospital Authority* is quoted for the effect of annuity agreements. Again, on p. 9, numerous cases are cited to show that annuity and insurance contracts are construed under contract law principles. Note 2 on p. 10 refers to the payout phase of CREF, apparently without recognition that there is an earlier period when there are no retirement equities because the accumulated funds may first be paid out in full on death or transferred in part or in full to TIAA, all under CREF's own rules. In CREF's case, clearly, there is no annuity contract until retirement unless form is elevated so far above substance that the latter is given no significance at all. (Cf. TIAA-CREF's position reported in note 26.) The argument on p. 11 that the contract cannot be modified without a writing signed by a CREF representative depends at least on the contract being an annuity contract during accumulation — the first question to be resolved. See also p. 12, fn. 3.

30. *Transferability,* note 5 above, Appendix A (Section 1.4 of this volume, Appendix A).

31. *Transferability,* note 5 above, Appendix A.

32. Compare Dewey, Ballantine opinion, note 7 above, p. 17 (Sec. 1.4 of this volume, p. 100), "TIAA has a *material proprietary interest* in the investment of its assets and its consent would be required under the statute" (emphasis added), with MacDonald's statement to the Senate Finance Committee (note 26 above, p. 3) that the TIAA-CREF system is "an arm of higher education" and with the Ad Hoc Committee Report (note 1 above, p. 15), "There was general agreement by the Committee to this statement: *The principal purpose of TIAA-CREF is and should be to serve educational institutions through the provision of pensions and related plans for retirement income and for insurance for faculty and staff"* (emphasis in original).

33. Ad Hoc Committee Report, note 1 above, p. A-1, note.

34. Dewey, Ballantine opinion, note 7 above, pp. 5, 23 (Section 1.4 of this volume, pp. 86, 106).

35. See *Restatement of Trusts* (Second), Section 227 (c); *Scott on Trusts,* Section 227.9 (3rd ed., 1967, with 1984 Supp.). Common trust statutes will not help; they are limited to banks and

trust companies. But see the organic act for CREF, note 37 below, and accompanying text.

36. To show that commingled funds can be a trust res, Professor Clark uses *Community Services, Inc.* v. *United States,* 422 F.2d 1353 (Claims Ct. 1970), in which a somewhat similar arrangement with an insurance company for retirement annuities was described as a deposit administration group annuity contract. In a controversy between Community Services and the IRS, the Claims Court held the arrangement to be a trust, the trust res being the employer's contributions, though they were commingled with the funds of the insurer. On the crucial point, the necessary nature of a trust res, the case is precisely in point with the TIAA-CREF contracts. Apparently not understanding the proposition for which Clark was using *Community Services,* Dewey denies its applicability (pp. 24, 25), citing to the contrary *Mundell* v. *Gibbs,* 70 Misc. 2d 174, 332 N.Y.S.2d 364 (1970), in which the court said there was no trust res, the insurer's obligations being to make certain payments out of its general funds. The question whether commingled funds could be a trust res was neither raised nor discussed in *Mundell.*

37. New York Laws of 1952, Chapter 124, Section 4.

38. See note 26 above, and text related thereto.

39. *Transferability,* note 5 above, p. A-7 (Section 1.3 of this volume, p. 78).

40. Section 201(b): "Type B—A not-for-profit corporation of this type may be formed for any one or more of the following non-business purposes: charitable, educational, religious, scientific, literary, cultural or for the prevention of cruelty to children or animals. Type C—A not-for-profit corporation of this type may be formed for any lawful business purpose to achieve a lawful public or quasi-public objective. . . . If a corporation has among its purposes any purpose which is within Type C, such corporation is a Type C corporation."

41. Class B was presumably chosen by CREF because the language defining it parallels the language of 26 U.S.C. Section

501(c)(3), under which TIAA and CREF claimed exemption from federal income taxation. Whatever the reason for the choice, it seems inept; Class C fits better.

42. *Transferability,* pp. A-7, 8 (Section 1.3 of this volume, pp. 78, 79).

43. See generally, E. Levi, *An Introduction to Legal Reasoning* (1949), 4, 6, and B. Cardozo, *The Nature of the Judicial Process* (1921), 40. See also L. Green, *Judge and Jury* (1930), 226: "There is no *one* way of stating in terms of legal theory a desired conclusion. Legal theory is too rich in content not to afford alternative ways, and frequently several of them, for stating an acceptable judgment" (emphasis in original).

44. See Schmitt and Hobbie, note 26 above.

45. Letter of March 20, 1987, to author from David E. Watts of Dewey, Ballantine.

46. Dewey, Ballantine opinion, note 7 above, pp. 31–32 (Section 1.4 of this volume, pp. 115–116).

47. 29 U.S.C. 1144, Section 514.

48. 482 N.Y.S.2d 875, 876 (1984).

49. 509 F.Supp. 388, 391 (E.D. Cal. 1981).

50. In a reply to Dewey's opinion. Draft of Feb. 11, 1987, in possession of author (reprinted in Section 1.5 of this volume).

51. 605 F.Supp. 421 (E.D. Mo. 1985).

52. 605 F.Supp. 429 (E.D. Mo. 1985).

53. 605 F.Supp. 428 (E.D. Mo. 1985).

54. 507 F.Supp. 618 (S.D. Texas, Houston Div. 1981).

55. 507 F.Supp. 620 (S.D. Texas, Houston Div. 1981).

56. Ad Hoc Committee Report, note 1 above, p. 3.

57. Ad Hoc Committee Report, note 1 above, pp. 77–80, 83. The Ad Hoc Committee considered an equity real estate fund

and recommended further study of the possibility. A successful real estate fund is at this time only a remote possibility for CREF. It may be noted, however, that several groups of mutual funds are now launching real estate funds for use in IRAs and Keogh plans.

58. Some participants would probably opt for a locked-in annuity model, which should remain an option but not be the only one. I am not hostile to the present TIAA individual deferred annuity model, as such. For many academics, the additional return said to be made possible by the TIAA lock in (in conversation, estimated at 0.1 percent per annum) is attractive for some part of retirement funds, even at the price of locking in the assets permanently, if that is necessary for either practical or legal reasons. My contentions here are only (1) that a way to unlock the funds without losing the added return should be sought, and (2) that an academic should have the opportunity to select options that do not involve locking up the assets, even if the extra return must be traded for them.

59. Dewey, Ballantine opinion, note 7 above, p. 25 (Section 1.4 of this volume, p. 108). If one reads the opinion charitably, it may be read as applying the adjective *enormous* only to the TIAA problem. But the letter overstates the difficulties in calculating the appropriate amounts for transfers from CREF.

60. Ad Hoc Committee Report, note 1 above, p. 77.

61. For a brief introduction to tax law constraints, see Ad Hoc Committee Report, note 1 above, p. 111.

62. Dewey, Ballantine opinion, note 7 above, p. 27 (Section 1.4 of this volume, p. 110).

63. There might be some adverse selection if males were to withdraw from TIAA and CREF to get the advantage of separate-sex annuity tables. (TIAA and CREF now use unisex tables; not all other insurers do, as yet.) Because a large proportion of male annuitants take joint and survivor annuities, however, that advantage from opting out of TIAA and CREF does not exist for most retirees.

64. Ad Hoc Committee Report, note 1 above, pp. 70, 72.

65. For the same reason, I consider the 10 percent cashout privilege at retirement (Retirement Transition Benefit, or RTB) to present serious problems of inequity. Unless that benefit can be valued at market, it should not be allowed for TIAA accumulations, even though the privilege does not seem to have been much abused. For CREF accumulations, there is no problem. But the sometimes suggested 25 percent RTB would be even more objectionable when applied to TIAA accumulations. The cashability of the supplemental retirement annuity accumulations is similarly objectionable, to the extent that the accumulations are in TIAA and in a nonsegregated portfolio.

66. Dewey, Ballantine opinion, note 7 above, pp. 28–30 (Section 1.4 of this volume, pp. 111–113).

67. According to an international memorandum of May 22, 1986, entitled "TIAA Investment Portfolio Market Value Estimates," outside consultants are used for part of the process. In recent years, "the method used for these market value estimates involves an evaluation of every item in the investment portfolio, according to the Ad Hoc Committee Report (note 1 above, p. 68).

68. The individual accumulations are already calculated by vintage (at book value), in order to credit them with the appropriate interest earnings. See TIAA-CREF, *Some Thoughts About the CREF Transfer-to-TIAA Option* TIAA-CREF (1986), p. 8.

69. Ad Hoc Committee Report, note 1 above, p. 67. The statement is made that under a policy permitting cashouts or transfers, "The present predictability of TIAA's cash flow *could be* impaired or eliminated," requiring modifications in investment policy "which *could* result in lower long-term rates of return" (emphasis added). Much of the need for liquidity in ordinary life insurance companies comes from the right to borrow against the cash value. Borrowing from funds accumulated for retirement is undesirable, and should be allowed, if at all, only in narrowly defiined emergency situations. There is no reason in experience to suppose that great instability would result from transferability from TIAA to other custodians.

70. Ad Hoc Committee Report, note 1 above, p. 84.

71. In *Securities and Exchange Commission* v. *Variable Annuity Life Ins. Co. of America et al.*, 359 U.S. 65 (1959), Justice Douglas erroneously but, of course, authoritatively made the transfer of investment risk the defining characteristic of insurance for purposes of the federal securities laws. He did so, however, in the context of contracts that also transferred a mortality risk for a part of their duration. In the TIAA accumulation phase, only investment risk is transferred, and even that transfer is more show than substance.

72. Dewey, Ballantine opinion, note 7 above, p. 29 (Section 1.4 of this volume, p. 112).

73. Section 3204(a)(3).

74. Perhaps a lesson can be learned from the cases on change of beneficiaries in life insurance. No matter how emphatically the insurance contract may specify that any change in the policy terms must be endorsed on the policy before the change is effective, the courts will be satisfied with less, such as when the insured has done all that he or she can, or (under some cases) when the insured has engaged in conduct that is directed toward making the change and establishes his intentions beyond doubt. So also here? See R. Keeton, *Basic Text on Insurance Law*, (1971), 253.

75. Section 208(c)5.

76. National Association of Insurance Commissioners, *Model Laws, Regulations and Guidelines* (1977), 805-1–805-4.

77. Ibid. 805-5–805-8.

78. See Ad Hoc Committee Report, note 1 above, App. A, pp. 111–12 for some tax considerations.

79. Ad Hoc Committee Report, note 1 above, pp. 70, 113. The relevant section is N.Y. Ins. Law Section 4223(a)(1)(B), which requires that an annuity contract contain, among others, the following provision: "If a contract provides for a lump sum settlement at maturity, or at any other time, that upon surrender of the contract at or prior to the commencement of any annuity

payments, the company will pay in lieu of any paid-up annuity benefit a cash surrender benefit of such amount as is specified in subsections (e), (g) and (i) of this section. The company shall reserve the right to defer the payment of such cash surrender benefit for a period of six months after demand therefor with surrender of the contract."

Section 1.3

1. Section 7-1.9 Revocation of trusts (a) Upon the written consent, acknowledged or proved in the manner required by the laws of this state for the recording of a conveyance of real property, of all the persons beneficially interested in a trust of property, heretofore or hereafter created, the creator of such trust may revoke or amend the whole or any part thereof by an instrument in writing acknowledged or proved in like manner, and thereupon the estate of the trustee ceases with respect to any part of such trust property, the disposition of which has been revoked. If the conveyance or other instrument creating a trust of property was recorded in the office of the clerk or register of any county in this state, the instrument revoking or amending such trust, together with the consents thereto, shall be recorded in the same office of every county in which the conveyance or other instrument creating such trust was recorded.

2. "Report to Carnegie Corporation of New York and Carnegie Foundation for the Advancement of Teaching from TIAA" (1957), p. 1.

3. Report, "A Comprehensive Plan of Insurance and Annuities for College Teachers," The Carnegie Foundation for the Advancement of Teaching (1916), p. 15.

4. "A Report to the Trustees of the Carnegie Foundation by the Commission Chosen to Consider a Plan of Insurance and Annuities" (1917), p. 11.

5. Report (note 2 above), p. 3.

6. *Scott on Trusts,* Vol. 1 (24) (1967).

7. *Restatement of the Law of Trusts,* Second, Vol. 1, p. 66.

8. *Coleman* v. *Golkin, Bomback & Co., Inc.,* 562 F.2d 166, 169 (C.A. 2 1977).

9. 422 F.2d 1353 (Claims Ct. 1970).

10. 422 F.2d, p. 1356–57.

11. 683 F.2d 520 (C.A.D.C. 1982).

12. 683 F.2d, p. 533.

13. Retirement Unit-Annuity Certificate (CREF), p. 1.

14. TIAA guarantees 2.5 percent interest on the funds transferred to it. However, this miminal return has no practical effect on TIAA obligations today. TIAA holds long-term assets paying substantially more than this, and Courts have ruled that this nominal obligation does not prohibit TIAA from taking steps consistent with public policy to modify its rules (*Spirt* v. *Teachers Insurance & Annuity Association,* 691 F.2d 1054 (2d Cir. 1982), 735 F.2d 23 (2d Cir. 1984)). Even if, far in the future, TIAA could not earn this rate of return, it would have no source of corporate funds, other than the funds supplied to it by its participants, to meet those obligations.

15. 37 McKinney's Consolidated Laws of New York, *Not-for-Profit Corporation Law,* p. 162.

16. See Revisers' Notes, above, which describe the increased flexibility authorized by the statute as follows:

> As compared with trust law, the section gives the directors greater freedom of investment, including the pooling of two or more funds. In addition, the section removes some practical obstacles to the investment of endowment or similar funds in growth, rather than fixed income, securities. This is done by authorizing directors to include in the income of such funds that portion of the realized appreciation of principal as they deem prudent. The directors may therefore, after taking into account the effect of such factors as inflation, properly protect the availability of current income by realization of increased value of securities and similar properties in the fund.

17. For a discussion of the law governing the delegation of investment responsibilities both within and outside the corporation, see Cary and Bright, "The Delegation of Investment Responsibility for Endowment Funds," 74-1 *Col. L. Rev.* 207 (1974).

18. Were a court to hold that Section 513(a) makes EPTL Section 7-1.9 unavailable to the parties, they, either as individuals or in conjunction with the attorney general, might then bring an action to compel TIAA-CREF to take the steps authorized in Not-for-Profit Corporation Law Sections 513 and 514 for the improved management of the funds. Their standing to bring such a suit is established under the rules set out in *Alco Gravure, Inc.* v. *Knapp Foundation*, 64 N.Y.2d 458, 479 N.E.2d 752, 490 N.Y.S.2d 116 (1985).

19. See, for example, comment in *Restatement of the Law of Trusts, Second*, Vol. 1, p. 40:

> Even though the insurance company is not a trustee, however, many of the rules applicable to trusts are applicable to this kind of contract, rather than the rules which are applicable to ordinary debts. Thus, just as a restraint on the alienation of the interest of a beneficiary under a trust may be valid (see Section 152, 153), so a restraint on the interest of the beneficiary of an insurance policy may be valid, since the policy permitting spendthrift trusts is equally applicable to life insurance contracts. See Section 152, Comment p. So too, just as a court may permit or direct the trustee to deviate from a term of the trust if owing to circumstances not known to the settlor and not anticipated by him compliance would defeat or substantially impair the accomplishment of the purposes of the trust (see Section 167), and in particular may permit or direct the trustee to apply income and principal from the trust estate for the necessary support of a beneficiary of the trust before the time when by the terms of the trust he is entitled to the enjoyment of such income or principal, provided the interest of no other beneficiary of the trust is impaired thereby (see Section 168), so the court may permit or direct a similar deviation in the case of a life insurance policy.

It is not novel to the law of New York to use the trust label in order to achieve some desired result. Thus under Debtor and Creditor Law Section 21-a employer contributions to an employee pension fund are deemed to be held in trust in order that the employee will have a priority over general creditors in the event of the employer's insolvency.

20. Paragraph (a) of EPTL Section 7-1.9 is basically declaratory of existing law (*Scott on Trusts*, Vol, 4, Section 329A (1967)).

21. "Report of the TIAA-CREF Ad Hoc Committee on Goals and Objectives to the Joint Boards of Trustees of TIAA-CREF" (1984) pp. 3, 65–66.

22. The report reads as follows at pages 65–66:

The absolute dedication to the support of life annuity payments of funds accumulated in TIAA-CREF deferred annuities could not be assured following cashouts or transfers of existing TIAA-CREF annuity accumulations to other financial vehicles. An initial transfer vehicle might offer or require life annuity options, but the original contractual provisions under which the funds were accumulated cannot necessarily control if the annuity contract has been terminated. Subsequent transfers of the same funds could be made, and it might become quite easy to escort funds through a simple series of tax-free transfers that, for example, end up in an IRA under which cash amounts may be withdrawn at any time, and without penalty after age 59-½.

Section 1.4

1. Our opinion is directed to the Clark Opinion's conclusion that an institution and one of its employee-participants in TIAA or CREF could jointly require a transfer of assets held by TIAA or CREF to a third party investment manager without the consent of TIAA or CREF. We do not address other questions, such as whether it would be legal, practical, appropriate and desirable for TIAA or CREF to consent to such transfers under any particular circumstance.

2. CREF is specifically authorized by the terms of the special act by which it was formed to provide retirement equities "with such participation rights and on such other terms and conditions as said corporation may from time to time approve and adopt." Section 4 of Chapter 124, Laws of New York of 1952. This provision clearly authorizes the limitation of amendments stated in the CREF contracts, and any premature transfer would of course require an amendment of the contract.

3. The statute clearly applies to TIAA, which is formed under the New York Insurance Law. There may be some question as to its direct application to CREF, which is subject to specified provisions of the New York Insurance Law under the special act of the New York Legislature. However, in view of the general applicability of the statute to annuity contracts, it appears likely that the same result as provided by the statute would be reached by giving effect to CREF's similar contractual requirement, especially since CREF annuity contracts are subject to the approval of the New York Department of Insurance, which requires such a contractual provision.

4. The only "property" that is separately allocable to a particular participant and that could therefore constitute a res for a separate trust for such participant is the promise of TIAA or CREF to make future payments of an annuity in the amounts and at the times prescribed by the annuity contract. However, the right to receive such future payments, even if deemed to be held in trust by some person, would not provide any current funds for investment by a third party investment manager.

5. Any holder of long-term bonds, or of a Baldwin-United annuity contract, during the interest rate fluctuations of the last decade would recognize the burden of TIAA's guarantee to pay an annuity based upon stated principal values, without regard to any lower value of TIAA's assets based on their investment during periods of lower interest rates.

6. See, for example, Comments, CCH Pension Plan Guide, Paragraphs 467.131 and 2450.25.

7. The arrangements for payment of an accumulated account value on death in the case of both CREF and TIAA, and for transfers from CREF to TIAA at retirement or at an age where retirement might be in contemplation, might in theory adversely affect other participants. However, the impact of these provisions is relatively predictable and limited in extent, and is not significantly subject to adverse selection or disintermediation. Similarly, in the case of the supplemental retirement annuity contracts that permit cash surrender and that are issued under limited circumstances by CREF and TIAA, the potential adverse effect on other participants is substantially limited by the front-end charges imposed on the issuance of such contracts, which charges inure to the benefit of all participants, and by the practical limitations on cash surrenders resulting from tax considerations and the loss of annuitization.

8. Other clauses of Section 514(b) set forth additional exceptions to the general preemption rule of Section 514(a), including exceptions for state criminal laws and certain state laws relating to a "multiple employer welfare arrangement" (which is defined as a fully insured welfare plan and would not include an annuity arrangement which is considered a pension plan under Section 3(2) of ERISA).

The only judicially created exceptions to the preemption rule are those relating to divorce and separation decrees and family support orders. See, for example, *Ball* v. *Johns-Manville Corp. Retirement Plan*, 522 F.Supp. 718 (D. D.C. 1981).

9. The Department of Labor has also taken the position that state laws restricting the types of assets in which a trust may invest are preempted by ERISA with respect to employee benefit plans. See Department of Labor Regulations Section 2550.404a-1 and the preamble thereto (issued in the Federal Register of June 26, 1979, 44 Fed. Reg. 37225).

10. Under the exception in Section 514(b)(2)(A) of ERISA, the New York State Insurance Law would not, of course, be preempted.

11. Prohibited Transaction Exemption 81-82 issued by the Department of Labor on September 15, 1981 (at Section II of the preamble).

Section 1.5

1. New York Not-for-Profit Law, Section 514. Delegation of investment management: (a) Except as otherwise provided by the applicable gift instrument, the governing board may (1) delegate to its committees, officers or employees of the corporation or the fund, or agents, including investment counsel, the authority to act in place of the governing board in investment and reinvestment of institutional funds, (2) contract with independent investment advisors, investment counsel or managers, banks, or trust companies, so to act. . . .

ERISA Section 402(c)(3) . . . (c) Any employee benefit plan may provide . . . that a person who is a named fiduciary with respect to control or management of the assets of the plan may appoint an investment manager or managers to manage (including the power to acquire and dispose of) any assets of a plan.

2. In this regard, trusts are frequently used as devices to accumulate wealth to be at some future date paid out or converted into another form of property holding to achieve a specific purpose. For example, trusts are used to purchase life insurance or a future annuity or to defray such family expenses as school tuitions, maintenance in old age, hospitalization and the like. The laws governing the administration of the trust are separate and distinct from the laws that govern any nontrust interest into which the trust funds have been converted.

3. *Charles, Henry & Crowley Co.* v. *Home Insurance Co.*, 349 Mass. 723 (issue was whether damage caused by a rock through a window followed by a theft was covered under a jeweler's block policy); *Green Bus Lines, Inc.* v. *Consolidated Mutual Insurance Co.*, 426 N.Y.S.2d 981 (issue was whether insured's indemnification policy covered liability for injuries to employees using solvents); *Michigan Millers Mutual Insurance Co.* v. *Christopher*, 413 N.Y.S.2d 264 (issue was whether insured who shot and killed an intruder

was covered for potential liability under his homeowner's policy). It is difficult to see how under any framing of the issues here these cases are relevant.

Other cases cited in the Dewey opinion illustrate the point that I make herein that an insurance contract exists when the company owns the contributed funds and bears the risks of mortality and investment. *Uhlman* v. *New York Life Insurance Co.*, 109 N.Y. 421 (company, not the policyholders, owns the funds and the dividend that the holders may receive depends on many contingencies all under the control of the company); *Holmes* v. *John Hancock Mutual Life Ins. Co.*, 288 N.Y. 106 (contract for deferred payment of benefits not subject to rule against perpetuities). One case in this group of cases involving the payout of insurance proceeds, *Matter of Nires*, 290 N.Y. 78, deserves special note because the three dissenters of the seven-judge New York Court of Appeals would have applied a trust remedy to a payout arrangement that everyone agreed was an insurance contract and not a trust. The issue involved a mother's petition to obtain an allowance for support of minor children from accumulated interest on the proceeds of their father's life insurance policy left on deposit with the company. The court held that a trust was not created primarily because the interest was not determined by what the principal actually earns but by applying a fixed three per cent rate and thus "The beneficiaries have no share in the increase or decrease in value of the assets."

Connick v. *TIAA*, 784 F.2d 1018, is representative of a number of cases holding that a teacher upon retirement cannot demand a lump sum payment of TIAA-CREF benefits. The situation here is entirely different in that the teacher is not acting alone but in conjunction with his employer and annuitization at retirement continues to be the objective.

4. See Schmitt and Hobbie, *Teachers Insurance and Annuity Association-College Retirement Equity Fund (TIAA-CREF) and the Tax Bill (H.R. 3838): Issues and Analysis,* Congressional Research Service, Library of Congress, January 28, 1986, revised March 13, 1986.

5. *Tax Notes,* March 10, 1986, pp. 999–1000.

6. "The comparison of TIAA with stock and mutual commercial insurance companies may have some validity as to form, but certainly not as to substance. . . . But the very factor that makes it appropriate to analogize mutual insurance companies to stock companies for tax purposes, the growth of uncommitted surplus, sharply distinguishes them from TIAA. In contrast to TIAA, mutual companies can accumulate surplus reserves that can be, and frequently are, used for purposes not related to the classes of beneficiaries or purposes to which the funds were initially attributable. However, virtually all of TIAA's assets and operations (and the entire reserves that are here at issue) involved pension funds under section 403(a) or (b) of the Code, an area to which a general policy of tax deferral applies" (Willard, *Tax Notes,* March 10, 1986, p. 999).

7. Citations, almost without end, can be found to support the proposition that a trust can exist even if not so labeled. See generally, *Scott on Trusts,* Vol. 1, p. 24 (1967); *Restatement of the Law of Trusts,* Second, Vol. 1, p. 66.

8. The New York Court of Appeals has recognized this principle at least since 1885. See *Barry* v. *Lambert,* 98 N.Y. 300, 306 (1885) ("No difficulty arises from the blendings of the money of the estate, with that of another person in the same loan, for the units of which it is composed being of equal value it is clearly severable and distinguishable, and sufficient data are given to enable such severance to be made.") See generally, Annotation, Investment of Trust Funds in Share or Part of Single Security or Group or Pool of Securities, 125 A.L.R. 669.

9. 422 F.2d 1353 (Claims Ct. 1970).

10. 683 F.2d 520 (C.A.D.C. 1982).

11. There are a great number and variety of cases that might have been selected to illustrate the conceptual difference between a trust and contract. These two were chosen because they presented situations quite similar to the facts at issue here. As I stated in Note 3, above, I believe that a number of the cases cited in the Dewey opinion provide excellent illustrations of the point I am making. See in particular *Matter of Nires,* 290 N.Y.

78 to the effect that there is no trust when the "beneficiaries have no share in the increase or decrease in value of the assets." The Dewey opinion cites *Mundell* v. *Gibbs,* 70 Misc. 2d 174, 332 N.Y.S.2d 364, as being in opposition to the argument made in the *Community Services* case. To the contrary, *Mundell* affirms the proposition that there is no trust when the contributions are paid into the general funds of the insurance company.

12. CREF recently sent to all its participants an endorsement to his or her certificate effective on January 1, 1987, amending the method of valuing accumulation units. The explanatory statement speaks of the units as being owned by the participant.

13. At one point it appears that the Dewey opinion views CREF's claimed ownership of the funds as rendering CREF immune from accountability to anyone for its administration of the funds during the accumulation phase. The opinion at page 30 finds "astonishing" a suggestion that I made in a footnote that the parties might seek to have CREF transfer the funds to an outside manager under the authority of Section 514 of the *New York Not-for-Profit Corporation Law.* CREF's administration of funds is reviewable by the New York Attorney General under Section 112 of that Law. New York case law has adopted a sufficiently broad definition of the party-in-interest rule to allow a teacher and college here to participate in and even initiate such a review. *Alco Gravure, Inc.* v. *Knapp Foundation,* 64 N.Y.2d 458, 479 N.E.2d 752, 490 N.Y.S.2d 116 (1985). Section 514 does not require a corporation to transfer funds to outside investment managers. It does, however, authorize such a transfer and thereby certifies that such a procedure, if properly used, is prudent. It is hardly "astonishing" to suggest that dissatisfied parties may, upon making proof that their dissatisfaction is justified, request a court for a show cause order as to why the corporation should not use the prudent management techniques set out in the statutes to improve performance.

14. 281 N.Y. 115, 22 N.E.2d 305.

15. This principle is recognized in *Not-for-Profit Corporation Law,* Section 102(17) which states that "institutional fund" does not

include "(ii) a fund in which a beneficiary that is not a not-for-profit corporation has an interest (other than possible rights that could arise upon violation or failure of the purposes of the fund)." The Comment in the Uniform Management of Institutional Funds Act, 7A ULA 713, to the section from which the New York law is derived explains it as follows: "A fund held by an institution for the benefit of any noninstitutional beneficiary is also excluded. The exclusion would apply to any fund with an individual beneficiary such as an annuity trust or a unitrust. When the interest of a noninstitutional beneficiary is terminated, the fund may then become an institutional fund."

16. See, for example, Keeton, *Basic Insurance Law,* paragraph entitled "AUTHORITY" in form policy on p. 1049 (1977).

17. *Central States, Southeast and Southwest Areas Pension Fund* v. *Central Transport, Inc.,* 472 U.S. 559, 570, 86 L. Ed. 2d 447, 454, 105 S. Ct. 2833 (1985).

18. *Shaw* v. *Delta Air Lines, Inc.,* 463 U.S. 85, 103 S. Ct. 2890, 77 L. Ed. 2d 490 (1983).

19. *Lane* v. *Goren,* 743 F.2d 1337, 1339 (9th Cir. 1984) (California statute regulating discriminatory employment practices of the trustee not preempted).

20. *Savings and Profit Sharing Fund of Sears Employees* v. *Gago,* 717 F.2d 1038, 1040 (7th Cir. 1938) (Wisconsin court order awarding divorced spouse a share in beneficiary's pension fund not preempted).

21. *Rebaldo* v. *Cuomo,* 749 F.2d 133, 139 (2d Cir. 1984). N.Y. EPTL Section 7-1.9 is a "statute of general application," which encompasses all trusts; it in no way singles out employee benefit trusts or subjects them to special rules.

22. For a detailed exposition of this analysis, see Kilberg and Inman, "Preemption of State Laws Relating to Employee Benefit Plans: An Analysis of ERISA Section 514," 62 *Texas L. Rev.* 1313, 1327–31 (1984).

23. *Sasso* v. *Vachris,* 66 N.Y.2d 28, 33, 494 N.Y.S.2d 856, 859, 484 N.E.2d 1359, 1362 (1985) ("Analysis begins with the pre-

sumption that the State law has not been preempted by Federal statute (ERISA) in the absence of persuasive evidence to the contrary.")

24. See, for example, *Central States, Southeast and Southwest Areas Pension Fund* v. *Central Transport, Inc.,* 472 U.S. 559, 105 S. Ct. 2833, 86 L. Ed. 2d 447 (1985).

25. 463 U.S. 85, 103 S. Ct. 2890, 77 L. Ed. 2d 490 (1983).

26. Section 338, *Restatement of the Law of Trusts* 2d.

> Consent of Beneficiaries and Settlor
> (1) If the settlor and all the beneficiaries of a trust consent and none of them is under an incapacity, they can compel the termination or modification of the trust, although the purposes of the trust have not been accomplished.

27. *Scott on Trusts,* Section 338.

Section 2.2

1. See, generally, W. Graebner, *A History of Retirement,* Yale University Press (1980); also L. M. Friedman, *Your Time Will Come: The Law of Age Discrimination and Mandatory Retirement,* Russell Sage Foundation (1985), p. 73 et seq.

2. See, generally, *Faculty Tenure: A Report and Recommendations by the Commission on Academic Tenure in Higher Education* (1973) and, at p. 93, W. P. Metzger, "Academic Tenure in America: A Historical Essay."

3. Although on almost every aspect of tenure the policies and practices of different academic institutions may vary widely, their central features have enough in common to merit referring to a tenure system. It is not only the substance, but the form of the tenure contract that varies among institutions. Normally, the contract is expressed in principles adopted by the academic institutions and accepted by its faculty. The contract terms can, however, be readily reduced to a formal agreement signed by the academic institution and its tenured faculty member.

4. Tenure, so highly developed in institutions of higher education, is not entirely unique to them. See "Due Process in Decisions Relating to Tenure in Higher Education," a report of the Special Committee on Education and the Law in Vol. 39 of *The Record* of The Association of the Bar of the City of New York (1984), p. 392.

5. The tenure contracts in actual use do not so neatly express this arrangement. This lack of contractual neatness may create difficulties in the proof, but it does not negate the existence, of the arrangement itself. This lack of neatness also tends to create a misconception in academia that the so-called contract system (involving contracts with faculty for a term of years) is legally to be distinguished from the tenure system (which involves contracts until retirement). Legally, however, both systems are contract systems. Colleges and universities might find it desirable, accordingly, to describe the terms of the tenure arrangement more clearly and fully than they have in the past and do so in a formal agreement.

6. Retirement is a career change, but it does not require cessation of all activity. Hence, retirement does not preclude new arrangements to involve retired faculty in continuing activity at their institution, or elsewhere.

7. U.S. Constitution Art. I, Sections 2 and 3 and Art. II, Section I.

8. U.S. Constitution Art. XXVI, Section 1 (the Twenty-Sixth Amendment).

9. 42 U.S.C.A. Section 402, 416(1).

10. Internal Revenue Code Section 401(a)(9) (pension plan) and Sec. 408(a) and (f) (IRA).

11. See Select Committee on Aging of the U.S. House of Representatives, *Federal Responsibility to the Elderly: Executive Programs and Legislative Jurisdiction* (1977). See also, E. A. Kutza *"The Benefits of Old Age,"* University of Chicago Press (1981), passim, but particularly pp. 30–54.

12. 50 U.S.C.A. App. Sec. 453.

13. See note 50 below.

14. For an example of the use of age as a criterion in regulations, see the FAA regulations prohibiting persons from serving as pilots or first officers on a commercial flight after their sixtieth birthday. 14 CFR Sec. 121.383(c) (1985).

15. For thoughtful analyses and differing perspectives of age as a criterion for differing social purposes, see particularly B. L. Neugarten (ed.), *Age or Need: Public Policies for Older People,* Sage Publications (1982); E. A. Kutza and N. R. Zweibel: "Age as a Criterion for Focusing Public Programs," pp. 55–99; F. L. Cook: "Assessing Age as an Eligibility Criterion," pp. 171–203; and C. D. Austin and M. B. Loeb: "Why Age Is Relevant in Social Policy and Practice," pp. 263–288.

16. See R. H. Binstock and E. Shanas, *Handbook of Aging and the Social Sciences,* Van Nostrand Reinhold Company (1985), p. 697, where it is said, "The relationship between chronological age and health and illness is well-known and well-documented in life tables and epidemiological reports on the distribution of disease and impairment. Chronological age is a basic and the best single general predictor of mortality as indicated by death rates; age is also associated with morbidity as indicated by an age-related incidence and prevalence of disease and disability."

17. Rand Corporation, *Geriatrics in the United States: Manpower Projections and Training Considerations* (1980), p. v.

18. See, for example, "The Biological Facts of Aging" in J. W. Walker and H. L. Lazer, *The End of Mandatory Retirement,* Wiley (1978), p. 147 et seq.

19. See, for example, *Mass. Board of Retirement* v. *Murgia,* 427 U.S. 307, 311 (1976): "The testimony clearly established that the risk of physical failure, particularly in the cardiovascular system, increases with age, and that the number of individuals in a given age group incapable of performing stress functions increases with the age of the group."

20. The percentage estimates vary but all of them are substantial in size. See 63 *Milbank Memorial Fund Quarterly, Health and*

Society (1985) wherein J. Rosenwaike, "A Demographic Portrait of the Oldest Old," p. 201, said, "More than 70 percent of those aged 85 and over require assistance in connection with some of their normal daily activities, whereas only 10 percent of those aged 65 to 74 are in this category" [citation omitted]; and in R. Suzman and M. W. Riley, p. 181, the calculation indicates that, of those aged eighty-five and over, 57 percent are either institutionalized or "need the help of another to function in daily life."

21. "The National Center for Health Statistics projects that the proportion of people aged sixty-five and older who are limited in their daily activities because of chronic illness may increase from 38 to 64 percent over the next twenty years" (*Report by the U. S. General Accounting Office to the Chairman of the Senate Committee on Labor and Human Resources,* December 7, 1982, GAO/1PE-83-1).

22. Some still consider it unfair, however. See, for example, Friedman, note 1 above, p. 33. It is not easy to understand, however, if the use of chronological age as a criterion for retirement is unfair, why does it then become fair to use chronological age as the criterion for other social goals such as benefits for the elderly or for the military draft? When do age distinctions that perform desired social functions become age discrimination? For a discussion of this dilemma, see B. L. Neugarten, "Age Distinctions and Their Social Functions," 57 *Chicago Kent Law Review* 809 (1981) and D. W. Nelson, "Alternative Images of Old Age as the Bases for Policy" in Neugarten, Ed., *supra,* note 15, pp. 131–169.

23. See *Weiss* v. *Walsh,* 324 F. Supp. 75 (1971) where, at page 77, it was said, "Notwithstanding great advances in gerontology, the era when advanced age ceases to bear some reasonable statistical relationship to diminished capacity or longevity is still future. It cannot be said, therefore, that age ceilings upon eligibility for employment are inherently suspect, although their application will inevitably fall unjustly in the individual case. If the precision of the law is impugnable by the stricture of general applicability, vindication of the exceptional individual

may have to attend the wise discretion of the administrator." See also, *Mass. Board of Retirement* v. *Murgia*, 427 U.S. 307 (1976) (state police officers), *Vance* v. *Bradley*, 440 U.S. 93 (1979) (foreign service officers) and *Retail Clerks Union* v. *Retail Clerks Int'l. Assoc.*, 359 F. Supp. 1285 (1973) (labor union officers), all of which involved so-called "mandatory retirement."

24. Relevant are such considerations as creativity, intellectual rigor, skill in communication, ingenuity in problem solving, memory, judgment, motivation, perseverance, flexibility, "up-to-dateness," vitality, resilience and leadership.

25. Thus in *Trafelet* v. *Thompson*, 594 F.2d 623, 628 (1979), in a decision upholding the constitutionality of a statutory retirement age of 70 for judges, the court said, "There are good reasons to consider individualized evaluations an inadequate substitute for a maximum age limitation. Fitness to be a policeman is more susceptible of objective evaluation than fitness to be a judge, because decline in the intellectual ability and the personality factors essential for effective judicial performance are more difficult to measure than decline in physical condition."

26. See, for example, the comment in another context of the Federal Court of Appeals in *Hahn* v. *The City of Buffalo*, 770 F.2d 12 (1985) at p. 15: "It seems somewhat anomalous for the lawfulness of maximum age limits . . . to depend on the particular evidence presented at various court trials throughout the country."

27. See, for example, a dictum in a dissent by Justice Rehnquist in *Cleveland Board of Education* v. *La Fleur*, 414 U.S. 632 (1974). There, at page 659, in arguing that the majority opinion ultimately could "lead to the invalidation of mandatory retirement statutes for governmental employees," he added, "In that event federal, state and local bodies will be remitted to the task, thankless both for them and for the employees involved, of individual determinations of physical impairment and senility."

28. See the introduction to this essay. However, there is an exception which contemplates performance evaluation after notice and hearing prior to the dismissal of tenured faculty for grave

cause. The impracticality and offensiveness of such evaluations, even when an identifiable cause is the issue, is the reason that such evaluations are rarely invoked. The due process requirements with which such evaluations are surrounded underscore the truly formidable nature of the task. See "Due Process in Decisions Relating to Tenure in Higher Education," 39 *The Record* of The Association of the Bar of the City of New York (1984), p. 392.

29. As John G. Kemeny, the former president of Dartmouth College, has written to the author, "Ideally I would institute that [a periodic review of tenured faculty] starting with age sixty, so that faculty members could count on a quarter of a century of having all the benefits of tenure. Unfortunately, I was told by legal counsel that starting a review process at sixty would violate the age discrimination laws. Therefore I would see no alternative but to review all tenured faculty members periodically. And here is where I see an unsolvable dilemma. If tenured faculty members are reviewed periodically (say every seven years), and if the result of such a review could be dismissal of the faculty member, then tenure loses its meaning."

30. See "At Will Employment and the Problem of Unjust Dismissal," 36 *The Record* of the Association of the Bar of the City of New York (1981), p. 170.

31. Retirement pursuant to a criterion of age need not, of course, be part of the faculty employment bargain. A few institutions offer their faculty term contracts for a limited number of years with a performance review prior to contract renewal. The dominant mode, however, is the tenure system with retirement at an agreed-upon date and it is to the reasonableness of that agreement that this essay is directed.

32. When a classification based on age has a rational basis for general application, it is neither arbitrary, nor an abuse of discretion, nor a denial of equal protection of the laws, to apply it even though in individual cases it may seem to work a hardship or appear to be unsound. See: *Mass. Board of Retirement* v. *Murgia,* 427 U.S. 307 (1976), and *Vance* v. *Bradley,* 440 U.S.

93 (1979). Unless it is "reasonably necessary," however, a classification may not come within the bona fide occupational qualification exemption of the federal Age Discrimination in Employment Act. See *Western Airlines* v. *Criswell*, (1985), 53 *Law Week* 4766, 4772.

33. 29 U.S.C.A. Secs. 101, 102, and 103.

34. One might say that the tenure contract is a contract of the faculty, by the faculty and for the faculty.

35. For example, the American Association of University Professors, the American Federation of Teachers, and the National Educational Association.

36. See, for example, the comments of Senators Heinz, Cranston and Glenn on "mandatory retirement," 131 Cong. Rec. (January 24, 1985) at pages S.5290 to S.5293 and Senator Cranston, 131 Cong. Rec. (January 24, 1985) at pages S.572 to S.578. The concerns expressed are with "involuntary retirement" or "discharge" solely by reason of age, or the absence of "choice" by the employee.

37. *San Antonio Independent School District* v. *Rodriguez*, 411 U.S. 1, 28 (1973).

38. If such a new benefit — undesirable as it may be — were to be granted by statute, there is something to be said for drafting the legislation so that the burden of proof, and the burden of going forward, is placed on the employee. It would, then, be the employees' task to establish both their continuing fitness to perform the functions for which they were employed and the institution's continuing need for their services.

39. 29 U.S.C.A. Sec. 621. Although the distinction is often obscured, age classification and age discrimination are different phenomena.

40. There was for two and a half years a specific exemption from the 1978 amendment to ADEA for tenured faculty who were between the ages of sixty-five and seventy. The termination of that express exemption from the 1978 amendment, for

a limited group of faculty, does not, however, mean that tenured faculty do not come within other exclusions contemplated in the ADEA. The fundamental relationship between the tenure contract and ADEA remains to be judicially clarified.

41. Only, for example, discrimination by employers of twenty or more persons. Section 630(b).

42. See, Section 631(a).

43. See, Section 621(b).

44. See, Section 623(f) and Section 631(c).

45. See above, under the heading: "The Retirement Arrangement" (Section 2.2.1 of this volume).

46. 29 U.S.C.A. sec. 623(a)(2).

47. To this effect, see *EEOC* v. *Wyoming,* 460 U.S. 226 (1983), pp. 232–3.

48. Alabama, Colorado, Mississippi, Missouri, Oklahoma, and Virginia.

49. Arkansas, North Carolina, and South Dakota.

50. Alabama, Arizona, Connecticut, Delaware, Georgia, Indiana, Kansas, Kentucky, Louisiana, Maryland, Massachusetts, Minnesota, Mississippi, Missouri, Nebraska, North Carolina, Ohio, Oregon, Rhode Island, South Carolina, South Dakota, Tennessee, Virginia, Washington, West Virginia, and Wyoming.

51. Alaska, Indiana, New Hampshire, and Connecticut (if entitled to pension benefits). See, also, South Dakota where age discrimination is prohibited in the state career civil service, but faculty under the jurisdiction of the Board of Regents are exempted.

52. California, Massachusetts, New Jersey, New York, and Vermont.

53. After adjusting for duplications, the number of states is thirty-five.

54. See *Levine* v. *Fairleigh Dickinson University,* 646 F.2d 825 (3rd Cir. 1981) where the university conceded it had not continued Dr. Levine in his full-time non-tenured status "solely on the basis of his age" (p. 828).

55. Relevant is the discussion in the majority opinion in *United Airlines, Inc.* v. *McCann,* 434 U.S. 192, 203–208 (1977).

Section 2.3

1. As used herein, the phrase *mandatory retirement* refers to involuntary retirement by reason of age. It does not include involuntary retirement for reasons other than age or retirement that is consensual.

2. At the time of this writing, July 1985, three such bills were pending in the United States Congress: H.R. 522; S. 2; and S. 1054, 99th Cong., 1st Sess, 1985. Section 2(3) of H.R. 522 would permit mandatory retirement of tenured faculty until the year 2000. The two Senate bills do not include specific exceptions for tenured faculty.

3. As of July 1985, there appears to be one such state— Wisconsin.

4. The ADEA did not originally reach public sector employers but was amended to do so in 1974 (Pub. L. 93-259, Sec. 288a(1)-(4), 88 Stat. 74). The constitutionality of the amendment applying the federal ADEA to state and local governments was upheld by the Supreme Court in *E.E.O.C.* v. *Wyoming,* 460 U.S. 226, 103 S. Ct. 1054, 75 L. Ed. 2d 18 (1983).

5. The statute involved in *E.E.O.C.* v. *Wyoming* required game wardens in the state to retire at age fifty-five. The Supreme Court specifically held that the state could, under federal law, continue to require retirement of game wardens at fifty-five if it could establish that age is a bona fide occupational qualification for the job (460 U.S. 240, 103 S. Ct. 1062, 75 L. Ed. 2d 31). Many state age discrimination statutes contain exemptions allowing mandatory retirement and other age restrictions on the employ-

ment of certain classes of individuals. See, for example, Wisc. Stat. Ann. Secs. 111.33(2)(b)(2)(f) (Supp. 1984) (law enforcement and firefighters) and 111.33(b)(2)(g) (Supp. 1984) (school bus drivers) and Utah Code Ann. Sec. 34-35-6(1)(f)(iii) (Supp. 1983) (judges). Many states also have statutes that set mandatory retirement ages for certain classes of state employees. State laws that make special provisions for classes of persons other than tenured faculty are not discussed in this paper.

6. That section provides,

> (1) Nothing in this chapter shall be construed to prohibit compulsory retirement of any employee who has attained 65 years of age but not 70 years of age, and who, for the 2-year period immediately before retirement, is employed in a bona fide executive or a high policymaking position, if such employee is entitled to an immediate nonforfeitable annual retirement benefit from a pension, profit-sharing, savings, or deferred compensation plan, or any combination of such plans, of the employer of such employee, which equals, in the aggregate, at least $44,000.

The Older Americans Act (Pub. L. 98-459, 98 Stat. 1767) increased the dollar limit in the above section from $27,000 to $44,000, effective October 9, 1984.

7. Compare 434 U.S. 199–202 with 434 U.S. 211–216 (Marshall, J., dissenting).

8. See, in this connection, *Waukesha Engine Div.* v. *Dept. of Industry,* 39 FEP Cases 733 (1985).

9. See note 10, below, for state statutes prohibiting age discrimination in employment. See note 11, below, for state age discrimination statutes applicable to public employment. See notes 39 through 42, below, for state statutes providing for mandatory retirement of tenured faculty at public colleges and universities.

10. Alaska (Alaska Stat. Ann. Sec. 18.80.220(a)(1) (1984)); Arizona (Ariz. Rev. Stat. Ann. Sec. 41-1463B.1 (Supp. 1984));

Arkansas (Ark. Stat. Ann. Sec. 12-3502(a) (1979)); California (Cal. Gov't. Code Sec. 12941 (1982)); Connecticut (Conn. Gen. Stat. Ann. Sec. 46a-60(a)(1) (Supp. 1984)); Delaware (Del. Code Ann. tit. 19, Sec. 711(a)(1) (1979)); Florida (Fla. Stat. Ann. Sec. 760.10(1)(a) (Supp. 1984); see also Fla. Stat. Ann. Sec. 112.043 (1982)); Georgia (Ga. Code Ann. Sec. 34-1-2(a) (1982) and Ga. Code Ann. Secs. 45-19-21 and 45-19-29(1) (1982)); Hawaii (Hawaii Rev. Stat. Sec. 378-2(1) (Supp. 1983)); Idaho (Idaho Code Sec. 67-5909(1) (Supp. 1984)); Illinois (Ill. Rev. Stat. Ch. 68, Sec. 2-1-2(A) (Supp. 1984)); Indiana (Ind. Code Ann. Sec. 22-9-2-2 (Burns 1974)); Iowa (Iowa Code Ann. Sec. 601A.6.1.a (West 1975)); Kansas (Kan. Stat. Ann. Sec. 44-1111 (1984)); Kentucky (Ky. Rev. Stat. Sec. 344.040(1) (1983)); Louisiana (La. Rev. Stat. Ann. Sec. 23:972A(1) (West Supp. 1984)); Maine (Me. Rev. Stat. Ann. tit. 5, Sec. 4572.1.A (1979)); Maryland (Md. Ann. Code art. 49B, Sec. 16 (1979)); Massachusetts (Mass. Gen. Laws Ann. Ch. 151B, Secs. 4-1B and 1C (West 1984)); Michigan (Mich. Comp. Laws Ann. Sec. 37.2202(1)(a) (West Supp. 1984)); Minnesota (Minn. Stat. Ann. Sec. 363.03 subd. 1(2) (West Supp. 1984)); Montana (Mont. Code Ann. Sec. 49-2-303(1)(a) and Mont. Code Ann. Sec. 49-3-201 et seq. (1983)); Nebraska (Neb. Rev. Stat. Sec. 48-1004(1)(a) (Reissue 1984)); Nevada (Nev. Rev. Stat. Sec. 281.370 (1983) and Nev. Rev. Stat. Ann. Sec. 613.330-1(a) (1983)); New Hampshire (N.H. Rev. Stat. Ann. Sec. 354-A:8I (Supp. 1981)); New Jersey (N.J. Stat. Ann. Secs. 10:3-1 and 10:5-12(a) (1976) as amended by L. 1985, c. 73, signed March 11, 1985 (effective January 1, 1984, for public employees and October 1, 1985, for private sector employees)); New Mexico (N.M. Stat. Ann. Sec. 28-1-7A (1983)); New York (N.Y. Exec. Law Sec. 296 subd. 3-a(a) (McKinney Supp.) 1984)); North Carolina (N.C. Gen. Stat. Sec. 126-16 (Supp. 1984)); North Dakota (N.D. Cent. Code Sec. 14-02.4-03 (Supp. 1983) and N.D. Cent. Code Sec. 34-01-17 (1980)); Ohio (Ohio Rev. Code Ann. Sec. 4112.02(A) (Page Supp. 1983) and Ohio Rev. Code Ann. Sec. 4101.17(A) (Page 1980)); Oregon (Or. Rev. Stat. Sec. 659.030(1)(a) and (b) (1981)); Pennsylvania (Pa. Stat. Ann. tit. 43, Sec. 955(a) (Purdon Supp. 1984)); Rhode Island (R.I. Gen.

Laws Sec. 28-5-7(A) (Supp. 1984)); South Carolina (S.C. Code Ann. Sec. 1-13-80(a)(1) (Law Co-op. Supp. 1983)); Tennessee (Tenn. Code Ann. Sec. 4-21-105(a)(1) (Supp. 1984)); Texas (Tex. Rev. Civ. Stat. Ann. art. 5221k, Sec. 5.01(1) (Vernon Supp. 1984)); Utah (Utah Code Ann. Sec. 34-35-6(1)(a) (Supp. 1983)); Vermont (Vt. Stat. Ann. tit. 21, Sec. 495(a)(1) (Supp. 1984)); Washington (Wash. Rev. Code Ann. Secs. 49.60.180 and 49.44.090 (Supp. 1984)); West Virginia (W. Va. Code Sec. 5-11-9(a) (1979)); Wisconsin (Wis. Stat. Ann. Secs. 111.321 and 111.322(1) (Supp. 1984)); Wyoming (Wyo. Stat. Sec. 27-9-105(a) (Supp. 1984)).

11. Alaska Stat. Ann. Sec. 18.80.300(1) and (3) (1984); Ariz. Rev. Stat. Ann. Sec. 41-1461.1, 2 and 5 (Supp. 1984); Cal. Gov't Code Sec. 12926(c) (1982); Conn. Gen. Stat. Ann. Sec. 46a-51(10) (Supp. 1984); Del. Code Ann. tit. 19, Sec. 710(2) (1979); Fla. Stat. Ann. Sec. 760.02(5) and (6) (Supp. 1984) (see also Fla. Stat. Ann. Secs. 112.043 and 112.044(3)(a)1 (1982) (public sector only)); Ga. Code Ann. Sec. 34-1-2 (1982) (private sector) and Ga. Code Ann. Sec. 45-19-20, et seq. (public sector); Hawaii Rev. Stat. Sec. 378-1 (Supp. 1983); Idaho Code Sec. 67-5901 (Supp. 1984); Ill. Rev. Stat. Ch. 68, Sec. 2-101(B)(1) (Supp. 1984); Ind. Code Ann. Sec. 22-9-2-1 (Burns 1974); Iowa Code Ann. Sec. 601A.2.5 (West 1975); Kan. Stat. Ann. Sec. 44-1112(d) (1984); Ky. Rev. Stat. Secs. 344.010(1) and 344.030(1) (1983); La. Rev. Stat. Ann. Sec. 23:971(1) (Supp. 1984); Me. Rev. Stat. Ann. tit. 5, Secs. 4553.4 and 4553.7 (1979); Md. Ann. Code art. 49B, Sec. 15(b) (1979); Mass. Gen. Laws Ann. Ch. 151B, Sec. 4-1B (West 1984); Mich. Comp. Laws Ann. Secs. 37.2201(a) and 37.2103(f) (West Supp. 1984); Minn. Stat. Ann. Sec. 363.01 subd. 15 (West Supp. 1984) and subd. 7 (West 1966); Mont. Code Ann. Sec. 49-2-101(8) and (15) (1983) (private sector) and Mont. Code Ann. Sec. 49-3-201 (1983) (public sector); Neb. Rev. Stat. Sec. 48-1002 (Reissue 1984); Nev. Rev. Stat. Secs. 613.310-1 and 613.310-4 (1983) (public and private sectors) and Nev. Rev. Stat. Sec. 281.370 (public sector); N.H. Rev. Stat. Ann. Sec. 354-A:3(5) (Supp. 1981); N.J. Stat. Ann. Sec. 10:3-1 (1976) (public sector) and 10:5-5e (1976) (public and private sectors) as amended

by L. 1985, c. 73, signed March 11, 1985 (effective January 1, 1984, for public employees and October 1, 1985, for private sector employees); N.M. Stat. Ann. Sec. 28-1-2A and B (1983); N.Y. Exec. Law Sec. 296 subd. 3-a, et seq. (applicability to both sectors apparent); N.D. Cent. Code Secs. 14-02.4-02-5 and 14-02.4-02-9 (Supp. 1983); Ohio Rev. Code Ann. Sec. 4112.01(A)(2) (Page 1980); Or. Rev. Stat. Sec. 659.010(6) (1981); Pa. Stat. Ann. tit. 43. Sec. 954(b) (Purdon Supp. 1984); R.I. Gen. Laws Sec. 28-5-6(B) (Supp. 1984); S.C. Code Ann. Sec. 1-13-30(d) and (e) (Law Co-op. Supp. 1983); Tenn. Code Ann. Sec. 4-21-102(4) (Supp. 1984); Tex. Rev. Civ. Stat. Ann. art. 522lk, Sec. 2.01(5) (Vernon Supp. 1984); Utah Code Ann. Secs. 34-35-2(5) and 67-19-4 (Supp. 1983); Vt. Stat. Ann. tit. 21, Sec. 495d(1) (1978); Wash. Rev. Code Ann. Sec. 49.60.040 (Supp. 1984); W. Va. Code Sec. 5-11-3(d) (1979); Wis. Stat. Ann. Sec. 111.32(6)(a) (Supp. 1984); Wyo. Stat. Ann. Sec. 27-9-102 (Supp. 1984).

12. Ark. Stat. Ann. Secs. 12-3501 and 12-3502; N.C. Gen. Stat. Sec. 126-16 (Supp. 1984).

13. Colorado has a statute that prohibits discharge from employment of any person between eighteen and sixty on the basis of age (Colo. Rev. Stat. Sec. 8-2-116 (1974). (See also note 45, below.)

South Dakota law prohibits discrimination on the basis of age only in the state career civil service (S.D. Codified Laws Sec. 3-6A-15 (1980)). That section does not apply to faculty under the jurisdiction of the state board of regents (S.D. Codified Laws Ann. Sec. 3-6A-13(5) (Supp. 1984)).

Alabama, Mississippi, Missouri, Oklahoma, and Virginia do not have state statutes prohibiting age discrimination in employment. (But see notes 29, 34, and 36, below.)

14. The abbreviation *BFOQ* refers to a provision like the one in federal law that allows age discrimination if age is a bona fide occupational qualification. The abbreviation *BFE/HPP* refers to an exemption similar to that in the federal ADEA that allows mandatory retirement at age sixty-five of certain bona fide executives and others in high policy-making positions.

These states have BFOQs in their statutes applicable to
private sector employment: Alaska (Alaska Stat. Ann. Sec.
18.80.220(a)(1) (1984)); Arizona (Ariz. Rev. Stat. Ann. Sec.
4-1463F.4 (Supp. 1984)); Connecticut (Conn. Gen. Stat. Ann.
Sec. 46a-60(b)(1)(C) (Supp. 1984)); Delaware (Del. Stat. Ann.
tit. 19, Sec. 711(e)(1) (1979)); Florida (Fla. Stat. Ann. Sec.
760.10(8)(a) (Supp. 1984)); Georgia (Ga. Code Ann. Sec. 34-
1-2(a) (1982)); Hawaii (Hawaii Rev. Stat. Sec. 378-3(2) (Supp.
1983)); Idaho (Idaho Code Sec. 67-5910 (2)(a) (Supp. 1984));
Illinois (Ill. Rev. Stat. Ch. 68, Sec. 2-104(A) (Supp. 1984));
Iowa (Iowa Code Ann. Sec. 601A.6.1.a (West 1975)); Kansas
(Kan. Stat. Ann. Sec. 44-1113(b)(2) (1984)); Kentucky (Ky.
Rev. Stat. Sec. 344.080 (1983) (dealing with advertisements and
applications)); Louisiana (La. Rev. Stat. Sec. 23:972F(1) (West
Supp. 1984)); Maine (Me. Rev. Stat. Ann. tit. 5, Sec. 4572A
(1979)); Maryland (Md. Ann. Code art. 49B, Sec. 16(g)(1)
(1979)); Massachusetts (Mass. Gen. Laws Ann. Ch. 151B, Sec.
4-1B (West 1984)); Michigan (Mich. Comp. Laws Ann. Sec.
37.2208 (West Supp. 1984)); Minnesota (Minn. Stat. Ann. Sec.
363.03 subd. 1 (West Supp. 1984)); Montana (Mont. Code Ann.
Sec. 49-2-303(1) and (2) (1983)); Nebraska (Neb. Rev. Stat.
Sec. 48-1003(2) (Reissue 1984)); Nevada (Nev. Rev. Stat. Sec.
613-350-1 (1983)); New Hampshire (N.H. Rev. Stat. Ann. Sec.
354-A:8I (Supp. 1981)); New Jersey (N.J. Stat. Ann. Sec.
10:5-2.1 (Supp. 1984) as amended by L. 1985, c. 73, signed
March 11, 1985 (effective October 1, 1985)); New Mexico (N.M.
Stat. Ann. Sec. 28-1-7A 1983)); New York (N.Y. Exec. Law
Sec. 296 subd.3-a(d) (McKinney Supp. 1984)); North Dakota
(N.D. Code Secs. 14.02.4-03 (Supp. 1983) and 34-01-17 (1980));
Ohio (Ohio Rev. Code Ann. Sec. 4112.02 (O)(1) (Page Supp.
1983)); Oregon (Or. Rev. Stat. Sec. 658.030(1)(a) (1981));
Pennsylvania (Pa. Stat. Ann. tit. 43, Sec. 955 (Purdon Supp.
1984)); Rhode Island (R.I. Gen. Laws Sec. 28-5-7(D) (Supp.
1984) (with approval of human rights commission)); South
Carolina (S.C. Code Ann. Sec. 1-13-80(h)(7)(i) (Law Co-op.
Supp. 1983)); Tennessee (Tenn. Code Ann. Sec. 4-21-125(1)
(Supp. 1984)); Texas (Tex. Rev. Civ. Stat. Ann. art. 522lk,
Sec. 5.07(a)(1) (Vernon Supp. 1984)); Utah (Utah Code Ann.
Sec. 34-35-6(2)(a) (Supp. 1983)); Vermont (Vt. Stat. Ann. tit.

21, Sec. 495(a) (Supp. 1984)); Washington (Wash. Rev. Code Ann. Sec. 49.60.180 (Supp. 1984)); and West Virginia (W. Va. Code Sec. 5-11-9(a) (1979)).

The following states have BFE/HPP provisions in their age discrimination statutes applicable to private employment: Arizona (Ariz. Rev. Stat. Sec. 41-1463K (Supp. 1984)); California (Cal. Govt. Code Sec. 12942(c) (Supp. 1984)); Connecticut (Conn. Gen. Stat. Ann. Sec. 46a-60(b)(1)(B) (Supp. 1984)); Delaware (Del. Stat. Ann. tit. 19, Sec. 711(i) (1979)); Georgia (Ga. Code Ann. Sec. 34-1-2(a) (1982)); Idaho (Idaho Code Sec. 67-5910(20)(b) (Supp. 1984)); Illinois (Ill. Rev. Stat. Ch. 68, Sec. 2-104 (E)(2) (Supp. 1984)); Iowa (Iowa Code Ann. Sec. 601A.13.1.a (West 1975)); Massachusetts (Mass. Gen. Laws Ann. Ch. 151B, Sec. 4-17(b) (West 1984)); Minnesota (Minn. Stat. Ann. Sec. 181.81 (West Supp. 1984)); New Jersey (N.J. Stat. Ann. Sec. 10:5-12 (Supp. 1984) as amended by L. 1985, c. 73, signed March 11, 1985 (effective October 1, 1985)); New Mexico (N.M. Stat. Ann. Sec. 28-1-7A (1983)); New York (N.Y. Exec. Law Sec. 296 subd. 3-a(e) (McKinney Supp. 1984)); North Dakota (N.D. Cent. Code Sec. 14-02.4-03 (Supp. 1983)); Ohio (Ohio Rev. Code Ann. Sec. 4112.02(O)(3) (Page Supp. 1983)); South Carolina (S.C. Code Ann. Sec. 1-13-80(h)(8) and (9) (Law Co-op. Supp. 1983)); Tennessee (Tenn. Code Ann. Sec. 4-21-126(c) (Supp. 1984)); and Texas (Tex. Rev. Civ. Stat. Ann. art. 5221K, Sec. 1.04(a) (Vernon Supp. 1984)).

15. Ariz. Rev. Stat. Ann. Sec. 41-1465 (Supp. 1984) (40–70); Del. Code Ann. tit. 19, Sec. 710(7) (1979) (40–70); Ga. Code Ann. Sec. 34-1-2(a) (1982) (40–70); Idaho Code Sec. 67-5910(7) (Supp. 1984) (40–70); Ill. Rev. Stat. Ch. 68, Sec. 101-3(A) (Supp. 1984) (40–70); Ind. Code Ann. Sec. 22-9-2-1 (Burns Supp. 1984) (40–70); Kan. Stat. Ann. Sec. 44-1112(a) (1984) (40–70); Ky. Rev. Stat. Sec. 344.010(4) (1983) (40–70); La. Rev. Stat. Ann. Sec. 23:971(1) (Supp. 1984) (40–70); Neb. Rev. Stat. Sec. 48-1003(1) (Reissue 1984) (40–70); Nev. Rev. Stat. Sec. 613-350-3 (1983) (40–69); N.D. Cent. Code Sec. 14.02.4-02-1 (Supp. 1983) (40–70); Ohio Rev. Code Ann. Secs. 4112.01 (A)(14) (Page Supp. 1983) and 4101.17 (Page 1980) (40–70);

Or. Rev. Stat. Sec. 659.010(6) (1981) (18–70); Pa. Stat. Ann.
tit. 43, Sec. 954(h) (Purdon Supp. 1984) (The Pennsylvania
statute applies to individuals between forty and seventy and to
anyone else who may be protected by subsequent amendment
to the federal ADEA.); R.I. Gen. Laws Sec. 28-5-6(I) (Supp.
1984) (40–70); S.C. Code Ann. Sec. 1-13-30(c) (Law Co-op
Supp. 1983) (40–70); Tenn. Code Ann. Secs. 4-21-101(b) and
4-21-126(a) (Supp. 1984) (40–70); Tex. Rev. Civ. Stat. Ann.
art. 5221k, Sec. 1.04 (Vernon Supp. 1984) (40–70); Wash. Rev.
Code Ann. Sec. 49.44.090 (Supp. 1984) (40–70); W. Va. Code
Sec. 5-11-3(q) (1979) (40–65); Wyo. Stat. Sec. 27-9-105(b)
(Supp. 1984) (40–70).
     The upper age limit in New York was eliminated for the
private sector effective January 1, 1986. (See 1984 N.Y. Laws
Ch. 296, Secs. 1 and 12.)

16. As previously mentioned, the federal ADEA applies to
employers with twenty or more employees (29 U.S.C. Sec.
630(b)). Many state age discrimination provisions extend to
employers with a smaller number of employees and thus may
provide protection for individuals whom federal law does not
reach. It is unlikely, however, that many tenured college and
university professors are employed by entities that are too small
to be covered by federal law. For that reason, provisions in state
statutes that limit the applicability of age discrimination restrictions to those having a certain number of employees are not
discussed herein.

17. The statutes in Alaska, California, Connecticut, Florida,
Hawaii, Iowa, Maine, Maryland, Massachusetts, Michigan,
Minnesota, Montana, New Hampshire, New Jersey, New Mexico, New York, Utah, Vermont, and Wisconsin do not have
upper age limits in their age discrimination statutes applicable
to private sector employment. As previously noted, the age limits
in the New York law applicable to private sector employment
were eliminated, effective January 1, 1986.

18. See notes 11 and 12, above.

19. These states have BFOQs in their statutes applicable to
public employment: Alaska (Alaska Stat. Ann. Sec. 18.80.

220(a)(1) (1984)); Arizona (Ariz. Rev. Stat. Ann. Sec. 4-1463F.4 (Supp. 1984)); Arkansas (Ark. Stat. Ann. Sec. 12-3503(a) (1979)); Connecticut (Conn. Gen. Stat. Ann. Sec. 46a-60(b)(1)(C) (Supp. 1984)); Delaware (Del. Stat. Ann. tit. 19, Sec. 711(e)(1) (1979)); Florida (Fla. Stat. Ann. Secs. 112.044(3)(f)1 (1982) and 760. 10(8)(a) (Supp. 1984)); Hawaii (Hawaii Rev. Stat. Sec. 378–3(2) (Supp. 1983)); Idaho (Idaho Code Sec. 67-5910 (2)(a) (Supp. 1984)); Illinois (Ill. Rev. Stat. Ch. 68, Sec. 2-104(A) (Supp. 1984)); Iowa (Iowa Code Ann. Sec. 601A.6.1.a (West 1975)); Kansas (Kan. Stat. Ann. Sec. 44-1113(b)(2) (1984)); Kentucky (Ky. Rev. Stat. Sec. 344.080 (1983) (dealing with advertisements and applications)); Louisiana (La. Rev. Stat. Sec. 23:972F(1) (West Supp. 1984)); Maine (Me. Rev. Stat. Ann. tit. 5, Sec. 4572A (1979)); Maryland (Md. Ann. Code art. 49B, Sec. 16(g)(1) (1979)); Michigan (Mich. Comp. Laws Ann. Sec. 37.2208 (West Supp. 1984)); Minnesota (Minn. Stat. Ann. Sec. 363.01-1 (West Supp. 1984)); Montana (Mont. Code Ann. Sec. 49-3-103(1) (1983)); Nebraska (Neb. Rev. Stat. Sec. 48-1003(2) (Reissue 1984)); Nevada (Nev. Rev. Stat. Sec. 613-350-1 (1983)); New Hampshire (N.H. Rev. Stat. Ann. Sec. 354-A:8I (Supp. 1981)); New Jersey (N.J. Stat. Ann. Sec. 10:5-2.1 (Supp. 1984) as amended by L. 1985, c. 73, signed March 11, 1985 (effective January 1, 1984)); New Mexico (N.M. Stat. Ann. Sec. 28-1-7A (1983)); New York (N.Y. Exec. Law Sec. 296 subd. 3-a(d) (McKinney Supp. 1984)); North Carolina (N.C. Gen. Stat. Sec. 126-16 (Supp. 1984)); North Dakota (N.D. Code Secs. 14.02.4-03 (Supp. 1983) and 34-01-17 (1980)); Ohio (Ohio Rev. Code Ann. Sec. 4112.02(O)(1) (Page Supp. 1983)); Oregon (Or. Rev. Stat. Sec. 659.030(1)(a) (1981)); Pennsylvania (Pa. Stat. Ann. tit. 43, Sec. 955 (Purdon Supp. 1984)); Rhode Island (R.I. Gen. Laws Sec. 28-5-7(D) (Supp. 1984) (with approval of human rights commission)); South Carolina (S.C. Code Ann. Sec. 1-13-80(h)(7)(i) (Law Co-op. Supp. 1983)); Tennessee (Tenn. Code Ann. Sec. 4-21-125(1) (Supp. 1984)); Texas (Tex. Rev. Civ. Stat. Ann. art. 5221k, Sec. 5.07(a)(1) (Vernon Supp. 1984)); Utah (Utah Code Ann. Sec. 34-35-6(2)(a) (Supp. 1983)); Vermont (Vt. Stat. Ann. tit. 21, Sec. 495(a) (Supp. 1984)); Washington (Wash. Rev. Code Ann. Sec. 49.60.180 (supp. 1984)); and West Virginia (W. Va. Code Sec. 5-11-9(a) (1979)).

The following states have BFE/HPP provisions in their age discrimination statutes applicable to public employment: Arizona (Ariz. Rev. Stat. Ann. Sec. 41-1463K (Supp. 1984)); Arkansas (Ark. Stat. Ann. Sec. 12-3505(b) (1979)); California (Cal. Govt. Code Sec. 12942(c) (Supp. 1984)); Connecticut (Conn. Gen. Stat. Ann. Sec. 46a-60(b)(1)(B) (Supp. 1984)); Delaware (Del. Stat. Ann. tit. 19, Sec. 711(i) (1979)); Idaho (Idaho Code Sec. 67-5910(20(b) (Supp. 1984)); Illinois (Ill. Rev. Stat. Ch. 68, Sec. 2-104(E)(2) (Supp. 1984)); Iowa (Iowa Code Ann. Sec. 601A.13.1.a (West 1975)); Massachusetts (Mass. Gen. Laws Ann. Ch. 151B, Sec. 4-17(b) (West 1984)); Minnesota (Minn. Stat. Ann. Sec. 181.81 (West Supp. 1984)); New Jersey (N.J. Stat. Ann. Sec. 10:5-12 (Supp. 1984) as amended by L. 1985, c. 73, signed March 11, 1985 (effective January 1, 1984)); New Mexico (N.M. Stat. Ann. Sec. 28-1-7A (1983)); North Dakota (N.D. Cent. Code Sec. 14-02.4-03 (Supp. 1983)); Ohio (Ohio Rev. Code Ann. Sec. 4112.02(O)(3) (Page Supp. 1983)); South Carolina (S.C. Code Ann. Sec. 1-13-80(h)(8) and (9) (Law Co-op. Supp. 1983)); Tennessee (Tenn. Code Ann. Sec. 4-21-126(3) (Supp. 1984)); and Texas (Tex. Rev. Civ. Stat. Ann. art. 5221k, Sec. 1.04(a) (Vernon Supp. 1984)).

20. Ariz. Rev. Stat. Ann. Sec. 41-1465 (Supp. 1984) (40–70); Ark. Stat. Ann. Sec. 12-3505(a) (1979); Del. Code Ann. tit. 19, Sec. 710(7) (1979) (40–70); Ga. Code Ann. Sec. 45-19-28 (1982) (40–70); Idaho Code Sec. 67-5910(7) (Supp. 1984) (40–70); Ill. Rev. Stat. Ch. 68, Sec. 1-103(A) (Supp. 1984) (40–70); Ind. Code Ann. Sec. 22-9-2-1 (Burns Supp. 1984) (40–70); Kan. Stat. Ann. Sec. 44-1112(a) (1984) (40–70); Ky. Rev. Stat. Sec. 344.010(4) (1983) (40–70); La. Rev. Stat. Ann. Sec. 23:971(1) (Supp. 1984) (40–70); Neb. Rev. Stat. Sec. 48–1003(1) (Reissue 1984) (40–70); N.C. Gen. Stat. Sec. 126-16 (Supp. 1984) (40–70); N.D. Cent. Code Sec. 14.02.4-02-1 (Supp. 1983) (40–70); Ohio Rev. Code Ann. Secs. 4112.01 (A)(14) (Page Supp. 1983) and 4101.17 (Page 1980) (40–70); Or. Rev. Stat. Sec. 659.010(6) (1981) (18–70); Pa. Stat. Ann. tit. 43, Sec. 954(h) (Purdon Supp. 1984) (The Pennsylvania statute applies to individuals between forty and seventy and to anyone else who may be protected by subsequent amendment to the federal ADEA.); R.I. Gen. Laws

Sec. 28-5-6(I) (Supp. 1984) (40–70); S.C. Code Ann. Sec. 1-13-30(c) (Law Co-op Supp. 1983) (40–70); Tenn. Code Ann. Secs. 4-21-101(b) and 4-21-126(a) (Supp. 1984) (40–70); Tex. Rev. Civ. Stat. Ann. art. 5221k, Sec. 1.04 (Vernon Supp. 1984) (40–70); Wash. Rev. Code Ann. Sec. 49.44.090 (Supp. 1984); W. Va. Code Sec. 5-11-3(q) (1979) (40–65); Wyo. Stat. Sec. 27-9-105(b) (Supp. 1984) (40–70).

21. Alaska, California, Connecticut, Florida, Hawaii, Iowa, Maine, Maryland, Massachusetts, Michigan, Minnesota, Montana, Nevada, New Hampshire, New Jersey, New Mexico, New York, Utah, Vermont, and Wisconsin have no upper age limits in their age discrimination statutes applicable to public employment.

22. However, this may not be the case in Georgia. The Georgia age discrimination statutes applicable to both the public and private sectors have upper age limits of seventy (Ga. Code Ann. Secs. 34-1-2(a) and 45-19-28 (1982)), and Georgia law allows compliance with the terms of a bona fide retirement plan (Ga. Code Ann. Secs. 34-1-2(a) and 45-19-35(d)(5) (1982)). However, the age discrimination statute applicable to the private sector also provides that, "When the retirement or insurance benefit program of any employer shall prohibit the employment of any person because of excessive age, such person shall have the authority, as a condition of employment, to waive the right to participate in any such program and receive any benefits therefrom" (Ga. Code Ann. Sec. 34-1-2(a) (1982)). Under this provision, an individual in the private sector might be able to waive any benefits and thereby avoid being subjected to mandatory retirement, perhaps even beyond the age of seventy. No waiver provision exists for the BFRP exemption in the age discrimination statute applicable to public employment.

23. Two of the five have unrestricted BFRP exemptions: Maryland (Md. Ann. Code art. 49B, Sec. 16(g)(4) (1979)) and Michigan (Mich. Comp. Laws Ann. Sec. 37.2103(a) (Supp. 1984)). New Mexico allows mandatory retirement at sixty-five or above if it is in accordance with a bona fide retirement plan that meets the terms of ERISA (N.M. Stat. Ann. Sec. 28-1-9 (1983)). (See

note 46, below.) Iowa allows compliance with a bona fide retirement plan provided such plan does not call for mandatory retirement before the age of seventy (Iowa Code Ann. Sec. 601A.13.1
(1975)). Minnesota permits mandatory retirement at age seventy
and above if established by law or provided for in a published
retirement policy (Minn. Stat. Ann. Sec. 363.02, subd. 6 and
Sec. 181.81 (West Supp. 1984)).

24. See *United Airlines* v. *McCann,* above. Thus, states that do
not have upper age limits but do have BFRP exemptions usually
do not offer to tenured faculty as a group more protection from
mandatory retirement than does federal law. Of course, to the
extent that a BFRP exemption allows mandatory retirement only
in accordance with the terms of a bona fide retirement plan,
state age discrimination statutes with BFRPs but without upper age limits may provide more protection than does federal
law for individual faculty members who are seventy or older
and who are subjected to involuntary retirement that is not in
accordance with the terms of a bona fide retirement plan.

25. The Montana age discrimination law has a BFRP exemption (Mont. Code Ann. Sec. 49-3-1-3(2) (1983)). Nonetheless,
the statute was held to have repealed by implication state statutes
setting mandatory retirement ages for public employees (*Taylor*
v. *Department of Fish, Wildlife, and Parks,* 666 P.2d 1228 (1983)
(game wardens); *Dolan* v. *School Dist. No. 10, Deer Lodge Cty.,*
195 Mont. 340, 636 P.2d 825 (1981) (schoolteachers and prin-
cipals)). It is not clear whether a private sector retirement plan
that imposes a mandatory retirement age would be considered
in violation of the statute. (See 636 P.2d 825, 830: "This decision does not affect pension plans nor seniority systems whereby
an employee has agreed, as part of the employment, to retire
at a certain age.")
    Utah law has a BFRP (Utah Code Ann. Sec. 34-35-6(3)
(Supp. 1983)), but it also expressly prohibits mandatory retirement for everyone except judges, "notwithstanding any statutory
provision to the contrary" (Utah Code Ann. Sec. 34-35-6(1)(f)(iii)
(Supp. 1983)). In a recent opinion, the attorney general for the
state of Utah concluded that the Utah Anti-Discrimination Act

precludes mandatory retirement based on age even when done pursuant to a bona fide retirement plan (Informal Opinion No. 84-62 (November 1, 1984)).

One of the age discrimination statutes in Florida has a BFRP that does not prohibit mandatory retirement (Fla. Stat. Ann. Secs. 112.043 and 112.044(3)(f)2 (Supp. 1984) (applicable to public employment)). However, the other Florida age discrimination statute, which applies to both sectors, has a BFRP with language prohibiting mandatory retirement (Fla. Stat. Ann. Secs. 760.10(1)(a) and 760.10(b) (1982)). In a recent opinion, the Florida attorney general concluded that mandatory retirement is unlawful in the public sector, notwithstanding the BFRP in Sec. 112.044(3)(f)2 (Op. Att'y Gen. 84-60 (June 26, 1984)).

26. Connecticut (Conn. Gen. Stat. Ann. Sec. 46a-60(b)(1)(E) (Supp. 1984) (Connecticut law does contain an exception that allows the termination of any person who has attained the age of seventy and who is entitled to benefits under a pension or retirement plan provided for state employees (Conn. Gen. Stat. Sec. 46a-60(b)(1)(A) (Supp. 1984)).)); Hawaii (Hawaii Rev. Stat. Sec. 378-3(4) (Supp. 1984) (The BFRP in Hawaii law prohibits mandatory retirement but provides a grace period for existing plans until April 30, 1986.)); Maine (Me. Rev. Stat. Ann. tit. 5, Sec. 4573.1-A.B(2) (1979) (The Maine statute expressly prohibits mandatory retirement even of those individuals who are exempted from the provisions of the federal ADEA.)); Massachusetts (Mass. Gen. Laws Ann. Ch. 151B, Sec. 4-17(a) (West 1984)); New Jersey (N.J. Stat. Ann. Sec. 10:5-2.1 (Supp. 1984) as amended by L. 1985, c. 73, signed March 11, 1985 (effective January 1, 1984, for public employees and October 1, 1985, for private sector employees)); Vermont (Vt. Stat. Ann. tit. 22, Sec. 495(f) (Supp. 1984)); and Wisconsin (Wis. Stat. Ann. Sec. 111.33(2)(b) (Supp. 1984)).

27. Alaska, California, New Hampshire, and New York have neither upper age limits nor BFRP exemptions in their age discrimination statutes applicable to private employment. As previously noted, the age limits in the New York law applicable to the private sector were eliminated effective January 1, 1986.

28. Alaska, California, New Hampshire, Nevada, and New York have neither upper age limits nor BFRP exemptions in their age discrimination statutes applicable to public employment. (But see note 31, below.)

29. Connecticut, Hawaii, Maine, Massachusetts, New Jersey, Vermont, and Wisconsin (no upper age limits and BFRP provisions that prohibit involuntary retirement) plus Alaska, California, Nevada, New Hampshire, and New York (neither upper age limits nor BFRP provisions).

30. Connecticut, Hawaii, Maine, Massachusetts, New Jersey, Vermont, and Wisconsin (no upper age limits and BFRP provisions that prohibit involuntary retirement), plus Alaska, California, New Hampshire, and New York (neither upper age limits nor BFRP provisions).

As noted above, Connecticut law does permit the termination of any person who has attained the age of seventy and who is entitled to benefits under a pension or retirement plan provided for state employees. (See note 26, above.)

31. Alaska Stat. Ann. Sec. 18.80.300(3) (1984); N.H. Rev. Stat. Ann. Sec. 354-A:3(5) (Supp. 1981). It is not entirely clear whether the exclusion applies only in the private sector or whether it operates to exempt public colleges and universities as well. Both state statutes apply to the state as employer. (See note 10, above.)

According to the Alaska Human Rights Commission, the University of Alaska is covered by the Alaska age discrimination statute (Janet L. Bradley, Executive Director, Alaska Human Rights Commission, letter to Thomas C. Woodruff, Executive Director, Commission on College Retirement (hereafter, Dr. Woodruff), May 6, 1985).

The New Hampshire Commission for Human Rights takes the position that the state age discrimination law applies to all public educational institutions (Merryl Gibbs, Executive Director, New Hampshire Commission for Human Rights, letter to Dr. Woodruff, March 19, 1985).

32. Conn. Gen. Stat. Ann. Sec. 46a-60(b)(1)(A) (Supp. 1984). (See, also, South Dakota Codified Laws, Ann., Sec. 3-6A-13 (5); and Indiana Code Ann. Secs. 22-9-2-10, and 22-9-2-1(1).)

33. California allows mandatory retirement of tenured faculty only if the institution provides for continuation in a nontenured status on a year-to-year basis (Cal. Gov't. Code Sec. 12942(a) (Supp 1984)). Massachusetts, New Jersey, New York, and Vermont permit mandatory retirement of tenured faculty at seventy or above (Mass. Gen. Laws Ann. Ch. 151B, Sec. 4-17(c) (West 1984); N.J. L. 1985, c. 73, signed March 11, 1985 (effective January 1, 1984, for public employees and October 1, 1985, for private sector employees); N.Y. Exec. Law Sec. 296 subd. 3-a(f) (McKinney Supp. 1984); Vt. Stat. Ann. tit. 21, Sec. 495g (Supp. 1984)).

34. See note 25, above.

35. See note 25, above.

36. See note 22, above.

37. Each of these states, as well as the federal law, provides other exceptions that may, in appropriate cases, be applicable to tenured faculty. For example, seven of the eight states (Florida, Georgia, Hawaii, Maine, Montana, Nevada, and Utah) have statutes that include a BFOQ provision. (See notes 14 and 19, above.)

38. Of course, individual employers, both public and private, are free to adopt retirement policies to the extent not prohibited by federal and applicable state laws. The retirement policies agreed to by individual employers with their employees, including institutions of higher learning, are beyond the scope of this paper.

39. Alabama, Arizona, Connecticut, Delaware, Georgia, Indiana, Kansas, Kentucky, Louisiana, Maryland, Massachusetts, Minnesota, Mississippi, Missouri, Nebraska, North Carolina, Ohio, Oregon, Rhode Island, South Carolina, South Dakota, Tennessee, Virginia, Washington, West Virginia, and Wyoming. (See, also, notes 31, 32, and 33, above.)

40. Delaware (Del. Code Ann. tit. 29, Secs. 5501(a)(1)(b); 5505; and 5521 (1983) (Faculty at state colleges and universities, with the exception of certain employees of the University of Delaware,

must retire on the last day of the contract year in which they attain the age of seventy.)); Georgia (Ga. Code Ann. Secs. 47-3-1(28)(k); 47-3-60; and 47-3-10(b) (1982) (Faculty in the state university system must retire at the close of the school year in which they attain the age of seventy.)); Kansas (Kan. Stat. Ann. Sec. 74-4925(1)(d) (1984) (Faculty at state colleges and universities must retire no later than the academic year following their seventieth birthday.)); Kentucky (Ky. Rev. Stat. Sec. 161.000 (Supp. 1984) (Most state college and university faculty, not including those at the University of Kentucky, must retire as of July 1 following their seventieth birthday.)); Mississippi (Miss. Code Ann. Secs. 25-9-103(e) and 25-11-111(f) (Supp. 1983) and Miss. Code Ann. Sec. 25-11-101, et seq. (1972) (Public college and university faculty, except those excluded by the ADEAA of 1978, must retire at seventy.)); Missouri (Mo. Rev. Stat. Sec. 169.060 (Supp. 1983) (Faculty at public colleges and universities, not including the University of Missouri, must retire on July 1 following the school year in which they turn seventy.)); Rhode Island (R.I. Gen Laws Secs. 36-10-9 and 16-17-1 (Supp. 1984) (State college and university faculty must retire on the first day of the calendar month next succeeding their seventieth birthday.)); South Carolina (S.C. Code Ann. Secs. 9-1-1530 (Supp. 1983) and 9-1-10(4) (1977) (Faculty at state colleges and universities must retire at seventy but, with approval, may be continued to age seventy-two.)); South Dakota (S.D. Codified Laws Ann. Secs. 3-6A-36.1 and 3-6-28 (1979) (All state employees, including college and university faculty, must retire at seventy.)); Tennessee (Tenn. Code Ann. Sec. 8-36-205(4) and (5) (1980) (College and university faculty may be retired involuntarily at sixty-five and must be retired at seventy but may, with approval, complete the school year.) (See note 52, below.)); Virginia (Va. Code Sec. 51-111.54 (Supp. 1984) (State college and university faculty must retire at seventy but may, with approval, continue to the last day of the fiscal year.)); West Virginia (W. Va. Code Sec. 18-7A-25a (1979) (Faculty must retire no later than six months after attaining age seventy.)); Wyoming (Wyo. Stat. Secs. 9-3-414 and 9-3-402(a)(v), (xviii), (xix), and (xxi) (1984) (State employees, including faculty, must be retired at sixty-six.) (But see *E.E.O.C.* v. *Wyoming,* note 4, above.))

41. Alabama (Ala. Code Sec. 16-25-14(a)(3) (Supp. 1984) as amended by Act 85-208 (signed March 25, 1985) (Faculty at public colleges and universities must retire at age seventy but, with approval, may continue year to year.)); Arizona (Ariz. Rev. Stat. Ann. Secs. 38-759; 38-759.01B; 38-781.07; 38-781.36B; and 15-1628 (Supp. 1984) (Faculty at state colleges and universities must retire at seventy but, with approval, may continue year to year.)); Connecticut (Conn. Gen. Stat. Ann. Secs. 5-164(b) and 5-160(g) (Supp. 1984) (Members of state employees' retirement plan must retire at seventy but may continue, with approval, year to year.); cf. Conn. Gen. Stat. Secs. 5-160(g); 5-154(u) and (v); 5-158f; and 5-156 (Supp. 1984) (providing for alternative retirement plan that does not impose mandatory retirement)); Indiana (Ind. Code Ann. Secs. 4-15-8-2 and 21-6.1-1-1 et seq. (Burns Supp. 1984) (Some state employees must retire at seventy; members of the teachers' retirement system must retire at the end of the school year in which they attain seventy-one but may be continued on the basis of a physician's certificate of mental and physical ability to teach.)); Louisiana (La. Rev. Stat. Ann. Sec. 42:691 (Supp. 1984) (All public employees, including college and university faculty, must retire at seventy but may be continued, with approval, if advantageous to the public service because of expert knowledge and qualifications.)); Maryland (Md. Ann. Code art. 73B, Sec. 11(1)(b)(i),(iii), and (iv); Sec. 86(1)(b) and (c); Sec. 110(k)(1)-(3); Sec. 117(1)(b); and Sec. 145(1)(b) and (c) (1983) (State college and university faculty must retire at seventy but, with approval, may continue year to year.)); Massachusetts (Mass. Gen. Laws Ann. Ch. 32, Secs. 1, 3(2)(g); 5(1)(a); and 90F (West Supp. 1984) (Faculty who are members of the public employees' retirement system must retire at age seventy but may continue if mentally and physically capable of performing their duties.)); Minnesota (Minn. Stat. Ann. Sec. 354.44 subd. 1a (1982) (Faculty in the state university system, not including the University of Minnesota, must retire at seventy but may be employed thereafter as

substitutes or on a part-time basis.)); Nebraska (Neb. Rev. Stat. Sec. 85-606 (Supp. 1984) (State college and university faculty must retire at seventy but, with approval, may continue year to year.)); Oregon (Or. Rev. Stat. Secs. 237.129999(2) and 237.133(1)(a) (1981) (College and university faculty must retire at seventy but, with approval, may be continued to age seventy-five.); see also Or. Rev. Stat. Sec. 237.139 (granting special authority to the state board of higher education to request permission to hire persons above the mandatory retirement age)); Washington (Wash. Rev. Code Ann. Sec. 28B.10.420 (Supp. 1984) (Faculty at public colleges and universities must be retired at age seventy but may be reemployed, on the basis of outstanding qualifications, on a part-time basis.); cf. Wash. Rev. Code Ann. Sec. 41.04.350(2) (allowing public employers to waive mandatory retirement requirements)).

42. See, for example, Ohio Rev. Code Ann. Secs. 3307.01(A) and (B) and 3307.37 (1980), providing that college and university faculty may be involuntarily retired upon attaining age seventy. A new statute in North Carolina eliminates mandatory retirement for most public employees but specifically authorizes the board of governors of the University of North Carolina system to require retirement at age seventy until July 1, 1998 (1984 N.C. Sess. Laws Chapter 1019, Sec. 2). See also Ky. Rev. Stat. Sec. 164.220(3), authorizing the board of trustees of the University of Kentucky to establish a mandatory retirement age for faculty at that institution.

43. See note 31, above.

44. As indicated in note 6, above, the dollar limit in the BFE/HPP in the federal law was recently increased from $27,000 to $44,000. At the time of this writing, all state law BFE/HPP exemptions, including that of Arizona, contained a dollar limit of $27,000. If past practice is indicative of future performance, some state legislatures will follow the federal lead and raise their BFE/HPP limits, and others will not.

45. Compare the antibias rules of the Colorado Department of Personnel, which prohibit age discrimination in public employment (4 Code of Colorado Regulations Sec. 801-1 (1983)).

46. At the time of this writing, three bills that would prohibit age discrimination in employment were being considered by the Missouri legislature: S.B. 133; S.B. 196; and H.B. 32, 83rd Gen. Assembly, 1st Reg. Sess. (1985).

47. Legislation recently enacted in Montana removed mandatory retirement provisions from all state-administered public retirement systems (Chapter 86, L. 1985 (signed March 18, 1985)).

48. At the time the lawsuit that led to *Board of Regents* v. *Oakley* was filed, the age limits (forty and sixty-nine) in Section 613.350-3 had not yet been enacted. The Nevada Supreme Court decided the *Oakley* case only on the basis of Section 281.370 and without taking into consideration the restrictions of Section 613.350-3, which were not in existence when the suit was filed. No Nevada case has yet arisen that would determine whether the provisions of Section 281.370 and Section 613.350-3 are in conflict and, if so, which one would prevail. The question is moot, at least for the time being, with regard to the University of Nevada System, which repealed its mandatory retirement policy after the *Oakley* decision and declined to reinstate it for faculty age seventy and over — even after it was pointed out to the board of regents that Section 613.350 was enacted after the case arose and could possibly be controlling (Donald Klasic, General Counsel, University of Nevada System, letter to Dr. Woodruff, March 29, 1985).

49. See note 31, above.

50. Employee Retirement Income Security Act of 1974 (29 U.S.C. Section 1001 et seq. (1976 and Supp. 1983)).

51. At the time of this writing, there was pending in the Oklahoma legislature a bill which would prohibit age discrimination in employment. Engrossed H.B. 1081, 40th Leg., 1st Reg. Sess. (1985) would protect individuals forty to seventy (Sec. 2) and includes a BFOQ (Sec. 8) and a BFE/HPP (Sec. 9).

52. Although the Tennessee statute providing for involuntary retirement of faculty at age sixty-five might be "as otherwise provided by law" and thus not in contravention of the state age dis-

crimination legislation, involuntary retirement based on age before age seventy would constitute a violation of the federal ADEA.

53. Compare Executive Order 1-82 (January 16, 1982), prohibiting discrimination on the basis of age, inter alia, in state employment in Virginia.

54. At the time of this writing, S.B. 93, 1986–86 Leg., 87th Reg. Sess., which would add a BFE/HPP to Wisconsin law, was pending in the Wisconsin legislature.

55. But see *E.E.O.C.* v. *Wyoming,* note 4, above. See also note 52, above. By Executive Order 19984-1, the Governor of Wyoming has directed all state agencies to comply with the federal ADEA. A modification of the Wyoming mandatory retirement law is expected during a recodification of the retirement statutes in the 1986 legislative session (Jeffery E. Gardner, Deputy Director, Wyoming Retirement System, letter to Dr. Woodruff, March 21, 1985).

Section 4.1

1. C. L. Macken, "1982 Long-Term Care Survey: National Estimates of Functional Impairment Among Elderly Medicare Beneficiaries Living in the Community," Paper presented at the Gerontological Society of America annual meeting, San Antonio, November 19, 1984; A. Sirocco, "An Overview of the 1982 National Master Facility Inventory Survey of Nursing and Related Care Homes," U.S. Department of Health and Human Services, *Advance Data* 111 (September 20, 1985); B. A. Feller, "Americans Needing Help to Function at Home," U.S. Department of Health and Human Services, *Advance Data* 92 (September 14, 1983).

2. J. F. Van Nostrand and others, "The National Nursing Home Survey: 1977 Summary for the United States," U.S. Department of Health, Education, and Welfare, DHEW Publication No. (PHS) 79-1794; W. G. Weissert, "Estimating the Long-Term Care Population: Prevalence Rates and Selected Characteristics," *Health Care Financing Review,* 6 (Summer 1985): 83–91.

3. J. F. Van Nostrand and others (see note 2, above); B. Bloom, "Current Estimates from the National Health Interview Survey: United States, 1981," National Center for Health Statistics, *Vital and Health Statistics,* Series 10, No. 141, U.S. Department of Health and Human Services Pub. No. (PHS) 83-1569 (October 1982); U.S. Bureau of the Census.

4. J. F. Van Nostrand and others (see note 2, above); B. Bloom (see note 3, above); K. Liu and K. Manton, "The Characteristics and Utilization Pattern of an Admission Cohort of Nursing Home Patients," *The Gerontologist,* 24 (1984): 70-76.

5. K. Liu and K. Manton (see note 4, above).

6. L. F. Lane, "The Potential of Private Long Term Care Insurance," *Pride Institute Journal,* 4 (Summer 1985): 15-24.

7. Katharine R. Levit, H. Lazenby, D. R. Waldo, and L. M. Davidoff, "National Health Expenditures, 1984," *Health Care Financing Review,* 7 (Fall 1985): 1-36.

8. M. A. Cohen, E. J. Tell, and S. S. Wallack, "The Lifetime Risk and Costs of Nursing Home Use Among the Elderly," *Medical Care,* 24 (Dec. 1986) (12): 1161-72.

9. Computed from National Nursing Home Survey and Cohen and others, (Assumes per diem nursing home expense of seventy dollars.) "The Financial Capacity of the Elderly to Finance Long-Term Care," *The Gerontologist,* 27 (1987): 494-502.

10. D. M. Topolnicki, "When a Nursing Home Becomes Your Poor House," *Money* (March 1986): 175-82.

11. Computed from Commission on College Retirement survey on retirement income of college and university employees, and M. A. Cohen, E. J. Tell, J. N. Greenberg, and S. S. Wallack, "The Financial Capacity of the Elderly to Finance Long-Term Care," *The Gerontologist,* 27 (1987): 494-502. (Assumes per diem nursing home expense of seventy dollars.)

Section 4.3

1. Risk sharing is not a function that requires an overarching

consortium of plans. Long-term-care costs do not have disper-
sion as wide as acute-care costs; the experience of continuing-
care retirement communities implies that risk sharing for long-
term care can be successfully accomplished with populations as
small as a few hundred (S. S. Wallack and E. J. Tell, "New
Approaches to the Finance and Delivery of Health Care to the
Elderly," *Health Care Cost Management,* Brookfield, Wis.: International Foundation of Employment Benefit Plans, 1987).

2. A prototype employer-sponsored plan, designed for possible adoption by a particular employer, is included as Appendix
B in "A Plan to Create Comprehensive Group Long-Term-Care
Insurance for College and University Personnel," Discussion
Draft published by the Commission on College Retirement
(1986). When considered in contrast to the consortium plans
described in this section, it can illustrate the flexibility, advantages, and disadvantages of an employer-specific long-term-care
insurance plan.

3. K. Rak, "Is the Medicare Home Health Boom Over?,"
. . . *home health line* 11 (June 9, 1986).

4. If it were practical, it would be preferable to have potential
beneficiaries join a managed care organization when they are
healthy and to give this organization responsibility for the full
spectrum of acute and long-term care in exchange for a fixed
per-enrollee payment (full capitation). This arrangement would
encourage more efficient substitution of services, both among
various long-term-care services, and across acute, preventive,
and long-term care. Such an approach would give the managed
care organization financial incentives to keep the individual functional and healthy. However, this system cannot be generally
recommended at this time. Providers lack experience with such
approaches, and few would be willing to take on these risks;
mechanisms must be developed to assure that providers do not
enroll only low-risk or low-cost beneficiaries; and Medicare
regulations currently preclude differential capitation payments
in recognition of heavy care needs—payments that may be
necessary for provider viability.

5. See note 2, above.

Case Index

A

Accord, Alexandre v. *Chase Manhattan Bank,* 61 A.D.2d 537, 402 N.Y.S.2d 21 (1st Dept 1978), and distribution of retirement annuities, 70

Accord, Johnson v. *Spicer,* 107 N.Y.185, 13N.E. 753f (1887), and relationships governed by common law equitable principles, 77

Adams v. *James,* 526 F. Supp. 80 (M.D. Ala. 1981), and involuntary retirement, 149–150

Application of Roth, 73 A.D.2d 560, 423 N.Y.S.2d 25 (1979), 74

B

Board of Regents v. *Oakley,* 97 Nev. 605, 637 P.2d 1199 (1981), and mandatory retirement of public university faculty, 157–158

Board of Trustees of Community College District No. 508 v. *Human Rights Commission,* 88 Ill. 2d 22, 429 N.E.2d 1207 (1981), and mandatory retirement of tenured faculty, 153

C

Charles, Henry & Crowley Co. v. *Home Insurance Company,* 349 Mass. 723, 212N.E.2d 240 (1965), and rules governing the construction of contracts, 69–70

Chatham County Hospital Authority v. *John Hancock Mutual Life Insurance Co.,* 325 F. Supp. 614 S.D. Ga. (1971), and annuity agreement and trust, 67

Chicago Bd. of Options Exchange, Inc. v. *Connecticut General Life Ins. Co.,* 713 F.2d 254 (7th Cir. 1983), and insurer as fiduciary for guaranteed benefits, 87

Christiansen v. *National Savings and Trust Co.,* 683 F.2d 520 (D.C. Cir. 1982): and analysis of trust and contract, 96–97; and expectations of employees on investment proceeds, 67; and relationship of HMO and contributed funds, 57–58

Community Services, Incorporated v. *United States,* 422 F.2d 1353 (Ct. Cl. 1970): and analysis of trust and contract, 78–79, 96–97; and retirement plan as trust, 56–57

Connick v. *Teachers Insurance and Annuity Association & College Retirement Equities Fund,* 784 F.2d 1018 (9th Cir. 1986), and distribution of retirement annuities, 70

D

Dodge's Trust, 25 N.Y.2d 273, 303 N.Y.S.2d 847 (1969), *In Re,* 72

Dolan v. School Dist. No. 10, Deer Lodge Cty., 195 Mont. 340 636 P.2d 825 (1981), and mandatory retirement age for public employees, 157

E

E.E.O.C. v. Wyoming, 460 U.S. 226, 103 S. Ct. 1054, 75 L. Ed. 2d 18 (1983): and involuntary retirement imposed by age, 145–146; and preemption of state law by federal law, 144

Eversole v. Metropolitan Life Ins. Co., 500 F. Sup. 1162 (D. Cal. 1980), and state insurance laws and fraud against policyholders, 86

G

Green Bus Lines, Inc. v. Consolidated Mutual Insurance Co., 426 N.Y.S.2d 981 (1980), and rules governing the construction of contracts, 69–70

Gross v. Lynnwood, 90 Wash. 2d 395, 583 P.2d 1197 (1978), and age discrimination in employment, 163

H

Hollenbeck v. Falstaff Brewing Corp., 605 F. Supp. 421 (E.D. Mo. 1985), and preemption of state law by federal law, 34

Holmes v. John Hancock Mutual Life Insurance Co., 288 N.Y. 106 (1942), and insurance fund as trust, 69

L

Landau, N.Y.L.J., March 3, 1981, at 6 col. 1, *rev'd on other grounds*, 87 A.D.2d 755, 449 N.Y.S.2d 2 (1982), *In Matter of*, 72

Lane v. Goren, 743 F.2d 1337, 1339 (9th Cir. 1984), and preemption of state law by federal law, 101

M

Marshall v. Chase Manhattan Bank, 558 F.2d 680 (2d Cir. 1977), and pre-emption of state law by federal law, 85

Metropolitan Life Insurance Co. v. Massachusetts, 105 S. Ct. 2380 (1985), and preemption of state law by federal law, 85–86

Michigan Millers Mutual Insurance Co. v. Christopher, 413 N.Y.S.2d 264 (1979), and rules governing the construction of contracts, 69–70

Mongomery v. Lowe, 507 F. Supp. 618 (S.D. Texas, Houston Div. 1981), and preemption of state law by federal law, 34

Mordecai Trust, 24 Misc.2d 668, 201 N.Y.S.2d 899 (1960), *aff'd.*, 12 A.D.2d 449, 210 N.Y.S.2d 478 (1960), *In Re*, 73

Mundell v. Gibbs, 70 Misc.2d 174, 332 N.Y.S.2d 364 (1970), and application of trust agreement, 78–79

N

Nires, 290 N.Y. 78 (1943), *In re*, 69

O

O'Neil v. Marriott Corp., 538 F. Sup. 1026 (D. Md. 1982), and preemption of state law by federal law, 85

Orzel v. City of Wauwatosa Fire Dept., 697 F.2d 743 (7th Cir. 1983), and preemption of state law by federal law, 144

P

Provience v. Valley Clerks Trust Fund, 509 F. Supp. 388, 391 (E.D. Cal. 1981), and preemption of state law by federal law, 33

R

Rosner v. Caplow, 90 A.D.2d 44, 456 N.Y.S.2d 50 (1982), *aff'd.*, 60 N.Y.2d 880, 470 N.Y.S.2d 367 (1983), and revocation or amendment as set forth in instrument, 72–74

S

St. Joseph's Hospital v. *Bennett,* 281 N.Y. 115, 22 N.E.2d 305 (1939): and charitable trust principles, 60–61, 78, 97; and freedom of investment, 65–66

Saruf v. *Miller,* 90 Wash. 2d 880, 586 P.2d 466 (1978), and age discrimination in employment, 163

Sasso v. *Vachris,* 482 N.Y.S.2d 875, 876 (1984), application of business corporation law to employee benefit trust, 33

Shaw v. *Delta Air Lines, Inc.,* 463 U.S. 85, 103 S. Ct. 2890, 77 L. Ed. 2d 490 (1983), and preemption of state law by federal law, 103

Simonds v. *Simonds,* 45 N.Y.2d 233, 408 N.Y.S.2d 359 (1978), and relationships governed by common law equitable principles, 77

Simpson v. *Alaska State Commission for Human Rights,* 423 F. Supp. 552, *aff'd* 608 F.2d 1171 (9th Cir. 1979): and age discrimination law without upper age limit, 146, 150; and state age discrimination laws and federal legislation, 144–145

Spinak v. *University of Akron,* 3 O. App. 3d 388, 445 N.E.2d 692 (Ct. App. Ohio 1981), and mandatory retirement of faculty, 159–160

T

Taylor v. *Department of Fish, Wildlife, and Parks,* 666 P.2d 1228 (1983), and mandatory retirement age for public employees, 157

U

Uhlman v. *New York Life Insurance Co.,* 109 N.Y.421 (1888), and insurance fund as trust, 68–69

United Air Lines v. *McCann,* 434 U.S. 192, 98 S. Ct. 444, 54 L. Ed.2d 402 (1977): and involuntary retirement based on preexisting plan, 143; and mandatory retirement with bona fide retirement plan, 145

University of South Carolina v. *Batson,* 271 S.C. 242, 246 S.E.2d 882 (1978), and mandatory retirement of tenured faculty, 161

Subject Index

A

Academy of Independent Scholars, retired faculty in, 277
Accumulation phase: defined, 2, 7; description of, 16–23; differences in, of TIAA and of CREF, 22–23; as trust or as insurance, 25–34
Activities of daily living (ADL), and eligibility for long-term care insurance benefits, 236–238, 257–261
Administrative services, implementation of, for pension program, 265–270
Affordability, as goal of long-term care insurance plan, 223
Age: as basis for dismissal, 108; as criterion for fixed retirement date, 107–109, 112–113; as criterion for pension planning, 107; as criterion for retirement, 115–140; and involuntary retirement, 108; permissible use of, under age discrimination laws, 108. *See also* Retirement age
Age Discrimination in Employment Act (ADEA), 133–135; application of, to states, 149; exceptions to, 143–144; involuntary retirement and, 141–146; seventy as retirement age in, 113
Age discrimination laws, 138; civil rights and, 131, 133; federal, 133–

135, 142–246; involuntary dismissal and, 108; permissible uses for age in, 108; state, 135–137, 144–164
Aging: as individual process, 116–117, 122–123; risk of impaired functioning in, 122
Alabama: age discrimination laws, 149–150; TIAA-CREF plans in, 201
Alaska: age discrimination laws, 148, 150; cost-of-living adjustments for pension plans in, 194
American Association of Retired Persons (AARP), 219, 280
American Association of University Professors (AAUP), 205
American Mathematical Society, retired faculty in, 278
American University, retired faculty in, 278
Arizona: age discrimination laws, 150; TIAA-CREF plans in, 201
Arkansas: age discrimination laws, 146, 150; TIAA-CREF plans in, 201
Association of American Colleges (AAC), 205

B

Barthel Self-Care Ratings, 259
Blue Cross, Blue Shield, 57–58

Bona fide executives/high policy-making positions (BFE/HPP), in state and federal age discrimination laws, 143–164
Bona fide occupational qualification (FBOQ), in state and federal age discrimination laws, 143–164
Bona fide retirement plan (BFRP), in state and federal age discrimination laws, 145–164
Bortz, W. K., 64
Brandeis University, long-term care insurance plan proposed by, 224–254, 257–262
Brandeis University Health Policy Center, 214–215
Business Corporation Law, New York, 33

C

California: age discrimination laws, 148, 150–151; cost-of-living adjustments for pension plans in, 194
California, University of (Los Angeles), retired faculty in, 279
"Caring for the Disabled Elderly: Who Will Pay?", 256
Carnegie, A., 54–55
Carnegie Corporation, 55; creation of TIAA by, 22; and Harvard study of long-term care insurance, 255; support of NACUBO by, 271
Carnegie Foundation for the Advancement of Teaching, creation of TIAA by, 2, 14, 54–55
Center for College Retirement Information, 271
Chronological age. See Age: Retirement age
Civil rights, age discrimination laws and, 131, 133
Civil Service Commission, 57–58
Clark, E., 26–34, 53, 64, 90
College Retirement Equities Fund (CREF). See TIAA-CREF
Colleges. See Higher education institutions
Colorado: age discrimination laws, 151; cost-of-living adjustments for pen-

sion plans in, 194; lack of social security protection in, 181; TIAA-CREF plans in, 201
Commission on College Retirement, 7–13; Clark's first opinion to, 53–63; Clark's second opinion to, 90–106; continued activities working paper by, 273–280; continued activity of retirees recommendations by, 275–280; on difficulty of financial planning for higher education institutions, 263–264; financial planning recommendations of, 267–271; on long-term care insurance, 217–220; long-term care insurance plan proposed by, 224–254, 257–262; on pension program, 169–170; pension program recommendations by, 170–171, 203–212; retirement age policy of, 108–109, 110–114; revised transferability of funds policy of, 105–106; on "Special Rule for Tenured Faculty" of ADEA, 165–166; transferability of funds policy statement by, 1–6
Community-based care, long-term care insurance benefits for, 239–246
Competitive medical plans (CMPs), 244
Congress: age as criterion of eligibility in, 120–121; and public policy over contracts, 130; and relationships of TIAA-CREF, 25–26
Connecticut: age discrimination laws, 148, 151; cost-of-living adjustments for pension plans in, 194; lack of social security protection in, 181; TIAA-CREF plans in, 201
Consortium of Long-Term-Care Plans, 225, 227–229
Constitution, U.S., age as criterion of voter eligibility in, 120
Consumer price index (CPI), and inflation adjustment for long-term care insurance plan, 247
Continuing care retirement communities (CCRCs), 244
Contribution rates: level percentage approach to, 183–185; step-rate approach to, 183–185

Cook, T. J., 182
Core pension plan, 170, 204-205

D

Defined benefit plans: advantages of,
177; assessment of, in public institutions, 191-193; assurance of benefits
in, 191-192; coverage and benefits
of, in public institutions, 190-191;
inadequate funding of, 193; lack of
portability of, 192-193; rates for,
205; severance benefit in, 171, 211;
and standards for funding, reporting, and disclosure, 171, 211-212;
summary of, in public institutions,
193-200; term defined, 177
Defined contribution plans: advantages
of, 177; rates for, 204-205; summary of, 189-190; term defined, 177
Delaware: age discrimination laws,
151; TIAA-CREF plans in, 201
Dewey, Ballantine, Bushby, Palmer &
Wood: and conceptualization of relationships of TIAA-CREF, 25-34;
and confusion of terms, 77-79; on
elements of trust, 66-68; on errors
regarding contract terms, 75-77; on
legal problems with transferability of
funds, 46-47; on problems with old
money, 37, 38, 41; transferability of
funds opinion by, 64-89
Disabilities: figures on health care and,
217-220; and full long-term care insurance plan, 225-227; and impairment levels in long-term care insurance plan, 237-238; long-term,
and social security, 180
District of Columbia, TIAA-CREF
plans in, 201

E

Elderly: as vulnerable group, 122; in
work force, 116. *See also* Aging
Eligibility, for benefits in long-term care
insurance plan, 236-238, 257-261
Emeriti Center, retired faculty in, 279
Emeritus College, retired faculty in,
277

Employee Retirement Income Security
Act (ERISA), 24; preemption provision of, 32-34, 84-88, 98-104;
trust obligations in, 77-79
Employer pension plans, 175-177
Estates, Powers, and Trusts Law, New
York (EPTL), 27, 32-34; applicability of, to TIAA-CREF, 53-54,
60-63, 64-65, 71-75, 77-78, 96-9

F

Faculty, tenured: continued activity
after retirement by, 273-280; government intervention in retirement
of, 131-133; mandatory retirement
protection by law for, 146-147; participation in research after retirement by, 277; as partners with higher
education institutions, 127-129,
132-133, 283-284; as percent of
total faculty, 115; performance appraisals as criterion for retirement
of, 123-127; retirement age for,
115-140; retirement of, for reasons
other than competence, 128-129; in
second careers after retirement,
279-280; sense of identity and worth
after retirement by, 273, 275; teaching after retirement by, 276-279
Federal Employees Health Benefits Act
of 1959, 57-58
Federal government: age as criterion of
eligibility in, 120-121; age discrimination laws and, 133-135; intervention in faculty retirement, 131-133,
140; intervention in retirement age
by, 109, 113-114; involuntary
retirement laws, 141-146, 165-166;
public policy over contracts in,
129-130
Financial planning, 263-271; advantages of establishing an organization
for, 269; choices in, 268-270; complexity of, 263, 265-266; difficulty
of, 263; implementation of, for pension program, 265-270
Financial planning services: for pension
plan employees, 170-171, 209-211;
pension plans with, 170-171

Fixed retirement date: age as criterion for, 112–113; commission policy on, 108–109, 111–112; early retirement and, 111

Flexibility, of pension plans, 169–170, 207–209

Florida: age discrimination laws, 148–149, 151–152; cost-of-living adjustments for pension plans in, 195; mandatory retirement prohibition in, 136; TIAA-CREF plans in, 201

Fox, A., 176

G

Georgia: age discrimination laws, 148–149, 152; cost-of-living adjustments for pension plans in, 195

Group Hospitalization, Inc., 57–58

Gunning, F. P., 64

H

Harvard University, study of long-term care insurance by, 255–256

Hastings College of Law, retired faculty in, 278

Hawaii: age discrimination laws, 148–149, 152–153; mandatory retirement prohibition in, 136

Health maintenance organizations (HMOs), 244

Health Policy Center's Long-Term-Care Group, 214–215

Higher Education Act of 1965, 144

Higher education institutions: employee population, 180; employees in retirement plans, 182–183; and employer-sponsored long-term care plans, 252–253; encouragement of continued activity of retirees by, 273–280; and faculty retirement for reasons other than competence, 128–129; financial planning in, 263–271; fixed retirement date selection by, 112–113; flexibility with retirement in, 139; functions of, 282; and long-term care insurance plan, 229–230; mobility in, 130–131; as partners with tenured faculty,

127–129, 132–133, 283–284; pension investment options of, 8; planning for faculty retirement by, 118–120; private, and pension benefits, 181–190; public, and pension benefits, 190–200; roles of, 282

Home-based care: findings on, 217–220; long-term care insurance benefits for, 239–246

House of Representatives, age as criterion of eligibility for, 120

I

Ibbotson, R. G., 179

Idaho: age discrimination laws, 153; cost-of-living adjustments for pension plans in, 195

Illinois: age discrimination laws, 153; lack of social security protection in, 181

Independence, maximum, as goal of long-term care insurance plan, 222

Indiana: age discrimination laws, 153–154; TIAA-CREF plans in, 201

Individual Retirement Account: age as criterion of eligibility in, 120–121; coordination of retirement with, 118

Inflation: adjustments for long-term care insurance plan, 246–247; adjustments in pension programs, 170, 205–207; effect of, on investments, 268; hedge against, with TIAA-CREF, 19; maintaining pension benefit value during, 177–179

Inflation, TIAA-CREF's vulnerability to, 188–189

Information services, implementation of, for pension program, 265–270

Institute for Living in Retirement, retired faculty in, 278

Institute for Retired Professionals, retired faculty in, 278

Insurance benefits: criteria for, 222–223; services offered with, 239–246

Insurance Department, New York, 49, 55

Insurance law: purpose of, 46–47; and transferability of funds of TIAA-CREF, 45–52

Insurance Law, New York, 46–48
Internal Revenue Code, age as criterion of eligibility in, 120
Internal Revenue Service (IRS), 79; on deductability of retirement plans, 56–57; and TIAA-CREF's relationships, 31–32
Investment, mortality risk vs. risk in, 20–22
Iowa: age discrimination laws, 154; TIAA-CREF plans in, 201
Ivanick, C. T., 64

J

Job security: in tenure system, 116, 127, 283; value of, 130
Joint Statement of Principles on Academic Retirement, 205

K

Kahn, 260
Kansas: age discrimination laws, 154; retirement offices on campuses in, 280; TIAA-CREF plans in, 201
Katz Index of ADL, 258
Kentucky: age discrimination laws, 154; TIAA-CREF plans in, 201
King, F. P., 182

L

Labor force: home care and women in, 220; older population in, 116–117
Law: and transferability of funds of TIAA-CREF, 45–52. *See also* New York law
Law of Trusts, The, 66, 77
Life Insurance Company of Virginia, 56–57
"Long-Term Care: Three Approaches to University-Based Insurance," 255
Long-term care insurance plan, 213–262; administration of, 227–229; automatic coverage in, 230–231, 233; background on, 213–214; basic plan, 226–227; benefits of, 239–241; eligibility criteria for, 236–238, 257–261; employee participation in, 229–231; and employer-sponsored plans, 229–230, 252–253; financing, 246; full plan, 225–226; goals of, 221–223; Harvard study of, 255–257; inflation adjustments for, 246–247; other employee benefits and, 253–254; portability of, 234–235; preliminary cost estimates of, 249–251; premiums for, 231–234; reimbursement of providers by, 244–246; services offered under, 240–246; spouse coverage in, 231, 234; system management of, 241–244; and transition issues, 252; unexpected development adjustments, 247–249; value of, 215; voluntary participation in, 230–231, 233
Louisiana: age discrimination laws, 154–155; cost-of-living adjustments for pension plans in, 195; lack of social security protection in, 181; pension replacement rates in, 191

M

MacDonald, J. G., 90
McGrath, J. P., 64
McKinney, 65, 70, 71, 83
Maine: age discrimination laws, 148–149, 155; cost-of-living adjustments for pension plans in, 195; lack of social security protection in, 181; mandatory retirement prohibition in, 136; TIAA-CREF plans in, 201
Managed care organizations, defined, 214
Maryland: age discrimination laws, 155; cost-of-living adjustments for pension plans in, 195; pension replacement rates in, 191; TIAA-CREF plans in, 201
Massachusetts: age discrimination laws, 148, 155–156; cost-of-living adjustments for pension plans in, 195; lack of social security protection in, 181
Medicaid program: functions of, 218–219; for per-patient care, 244; as public funding of long-term care, 213; rates for, 245

Medicare program: approved organizations by, 244; coordination of retirement with, 118; functions of, 218–219

Mental impairment, and eligibility for long-term care insurance, 259–261

Mental Status Questionnaire (MSQ), 260

Michigan: age discrimination laws, 156; TIAA-CREF plans in, 201

Michigan, University of, retired faculty in, 277

Minnesota: age discrimination laws, 156; TIAA-CREF plans in, 201

Mississippi: age discrimination laws, 156; cost-of-living adjustments for pension plans in, 196

Missouri: age discrimination laws, 157; cost-of-living adjustments for pension plans in, 196

Montana, age discrimination laws, 148–149, 157

Mortality risk, investment risk vs., 20–22

Munnell, A. H., 199

N

National Association of College and University Business Officers (NACUBO), 271

National Association of Insurance Commissioners, Model Law of, 47

National Nursing Home Survey, 250

NCTCS, 258

Nebraska: age discrimination laws, 157; TIAA-CREF plans in, 201

Nevada: age discrimination laws, 148–149, 157–158; lack of social security protection in, 181; TIAA-CREF plans in, 201

New Deal legislation, public policy over contracts in, 129–130

New Hampshire: age discrimination laws, 148, 158; TIAA-CREF plans in, 201

New Jersey: age discrimination laws, 148, 158; cost-of-living adjustments for pension plans in, 196; TIAA-CREF plans in, 201

New Mexico: age discrimination laws, 158; cost-of-living adjustments for pension plans in, 196

New money, handling, in transferability of funds, 35–36

New School for Social Research, retired faculty in, 278

New York: age discrimination laws, 148, 159; pension replacement rates in, 191; TIAA-CREF plans in, 201

New York law, on transferability of funds, 53–63, 69–71

NHIS, 258

Norris-LaGuardia Act, public policy over contracts in, 130

North Carolina: age discrimination laws, 146, 159; cost-of-living adjustments for pension plans in, 196; TIAA-CREF plans in, 201

North Dakota: age discrimination laws, 159; TIAA-CREF plans in, 201

Not-for-Profit Corporation Law, New York, 28, 65; as applicable to TIAA-CREF, 60–61, 93, 96–97

Nursing home care: findings on, 217–220; long-term care insurance benefits for, 239–246

O

OARS, 260

Ohio: age discrimination laws, 159–160; cost-of-living adjustments for pension plans in, 197; lack of social security protection in, 181

Oklahoma: age discrimination laws, 160; TIAA-CREF plans in, 201

Old money, problems with, 36–45, 51

Oregon: age discrimination laws, 160; cost-of-living adjustments for pension plans in, 197; TIAA-CREF plans in, 201

P

Payout phase, description of, 16–23

Pennsylvania: age discrimination laws, 160; TIAA-CREF plans in, 201

Pension benefits: at private institutions, 181–190; at public institutions, 190–

200; comparison of, for four-job worker and one-job worker, 199; establishment of, 173–177; and full long-term care insurance plan, 226; graduated, 179; and index bond as investment instrument, 178, 206; indexing, 170, 178–179, 205–207; maintaining the value of, 177–179; and performance indexing, 178–179, 207

Pension program: ADEA and, 143; age as criterion of eligibility in, 121; assumptions and planning for, 107; commission findings on, 169–170; commission recommendations for, 170–171, 203–212; core pension plan in, 170, 204–205; cost-of-living adjustment provisions by state, 194–198; current retirement plans and higher education employees, 172–202; goal of, 167; principles of, 168–169

Performance appraisals: as criterion for retirement, 123–127; difficulties with, 124–126; kinds of, 123–124; measures used in, 125–126; tenure system and, 116, 126

Portability: of long-term care insurance plan, 234–235; of pension plans, 169

Postretirement: continued activity in, 110–111, 118, 132, 273–280; employment, 108; fixed retirement date and, 108, 111

Presidency, age as criterion of eligibility for, 120

President's Commission on Pension Policy, 174

R

Research, participation of retired faculty in, 277

Retirement: arrangement, 117–120; concept of, 107; considerations in planning, 275; inflexibility of, 169; involuntary, 117, 141–166; office of services for, 275; phased, 128, 188, 276–277; states barring involuntary, 136–137. See also Postretirement

Retirement age: ADEA and, 133–135;

commission policy on, 110–114; for higher education personnel, 107–114; state laws and, 146–149; for tenured faculty, 115–140; uncapping, 140–142, 147–148, 165

Retirement Annuity Contract, 20–22

"Retirement Benefits for University Evaluating the Tradeoffs," 255

Retirement, early: bridge plan, 188; commission policy on, 108; disincentive for, under TIAA-CREF, 187; fixed retirement date and, 111; incentive plans for, 187–188; increased pension contribution plan for, 187–188; lump-sum arrangement for, 187; phased retirement plan as, 188

Retirement income: establishing the initial benefit for, 173–177; goals of, 172–173; maintaining the value of benefits in, 177–179; as major asset for faculty, 1–2

Retirement program: current, for higher education employees, 172–202; elements of, 168; fixed retirement date in, 111–112, 118; flexibility of, 282–283; in higher education employee population, 180; objectives of, 110–111; phased, 108–111

Retirement Transition Benefit (RTB), defined, 18

Rhode Island: age discrimination laws, 160–161; TIAA-CREF plans in, 201

Rivlin, A. M., 256

Ruebhausen, O. M., 53, 90, 166

S

Savings plans, as component of retirement program, 266

Scott, A. W., 66, 77

Senate, age as criterion of eligibility for, 120

Severance benefits, in pension plans, 171

Severs, C. A., III, 64

Sherwood, 258–259

Short Portable Mental Status Questionnaire (SPMSQ), 260

Sinquefield, R., 179
Social Health Maintenance Organization (SHMO), 254, 258
Social security: age as criterion of eligibility for, 120; coordination of retirement with, 118; coverage for nonparticipating employees, 171, 212; as part of retirement plan, 180–181; pension plans and, 171; replacement rates, 175–176
Social/HMOs, 244, 261–262
South Carolina: age discrimination laws, 161; cost-of-living adjustments for pension plans in, 197
South Dakota: age discrimination laws, 161; cost-of-living adjustments for pension plans in, 197
Southern Illinois University (Carbondale), retired faculty in, 277
Spendthrift provision, in TIAA-CREF, 19–20, 22, 29
Standard of living: before and after retirement, 207–208; maintenance of, as goal of long-term care insurance plan, 221–222; pension benefits and, 168–169, 170
Standards, in pension plans, 171
State government: ADEA application to, 149; age as criterion of eligibility in, 121; age discrimination laws, 135–137, 144–164; intervention as peril to academic freedom, 140; intervention in retirement age by, 109, 113–114; involuntary retirement laws, 141–164
State preadmission screening (PAS), 260
Statutory grant of authority, 83–84
Supplemental retirement annuities (SRAs), 24
Supreme Court, New York, 78–79
Supreme Court, U.S., 33; on age discrimination, 131

T

Tax Reform Act of 1986, 93
Teachers Insurance and Annuity Association (TIAA). See TIAA-CREF

Tennessee: age discrimination laws, 161–162; cost-of-living adjustments for pension plans in, 197; TIAA-CREF plans in, 201
Tenure system, 113–114; academic freedom in, 128, 283; ADEA and contracts in, 133–135, 144; approval of contract in, 130–131; central features of, 115–116; contractual bargain in, 116, 127, 137; costs of, 128; diversity in, 113; fixed retirement date as contractual part of, 109, 112–114; gains of, 127–128; job security in, 116, 127, 283; nonfaculty personnel and, 114; performance appraisals and, 126; probationary period in, 115; state age discrimination laws and, 135–137
Texas: age discrimination laws, 162; pension replacement rates in, 191; TIAA-CREF plans in, 201
"TIAA-CREF: The Future Agenda," 105–106
TIAA-CREF: as annuity design innovator, 188–189; assessment of, 185–189; in Canada, 54–55; Clark's first opinion on, 53–63; Clark's second opinion on, 90–106; conceptualization of relationships with, 25–34; contribution rates under, 183–185; creation of, 2, 14–15, 18–19, 54–55; defined contribution plans of, 176–177; description of funds in, 16–23; Dewey, Ballantine, Bushby, Palmer & Wood's opinion on, 64–89; disincentive to retire under, 187; for employees at public institutions, 200–201; financial planning efforts of, 265–270; financial responsibilities of, 8–9; lack of flexibility in, 169, 186–187; monopoly by, 3–4, 36, 49–50; mortality risk vs. investment risk in, 20–22; primary purpose of, 7; rejection of commission conclusions by, 11–12; relevant terms in contracts of, 23–25; retirement coverage under, 181–183, 186; risk of investment under, 186; as servant to higher education employees, 26–27, 30; top

board of, 2, 4–5, 13; transferability of funds invested with, 1–106; as Type B corporation, 28–29, 60, 65; as Type C corporation, 28–29; vulnerability of, to inflation, 188–189; waiting period for participation in, 184

Transferability of funds, 1–106; Clark's first opinion on, 53–63; Clark's second opinion on, 90–106; commission policy on, 1–6, 7–13; commission's revised policy on, 105–106; conditions for, 9–10; and description of funds, 16–23; Dewey, Ballantine, Bushby, Palmer & Wood's opinion on, 64–89; fairness and, 39–40; and handling new money, 35–36; legal problems with, 45–49, 50–52; legal remedy for, 10; New York law on, 53–63, 69–71; in pension plans, 170, 209; and problems with old money, 36–45, 51; problems with, 80–83; reasons for, in TIAA-CREF, 10–11

U

Uncapping retirement age, 165; defined, 147–148; government intervention by, 140, 141–142

"Understanding How to Evaluate the Structures and Administration of University-or College-Based Long-Term Care Insurance," 255

United States Civil Service System, cost-of-living adjustments for pension plans in, 198

Universities. *See* Higher education institutions

Utah: age discrimination laws, 148–149, 162; cost-of-living adjustments for pension plans in, 198; mandatory retirement prohibition in, 136; TIAA-CREF plans in, 201

V

Vermont: age discrimination laws, 148, 162; TIAA-CREF plans in, 201

Virginia: age discrimination laws, 162–163; cost-of-living adjustments for pension plans in, 198; TIAA-CREF plans in, 201

W

Washington: age discrimination laws, 163; cost-of-living adjustments for pension plans in, 198; TIAA-CREF plans in, 201

Watts, D. E., 64

Wellness programs, for retirees, 276

West Virginia: age discrimination laws, 163; TIAA-CREF plans in, 201

Wharton, C. R., 106

Wiener, J. M., 256

Willard, D. S., 93–94

Wisconsin: age discrimination laws, 148–149, 163; mandatory retirement prohibition in, 136

Women, in labor force and home care, 220

"Working Paper on Continued Activities," 273–274

Wyoming: age discrimination laws, 164; pension replacement rates in, 191; TIAA-CREF plans in, 201

Y

Yale Law School, 26

Yale University, 53